AVICENNA'S METAPHYSICS IN CONTEXT

Avicenna's Metaphysics in Context

Robert Wisnovsky

Duckworth

First published in 2003 by
Gerald Duckworth & Co. Ltd.
61 Frith Street, London W1D 3JL
Tel: 020 7434 4242
Fax: 020 7434 4420
inquiries@duckworth-publishers.co.uk
www.ducknet.co.uk

A catalogue record for this book is available
from the British Library

ISBN 0 7156 3221 3

Typeset by Robert Wisnovsky and Hussein Rashid
Printed in Great Britain by
Bookcraft (Bath) Ltd, Midsomer Norton, Avon

Contents

Acknowledgements

So many people have helped me reach the stage of publishing a book about Avicenna's metaphysics that it is difficult to know how to thank them all. I suppose I should just describe my intellectual trajectory from its beginning.

Elizabeth Fine taught me Greek in high school, and introduced me to the beautiful strangeness of ancient texts. When I was a sophomore at Yale, Dimitri Gutas convinced me to enroll in first-year Arabic, and then, perhaps feeling responsible, was kind enough not to fail me. At Yale Abbas Amanat introduced me to Islamic history, and Gerhard Böwering supervised my senior thesis on the Ikhwān aṣ-Ṣafā᾿. A postgraduate year at Oxford studying with Fritz Zimmermann showed me how serious medieval Arabic thought could be. Even though this book preserves not a single sentence from my Princeton Ph.D. dissertation, "Avicenna on final causality", I owe a great debt to my doctoral supervisor, Hossein Modarressi: he guided me gently through the most difficult Avicennian texts, corrected my translations with care and suggested further avenues of inquiry. At Princeton Sarah Waterlow Broadie was the second reader of my dissertation, and Fadlou Shehadi and Parviz Morewedge were my external examiners. Also at Princeton, Stephen Menn introduced me to medieval philosophy, Michael Cook introduced me to *kalām*, and Jim Morris introduced me to Sufi thought; and courses on Aristotle's psychology and natural philosophy with, respectively, Myles Burnyeat and Pierre Pellegrin showed me the high level of philological and philosophical rigor which scholars of ancient philosophy demand of themselves. The world of the late-antique commentators on Aristotle opened up when Richard Sorabji hired me as his postdoctoral research assistant at King's College London. Through my work there I was introduced to Duckworth's editor, Deborah Blake, who has waited patiently for this book to ripen.

Wolfhart Heinrichs, Bill Graham, Bill Granara, Roy Mottahedeh, Bashi Sabra, Muhsin Mahdi, John Murdoch, Ayman El-Desouky and Wheeler Thackston have all been supportive and stimulating colleagues here at Harvard. In particular, my good friend and colleague Carl Pearson and I have had countless conversations about the history of Aristotelian and Neoplatonic philosophy, and I learned something important from every single one of them. Not only Carl but Sylvia Berryman, Ian Crystal, Richard Sorabji, Victor Caston, Everett Rowson, Thérèse-Anne Druart, Michael Marmura, Dimitri Gutas and Jules Janssens each spent much of their precious time reading and criticizing earlier versions of this work. Above all others, however, Stephen Menn has served as a paradigmatic mentor: patient and generous, but also severe and exacting. He knows how much I owe him.

I am also grateful to many other friends, colleagues and students who have guided me on particular issues and pointed me towards useful and interesting materials; these include Rahim Acar, Amos Bertolacci, Allan Gotthelf, Dag Hasse, Angela Jaffray, Yaron Klein, Christian Lange, Craig Martin, Sait Ozervarli, Amy Proferes, Ahmed al-Rahim, David Reisman, Will Robins, Jim Robinson, Joe Saleh, Jeff Spurr, Abe Stone, Moshe Taube and Hikmet Yaman. Hussein Rashid helped me enormously with the logistics of producing camera-ready copy.

My twelve-year-old son Simon Wisnovsky was born at the same time I started to wrestle with Avicenna's *Ilāhiyyāt*. My own experience, combined with that of his beloved Red Sox, should teach him that it is good simply to persevere. I am strengthened by the love I receive from Simon and from my two-year-old daughter Jasmine Parsons, as well as from my parents Mary and Joe Wisnovsky, from my brother Peter Wisnovsky, and from my in-laws Sheila, Emma and Anne Parsons. What I cannot even begin to express is my gratitude to my wife Laila Parsons. A historian of the modern Middle East, she started out skeptical of my project's value. After many long rigmaroles together, and also some acute editing on her part, she has now come to believe in its significance, and this has meant more to me than anyone else's opinion. I dedicate this book to her.

A Note on Transliteration and Citation

Throughout this volume individual Arabic and Persian letters have been transliterated according to the system adopted by the *International Journal of Middle Eastern Studies*. However, I have retained the sun letters when transliterating the Arabic definite article, and elided the *hamzat al-waṣl*, and for everything other than titles of books or individual names and terms, I have fully vocalized the transliterated text; thus *wa-s-sababu fī dhālika*, but also Arisṭūṭālīs, *aṭ-Ṭabīʿa*. The Greek long vowels have been transliterated as *ê* and *ô*, and the iota subscript as *-êi*, *-ôi* and *–âi*.

References to Plato's and Aristotle's works follow the standard page and line numbering of Stephanus and Bekker, respectively. When abbreviating their works I have adhered to the system adopted by the Ancient Commentators on Aristotle Project; thus Aristotle's *Posterior Analytics* is abbreviated as *An. Post.*, and Plato's *Parmenides* is abbreviated as *Parm.* Citations of the Greek commentaries on Aristotle's works all refer to the editions contained in the *Commentaria in Aristotelem Graeca* (*CAG*) (Berlin, 1882-1909), and follow their page and line numbering. My bibliography contains the particular editions I used when citing the Greek commentaries on Plato's works. When I refer to a commentary I follow the standard procedure of using the Latin preposition *in* before the abbreviated title of the work commented on; thus the commentary by Syrianus on Aristotle's *Metaphysics* appears as Syrianus, *in Metaph.*, and the commentary by Proclus on Plato's *Timaeus* appears as Proclus, *in Tim.*

For Laila

Introduction

My aim in this book is to present a history of the metaphysics of Abū ᶜAlī al-Ḥusayn ibn ᶜAbdallāh ibn Sīnā (born before 980 AD – died 1037 AD), known in the West by his Latinized name Avicenna.

Since 1937, when Amélie-Marie Goichon published *La distinction de l'essence et de l'existence d'après Ibn Sīnā (Avicenne)*, no serious book-length study specifically devoted to Avicenna's metaphysics has appeared. This is surprising enough given how influential Avicenna's metaphysical ideas were, but what makes it astonishing is that tremendous advances have taken place since Goichon's time in fields relevant to this topic. Those fields include – from the ultimate to the proximate, to use Avicenna's terms – the study of late-antique Greek philosophy and the study of classical Islamic doctrinal theology, or *kalām*; the study of the Greco-Arabic philosophical translations and the study of the philosophy of al-Fārābī; and the study of Avicenna's metaphysics and the study of his intellectual biography. I shall briefly review those advances in the order just described.

Two changes stand out in fields outside of, but contiguous to, Arabic philosophy. The first is the increasing accessibility of Greek philosophical texts from the late-antique period, the period that immediately preceded the Greco-Arabic translation movement and the birth of Arabic philosophy. Although many of these works have been available in their original Greek since the end of the nineteenth century, when the Teubner editions of the texts of Proclus and other Neoplatonists appeared, and when the Royal Prussian Academy published the 24-volume *Commentaria in Aristotelem Graeca*, it is only fairly recently that many of those texts have been translated, with notes and commentary, into modern European languages. I am thinking in particular of the Budé series of translations of the Neoplatonists into French, and the Ancient Commentators on Aristotle series of translations of the *CAG* into English. These translations, as well as the interpretive work that accompanies the translations and follows in their wake, have enabled even those scholars of Arabic philosophy who do know Greek to gain a vista of the whole late-antique philosophical landscape before venturing into the dark hollow of a Neoplatonic treatise or commentary.

The second major advance has been the increasing availability of *kalām* texts from the century or so immediately preceding Avicenna's birth. In the period when Goichon wrote her book those interested in classical Islamic theology were forced to rely on Islamic doxographies from later periods. These doxographies often reflect post-Avicennian concerns and their value as sources for pre-Avicennian *kalām* history is correspondingly limited. Since Goichon's time many *kalām* texts from the tenth century have been edited, and the often fragmentary evidence of *kalām* developments in the eighth and ninth centuries has now been collated and translated into German.[1] Even though what we have available to us is still only a small fraction of the literary output of the classical *mutakallimūn*, we are much better able than those in Goichon's time to construct an outline of the state of *kalām* in the period before Avicenna.

In the field of Arabic philosophy itself two important advances have taken place since Goichon wrote her book. The first is the large number of editions now available of the Arabic translations from the Greek, be they of Aristotle's texts or of texts wrongly attributed to Aristotle. Although some of these editions are more reliable than others, they nevertheless provide a wealth of evidence of how the translators went about rendering often obscure Greek terms into Arabic. The word choices made by different translators in different places at different times were philosophically significant because subsequent Arabic philosophers scrutinized these texts with great care. A Greco-Arabic Lexicon is currently under preparation, and several fascicles have already appeared.[2] Once completed, the Lexicon will help scholars gain an even more precise understanding of the history of the translations.

The second important advance in the field of Arabic philosophy has been the increasing availability of the philosophical works of al-Fārābī (d. 950). Avicenna referred to al-Fārābī as the Second Teacher, the first being Aristotle, and scholars have known for a long time that Avicenna was influenced by al-Fārābī's thought, either directly, through reading al-Fārābī's works themselves, or indirectly, through reading texts written by philosophers from the generation between al-Fārābī's death and Avicenna's birth. With more of al-Fārābī's texts now edited, scholars can determine with greater precision than Goichon could which philosophical items Avicenna borrowed from al-Fārābī and which ones he chose to leave behind.

Within Avicenna studies there have also been two important advances. Not only are edited versions of many more of Avicenna's texts now available than in Goichon's time, but individual scholars have been working on particular problems of Avicenna's metaphysics, presenting the results of their research in the form of articles in journals and collections, or as chapters in books which cover other philosophers in addition to Avicenna. Goichon was breaking new ground simply by basing her analysis on Avicenna's Arabic texts instead of their Latin translations. Now, close readings of brief passages or even chapters that bear on particular metaphysical topics have enabled scholars to paint detailed pictures of important aspects of Avicenna's metaphysics.[3]

The other advance that has been made in Avicenna studies is also a result of the far greater number of Avicenna's texts now available in edited form. Scholars

[1] van Ess 1991-1997.
[2] Endress and Gutas 1992-.
[3] e.g., Marmura 1979, 1981, 1984a, 1984b and 1992; and Jolivet 1984 and 1991.

of Avicenna's thought are now able to establish a fairly precise intellectual biography by collating those newly available texts with what Avicenna wrote about his life and career in his autobiography and in other works, and with what his student al-Jūzjānī wrote about him. In the past fifteen years or so, efforts to date particular texts and to periodize Avicenna's career have intensified, and scholars can now appeal to evidence of intellectual change from an earlier text to a later one, in order to explain what once seemed to be perplexing inconsistencies in Avicenna's thought. What is more, the close scholarly attention paid to Avicenna's intellectual biography means that we understand much better than before how Avicenna viewed his place in the history of philosophy.[4] It is now clear that Avicenna saw himself as the heir to a long tradition of Aristotelianism, contrary to the claim by some modern interpreters that mystical vision was the engine that drove his thought.

This is all, in a way, to help the reader locate me in my context, that is, the scholarly context in which this book appears. But of course I mean more by context than that, because my aim is to build upon all the scholarly advances I just described, with a view towards locating Avicenna's metaphysics in its own context more precisely than Goichon was able to do 65 years ago. I shall first give a summary of the contents of the book and then say how I think I have accomplished this goal.

My book revolves around the answers Avicenna and his predecessors gave to two pairs of questions: what is the soul and how is it related to the body as its cause, and what is God and how is He related to the world as its cause? The two pairs of questions are similar because any claims I make about how the soul causes the body will inevitably shape how I define the soul, just as any claims I make about how God causes the world will inevitably shape how I define God. In other words, my challenge is to come up with a definition of the soul which satisfies both my intuitions about what the soul is in and of itself, as well as my intuitions about what the soul is relative to its effect, the body. Similarly, my challenge is to come up with a definition of God which satisfies both my intuitions about what God is in and of Himself, as well as my intuitions about what God is relative to His effect, the world.

In order to respond to these challenges, Avicenna and his predecessors invented new concepts and distinctions and reinterpreted old ones. Part I, "Avicenna and the Ammonian Synthesis", is about the complicated history of one such concept, *entelekheia*, a Greek term often translated as "actuality". Aristotle invented the word and used it most prominently to define the soul (*psukhê*) as well as to define change (*kinêsis*). (Strictly speaking, Aristotle's definitions of the soul and change are really descriptions, not definitions, but that need not concern us here.) The soul, Aristotle claims, is the first *entelekheia* of a natural

[4] Gutas 1988.

instrumental body possessing life potentially. Change, he says, is the *entelekheia* of the potential insofar as it is potential. It is not immediately clear what Aristotle meant when he defined the soul and change in these ways. One of the main reasons for this is that the concept of *entelekheia* is so underdetermined. If I am unsure what exactly an *entelekheia* is, I will not be able to get a good sense of what a soul is or what change is. Most modern commentators on Aristotle agree that the best way to make sense of Aristotle's definitions of the soul and of change is to treat his uses of *entelekheia* in each case individually. They put to the side the question of what Aristotle thinks an *entelekheia* might be, and concentrate instead on what Aristotle thinks the soul is an *entelekheia of*, and on what Aristotle thinks change is an *entelekheia of*. The rationale behind this approach is that it is more important to determine Aristotle's concept of the soul and his concept of change, than it is to determine his concept of *entelekheia*.

The late-antique commentators were more reluctant than their modern counterparts to give up on *entelekheia*. They felt that their main challenge was to define what *entelekheia* meant in such a way that Aristotle's uses of it to define the soul and to define change could be seen to be identical at some basic metaphysical level. (Whether the underlying identity that binds together the two uses of *entelekheia* is strong or weak was a subject of disagreement.) This was a daunting task and occasionally the commentators fell back on the approach that would eventually be taken up by modern scholars. Why should the commentators have set themselves up for such frustration? They did this, I believe, because their hermeneutical commitment to viewing Aristotle's philosophy as systematic rather than aporetic was much stronger than that of Aristotle's interpreters today. Aristotle had divided *entelekheia* into two types, first and second, in his definition of the soul. According to most interpretations, the first *entelekheia* refers to a capability to perform some function, while the second *entelekheia* refers to the active exercise of that capability. The commentators, committed to viewing Aristotle as a system-thinker rather than a problem-thinker, felt an obligation to interpret Aristotle's definition of change in light of the first *entelekheia*/second *entelekheia* distinction: to decide whether change was a first or second *entelekheia*, and once that was done, to figure out what the remaining *entelekheia* applied to.

In Chapter 2 I survey the attempts by Alexander of Aphrodisias (fl. 205 AD) and Themistius (fl. 365 AD) to deal with the issue of how consistent Aristotle's use of *entelekheia* to define the soul is with his use of *entelekheia* to define change. Particularly significant, to my mind, are Alexander's promotion of the term *teleiotês* – completeness – as a gloss of *entelekheia*, and his appeals to Aristotle's discussion of what it is to be *teleion*, complete, in order to come up with a list of meanings for *teleiotês* that might then be transferred to *entelekheia*. I then argue that Themistius invents a new concept – I have called it "endedness" – which he adds to the semantic range of *teleiotês*. In other words, Themistius wants to interpret *teleiotês* in such a way that it refers not only to being *teleion*, or complete, but also to the various ways in which a thing can be directed towards or serve as a *telos*, or end.

In Chapters 3 and 4, I describe the attempts by Neoplatonic Aristotle-commentators from Syrianus (d. ca. 437 AD) to Philoponus (d. ca. 570 AD) – but whose central figure was Ammonius (d. ca. 521 AD), son of Hermeias – to add yet another new understanding of *teleiotês*. In addition to completeness and endedness, *teleiotês* was also held by the Neoplatonists to mean perfection. The Neoplatonists used *teleiotês*, now understood as perfection, to refer in a strict sense to superiority in the cosmic hierarchy. And since everything in the world was seen to be striving for perfection, the Neoplatonists also used *teleiotês* to refer to the goal or final cause of each thing's upward reversion (*epistrophê*) towards the well-being (*to eu einai*) that was peculiar to its species.

Concurrently, the Neoplatonic commentators promoted a new understanding of *to teleion* as the perfect. The perfect was seen by the Neoplatonists to refer not so much to something which is complete in a quantitative or qualitative way, or to something which is ended in the sense of being directed towards or serving as a *telos*, but instead to something which is *full* of existence. Because a thing which is full of existence can pass the existence it receives from what is above it in the cosmic hierarchy directly down to what is below it in the cosmic hierarchy, the Neoplatonists used the perfect to refer to the efficient cause of the existence (*to einai*) each thing received from above in the downward procession (*proödos*) of being.

By this stage it becomes clear that *teleiotês*, a term which had originally been fashioned to solve a problem of Aristotelian exegesis – squaring Aristotle's use of *entelekheia* to define the soul with his use of *entelekheia* to define change – had accrued so many new meanings that it was now an important concept in its own right; and that its usefulness in solving that particular exegetical problem was beginning to take a back seat to its usefulness in other contexts. In particular, *teleiotês* and *to teleion* were now being used by the Neoplatonists to integrate their metaphysics of reversion and procession with the Aristotelian concepts of final causation and efficient causation. Partly as a result of this development, discussions of causation came to be seen by the Neoplatonists to fall into the domain of metaphysics rather than into the domain of natural philosophy, as Aristotle had thought.

I argue in Chapters 3 and 4 that this new understanding of perfection and the perfect had profound consequences for the way the Neoplatonists responded to the metaphysical questions and challenges I outlined above. In Chapter 3, I discuss how the Neoplatonists' concepts of perfection and the perfect shaped their answer to the question, what is God and how is He related to the world? The Neoplatonists were in agreement that God should be described, as far as one was able, as One: as utterly simple and unique. But if, relative to the world, God is also seen to be *both* the original source of procession, *and* the ultimate goal of reversion, His combination of efficient causality and final causality would entail duality where there ought to be only unity. I argue that despite their vigorous efforts the Neoplatonists were unable to resolve this dilemma satisfactorily.

In a similar way I discuss in Chapter 4 how the Neoplatonists' new understanding of perfection and the perfect played out in their discussions of the soul and its relationship to the body. Since Alexander's time *teleiotês* had been the term commentators turned to when they wished to gloss Aristotle's use of *entelekheia* to define the soul. Yet now that *teleiotês* was seen by the Neoplatonists to be related to its effect as a final cause, the soul, as a *teleiotês*, should be seen to be related to the body as its final cause. Seeing the soul as the final cause of the body was not at all difficult to reconcile with Aristotle's conception of the soul, since he himself had said that the soul was related to the body as its final cause as well as its formal and efficient cause.

But what the Neoplatonists meant by final cause was significantly different from what Aristotle had meant by final cause. In particular, the Neoplatonists had divided Aristotle's four causes – the efficient, the final, the formal and the material – into causes which are separate from or transcend their effects, and causes which are inseparable from or immanent in their effects. The Neoplatonists reckoned that the efficient and final causes transcend their effects, whereas the formal and material causes are immanent in their effects. The result is that if the correct way to understand the soul's being an *entelekheia* is to see the soul as a *teleiotês*; if a *teleiotês* is related to its effect as a final cause; if therefore the soul is related to the body as a final cause; and if final causes are separate from their effects; then I can claim that the soul is separate from the body.

For a Neoplatonist this is a welcome conclusion, since a separate soul is far more consistent than an inseparable one with the Platonic picture of the soul as pre-existing the body's birth and surviving the body's death. But Neoplatonists whose job it was to comment on texts where Aristotle discusses the soul faced the exegetical challenge of integrating their understanding of the soul as a *teleiotês*, along with all its happy consequences, into Aristotle's descriptions of the soul, according to which – by Peripatetic accounts, at least – the soul is *not* separate from the body. I argue that the solutions some Neoplatonic commentators came up with to face this challenge are sophisticated and in some cases quite justifiable readings of Aristotle's theory of the soul.

In Chapter 5 I examine how all these Greek terms – *entelekheia*, *teleion*, *telos* and *teleiotês* – were translated into Arabic in the ninth and tenth centuries. The tendency among scholars has been to view the translations as a disruption in the history of philosophy: before the translations there was Greek philosophy, and after the translations there was Arabic (or Islamic) philosophy. Of course there is no denying that the translations did cause a certain amount of disruption. In fact translation movements have often forced important conceptual changes to take place in the history of philosophy. In the case of the Greco-Arabic translation movement, the ways the translators chose to render a particular Greek term or phrase into Arabic sometimes exposed new ways for an Arabic philosopher to conceptualize old problems which had stumped his Greek predecessors, sometimes flushed out problems which had been hidden to his Greek predecessors, and sometimes created entirely new problems which his Greek predecessors had never been forced to confront.

All this is true. But I argue that we can also detect a great deal of philosophical continuity between the translators and their immediate predecessors. One piece of evidence of this continuity is the fact that two distinct concepts in Aristotle's philosophy – actuality (*entelekheia*) and end (*telos*) – were conflated in the Arabic version of his *Metaphysics* and appear together as perfection (*tamām*). In other words, a Neoplatonic premise – that an *entelekheia*, since it is a *teleiotês*, is related to its effect as a final cause – is embedded in the very wording of the Arabic version of an Aristotelian text. To my mind this shows that the translators, particularly those active in the early stages of the translation movement, did not stand outside of the history of philosophy but were an integral part of the Neoplatonic continuum. I end Chapter 5 by discussing the philosophical impact the translators' word choices had on the writings of early Arabic philosophers such as al-Fārābī.

In Chapter 6 I examine the ways in which Avicenna stood as heir to this long series of interpretations of perfection and the perfect. In particular, I consider Avicenna's application of the concept of perfection to the soul, and – as in Chapter 4 – focus on the role perfection plays in his discussions of the soul's causal relationship with the body. Avicenna follows the later Greco-Arabic translators in using *kamāl* rather than *tamām* when defining the soul. Nevertheless, he uses *kamāl* and *tamām* interchangeably in other contexts, and in most cases, I argue, he understands *kamāl* and *tamām* in a Neoplatonic sense, that is, in the way that a Neoplatonist understood *teleiotês*, and not in the way that Aristotle understood *entelekheia*. This meant that Avicenna, like the Neoplatonists, understood that the manner in which *kamāl* and *tamām* related to their effects was as final causes; and in addition to the term *al-ᶜillatu l-ghāʾiyya*, which he takes from the later translators, Avicenna refers to the final cause as *al-ᶜillatu t-tamāmiyya* and *al-ᶜillatu l-kamāliyya*.

Avicenna also accepts and promotes the Neoplatonic distinction between the efficient and final causes, which are separate from their effects, and the formal and material causes, which are inseparable from their effects. I argue that Avicenna's clear acceptance of the Neoplatonic premise that the final cause is separate from its effect was crucial to his argument that the human rational soul survives the death of the body it originated in, and that in this respect his theory is similar to that of Neoplatonic commentators such as Philoponus, whose theories I described in Chapter 4.

I also argue that one other striking piece of evidence of Avicenna's Neoplatonic inheritance can be detected in the different ways he distinguishes between first and second perfections. In some contexts, the model he follows is that of Aristotle, holding that the first perfection refers to a capability to perform some function, while the second perfection refers to the active exercise of that capability. At other times, Avicenna says that the first perfection should be understood as that which is necessary for something to exist, while the second perfection should be understood as that which is necessary for something to exist well. To my mind this latter method of distinguishing between first and second perfections is clearly an echo of the Neoplatonists' distinction between existence (*to einai*) and well-being (*to eu einai*), the former passed down from above in the course of procession (*proödos*), the latter striven for from below in the course of reversion (*epistrophê*). I argue that Avicenna saw no fundamental discrepancy between the two ways he distinguished between first and second perfections, but that if pushed, he would regard the Neoplatonic method (i.e., necessary to exist/necessary to exist well) as basic, and the Aristotelian method (i.e., capability to perform some function/exercise of that capability) as derivative. This suggests that Avicenna's cosmology is best understood as being structured along Neoplatonic lines of procession and reversion.

In Part II, "The Beginnings of the Avicennian Synthesis", I begin by focusing on the role played by perfection and the perfect in more general discussions of causal relations. One of the many challenges facing an interpreter of Aristotle's teleology is determining how the final cause operates in tandem with the other three causes: the formal, the material and the efficient. Sometimes Aristotle simply identifies the final and formal causes and claims that they operate in tandem with the material cause. In organic things the form is the end and the end is the form. It is for the sake of the form "cow", for example, that the materials that make up a cow – flesh, blood, bone, sinew – come together. Those material elements, left on their own, would not make up a cow, Aristotle reckons; it is only the form that explains their coming together. (Yet not every end is a form. The Unmoved Mover, for example, is an end, but it is not a form, at least according to most interpreters.)

In other contexts Aristotle says that the final cause operates in tandem with the efficient and not the material cause. Health is the cause of hard work, he says, and hard work of health. But they are not causes of each other in identical ways. Hard work is the efficient cause of health, and health is the final cause of hard work. Among Neoplatonic commentators there was little debate over the fact that the efficient was the cause that most deserved to operate in tandem with the final. This was because, as mentioned already, both the efficient and the final causes were seen to be separate from their effects, while the formal and the material causes were seen to be inseparable from their effects. Since the Neoplatonists felt strongly that something that was separate from matter was superior to something that was inseparable from matter, it would therefore be demeaning for the final cause to be thought of as operating in tandem with the material cause.

Avicenna follows the lead of the Neoplatonists in regarding the efficient and the final as the causes that operate in tandem with each other. And like the Neoplatonists he saw as one of his primary challenges determining the precise nature of the complementarity between efficient and final causes. Avicenna goes to great length to show how the final cause and the efficient cause do not compete over the same *explanandum* but instead explain different *explananda* in a complementary way. The final cause, Avicenna says, has explanatory priority with respect to essence, while the efficient cause has explanatory priority with respect to existence.

I shall use Aristotle's example to explain what Avicenna means. Yesterday I worked hard in my garden with a view to attaining a state of health; with a view to becoming healthier, in other words. The idea of health was in my mind *before* I started working hard, because the idea of health was what got me off the sofa and out into the garden in the first place. But health only came into existence concretely – in my body, that is – *after* I had finished the hard work, because the hard work was what caused my body to be in a state of health. Put in Avicenna's terms, when health acts as a final cause, when it is conceived in the mind as a universal idea or essence to be striven for, it comes *before* the efficient cause, hard work. But the health that comes into concrete existence in my body comes *after* the efficient cause, hard work. The final cause, health, is prior to the efficient cause, hard work, with respect to essence, because the idea or essence of health comes before its effect, hard work. But the efficient cause, hard work, is prior to the final cause, health, with respect to existence because the existence of hard work comes before its effect, health.

Because Avicenna often uses the term *shayʾiyya*, "thingness", for essence in many of his discussions of how the final and efficient causes operate in tandem with each other, I try to explain what he meant by that strange term. In Chapter 7, I focus on ninth- and tenth-century debates about what it is to be a thing, and about how things are related to existents. These debates took place among *mutakallimūn* – that is, those engaged in formulating Islamic doctrine, or *kalām* – and philosophers such as al-Fārābī discussed the issue as well. I then examine Avicenna's assertions about things and existents in contexts outside the problem of final-efficient complementarity. I compare what Avicenna says in those contexts with what the *mutakallimūn* and al-Fārābī say, and find that in some important respects al-Fārābī's position is closer to the Muᶜtazilite *mutakallimūn*'s position than it is to Avicenna's position; and that Avicenna's position is closer to the position of the Ashᶜarite and Māturīdite *mutakallimūn*, than it is to al-Fārābī's position. This is surprising, given our expectation that a philosopher is much more likely to agree with another philosopher than he is to agree with a *mutakallim*, and given our expectation that a *mutakallim* is much more likely to agree with another *mutakallim* than he is to agree with a philosopher.

In examining those passages where Avicenna talks about thingness and essence in contexts outside the problem of final-efficient complementarity, I list Avicenna's most important assertions about how thingness and essence are related to existence, and find those assertions to be incompatible. Sometimes Avicenna claims that essence and existence are always found together, that one always entails the other, and that they should be seen to be on an equal footing, with neither prior to the other. Other times he seems to favor essence, implying that it is logically prior to existence. And sometimes he even appears to entertain the notion that there is a certain category of essence which is in no way connected to existence. This implies that essence and existence might not always be found together.

Next I turn to the passages where Avicenna talks about thingness and essence in the context of final-efficient complementarity. Chapter 8 focuses on a pressing philological question: whether, in those particular passages, the instances where Avicenna appears to use the term *shayʾiyya*, "thingness", should be emended to read *sababiyya*, "causality", instead. I argue that the weight of evidence compels us to retain *shayʾiyya*. Chapter 9 attempts to explain how Avicenna's application of the essence/existence distinction to the problem of final-efficient complementarity arose partly from his attempt to solve a specific problem of Aristotelian exegesis, namely, how to avoid circularity when holding that health and hard work are the causes of each other.

To Chapter 7's list of assertions about how thingness and essence are related to existence in passages outside of the context of final-efficient complementarity, I then add the assertions Avicenna makes about how thingness and essence are related to existence in passages devoted to the problem of final-efficient complementarity. I find that while Avicenna's assertions remain incompatible, there seems to be evidence of a development in his thinking. In works from his middle period Avicenna uses the terms *shayʾiyya* (thingness) as well as essence (*māhiyya*), whereas in works from his late period he relies solely on *māhiyya* (essence). I discuss the various reasons why Avicenna's views on this issue might have evolved. I argue that the most important reason was that with *māhiyya* rather than *shayʾiyya* Avicenna reckoned that he would have an easier time both upholding the universal applicability of the final cause, and establishing the final cause's primacy among the causes. This is because there were reasons for Avicenna to think that *māhiyya* was itself more universally applicable than *shayʾiyya*; and because *māhiyya*, if seen to be logically prior to existence, would provide a basis on which Avicenna could argue for the final cause's primacy.

In Chapter 6 I concluded that important pieces of evidence suggest that Avicenna's cosmology is best understood along Neoplatonic lines of procession and reversion. In Chapter 9 I described how Avicenna used his distinction between essence and existence to attack the problem of how final causes and efficient causes operate in tandem. The way Avicenna went about treating this issue suggested to me that he was partly motivated by a desire to resolve an issue of Aristotelian exegesis: avoiding the trap of circularity he might fall into when he held that the final and the efficient are causes of each other. In Chapter 10 I argue that Avicenna's attempts to solve the problem of final-efficient complementarity by using his essence/existence distinction should also be viewed in the broader context of his Neoplatonic cosmology of procession and return.

As I described in Chapters 3 and 6, the mechanism of procession is built around the idea that when something becomes perfect, when it has become so full of existence that it can pass the existence it receives from above directly down to what is below, the relation of the perfect thing to the imperfect thing below it is the relation of an efficient cause to its effect. I argue that Avicenna's assertion that the efficient cause is prior to the final in terms of existence, is compatible with this premise.

The mechanism of reversion, by contrast, is built around the idea that the perfection possessed by something higher in the cosmic hierarchy serves as a goal for something lower than it in the cosmic hierarchy. The perfection possessed by the higher thing acts as a final cause on the lower thing, in the sense that the lower thing strives to attain the higher thing's perfection by becoming as similar to the higher thing as it can be. Not so obvious is how this idea might be compatible with Avicenna's assertion that the final cause is prior to the efficient cause with respect to essence. Given that perfection and essence can each be understood as referring to a thing's substantial form, then perfection and essence will be identifiable at some level. It is by being as human as I can be that I revert upwards. This is because my being as human as I can be entails my being as rational as I can be, since rationality is what sets the species "human" apart from other species of animal such as "cow". My being as rational as I can be consists simply in my thinking about universal intelligibles as much as I can; and by thinking about universal intelligibles as much as I can, I revert upwards to the higher level of the Active Intellect, which is thinking about universal intelligibles all the time.

The perfection possessed by the Active Intellect serves as my goal while I am thinking about universal intelligibles, because I am not thinking about universal intelligibles for their own sake. Rather, I am thinking about universal intelligibles because by thinking about universal intelligibles I imitate the Active Intellect and thereby come to possess, or at least participate in, the perfection which the Active Intellect possesses. In the sense that it causes me to fulfill my humanity, in the sense that it causes my substantial form or essence to inhere in me to the greatest degree possible, the Active Intellect, as a final cause, is prior, in terms of essence, to the efficient cause of my thinking about universal intelligibles. This is because I – meaning my human rational soul –

am the efficient cause of the preparatory activities that enable me to think about universal intelligibles, and I would never have begun to serve as the efficient cause of those activities in the first place if the goal of reversion had not been there first.

With some effort, therefore, Avicenna can integrate his use of the essence/existence distinction (inherited from the *mutakallimūn*) to explain the problem of final-efficient complementarity (inherited from Aristotle), into his cosmology of return and procession (inherited from the Neoplatonists). But Avicenna still faces the same theological problem I described in Chapter 3. In Chapter 3 I argued that the Neoplatonists were unable to resolve the following dilemma. On the one hand, God is utterly simple and unique. On the other hand, God is both the original source of procession and the ultimate goal of reversion, and God's combination of efficient causality and final causality entails duality in Him rather than simplicity.

Avicenna tries to deal with this problem by arguing that God is perfect – that is, that He possesses perfection – yet is at the same time *above* perfection. In the sense that God possesses perfection God is related to the world as a final cause. God's perfection acts as a goal for all other beings. What is more, if God possesses perfection and is therefore perfect, and if the perfect is related to what is below it as an efficient cause, then God will also act as an efficient cause of all other beings. God's final causality is therefore identical, at least extensionally, with His efficient causality.

There is a flaw in this picture, however. The perfect acts as an efficient cause of what is below it by being so full of existence that it can pass the existence it receives from above directly down to what is below. Since there is nothing above God, He cannot receive any existence from above and pass it down to the Intellect below. Therefore Avicenna is forced to say that God does not just possess perfection, He is above perfection. Being above perfection, by Avicenna's reckoning, means having *too* much existence – so much so that it spills over and starts the cascade of procession downwards. But Avicenna's proposal – holding that God possesses perfection yet is also above perfection – not only fails *prima facie* to solve the duality problem, it raises the problem of consistency in his theology, and it flushes out yet another problem embedded in the premise that God is *both* an efficient and a final cause.

The consistency problem is this: if Avicenna thinks of God as being above perfection, then at least in one sense he seems to be holding God's efficient causality to be prior to his final causality. Perhaps it even forces him to hold that God is not a final cause at all, with the topmost of the celestial Intellects now serving in that role. How are we then to reconcile this picture with Avicenna's many unambiguous statements that the final is the primary cause and the noblest of the causes, that metaphysics consists in understanding the final cause, and that God Himself serves in the role of ultimate final cause?

The second problem is that as the possessor of perfection, as the ultimate final cause of reversion, God's quality of causal *self-sufficiency* takes center stage. As that which is above perfection, as the original efficient cause of procession, however, God's quality of causal *productivity* takes center stage. In the former case God is seen as isolated and transcendent. In the latter case God is seen as involved and creative. How are we then to reconcile these two aspects of the divine, the transcendent and the self-sufficient on the one hand, and the involved and productive on the other?

In Chapters 11 to 14 I describe how Avicenna went about devising a new way to solve the problem of retaining both of these divine characteristics – transcendent self-sufficiency and involved productivity – without implying any unwanted duality in God. To do this Avicenna constructed what I call a matrix of distinctions. The distinctions he used to build this matrix include the following: the distinction between necessary existence and possible existence; the distinction between in itself and through another; and the distinction between uncaused and caused. Ultimately Avicenna would reduce this matrix of distinctions to a single, overarching distinction: the distinction between an uncaused necessary of existence in itself (*wājib al-wujūd bi-dhātihi*), and a caused necessary of existence through another (*wājib al-wujūd bi-ghayrihi*).

Although Avicenna's matrix was new, many of the distinctions he used to construct it were old. Chapters 11, 12 and 13 are an inventory of the sources that he drew from to come up with his matrix. In Chapter 11, I review what Aristotle has to say about necessity, in the Arabic versions of *Metaphysics* 5.5, the chapter of his philosophical lexicon where he distinguishes between different ways of being necessary; *Physics* 2.9, where he discusses hypothetical necessity, the kind of necessity that operates down here in the world of coming-to-be and passing-away; *Metaphysics* 12.7, where he might be misunderstood as advocating the idea that God is a necessary being, when in fact he does not; and in *De Interpretatione* 12-13, where he discusses the relations between the modal operators "necessarily" (or "necessary that"), possibly (or "possible that") and "impossibly" (or "impossible that").

I argue that Avicenna owes a *conceptual* debt to *Metaphysics* 5.5, since he takes from that chapter the idea that what is necessary can be seen to be self-sufficient (that is, as not being dependent upon a cause); to be productive (that is, as necessitating its effect); and to be produced (that is, as necessitated by its cause). I also argue that Avicenna owes a *terminological* debt to *De Interpretatione* 12-13, since in those chapters, unlike *Metaphysics* 5.5 (where *to anankaion* – the necessary – is translated into Arabic as *al-muḍṭarr*), the translator chose to render *anankaion einai* – necessary that it be – as *wājib an yūjada*. Crucially, the Arabic translator of the *De Interpretatione* used the existential verb *w-j-d* to render what in Greek was a merely copulative *einai*. I end Chapter 11 by explaining how this translator's decision allowed Arabic interpreters such as Avicenna to think of possibility as contingency, that is, as causedness.

In Chapter 12 I discuss how al-Fārābī contributed to Avicenna's matrix of distinctions. In his *Commentary on the De Interpretatione* al-Fārābī came up with a distinction between *mumkin al-wujūd bi-nafsihi* and *wājib al-wujūd bi-nafsihi*. But this distinction was introduced by al-Fārābī in a discussion of *De Interpretatione* 9's problem of future contingents, and of the effect that God's foreknowledge of those future events might have on the question of determinism. I argue that this is not the context in which Avicenna devises and employs his matrix of distinctions, and that the influence of al-Fārābī's distinction on Avicenna was probably only terminological, and not conceptual.

I examine what the *mutakallimūn* have to say in Chapter 13. In contrast to al-Fārābī, who seems to have been most influenced by Muᶜtazilism, Avicenna's most important theological source was the Sunnī *kalām* of the Ashᶜarites and Māturīdites. In order to explain the nature of the eternality possessed by God and His attributes, Sunnī *mutakallimūn* moved away from earlier, pre-Avicennian attempts to argue that when we define an eternal thing as "that whose existence has no beginning in time" (*mā lā awwala li-wujūdihi*), what we really mean is that an eternal thing *is uncaused*; to later, post-Avicennian attempts to argue that when we define an eternal thing as "that which has never ceased to be nor will ever cease to be" (*mā lam yazal wa-lā yazālu*), what we really mean is that an eternal thing *cannot possibly not exist*, and that therefore an eternal thing *is necessary of existence*. This transformation was motivated by the Sunnī *mutakallimūn*'s desire to reconcile their use of eternality in proofs of the world's createdness, with their use of eternality in discussions of how the divine attributes (*ṣifāt*) relate to the divine Self (*dhāt*).

I argue that evidence from a number of texts from the last quarter of the tenth century, as well as from one of Avicenna's earliest works, the *Ḥikma ᶜArūḍiyya*, which he composed in 1001, shows that the separate influences of the Arabic Aristotle, al-Fārābī, and the *mutakallimūn* were combining to suggest the notion of the necessary of existence in itself to a number of thinkers. However, none of those other thinkers focused as intently as Avicenna did on creating a coherent matrix of distinctions that supported that notion.

Chapter 14 addresses the question of evolution in the ways Avicenna constructed his matrix of distinctions and the uses he put it to. As I just mentioned, Avicenna's new matrix of distinctions is first articulated in his *Ḥikma ᶜArūḍiyya*, one of his earliest works, and I examine his discussion there and in the *Mabdaᵓ wa-maᶜād*, another early work. I conclude by arguing that the tension which one scholar has detected between the different ways in which Avicenna applied the matrix of distinctions in the *Shifāᵓ*, *Najāt* and *Ishārāt* – works from his middle and late periods – is prefigured by a tension between the different ways he applied the matrix of distinctions in the *Ḥikma ᶜArūḍiyya* and in the *Mabdaᵓ wa-maᶜād*.

My treatment of Avicenna's metaphysics in this book is not definitive. Many more books will be required before justice is done to a subject as complex, wide-ranging and historically important as this. But I am still confident that I have moved the study of Avicenna's philosophy forward. Apart from the particular hypotheses argued for in each chapter, I hope by the end of the book to have convinced the reader of the general idea that Avicenna's metaphysics is best understood as bridging two periods in the history of philosophy. In one sense Avicenna's metaphysics is the culmination of what I call the Ammonian synthesis. By "Ammonian synthesis" I refer to the tendency, epitomized by the Aristotle-commentator Ammonius and his students, to incorporate the larger project of reconciling Plato's and Aristotle's philosophies (I call this the greater *sumphônia*), into the smaller project of forging a single, consistent doctrine out of the sometimes incongruent theories found in Aristotle's many treatises (I call this the lesser *sumphônia*).

All of this integrating spurred the thinkers of the Ammonian synthesis to invent new metaphysical tools, a crucial example of which is the concept of perfection. As a consequence, Avicenna's appeal to *kamāl* and Aristotle's appeal to *entelekheia* in explaining the soul's relationship to the body are superficially similar but profoundly different. To ignore perfection's complex history is to ignore the context in which Avicenna's metaphysics was born and developed. The lesson to be drawn is that further scholarship on other issues in Avicenna's philosophy will benefit from direct comparison with parallel treatments of those same issues by earlier philosophers of the Ammonian synthesis.

This point may seem underwhelming, if not obvious; but the tendency of some scholars has been to compare Avicenna directly with Aristotle, skipping (or treating only perfunctorily) the profound developments – particularly among the Neoplatonists – that took place during the 1,300 years that separated the two thinkers. And even when scholars do take Neoplatonism into account, their attention has been so fixed on pseudo-Aristotelian works such as the *Theology of Aristotle*, that whatever Neoplatonism is found in the philosophy of a thinker such as Avicenna is assumed to be directly attributable to those notorious treatises. One thing which my book shows is that Neoplatonism came to philosophers such as Avicenna not so much through a funnel (viz., the *Theology of Aristotle* and a few other pieces of pseudepigraphia) but through a sieve (viz., the many Aristotle-commentaries by philosophers of the Ammonian synthesis).

But what do I mean when I claim that Avicenna's metaphysics is the *culmination* of the Ammonian synthesis? By 1001, the Aristotle-commentators of the Ammonian synthesis had been so successful in folding the larger project of reconciling Plato and Aristotle into the smaller project of reconciling Aristotle with Aristotle, that to the 21-year-old Avicenna, then composing his first philosophical *summa*, an Ammonian interpretation (most importantly, of the human rational soul's separability) seemed like an entirely natural reading of

Aristotle's texts. At the same time the young Avicenna grew up and lived in the provinces – in Bukhārā, at the periphery of the Islamic world – and was almost entirely self-taught in philosophy. The 21-year-old prodigy thus found himself confronted by all the philosophical problems entailed by the Ammonian synthesis (most importantly, the conceptual duality that results from God's operating as both efficient and final cause), yet without having first been inculcated with the hermenutical commitments (most importantly, the need to reconcile Plato and Aristotle) which had originally created those problems, and which had still served to motivate his predecessor al-Fārābī, a student of the Aristotelian school in metropolitan Baghdad and the author of a treatise on the harmony of Plato and Aristotle.

This freedom from hermeneutical commitments enabled Avicenna to attack the old Ammonian problems by laying the groundwork for a new synthesis, an Avicennian synthesis between the Islamic theology of the classical *mutakallimūn* and the philosophy propounded by the Arabic heirs (most importantly, al-Fārābī) to that earlier, Ammonian synthesis. The *kalām* influence on Avicenna's distinction between essence and existence will be obvious enough, I hope. And though the language which Avicenna used to formulate his distinction between *necessary of existence in itself* and *necessary of existence through another* was undoubtedly shaped by the Arabic Aristotle, particularly in the digested form contained in al-Fārābī's writings, his attempt to apply that new distinction to the relationship between God and the world, was prefigured by earlier *kalām* debates about how best to describe the relationship between God and God's eternal attributes. The shelf-life of the Avicennian synthesis was even longer than that of the Ammonian synthesis. After some of Avicenna's works had been translated into Latin in Toledo in the second half of the twelfth century, his metaphysical ideas came to exert profound influence on Latin scholastic philosophy. More significantly, working out the implications of Avicenna's metaphysical distinctions was to become the predominant challenge of post-classical Islamic thought, particularly in the areas of epistemology, cosmology and theology; and evidence of the impact of Avicenna's metaphysics can be found in Arabic philosophical works from as late as the end of the nineteenth century. The history of the Avicennian synthesis is the subject of another book, however.

I ought to say a few words about the general approach I took when writing this book. One of the worries I had in devoting so much attention to the Aristotelian and Neoplatonic background to Avicenna's thought was that I risked being accused of secret membership in what Mahdi once described as the "charmed circle of source-hunters".[5] The source-hunter, by Mahdi's reckoning, sees

[5] Mahdi 1990, 700.

nothing original in the Arabic philosophical text he is reading, only worn coins, vestiges of earlier (and greater) Greek thinkers.

My aim in devoting such a great chunk of the book to the Aristotelian and Neoplatonic background to Avicenna's thought is not to prove that he had no original thoughts, or to support the traditional Western notion that the Arabic philosophers simply received Greek philosophy and then, three centuries later, handed it back – slightly scuffed – to Europe, where it presumably belonged. On the contrary, I hope that by describing as accurately and completely as I can the intellectual context in which Avicenna was situated, a more precise picture of his originality will emerge.

Sabra has spoken of the twin ills of reductionism and precursorism in the study of the history of Arabic science, and I believe his analysis applies just as acutely to the study of the history of Arabic philosophy. According to a reductionist, as with a source-hunter, Arabic philosophy will appear to be nothing but a "reflection, sometimes faded, sometimes bright or more or less altered, of earlier (mostly Greek) examples".[6] Precursorism is the opposite tendency. A precursorist sees nothing but glorious originality in an Arabic philosophical text, and traces later, supposedly original, European ideas back to their true Arabic roots.

The middle road between reductionism and precursorism is contextualism, and this is the approach I have tried to follow. More specifically, a contextualist approach requires that Arabic philosophy not be viewed through the lens of Greek philosophy or through the lens of medieval and early-modern European philosophy. Instead, contextualism demands that I try as hard as I can to see Arabic philosophy on its own terms.

In the case of a book on Avicenna's metaphysics, this means that my translations of and citations to Greek sources will, wherever possible, take into account the Greek sources' Arabic translations, since Avicenna read the Arabic translations and not the Greek originals. It also means that in addition to Aristotle I take into account the Greek commentaries on Aristotle, many of which were also translated into Arabic, since Avicenna read commentaries as well as the Aristotelian texts themselves.[7] What is more, I should take into account the works of al-Fārābī, since Avicenna thought of him as his Second Teacher. Finally, I should take into account works of *kalām*, and particularly tenth-century *kalām*, since Avicenna studied some theology as a youngster.[8]

Only after I have amassed the extant raw materials which Avicenna had before him, can I begin the task of the historian of philosophy: reconstructing the spectrum of philosophical options available to Avicenna on a given issue, and

[6] Sabra 1987, 223-224.

[7] *wa-naẓara fī n-nuṣūsi wa-sh-shurūḥi*: Ibn Khallikān, *Wafayāt al-aᶜyān wa-anbāᵓ abnāᵓ az-zamān* 1 (#182), 420,10-11.

[8] *[qad] ḥafiẓa ashyāᵓa min uṣūli d-dīni*: Ibn Khallikān, *Wafayāt al-aᶜyān wa-anbāᵓ abnāᵓ az-zamān* 1 (#182), 420,4-5.

explaining why he chose one option and not others. What I have found in Avicenna's metaphysics is – to use Sabra's terms once again – an active appropriation of his sources rather than a passive reception of them.

Part I

Avicenna and the Ammonian Synthesis

1. Aristotle
Perfection in the Definitions of the Soul and of Change

I should begin Part I with a word of warning. I intend to offer not so much my own interpretation of Aristotle's understanding of *entelekheia*, but rather a survey of *entelekheia*-interpretations of philosophers from Alexander of Aphrodisias to Avicenna. Although my hope is that Aristotle specialists will be interested in reading about how issues relating to *entelekheia* played out in late-antique and early-Arabic philosophy, I cannot say whether this will contribute to their debates about what Aristotle really thought about those issues. My goal is simply to begin contextualizing Avicenna's theory: to start proving, in other words, that his understanding of perfection and the perfect, and his application of those concepts to "hot" issues in late-antique and early-Arabic metaphysics, can be seen as justifiable, and even compelling, readings of Aristotelian philosophy, *given* the peculiar evolution of the interpretation-history which he was heir to, and *given* the subtle conceptual shifts which resulted from the word choices made by the Greco-Arabic translators. This is why I have gone into such detail describing the theories of Avicenna's predecessors, and why I have based my own translations, wherever possible, on the Arabic versions of his predecessors' Greek works.

Aristotle invented the term *entelekheia*, sometimes translated into English as "actuality", but also as "fulfillment", "perfection" and "completion". Aristotle uses the term most often when he applies it adverbially in constructions such as the dative *entelekheiâi* and the prepositional phrase *kat' entelekheian*. When used in this adverbial way *entelekheia* is roughly synonymous with *energeia*, "activity", in its analogous constructions *energeiâi* and *kat' energeian*. The terms *energeia* and *entelekheia* are most interchangeable when they are placed in opposition to the term *dunamis*, "potentiality", similarly applied in the dative *dunamei* and in the prepositional phrase *kata dunamin*. In their adverbial forms *entelekheiâi* and *energeiâi* mean something like "in actuality", while *dunamei* means something like "in potentiality".

Aristotle uses the term *entelekheia* less often – but more interestingly – in a nominal, as opposed to an adverbial sense. In other words, Aristotle not only says that something is *in* a state of actuality (X is *entelekheiâi*), but that something is *itself* an actuality (X is *entelekheia*), in which case *entelekheia* is used as a predicate, or – most rarely of all – that actuality is *itself* something or other (*entelekheia* is X), in which case *entelekheia* is the subject. When used in this nominal rather than adverbial way, *entelekheia* can be – and has been – understood as referring not only to the *state of being actual*, but also to the *process of becoming actual*. In other words, when used in the nominal rather than adverbial way, *entelekheia* has been interpreted by some scholars as referring not only to the state of actuality, but also to the process of actualization.

Of these nominal uses of *entelekheia*, the two most prominent occur in *De Anima* 2.1, where Aristotle defines what *psukhê* ("soul") is, and in *Physics* 3.1, where Aristotle defines what *kinêsis* ("motion" or, more generally, "change") is. In the *De Anima* translation incorrectly attributed to Isḥāq ibn Ḥunayn and edited by Badawī, Aristotle says:

L1

Arisṭūṭālīs, *Fī n-nafs*, 29,9-30,4
Aristotle, *DA* 2.1, 412a6-28

It is held that substance is one of several classes of things, and that one [type] is like matter, which in itself does not subsist as a particular thing; another is the shape and form by which a thing is made particular, such that it may be said to be *this* [thing, i.e., as opposed to that thing]; and the third is the compound of these two. Matter is a potentiality, and form is an "*entelekheia*", meaning perfection [*fa-l-hayūlā quwwatun mina l-qūwā wa-ṣ-ṣūratun hiya anṭalākhiyā ya*ᶜ*nī t-tamām = esti d'hê men hulê dunamis to d'eidos entelekheia*], this [i.e., *entelekheia*] being of two types: the first is like knowledge, and the other is like contemplating.

Now bodies are said to most warrant being substances, and especially natural ones, for these are prior to the rest. Among natural bodies are those which possess life, and those which do not possess life, life referring simply to that which nourishes itself, grows and decays. So every natural, living body will doubtless be a composite substance. And since it is the body which we describe as being such [i.e., that it has life in it], it follows that it [body] will not be a soul, because body is not predicated of a substrate, but instead is like substrate or matter.

The soul, then, must be substance as form of a natural body which possesses life potentially. Substance is "*entelekheia*", and "*entelekheia*" is of two types, the first being like knowledge, because sleeping and waking come about only through the soul's existence, and waking is equivalent to contemplating, whereas sleeping is equivalent to possessing [the capability to think] without activity [i.e., without actively using that capability]. As far as coming-to-be is concerned, knowledge is [also] likely to be prior. On account of this the soul is an "*entelekheia*", that is, the first perfection of a natural body possessing life potentially [*min ajli dhālika ṣārati n-nafsu anṭalāshiyā wa-huwa awwalu tamāmi jirmin ṭabī*ᶜ*iyyin dhī ḥayātin bi-l-quwwati = dio hê psukhê estin entelekheia hê prôtê sômatos phusikou dunamei zôên ekhontos*].[1]

[1] I address the problem of the Arabic *De Anima* translations in Chapter 5.

I should remind readers that my English translations are, wherever possible, drawn from the Arabic versions of the Greek texts, which is why I have rendered *tamām* here in L1 (and *kamāl* in L2) as "perfection" rather than as "actuality", since "perfection" is the English word that most precisely evokes Avicenna's understanding of those two Arabic terms. When discussing Aristotle's own uses of *entelekheia*, however, I have more often than not simply transliterated that Greek term; but I have also felt free to translate it variously – as actuality, actualization, perfection or completion – in order to illustrate the ambiguities and apparent inconsistencies which worried the Aristotle-commentators.

In any case, two issues can be distinguished already. The first is that Aristotle seems to think that *entelekheia* is indicative of the type of substance a thing is. Substance, according to Aristotle, may be viewed as matter, as form, or as the composite of matter and form. In L1 *entelekheia* is clearly meant to be tied to substance as form. More particularly, *entelekheia* seems intended to indicate the respect in which substance as form may be contrasted with substance as matter: just as matter is linked to a substance in its state of potentiality, so form is linked to a substance in its state of actuality.

So far so good. The second issue, however, clouds this picture. Aristotle thinks that *entelekheia* is divisible into two types, or modes – first *entelekheia* and second *entelekheia* – and that the soul is a first *entelekheia*. One of the examples Aristotle gives of first and second *entelekheiai* – knowledge (*epistêmê*) and contemplating (*theôrein*) – helps us, though not much, and the whole distinction comes across as underdetermined. Aristotle has already said that the soul is substance as form, and we are meant to see that as representing *entelekheia* – actuality – in contrast to the potentiality represented by substance as matter. Yet in the distinction between knowledge and thinking, it is contemplating, not knowledge, which seems closer to representing actuality. How then can Aristotle claim that the soul is an *entelekheia* because it represents actuality rather than potentiality, and then claim that the soul is a first *entelekheia*, which seems much closer to potentiality than it does to actuality?

Although scholars throughout the ages have offered various interpretations of Aristotle's distinction, there is something close to a consensus now that when Aristotle distinguishes between first and second *entelekheiai*, he means to refer not so much to the difference between potentiality and actuality, but to the difference between possessing (*hexis*) the capability to perform some function, and using (*khrêsis*) or exercising that capability.[2] The example Aristotle gives is thus meant to be understood this way: when we are merely knowledgeable, that is, when we possess the capability to contemplate but are not actively contemplating, our souls are in a state of first actuality. When we are contemplating, that is, when we are actively using our capability to

[2] How *entelekheia* applies to the soul is treated by Ross 1961, 166-167 and 213; Hamlyn 1968, 82-85; and Ackrill 1972-73. Ackrill is criticized by Charlton 1980.

contemplate, our souls are in a state of second actuality.[3] As we shall see, one reason why Aristotle is keen *not* to reduce the distinction between first and second *entelekheiai* to a simple distinction between potentiality and actuality is that he wants to avoid implying that the transitions from ignorance to knowledge, and from knowledge to contemplating, represent changes, and particularly alterations or changes of quality (*alloiôseis*). Instead, the contrast between ignorance and knowledge and knowledge and contemplating should be seen as indicating the presence or absence of a relation, namely, the relation to the object of thought.[4]

Given that the transition from first *entelekheia* to second *entelekheia* ought *not* to be seen as a change, it is a bit surprising that Aristotle should have chosen to use *entelekheia* to define change. Isḥāq ibn Ḥunayn's translation of *Physics* 3.1 has Aristotle saying that:

L 2
Arisṭūṭālīs, *aṭ-Ṭabīʿa*, 170,15-171,2
Aristotle, *Phys.* 3.1, 201a10-12

> So if each one of these types [of change, i.e., change of substance, change of quality, change of quantity, and change of place] is divisible into what is in [a state of] perfection and what is in [a state of] potentiality, change will consist in the perfection of what is in [a state of] potentiality in so far as it is such [*wa-idha qussima kullu wāḥidin min hādhihi l-ajnāsi ilā mā bi-l-kamāli wa-mā bi-l-quwwati kānati l-ḥarakatu kamāla mā* [or, *<wa-hiya> kamālu mā*] *bi-l-quwwati bi-mā huwa ka-dhālika* = *diêirêmenou de kath' hekaston genos tou men entelekheiâi tou te dunamei hê tou dunamei ontos entelekheia hêi toiouton kinêsis estin*].

What is different about Aristotle's nominal use of *entelekheia* in L2 to define change and his nominal use of *entelekheia* in L1 to define the soul? First of all, Aristotle seems unconcerned here in L2 with showing how *entelekheia* might refer to substance as form, as opposed to substance as matter. This is in contrast to L1, where an explicit connection is made between *entelekheia* and substance as form. In fact, in *Physics* 3.1, 201a4, Aristotle does make a contrast using form, but the contrast he makes is between form and privation (*sterêsis*), not between form and matter (*hulê*) as in L1.[5] What is more, this contrast (*Physics* 3.1, 201a4) is meant to illustrate the contraries between which one type of

[3] Other places where Aristotle opposes *epistêmê* (knowledge) and *theôrein* (contemplation) are *Metaph.* 9.6, 1048a34 and 9.8, 1050a12-14; *Phys.* 8.4, 255a34; *DA* 2.5, 417a29; *GA* 2.1, 735a11; and *EN* 7.3, 1146b31-35.

[4] *Phys.* 7.3, 247b1-248a7; at *DA* 2.5, 417b5-16 Aristotle allows for the possibility that the transition from ignorant to knowledgeable might be a special sort of *alloiôsis*.

[5] It is true that the term Aristotle uses for form here at *Physics* 3.1, 201a4, is just *morphê*, most often translated as "shape", and not *morphê kai eidos* as in L1; but in *Physics* 1.7-9 Aristotle often contrasts *eidos* with *sterêsis*, so it is reasonable to interpret the contrast at 201a4 as likewise indicating form as substance, and not some subsidiary notion of form as shape.

change – change of substance – takes place, and is not meant to illustrate the difference between actuality and potentiality as in L1.

Second, it is hard to avoid drawing the conclusion that when Aristotle uses *entelekheia* nominally in L2, saying that "change is an *entelekheia*", he might well have meant for *entelekheia* to refer not so much to a *state of being* as to a *process of becoming*, a meaning which would be counterintuitive in L1, that is, in the context of defining the soul. In other words, it is unclear in L2 whether change simply refers to the state of being changed which the changing thing itself possesses; or whether change refers to something outside of the changing thing – to something which the changing thing participates in but does not possess as a state – namely, the process by which the potentially changed thing comes to be actually changed. The main problem with seeing change as a process in which the changing thing participates is that it violates Aristotle's clearly stated rule that "There is no change above and beyond [i.e., outside of] the changing thing (*ouk esti de tis kinêsis para ta pragmata* = *wa-laysat ḥarakatun khārijatan ʿani l-umūri anfusihā*)" (*Phys.* 3.1, 200b32-33 = *aṭ-Ṭabīʿa*, 168,10-11).

Whether Aristotle intended that his definition of change in L2 be read as supporting the view that change is a state of being or a process of becoming was a major source of disagreement among medieval Latin thinkers.[6] In fact, it is still debated by Aristotle scholars: the process view held sway until the middle of the twentieth century; the state view then replaced it as the standard interpretation; and the pendulum now seems to have begun swinging back to the process view.[7] For my own purposes, what is important is not so much uncovering the *correct* interpretation of Aristotle's use of *entelekheia* to define change. Rather, my concern is that if a commentator decides to interpret Aristotle's use of *entelekheia* to define change as supporting the process view of change, he will have committed himself to saying that *entelekheia* in general includes process as well as state in its range of referents.

The third major difference between Aristotle's uses of *entelekheia* in L1 and in L2 is that in L2 Aristotle does not introduce the distinction between first and second perfections, unlike in L1, where the distinction is crucial to his definition of the soul. On the other hand, Aristotle does introduce a distinction in *Physics* 3.2 that – at first glance, at least – could be seen to be analogous to the first/second *entelekheia* distinction introduced in L1. In *Physics* 3.2 (and echoed

[6] Maier 1958 (Avicenna's theory is treated at 68-73). Following in Maier's footsteps are McCullough 1980, Weisheipl 1981, and Des Chene 1996, 17-52.

[7] The "process" or "actualization" interpretation of Aristotle's definition of *kinêsis* is expounded by Ross 1936, 537; and Peck 1972. The most ingenious – and certainly the most influential – recent defense of the "state" or "actuality" view has been the criticism of Ross' interpretation by Kosman 1969. Kosman's view is also held, or modified, by Owens 1978; Gill 1980, 130-133; Waterlow 1982, 112-119; and Hussey 1983, 55-65. Kosman's view is criticized in turn by Kostman 1987, and Graham 1988.

at *De Anima* 2.5, 417a16-17) Aristotle says that change is a state of being active (*energeia*) though in an incomplete or imperfect way (*atelês*):

L3
Arisṭūṭālīs, *aṭ-Ṭabīʿa*, 183,8-11
Aristotle, *Phys.* 3.2, 201b32-33

> Now change is thought to be a kind of activity, although an incomplete activity. The reason for this is that what is potentially changed – that whose activity is change – is incomplete [*wa-l-ḥarakatu maẓnūnun annahā fiʿlun mā illā annahu fiʿlun ghayru tāmmin wa-s-sababu fī dhālika anna mā huwa bi-l-quwwati mutaḥarrikun wa-huwa lladhī l-ḥarakatu fiʿluhu fa-huwa ghayru tāmmin = hê te kinêsis energeia men tis einai dokei atelês de aition d'hoti ateles to dunaton hou estin energeia*].

I shall leave aside for the moment the thorny question of the equivalence of *entelekheia* and *energeia*, a question which arises because – as mentioned at the beginning of the chapter – the times when the two terms seem most interchangeable are those when they are used adverbially, rather than nominally as in L3.[8] I shall also continue translating *teleion* and *ateles* as "complete" and "incomplete" until I discuss their use by the Neoplatonists, when the concepts of *entelekheia* and *teleiotês* become assimilated, and "perfect" and "imperfect" will become more apt.

Any attempt to square the incomplete/complete distinction implied in *Physics* 3.2 with the first/second distinction articulated in *De Anima* 2.1 will still have to confront a number of problems. This is mainly because Aristotle first introduces the incomplete/complete distinction not in L3 – where, in fact, it is merely implied – but in *Physics* 3.1, 201a4-9, where he lists four examples of paired contraries between which the four types of change take place. In the case of change of substance, the contraries are – as mentioned above – form and privation; in the case of change of quality, the contraries are black and white; in the case of change of location, the contraries are up and down; and in the case of change of quantity, the contraries are complete and incomplete. The incomplete/complete distinction seems primarily applicable, therefore, to one type of change – change of quantity – and only derivatively applicable (if applicable at all) to other types of change, or to change in general.

To sum up: if – as a Greek or Arabic commentator – my aim is to harmonize Aristotle's use of *entelekheia* in L1 and his use of *entelekheia* in L2, I will have to confront three major challenges.

[8] On the etymology of *entelekheia* and its differences with *energeia*, see Ross 1924, 245-246; Chen 1958; Blair 1967; Franzen and Georgulis 1972; and Graham 1989. Most recently, Stephen Menn (Menn 1994) has argued that a chronological progression can be detected in Aristotle's uses of the terms *dunamis*, *energeia* and *entelekheia*.

(1) Whereas in L1 *entelekheia* is identified with form and linked to substance as form, in L2 it is not; and even when Aristotle does say, in *Physics* 3.1, 201a4, that form is one of the contraries involved in a particular type of change – change of substance – the other contrary he mentions is privation (*sterêsis*), not matter, with which form is contrasted in L1.

(2) Whereas in L1 *entelekheia*'s identification with form is meant to contrast the state of actuality or perfection with the matter's state of potentiality, in L2 *entelekheia* can plausibly refer *either* to the state of actuality or perfection possessed by the changing thing *or* to the actualization or process of becoming actual or perfect, in which the changing thing participates.

(3) Whereas in L1 the distinction between first *entelekheia* and second *entelekheia* refers to the difference between possessing a capability to perform a function and exercising that capability, no distinction between two types of *entelekheia* is articulated in L2; and even the distinction between the incomplete and the complete hinted at in L3 and articulated in *Physics* 3.1, 201a4-9, seems applicable only, or at least primarily, to the contraries of quantitative change, and not to the states of possessing and using.

In the rest of this chapter I shall focus on the third challenge, reconciling the first/second distinction of *De Anima* 2.1 with the incomplete/complete distinction implied in *Physics* 3.1-2. This is for several reasons. First, Avicenna regards the discussion of the first challenge as a dead end, since he insists that determining whether or not something is a perfection will not tell us whether or not that thing is a substance. In other words, Avicenna holds that perfection is not necessarily linked to substantiality, a view I shall discuss in Chapter 6. Second, the early Peripatetic commentators' discussions of the second challenge came to revolve around their discussions of the third challenge; this will become clear as we proceed through Chapter 2. What is more, the later Neoplatonic discussions of the second challenge also came to revolve around a new, fourth challenge: determining whether or not (and if so, how) perfection was linked to causality; this will become clear in Chapters 3 and 4. The main point of listing the challenges above, of course, is simply to show that Aristotle's uses of *entelekheia* in L1 and L2 are not transparently identifiable, but warrant aggressive interpretation.

In order to come to grips with the third challenge – in order, that is, to reconcile the first/second distinction articulated in *De Anima* 2.1, with the incomplete/complete distinction hinted at in *Physics* 3.2 and articulated in *Physics* 3.1 – I, as a commentator, shall probably end up having to advocate either of two positions. On the one hand, I could (1) throw my hands up and say that the two distinctions are simply not identifiable. Try as I might to reconcile them, I must conclude in the end that the two distinctions apply to two different species of the overarching genus of *entelekheia*. The incomplete/complete distinction applies to one species of *entelekheia*, namely the kind whose specific difference is "predicable-of-change". And the first/second distinction applies to another species of *entelekheia*, namely the kind whose specific difference is "predicable-of-soul".

If, on the other hand, I wish to argue that the two distinctions are in fact reconcilable, I shall have to choose between two further alternatives. The first alternative (2a) has me saying that the two distinctions are identifiable in a strong sense. In other words, I could argue that either of the two distinctions applies equally to both species of the genus *entelekheia*. The incomplete/complete distinction applies equally to the species of *entelekheia* whose specific difference is "predicable-of-change" and to the species of *entelekheia* whose specific difference is "predicable-of-soul". Similarly, the first/second distinction applies equally to the species of *entelekheia* whose specific difference is "predicable-of-soul" and to the species of *entelekheia* whose specific difference is "predicable-of-change".

The second alternative (2b) has me saying that the two distinctions are identifiable in a weak sense. In other words, I could argue that only one of the distinctions applies to both species of the genus *entelekheia*, while the other applies merely to one species of *entelekheia*, either to the species whose specific difference is "predicable-of-change", or to the species whose specific difference is "predicable-of-soul". I could, for example, argue (2b[i]) that the first/second distinction can be construed broadly enough as to apply not only to the species of *entelekheia* whose specific difference is "predicable-of-soul", but also to the species of *entelekheia* whose specific difference is "predicable-of-change". The incomplete/complete distinction, by contrast, can only be construed so narrowly that it applies merely to change and not to the soul. In short, everything which is subject to the incomplete/complete distinction will also be subject to the first/second distinction; but not everything which is subject to the first/second distinction will be subject to the incomplete/complete distinction. For example, changes are subject to both the incomplete/complete and the first/second distinctions; but souls are subject only to the first/second distinction and not to the incomplete/complete distinction.

Conversely, I could argue (2b[ii]) that the incomplete/complete distinction can be construed broadly enough as to apply not only to the species of *entelekheia* whose specific difference is "predicable-of-change", but also to the species of *entelekheia* whose specific difference is "predicable-of-soul". The first/second distinction, by contrast, can only be construed so narrowly that it applies merely to the soul and not to change. In short, everything which is subject to the first/second distinction will also be subject to the incomplete/complete distinction; but not everything which is subject to the incomplete/complete distinction will be subject to the first/second distinction. For example, souls are subject to both the first/second and the incomplete/complete distinctions; but changes are subject only to the incomplete/complete distinction and not to the first/second distinction.

Let me give another example of (2b) in order to illustrate the kind of weak identity which I am referring to. Take the two distinctions cause/effect and agent/act. The cause/effect distinction can be construed broadly enough as to apply both to the species of the genus *existent* whose specific difference is "productive/produced *with* will" and to the species of the genus *existent* whose specific difference is "productive/produced *without* will". The agent/act distinction, by contrast, can only be construed so narrowly that it applies merely to the species of the genus *existent* whose specific difference is "productive/produced *with* will". Everything which is subject to the agent/act distinction will also be subject to the cause/effect distinction; but not everything which is subject to the cause/effect distinction will be subject to the agent/act distinction. For example, my taking my son bowling is subject to both the cause/effect distinction and the agent/act distinction, since my taking my son bowling is voluntary; but the brick's falling to the ground is subject only to the cause/effect distinction, since the brick's falling to the ground is involuntary.

What goes through my mind, as a commentator, when I am faced with choosing between these various positions? Position (1) involves my giving up on reconciling the incomplete/complete distinction implied in *Physics* 3.2 with the first/second distinction articulated in *De Anima* 2.1, and logically speaking this has to be my safest route. Any serious attempt to identify the two distinctions will, it seems, require me to pare down so many rough edges – including, as mentioned above, whether the basic distinction is one between the two contraries of quantitative change or one between possessing a capability and using that capability – that what was left of each distinction would be trivial. Instead, my claim would be more limited: *entelekheia* is an overarching concept which, when predicated of change, is distinguishable into incomplete and complete, and when predicated of the soul, is distinguishable into first and second.

In spite of the obvious advantages of this first option, the late-antique and Arabic commentators tended to prefer position (2), a position which left them the further choice between holding (2a) that the two distinctions were identifiable in a strong sense, and holding (2b) that the two distinctions were identical in a weak sense, with one distinction subsumed under the other. Needless to say, the commentators' hermeneutical commitment to viewing Aristotle as a system-thinker rather than as a problem-thinker (let alone as a thinker whose ideas may have evolved during his lifetime, or even – God forbid – as a thinker whose views on certain topics were hopelessly inconsistent) gave them a big push in the general direction of position (2), in that it inspired them to persevere in reconciling Aristotle's often incongruous applications of terms and distinctions between terms.

Hermeneutical commitments aside, adopting position (2) – either strongly identifying the two distinctions (2a), or subsuming one under the other (2b) – forced the commentators to confront not only the obvious philosophical problems pushing them to adopt position (1), but also the problematic implications that arose when they chose position (2) and attempted to solve those problems. What I mean is that the commentators' solutions to this challenge were often Pyrrhic, in that they led to further, unsavory commitments on the issues of the soul and change. The direst of these implications was first, that the soul – or at least the intellectual part – could be described as undergoing some kind of change when it makes the transition from knowledge to contemplation; and second, that change could be described as a process in which the changing thing participates, rather than as a state which the changing thing possesses. What I am arguing, in other words, is that these two unsavory commitments were the horns of a dilemma that emerged as a direct result of trying to square the first/second distinction with the incomplete/complete distinction.

Let me be more precise. Because the incomplete/complete distinction seems to apply only, or at least primarily, to quantitative change, since that is the only context in *Physics* 3 in which Aristotle articulates the distinction explicitly, I could draw the conclusion that when Aristotle describes in L1 the distinction between a soul in a state of first perfection and a soul in a state of second perfection, he is imagining that when I make the transition from the state of possessing the capability to think to the active exercise of that capability, my soul is undergoing a change from incomplete quantity or magnitude to complete quantity or magnitude. This is absurd, of course; commentators on Aristotle are agreed that the soul undergoes *no* type of change, let alone a quantitative change, when it passes from first to second perfection. The reason, mentioned above, is that according to Aristotle change occurs between two contraries, and knowledge and contemplation are not contraries, but rather indications of the presence or absence of a relation. In this case, the relation which is present or absent is the relation to the object of thought. When I am contemplating – when, that is, I am in a state of second perfection – the relation between my soul and the object of thought is present. When I am not contemplating – when, that is, I am in a state of first perfection – the relation between me and the object of thought is absent.

For example, when I am contemplating the Pythagorean theorem, my soul is in a state of second perfection, since the relation between my soul and the object of thought – the Pythagorean theorem – is present. But when I am watching television, my soul is in a state of first perfection, since the relation between my soul and the object of thought – the Pythagorean theorem – is absent. No change takes place: as just mentioned, the transition from *knowing* the Pythagorean theorem (i.e., the state of *possessing the capability* to think about the Pythagorean theorem), to *contemplating* the Pythagorean theorem (i.e., *actively exercising* that capability to think about the Pythagorean theorem) is not a change from one contrary to another, but rather the appearance of a relation where previously there had been none. In short, if I say that the first *entelekheia* of *De Anima* 2.1 is nothing other than the incomplete *entelekheia* of *Physics* 3.1, I shall have to conclude that when I am watching television and not contemplating the Pythagorean theorem – when, in other words, I am in a state of first perfection – my soul is itself a change or is somehow undergoing a change. This is because my soul's being in a state of first *entelekheia* is nothing other than my soul's being in a state of incomplete *entelekheia*, and incomplete *entelekheia* is – according to the implication of L3 – what change consists in. This is clearly unacceptable.

On the other hand, if I were to say that the complete *entelekheia* of *Physics* 3.1 is nothing other than the second *entelekheia* of *De Anima* 2.1, I would have to conclude that once something has finished changing quantitatively – say, a fruit which has expanded in magnitude to its full, complete and mature size – it is somehow actively using a capability which it merely possessed when it was incomplete and immature. This is because the fruit's being in a state of complete *entelekheia* is nothing other than the fruit's being in a state of second *entelekheia*, and second *entelekheia* is – according to the standard interpretation of L1 – using a capability which earlier one merely possessed. This too is unacceptable, for it is difficult to understand what it would mean to say that a ripe piece of fruit is actively using a capability which it merely possessed when it was unripe.

It seems hopeless, then, to argue in favor of the strong identity of position (2a), that is, to argue that the first/second distinction means nothing more or less than the incomplete/complete distinction, and vice versa; and that everything which is subject to the first/second distinction will also be subject to the incomplete/complete distinction, and vice versa.

This leaves me with position (2b), arguing that one distinction can be construed broadly enough as to apply *both* to the soul and to change, while the other can only be construed so narrowly that it applies merely to the soul *or* to change. To argue in favor of this position I shall have to choose between (2b[i]) expanding the notions of possessing a capability and using that capability so that they were no longer restricted to intellection, nor even to being ensouled in general; and (2b[ii]) expanding the notions of incompleteness and completeness so that they were no longer restricted to quantitative change, nor even to change in general.

According to (2b[i]), possessing and using can, if construed broadly enough, be understood as applying not only to knowledge and contemplation, and to being asleep and awake (Aristotle's other example of the distinction in L1), but also to incomplete and complete quantitative changes, and to incomplete and complete changes in general. According to (2b[ii]), incompleteness and completeness can, if construed broadly enough, be understood as applying not only to quantitative changes, and to changes in general, but also to non-kinetic transitions from possessing to using, such as intellection. Once I have undertaken either expansion, (2b[i]) or (2b[ii]), *entelekheia* could then be held to be basically divisible into the expanded distinction, an expanded distinction which would now subsume the non-expanded distinction.

Which distinction ought I, as a commentator, to choose for expansion, possessing/using or incomplete/complete? Neither is without difficulties. On the one hand, expanding the possessing/using distinction (2b[i]) seems like the obvious choice, since it is, after all, the only distinction which Aristotle explicitly applies to *entelekheia*; the incomplete/complete distinction is only expressly articulated in the context of the contraries of quantitative change, and not in the context of change in general; and even when Aristotle does imply that the incomplete/complete distinction applies to change in general, he uses the term *energeia* and not *entelekheia*, and says merely that change is an incomplete *energeia*, leaving us to guess what a complete *energeia* might be.

On the other hand, natural philosophy is a broader science than psychology, since its subject is all natural things, and not just natural things with souls. Because the incomplete/complete distinction seems to apply to at least one type of change, and perhaps to change in general, expanding the incomplete/complete distinction (2b[ii]) would appear to be the better choice, if *entelekheia* is to cover inanimate as well as animate things. One problem with this line of argument is that Aristotle's assertion at *Parts of Animals* 1.1, 641a22-b10, that the intellect is not a subject to be investigated by the natural philosopher, appears to eliminate the very transition – from knowledge to contemplation – which (2b[ii]) must account for.

Nevertheless, what appears to have been the decisive factor in prompting the commentators to choose (2b[ii]), expanding the incomplete/complete distinction, is that Aristotle simply provides more textual raw material with which to construct an interpretation along the lines of (2b[ii]) than he provides to construct an interpretation along the lines of (2b[i]). This was true for the ancient commentators, as we shall see, and it remains the case today: the most influential recent treatment of Aristotle on *kinêsis*, that of Kosman, is based on an expanded notion of completion or perfection.

This raw material came in two forms. First, Aristotle devotes an entire chapter of *Metaphysics* 5 – his philosophical lexicon – to discussing "the complete" (*to teleion*), a discussion which itself allows for an expanded notion of completeness (and, by implication, of incompleteness). Second, Aristotle uses two terms for completion or completeness – *teleiôsis* (which appears about two dozen times in the Aristotelian corpus) and *teleiotês* (which appears only four times) – in contexts similar to those in which he uses *entelekheia*.

Here is what Aristotle says about *to teleion*:

L 4

Aristāṭālīs, *Mā baᶜda ṭ-ṭabīᶜa II*, 621,9-622,13
Aristotle, *Metaph.* 5.16, 1021b12-1022a2

The complete [*at-tāmm = to teleion*] is spoken of in one way as that outside of which no part whatsoever can be found; for example a time-span: each thing's complete time-span consists of that outside of which no time at all can be found which is part of that time-span. Similar to this is that to which some kind of excellence applies, and that which is spoken of in the sense of goodness, whenever it has a superiority in its genus; for example a doctor is complete and a piper is complete when they have no deficiency in their special kind of excellence. In this way ["complete"] is said – by means of transference [*bi-ntiqāli l-qawl = metapherontes*] – of bad things. For we say "a complete liar" and "a complete thief" because we also apply the term "good" to them, as when we say a good thief and a good liar. Every single one of these complete things and all their substances are then said to be complete when, with respect to their particular kind of excellence, no part of their natural magnitude is deficient. Those things in which their worthwhile end exists are also said to be complete [*wa-ayḍan tuqālu tāmmatan allatī lahā tamāmun fāḍilun = eti hois huparkhei to telos, spoudaion on, tauta legetai teleia*], for they are complete by virtue of the end which they possess; and since an end is a kind of limit [*fa-idhi t-tamāmu ghāyatun mā mina l-ghāyāti = hôst' epei to telos tôn eskhatôn ti esti*] we transfer it to bad things, saying that a thing is completely ruined and completely destroyed when there is no deficiency in the destruction, but it is instead at the utmost degree of badness. For this reason passing away is also said, by way of transference, to be a completeness, because both are limits. For the end, and what something is on account of, are limits. [*fa-t-tamāmu wa-lladhī bi-sababihi yakūnu sh-shayʾu ghāyātun = telos de kai to hou heneka eskhaton*]. Those things which are themselves said to be complete are thus spoken of in these ways: some in the sense that no goodness is deficient in them, nor any superiority, nor is any part of them found outside them, and generally in the sense that nothing at all is superior in every one of the genera, nor is it outside them. As for the other ways, they are in respect of these, either by doing, or possessing, or being equivalent to something like this, or by being in another kind of relation to things which are said to be complete in the primary way.

I shall discuss in Chapter 5 the implications of the Arabic translations of *teleion* as *tāmm* and of *telos* as *tamām* in L4. For the moment what is of interest is Aristotle's series of claims about *to teleion*. In the first sentence he says that *to teleion* is that which has quantitative completeness or wholeness. That is, a thing is *teleion* when it has parts and when none of its parts is missing (though the example Aristotle gives in the second sentence is of temporal rather than spatial magnitude). Aristotle next claims that *teleion* applies to degrees of excellence in a particular field of endeavor: a doctor is complete when there is no degree of excellence in doctoring beyond what he has attained. In general, he says, things which have achieved their end – their *telos* – may be said to be complete. Even bad things such as dying or thieving can be said to be complete once they achieve their *telos*; although to be precise, they are "complete" only in a metaphorical or derived sense of the word. Here *telos* is assumed to be synonymous with *peras* (= *nihāya*, "terminus"), a position which Aristotle openly adopts in the next chapter, *Metaphysics* 5.17. There he says that a thing's terminus is that outside which nothing can be found, and he explicitly identifies the terminus with the *telos* of each thing.[9]

In *Metaphysics* 5 in general, it is sometimes unclear whether the first sense of a philosophical term which Aristotle lists is the philosophically basic sense, or simply the most commonly applied or primitive sense. In the case of Aristotle's discussion in *Metaphysics* 5.4 of the term *phusis* ("nature"), for example, the first sense offered ("the coming to be of growing things") is clearly the primitive sense, and the last sense offered ("the substance of things which have, in and of themselves, the principle of change") is clearly the most philosophically basic sense. That also seems to be the pattern with his discussion of *to teleion*. As expressed in the first sentence, the primitive sense of *teleion* is quantitative wholeness: the quality possessed by a whole none of whose parts is missing. Advocates of (2b[ii]) can appeal to that primitive sense of completeness to cover the contraries of quantitative change, given that the notion of quantitative wholeness seems easily applied to spatial magnitude.

The example Aristotle gives in the second sentence – a span of time – will cover change in general, if change is held to be a process in which the changing thing participates. Advocates of (2b[ii]) who are inclined to see change as a process (2b[ii]´) will argue that since change is an incomplete activity, change will consist in the dynamic quality of incompleteness that characterizes an unfinished time-span. The quality of incompleteness here is dynamic because it is temporal: with the passing of every moment, the process becomes measurably less incomplete, and more complete.

Even if I do not want to interpret change as a process, the use of *teleion* to describe a thing possessing a state – as opposed to a thing participating in a process – finds support in L4. In fact, as mentioned above, Aristotle indicates at the end of L4 that the sense in which *teleion* refers to a thing that possesses a state – the state of having attained its *telos* – is more philosophically basic than the sense in which *teleion* refers to a thing that has undergone spatial or temporal completion. Advocates of (2b[ii]) who are inclined to see change as a state (2b[ii]´´) can then argue that since change is an incomplete activity, change will consist in the particular type of incompleteness that a changing thing possesses. The quality of incompleteness here is static because it is logical, not physical: the changing thing possesses the state of incompleteness in the sense

[9] *Metaph.* 5.17, 1022a4-13 = *Mā baʿda ṭ-ṭabīʿa II*, 628,3-12.

that incompleteness is taken here to be the essential differentiating characteristic of a logical category – the category of "changing thing" – rather than taken to be a measurable characteristic of spatial and temporal quantities, such as the growth of the fetus in the womb or the time-span of any process of development.

In short, seeing change as a process in which the changing thing participates will require me to interpret the incompleteness of change as admitting of measurable degrees: at the beginning of the change, the incompleteness is at its greatest, and towards the end of the change, the incompleteness is at its least. Seeing change as a state possessed by the changing thing, on the other hand, will require me to interpret the incompleteness which the changing thing possesses as not admitting of measurable degrees: the changing thing possesses the differentiating characteristic of one logical category, while the changed thing possesses the differentiating characteristic of another logical category. Neither category admits of measurable degrees of difference, since the categories are logical, not physical: a thing is either in a state of incompleteness or it is in a state of completeness.

Regardless of how decisively the evidence provided by L4 supports the state interpretation of change over the process interpretation of change, an advocate of either (2b[ii]´) or (2b[ii]´´) could still mine that text for raw material with which to fashion an overarching incomplete/complete distinction which would subsume *entelekheia* as knowledge and contemplation as well as *entelekheia* as change. This is because *telos*, "end", can refer not only to "limit" or "terminus" (*peras*) but also to "purpose" or "that for the sake of which" (*to hou heneka*). What I mean is that a commentator could argue that when Aristotle asserts in L4 that "Those things in which their worthwhile end exists are also said to be complete, for they are complete by virtue of the end which they possess (*eti hois huparkhei to telos, spoudaion on, tauta legetai teleia˙ kata gar to ekhein to telos teleia* = *wa-ayḍan tuqālu tāmmatan allatī lahā tamāmun fāḍilun fa-innahā tāmmatun bi-tamāmihā lladhī huwa lahā*)" (*Metaph.* 5.16, 1021b23-25 = *Mā baᶜda ṭ-ṭabīᶜa II*, 622,2-3), he is referring to *telos* in the sense of purpose or that-for-the-sake-of-which (*to hou heneka*) and not to *telos* in the sense of limit or terminus (*peras*). This line can further be read as implying that *to teleion* refers to something which is "ended", either in the sense of *being directed towards an end* but not having attained it, or in the sense of *serving as an end* for something else.

The result of having so many meanings of *teleion* to choose from is that a commentator had more tools at his disposal with which to subsume the first/second distinction under the incomplete/complete distinction, regardless of whether he chose to advocate the process view of change (2b[ii]´) or the state view of change (2b[ii]´´). Change could be held to be an *entelekheia atelês* because it has not reached its *telos qua* "limit" or "terminus". The changing thing either remained in an unfinished process which had not reached its terminus (2b[ii]´) or itself possessed the state of not having reached its terminus (2b[ii]´´).

On the other hand, knowledge and contemplation could each be held to be *teleia* because both are "ended", that is, both have a *telos qua* "end" or "purpose". Knowledge, the first *entelekheia* of the *De Anima*, is "ended" in the sense of "having an end": it refers to a capability which *is directed towards* an end. Contemplation, the second *entelekheia* of the *De Anima*, is "ended" in the sense of "being an end": it refers to a function which *serves as an end*. Thus:

2b[ii]´

Phys. 1st: *entelekheia atelês* = incomplete process (e.g., "construction")
DA 1st: *entelekheia teleia* = ended capability (e.g., "knowledge")

Phys. 2nd: *entelekheia teleia* = completed process (e.g., "constructed")
DA 2nd: *entelekheia teleia* = ended exercise of capability (e.g., "contemplating")

or

2b[ii]´´

Phys. 1st: *entelekheia atelês* = state of incompleteness (e.g., "being constructed")
DA 1st: *entelekheia teleia* = ended capability (e.g., "knowledge")

Phys. 2nd: *entelekheia teleia* = state of completeness (e.g., "having been constructed")
DA 2nd: *entelekheia teleia* = ended exercise of capability (e.g., "contemplating")

Adding *teleion* to the mix certainly helps a commentator identify the complete *entelekheia* of the *Physics* with the second *entelekheia* of the *De Anima*. Both are *teleia*, after all; and even though they are *teleia* in different ways – the former is *teleia* in the sense of being completed, the latter is *teleia* in the sense of serving as an end – the shared characteristic of being *teleia* is enough to contrast them with the incomplete *entelekheia* of the *Physics*. Of course, that still leaves the commentator the task of accommodating the first *entelekheia* of the *De Anima*, which ought, according to this approach, to be viewed as *atelês* rather than *teleia*.

In spite of that very loose end, the commentators persevered in viewing *teleion*, both in the sense of quantifiably whole and in the sense of ended, as a useful tool in flushing out the evasive *entelekheia*. Fueling their enthusiasm for *teleion* was the possibility of appealing to Aristotle's use of the abstract nouns which derive from it – namely *teleiotês* and *teleiôsis*, translatable as "completeness" and "completion" – in contexts similar to those in which he uses *entelekheia*. As I mentioned earlier, Aristotle employs the terms so rarely that it would be foolhardy to claim that he applied them in any strict or consistent way in his work. But as with *to teleion*, so *teleiotês* and *teleiôsis* were seen by commentators as rough diamonds, so to speak, ready to be cut into sparkling new concepts with which to gloss *entelekheia*, and thereby to sort out the confusion surrounding Aristotle's seemingly inconsistent uses of that term.

Of the two terms, *teleiotês* is used less often. Aristotle seems to have understood *teleiotês* and *ateleia* as the abstract nouns corresponding to the substantive adjectives *to teleion* and *to ateles* which, as we saw, he applied to the contraries of change of quantity in *Physics* 3.1, 201a4-9. For example, in *Physics* 8.7 – foreshadowed at *Physics* 3.6, 207a21 – *teleiotês* and *ateleia* are linked to change of quantity. The *Physics* 8.7 passage is meant to distinguish between change of location and the other types of change:

L 5

Arisṭūṭālīs, *aṭ-Ṭabīʿa*, 887,6-12
Aristotle, *Phys.* 8.7, 261a32-37

We say that it appears that none of the other changes [i.e., other than circular locomotion] can be continuous. This is because all of the various types of change are only ever from one opposite to another opposite. For example, the two limits of coming-to-be and passing-away [i.e., change of substance] are the existent and the non-existent [*mawjūdun wa-lā-mawjūdun = to on kai to mê on*]; the two limits of alteration [i.e., change of quality] are the contrary affections; and the two limits of increase and decrease [i.e., change of quantity] are greatness or smallness, or completeness or incompleteness of magnitude [*aw kamālu l-ʿiẓam wa-naqṣānuhu = ê teleiotês megethous kai ateleia*].

Given Aristotle's apparently restricted use of *teleiotês* in passages focusing on change of quantity, *teleiôsis* might have appeared to a commentator as a better candidate for the abstract noun corresponding to a new, expanded notion of *to teleion*. In a passage in *Physics* 7.3, for example, Aristotle uses *teleiôsis* in a way that might help show how an expanded incomplete/complete distinction could cover the first/second distinction. In *Physics* 7.3 Aristotle is at pains to show that while the conditions preparatory to the acquisition of knowledge may involve changes – and specifically changes of quality, or alterations (*alloiôseis = istiḥālāt*) – the acquisition of knowledge is not itself a change. This is because, as mentioned above, states of the soul are indicative merely of the presence or absence of a relation, and therefore the transition between them cannot be categorized as a change of quality:

L 6

Arisṭūṭālīs, *aṭ-Ṭabīʿa*, 760,8-761,6
Aristotle, *Phys.* 7.3, 246a10-16

Again, states [*Ṭ* 760,8: *al-hayʾāt = hexeis*], whether of the body or of the soul, are not changes of quality. For some are excellences [*Ṭ* 760,9: *faḍāʾil = aretai*] and others are defects, and neither excellence nor defect is change of quality. Excellence is a kind of

> completion [*Ṭ* 761,4: *kamālun mā* = *teleiôsis tis*], for anything which has acquired its own special excellence and is then in its natural state is – at that moment – complete [*Ṭ* 761,5: *kāmilan* = *teleion*].

What made *teleiôsis* even better qualified to serve as the abstract noun for an expanded notion of *to teleion* was that Aristotle used *teleiôsis* not only to describe states which do not involve or presuppose change, as in L6 (as well as in L4, where excellence – *aretê* – is also held to be a kind of *teleiôsis*), but also to describe changes themselves. In other words, it seemed that *teleiôsis* could serve in precisely the contexts – the states of the soul as well as change – in which *entelekheia* figured so prominently. It might, then, seem surprising that most commentators chose to use *teleiotês* instead of *teleiôsis* to gloss *entelekheia*.

The reason they did so, I believe, is that when Aristotle did use *teleiôsis* in the context of change, he meant for it to describe types of change that are more easily understood as processes rather than as states, as completions rather than completenesses. Aristotle used *teleiôsis* most often to describe natural phenomena such as fetal development, a process which involves not only growth – that is, change of quantity – but also concoction or ripening – that is, change of substance or of quality (the commentators disagree). It would be a reasonable extrapolation to expect that Aristotle also thought of an infant's growth to a mature, adult size, as a *teleiôsis* which takes place after birth. And given Aristotle's use of *teleiôsis* to describe concoction generally, one has to assume that he would also regard the functioning of the soul's nutritive faculty in transforming food into blood, as well as pubescence (i.e., the sexual maturation of children into adults) as post-natal *teleiôseis*.

Admittedly, it is sometimes unclear whether in a few of those cases Aristotle also meant for *teleiôsis* to describe the end-state of the process of fetal development rather than the process itself. But it is certain that in most instances *teleiôsis* was meant to refer to a process.[10] What is more, if a fetus' development can be assigned to any of the four types of change, change of quantity will be the leading candidate; and if concoction can be assigned to any of the four types of change, it is probably substantial change, and possibly change of quality. It would be perfectly reasonable for a commentator to suppose, then, that Aristotle meant for *teleiôsis* to refer to the process of change generally – the passage between the beginning-state of *ateleia* and its contrary, the end-state of *teleiotês* – and not to only one of the four types of change.

[10] Passages where *teleiôsis* refers to a process are: *GA* 3.7, 757a32 (*teleiôsin* = *kamāl* at *Fī kawn al-ḥayawān*, 117,21); 4.4, 770b26 (*teleiôseis* = *tamām* at 152,25); and 5.10, 777b27 (*teleiôseis* = *at-tamām wa-l-kamāl* at 171,6); *HA* 6.3, 561a6; and 7.4, 583b24, 584a34 and 584b26; *Meteor.* 4.2, 379b18 and 21 and 4.3, 380a19; *Probl.* 10.41, 895a27; 20.7, 923b4; and 20.24, 925b29. Passages where *teleiôsis* refers to the end-state of a process are: *GA* 3.2, 753a10 (*teleiôsin* = *at-tamām* 106,16); and 4.8, 776b1(*bis*) (*teleiôsis* = *tamām* at 167,21[*bis*]).

The problem is that if I, as a commentator, wish to use *teleiôsis* as a gloss of *entelekheia*, I will also commit myself to understanding change as a process. And in fact, some of the commentators who allowed that change could be seen as a process used *teleiôsis* to gloss *entelekheia* when applied to change, and *teleiotês* to gloss *entelekheia* when applied to the soul. By contrast, those commentators wishing to see change as a state used *teleiotês* to gloss *entelekheia* when applied to both change and the soul, reserving *teleiôsis* to describe only the specific changes of quantity, quality and substance that obtain during fetal development and concoction – primarily, it seems, out of deference to Aristotle's use of *teleiôsis* in those contexts.

The conclusions one has to draw, therefore, are that Aristotle was inconsistent in his use of the terms *teleiôsis* and *teleiotês*, since both seemed applicable to the end-state of a change of quantity; and that Aristotle used *teleiôsis* to describe processes (fetal development, ripening or maturation, and concoction generally), the end-states of such processes, and states of excellence or perfection which involve no change but only the presence or absence of a relation. If, because of Aristotle's broader use of *teleiôsis*, I choose to use *teleiôsis* instead of *teleiotês* as a gloss of *entelekheia*, I shall also commit myself to viewing *entelekheia* as a process as well as a state.

How did the commentators deal with this problem? As I just mentioned, a commentator committed to seeing change as a process (2b[ii]´) could turn to *teleiôsis* as a gloss of *entelekheia* when he reckoned *entelekheia* referred to a process, namely the process of change; and could turn to *teleiotês* as a gloss of *entelekheia* when he reckoned *entelekheia* referred to a state, be it the state of having changed, the capability to function or the exercise of that capability. Thus:

2b[ii]´

Phys. 1st: *entelekheia atelês* = *teleiôsis qua* "process of completion" = incomplete process (e.g., "construction")

DA 1st: *entelekheia teleia* = *teleiotês qua* "state of being directed towards an end" = ended capability (e.g., "knowledge")

Phys. 2nd: *entelekheia teleia* = *teleiotês qua* "state of completeness" = completed process (e.g., "constructed")

DA 2nd: *entelekheia teleia* = *teleiotês qua* "state of serving as an end" = ended exercise of capability (e.g., "contemplating")

On the other hand, a commentator committed to seeing change as only a state (2b[ii]´´) could turn to *teleiotês* as a gloss of *entelekheia* regardless of whether *entelekheia* referred to the state of changing, the state of having changed, the capability to function or the exercise of that capability. Thus:

2b[ii]´´

Phys. 1st: *entelekheia atelês* = *teleiotês qua* "state of being completed" = state of incompleteness (e.g., "being constructed")
DA 1st: *entelekheia teleia* = *teleiotês qua* "state of being directed towards an end" = ended capability (e.g., "knowledge")

Phys. 2nd: *entelekheia teleia* = *teleiotês qua* "state of having been completed" = state of completeness (e.g., "having been constructed")
DA 2nd: *entelekheia teleia* = *teleiotês qua* "state of serving as an end" = ended exercise of capability (e.g., "contemplating")

Although the commentators' varied uses of Aristotle's concepts of *teleiôsis* and *teleiotês* succeed in providing common ground on which to reconcile the incomplete/complete distinction of the *Physics* with the *De Anima*'s first/second distinction, the horns of the process/state dilemma remain sharp. What I mean is this: I could, as a commentator, use *teleiotês* to gloss all instances of *entelekheia* (2b[ii]´´). That is, I could insist on understanding *entelekheia* as only ever referring to a state. This is consistent with Aristotle's insistence in *Physics* 3.1 that change is only ever *in* the changing thing.

The problem then arises, how do I distinguish the *teleiotês* that is possessed by a changing thing from the *teleiotês* that is possessed by a changed thing? I could, I suppose, claim that the *teleiotês* of the changing thing is *active*, while the *teleiotês* of the changed thing is *inactive*. That would be fine, but what am I to do with the *teleiotês* of one who possesses knowledge but is not actively contemplating, and the *teleiotês* of one who is actively contemplating? It seems that the criteria of activity and inactivity will get me into trouble here, since the *teleiotês* of one who possesses knowledge but is not actively contemplating is inactive, which implies that it is the end-state possessed by a changed thing; and since the *teleiotês* of one who possesses knowledge and is actively contemplating is active, which implies that it is the state of change possessed by a changing thing.

The result of using the criteria of activity and inactivity is that I have succeeded in implying precisely what I wanted to avoid: that knowledge is the end-state possessed by a changed thing, that acquiring knowledge is therefore a change, and that contemplating is itself a change. I could perhaps reconcile the inactive end-state of the changed thing with the inactive state of someone who is knowledgeable but is not actively contemplating, by saying that even though the acquisition of knowledge is not, properly speaking, a change, the conditions that are preparatory to the acquisition of knowledge – such as walking to class or taking a book out of the library – are changes. Nevertheless, I am left with seeing activity as binding together change and contemplation.

My only recourse, it seems, is to use Aristotle's own criterion in L3 and say that *teleiotês*, when understood as the state possessed by the changing thing, is incomplete, in contrast to the complete *teleiotêtes* of the changed thing, of someone who is knowledgeable but is not actively contemplating, and of someone who is actively contemplating. That still leaves me with the problem of explaining what an incomplete completeness is: either it is a self-contradiction, and therefore as meaningless as saying "a non-white whiteness" or "an unsmall smallness"; or it simply means an incompleteness, in which case the idea of *teleiotês* no longer serves to bind together the *entelekheia* that is descriptive of change and the *entelekheiai* that are descriptive of the changed thing's end-state and of the soul's states of possessing a capability and using that capability. It seems that I am left, after all that work, with option (1), namely, giving up on reconciling the first/second distinction articulated in L1 and the incomplete/complete distinction implied in L2.

The one way I could, as a commentator, still use the notion of completeness to bind together the *entelekheia* of L1 and the *entelekheia* of L2, is to appeal to the apparent distinction between *teleiotês* and *teleiôsis*. I can use *teleiotês* to refer to the end-state possessed by a changed thing, to the state of someone who is knowledgeable but is not actively contemplating, and to the state of someone who is actively contemplating. But because, as shown above, using activity and inactivity as criteria to distinguish between change itself and the end-state possessed by a changed thing leads to so many other problems (either implying that contemplating is a change, or propounding the absurd notion of an incomplete completeness), I can choose instead to call change a *teleiôsis* rather than a *teleiotês* (2b[ii]′). I will have retained the notion of completeness as an overarching gloss of *entelekheia*, but I will have paid a heavy price: because *teleiôsis* was so clearly used by Aristotle to refer to processes such as fetal development and growth, my use of *teleiôsis* will commit me to seeing change as a process in which the changing thing participates, rather than seeing change as a state possessed by the changing thing. Nevertheless, I will have avoided seeing contemplation as a change, since contemplation is a *teleiotês* and not a *teleiôsis*. I will also have avoided propounding the seemingly contradictory notion of an incomplete completeness and retained the idea of completeness as a gloss to explain *entelekheia*, though with a rider: I must now distinguish between *teleiôsis* as process of completion and *teleiotês* as state of completeness. In any case, historically, the attempt to resolve this dilemma is one of the main sources of the view that change is best understood as a process, an interpretation that, as mentioned above, reverberated throughout the Middle Ages and still does among Aristotle scholars.

My main purpose in Chapter 1 has been to show that Aristotle's uses of his new term *entelekheia* to define both motion and the soul are opaque and appear at first (or even second) glance to be inconsistent, and that they therefore invited energetic exegesis along the lines I have described. As I shall show in Chapters 2, 3 and 4, Alexander subscribed to the "completeness" rather than the "endedness" understanding of *teleiotês*; Themistius also subscribed to the "completeness" understanding of *teleiotês* but hinted that the distinction between the two types of endedness – I shall call them "autotelic" and "allotelic" endedness – might provide an escape route from a further complication; the Neoplatonists subscribed generally to the understanding of *teleiotês* as endedness but collapsed the two different types of endedness which Themistius appears to have advocated; and the Arabic translations collapsed endedness and end. This is the legacy left to Avicenna.

2. Alexander and Themistius
Attempts at Reconciliation

Reconstructing the views of Alexander of Aphrodisias (fl. 205 AD) is hampered by the loss of his commentary on the *Physics*. Nevertheless, we can get some idea of what he thought by sorting through the bits and pieces of physical doctrine contained in his *Quaestiones* as well as the citations contained in Simplicius' commentary on the *Physics*, and then comparing that material with what he says about *entelekheia*, *teleiôsis*, *teleiotês* and *to teleion*, in the context of the soul, of which there is much evidence, and with what he says about those concepts in other commentaries. In Alexander there seems to be an acute awareness of the problems that arise from Aristotle's use of *entelekheia* to define the soul and to define change, and a willingness to use the Aristotelian terms *teleiôsis* and *teleiotês* in ways different from Aristotle's in order to help resolve those problems.

Alexander is quite consistent in his uses of *teleiôsis* and *teleiotês*. Apart from one example, Alexander always uses *teleiôsis*, and never *teleiotês*, when he wishes to describe processes such as fetal development, growth to maturity, and concoction; in other words, when he wishes to refer to quantitative, substantial or qualitative changes that occur over periods of time.[1] Like Aristotle, Alexander also uses *teleiôsis* to refer to states. But unlike Aristotle, who almost always uses *teleiôsis* to refer to states such as "excellences" (*aretai*) that present themselves following transitions (such as not-contemplating to contemplating) which are *not* changes of quality (*alloiôseis*), Alexander uses *teleiôsis* to describe the state of completeness following changes of quantity, quality and substance.[2] In this respect Alexander seems to be following Aristotle's rare use of *teleiôsis* in the *Generation of Animals* to refer to the state of completeness following a developmental change.

But in contrast to Aristotle, who appealed to *teleiôsis* far more often than to *teleiotês*, Alexander assigns *teleiotês* the more prominent role. Not only does Alexander use *teleiotês* to describe states such as *aretai*, he appeals to *teleiotês* whenever he wishes to gloss *entelekheia*. Alexander even goes so far as to claim (incorrectly) that Aristotle himself identified *entelekheia* and *teleiotês*, saying in one passage, "The soul, therefore, is substance as form (*kata to*

[1] Alexander, *in Metaph.* 1.5 (*ad* 985b26), 38,18; *in Meteor.* 4.2 (*ad* 379b10), 186,14.16.31.35 and 187,7(*bis*); and 4.3 (*ad* 380a12), 188,24.25 and 189,5.34; *DA*, 36,6; *Quaest.* 3.14, 111,17.23.24; *in Sens.* 6 (*ad* 446b2), 125,15. At *in Meteor.* 4.2 (*ad* 379b10), 188,13 Alexander uses *teleiotês* to describe concoction, though given the uniqueness of its usage in that sense, my guess is that its appearance there is the result of a scribal error.

[2] Alexander, *in Metaph.* 5.16 (*ad* 1021b12), 410,19.

eidos). Aristotle calls the form 'perfection' (*teleiotês*) and 'actuality' (*entelekheia*)".[3]

Alexander's new uses of *teleiôsis* and particularly *teleiotês* can be seen more clearly in his commentary on L4. In that commentary Alexander distinguishes between three senses in which something may be said to be *to teleion*. The first sense (*in Metaph.* 5.16, 410,18-28) refers to something which has attained its *teleiôsis*, here understood as referring to temporal completeness, and thus to a kind of quantitative completeness. As I mentioned above, Alexander's use of *teleiôsis* in this sense finds only very limited support in Aristotle.

The second sense (*in Metaph.* 5.16, 410,28-411,18) in which something is said to be *teleion* is when it possesses an excellence (*aretê*) compared to other similar things. That is to say, a thing is *teleion* when it possesses a superiority to all other things alike it in species. Alexander's use of "species" (*eidos*) here, in contrast to the "genus" (*genos*) which appears in the text of L4, is possibly significant, since Alexander seems to be making two claims. First, excellence or superiority is a *teleiotês* in the sense that it signifies the furthest limit of formation, the maximum extent to which a form can inhere in a thing. Second, excellence or superiority is a *teleiotês* in the sense that it signifies the full exercise of the capability represented by the inherence of that form.

Although Alexander does not make this explicit, the implication of his use of "alike in species" rather than Aristotle's "alike in genus" is that, in logical terms, Alexander saw the *teleiotês* here as playing something like the role of the specific difference: the essential characteristic that differentiates one species of a genus from another species of that genus, the essential characteristic that makes a species the species it is. In the case of the species "human", the specific difference "rational" is what sets my species apart from other species subsumed under the genus "animal". Alexander's point appears to be that the more rational I am, the closer to my *teleiotês* as a human I shall be. However, I hesitate to make too much of Alexander's choice of terms here, because a strict understanding of genus, species and specific difference comes into ancient philosophy only after the appearance of Porphyry's *Isagoge*. My aim here is simply to show how Alexander's choice of species rather than genus provided Peripatetic cover for a post-Porphyrean move by Ammonius and his successors, which I shall describe in Chapters 3 and 4.

The third sense of *to teleion*, according to Alexander, refers to something which is in possession of its own end (*telos*). Whereas the first and second

[3] Alexander, *DA (Mantissa)*, 103,3-4. At Alexander, *DA* 16,1 the claim that Aristotle held the soul to be *teleiotês* as well as *entelekheia* is repeated. The editor suggests that this line might be a glossator's interpolation, though given its appearance in the *Mantissa*, where the *kai* is unlikely to be epexegetical (since the *kai* introduces *entelekheia*, not *teleiotês*), it seems reasonable to retain it. According to Todd 1974, 214n.27, Aristotle's "identification" of *entelekheia* and *teleiotês* is also attested to in a scholium (*Schol. in Arist.* 358a19). Alexander pairs *teleiotês* and *entelekheia* (without, however, claiming that Aristotle did it first) at *DA* 24,1-2 and 52,2-3.

senses of *teleion* refer to quantitative completeness (*teleiôsis*) and qualitative or substantial completeness (*teleiotês*), respectively, the third sense refers to a kind of endedness. Alexander calls this third sense a *teleiotês*. But here Alexander holds to a strict understanding of *telos*: he says (*in Metaph.* 5.16, 411,18-38, as well as *in Metaph.* 5.17, 413,31-34) that it refers to the terminus or limit of a process.[4] Alexander's strict understanding of *telos* here prevents him from using *teleiotês* to refer to endedness in the sense of *being directed at an end* or *serving as an end*, senses which Themistius would later appeal to in an effort to reconcile the first and second *entelekheiai* of *De Anima* 2.1 with the first and second *entelekheiai* implied in *Physics* 3.1 and 3.2.

The general impression one gets from Alexander's works is that *teleiotês* has replaced *teleiôsis* in importance as a philosophical term. In this respect Alexander's use of the two terms is the reverse of Aristotle's. What is Alexander's rationale for elevating *teleiotês* over *teleiôsis*? First of all, as I discussed above, Aristotle used *teleiôsis* not only to describe states such as excellence, he used it even more often to refer to changes – fetal development and concoction – which cannot possibly be applied to the soul. Alexander wants another term for completeness which can be used to gloss *entelekheia* but which will not imply that the soul is either a concoction or the result of a concoction. To do this he needs not only to understand *teleiotês* in a far broader sense than Aristotle understood it, but also to choose a term which covers all transitions or transformations leading up to the *teleiotês*. This new term must cover the four changes articulated in Aristotle's discussion of *kinêsis*, as well as transitions such as not-seeing to seeing and not-contemplating to contemplating, which Aristotle insists are not changes, and specifically, not changes of quality. The term Alexander chose is *metabolê*, used by Aristotle in a separate discussion of change in *Physics* 5.1 and 5.2.

In those chapters Aristotle settles on a new categorization of change to replace the one he had originally proposed in Book 3. In Book 5 Aristotle now says that *genesis*, or substantial change, is in a different category from the other types of *kinêsis* introduced in *Physics* 3. This is because *genesis* involves a transition from one *contradictory* to another (*ta kat' antiphasin*), that is, between two things so related that one and only one can be true at the same time (e.g., the transition from not-being to being). Quantitative change, qualitative change and locomotion, however, involve transitions between one *contrary* and another (*ta enantia*), that is, between two things within the same genus which differ from each other to the greatest possible degree (e.g., the transition from small to

[4] Here Alexander may also have had in mind *Metaph.* 10.4, 1055a10-18, where Aristotle says that everything which possesses a *telos* is called *teleion*, the sense of *telos* in this passage being identical to *peras* (i.e., end as limit rather than end as purpose or function). Aristotle also identifies *to teleion* in that passage as that which is greatest in a genus, not a species, reinforcing for Alexander the connection to L4.

large, black to white, and Boston to Los Angeles). Aristotle introduces the term *metabolê* to subsume both *genesis* and the three remaining types of *kinêsis*.

Alexander's innovation is to understand *genesis* so broadly – as applying not only to the coming-to-be of substantial forms in bodies, but also to the coming-to-be of intelligible forms in intellects – that he can now use *metabolê* to refer to quantitative change, qualitative change and locomotion; to the coming-to-be of substantial forms; and to the coming-to-be of intelligible forms. In other words, Alexander uses *metabolê* to cover all types of kinetic change, and all types of coming-to-be, including non-kinetic transitions such as that from not-contemplating to contemplating.

Let me be more specific. In his comments on *Metaphysics* 2.2 (*ad* 994a19-b6), Alexander says (*in Metaph.* 2.2, 153,14-28) that the *teleiotês* is the end-state following various *metabolai*: the *metabolê* from boy to man; the *metabolê* from learner to one with scientific knowledge; and the *metabolê* from not-contemplating to contemplating. That is to say, the *teleiotês* is the end-state following each of these types of *metabolê*, regardless of whether the *metabolê* is with respect to growth (*auxêsis*), as in the first case; with respect to quality (*alloiôsis*), as in the second case; or with respect to form (*kat' eidos*), as in the third case.[5]

The first problem with Alexander's account is his calling the transition from learner to possessor of knowledge an *alloiôsis*. As mentioned above, Aristotle is pretty insistent that while the conditions preparatory to this transition may be *alloiôseis*, the transition itself is not an *alloiôsis*. But this really is an unsolvable problem for Alexander. He cannot claim that the transition from learner to someone with scientific knowledge is a *genesis*, because the transition consists neither in the coming-to-be of a substantial form (the possessor of knowledge is as human as he was when he was a learner), nor in the coming-to-be of an intelligible form (this is reserved for the transition from not-contemplating to contemplating). The result is that Alexander is left with *alloiôsis*. To be fair, there is a line in *De Anima* 2.5 (417b5-7) where Aristotle seems to allow for the possibility that the transition from learner to possessor of knowledge can be seen as a special kind of *alloiôsis*, so Alexander does have some Aristotelian cover.

The other problem arises from Alexander's nifty move of understanding *metabolê kat' eidos* as referring to the coming-to-be in the intellect of an intelligible (*noöumenon*). When Aristotle discusses *genesis* in *Physics* 5 and

[5] Alexander recapitulates this list of examples at *in Metaph.*, 154,25-155,5 and 155,15-30. One slight lexicographical problem can be detected: unlike in his comments on *Metaphysics* 2.2, Alexander's comments on *Metaphysics* 5.16 use *teleiôsis*, not *teleiotês*, to describe the completed state following a quantitative change. Perhaps this is because Aristotle himself uses *teleiôsis* in *Metaphysics* 5.16, though Aristotle uses it in the context of the second type of completeness, the completeness that is reducible to superiority or excellence (*aretê*) in a genus or species. Other places where Alexander uses *teleiotês* to refer to an end state following a *metabolê* are *Quaest.* 1.7, 16,2-3 and 3.3, 86,21-34; and *DA* 82,2.

distinguishes it from the three kinetic changes, he had in mind the coming-to-be of a substantial form, not the coming-to-be of an intelligible form. Alexander could argue in his defense that Aristotle himself maintains that when someone thinks of an intelligible form, his intellect "becomes" that intelligible form (e.g., *DA* 3.2, 426a16 and 3.4, 430a3). Alexander could then claim that he is simply making the logical inference that the intellect undergoes a kind of substantial *genesis*; and that therefore the transition from not-contemplating to contemplating is a *metabolê kat' eidos*.

Where this line of defense seems most vulnerable is in Alexander's claim that because the intellect undergoes a *metabolê kat' eidos*, the intelligible form is the *teleiotês* of the intellect's *metabolê* from not-contemplating to contemplating. This is an idea found elsewhere in Alexander's work.[6] But it seems to me that Alexander also has another type of *teleiotês* in mind here, and is conflating the two types of *teleiotês* into one. The other type of *teleiotês* Alexander has in mind here is the *good* of each thing, a quasi-moral objective.[7] The presence of the intelligible form in the intellect following the transition from not-contemplating to contemplating signifies a *teleiotês both* in the sense that intellectual activity is the human good, *and* in the sense that intellectual activity is the end-state following the intellect's *metabolê kat' eidos*. The two types of *teleiotês* are not identical: the former *teleiotês* signifies the full and complete inherence of a *substantial* form (in this case, "humanness"), while the latter *teleiotês* signifies the full and complete inherence of an *intelligible* form.

This problem becomes acute when I try to distinguish what happens during self-intellection from what happens during my intellection of other concepts. At the most abstract level, I can see that (1) if I am thinking about "intellect" (*nous*), the coming-to-be in my intellect of the *intelligible* form of "intellect" (the *noöumenon* of *nous*) will be numerically identical to the coming-to-be in my intellect of the *substantial* form of "intellect" (the *eidos* of *nous*). By thinking about "intellect" my intellect becomes an intellect. Therefore the *teleiotês qua* complete inherence of the intelligible form "intellect" in my intellect will be one and the same as the *teleiotês qua* complete inherence of the substantial form "intellect" in my intellect.

What about (2) when I am thinking about "human"? Is the coming-to-be in my intellect of the intelligible form "human" (the *noöumenon* of *anthrôpos*) numerically identical to the coming-to-be in my intellect of the substantial form "human" (the *eidos* of *anthrôpos*)? On the one hand, I am committed to the view that my intellect "becomes" whatever it is thinking about. By thinking about the intelligible form "human", my intellect will itself *become* human. In that sense the coming-to-be in my intellect of the intelligible form "human" is

[6] e.g., Alexander, *DA* 84,19-24.

[7] Alexander, *in Metaph.* 1.1 (*ad* 980a21) 1,4-9 and 411,5; *DA (Mantissa)* 151,31-152,4; and *De fato* 17, 198,1-2 and 36, 211,15.

identical to the coming-to-be in my intellect of the substantial form "human". Therefore the *teleiotês qua* complete inherence of the intelligible form "human" in my intellect will be identical to the *teleiotês qua* complete inherence of the substantial form "human" in my intellect.

On the other hand, common sense dictates that it is not my intellect but my soul-body composite, which most warrants possessing the substantial form "human". In this sense the coming-to-be in my soul-body composite of the substantial form "human" is identical neither to the coming-to-be in my intellect of the intelligible form "human" nor to the coming-to-be in my intellect of the substantial form "human". Therefore the *teleiotês qua* complete inherence of the substantial form "human" in my soul-body composite will be identical neither to the *teleiotês qua* complete inherence of the intelligible form "human" in my intellect nor to the *teleiotês qua* complete inherence of the substantial form "human" in my intellect.

Of course, there is a sense in which I, as a human, have achieved a kind of perfection whenever I contemplate anything. But as mentioned above, this is a different type of *teleiotês*. It refers to a quasi-moral good, and not to an end-state following a transition. My soul-body composite possesses its *teleiotês qua* complete inherence of the substantial form "human" as long as it is alive, regardless of whether I am contemplating or not. But my soul-body composite possesses its *teleiotês qua* moral good only when I am actively contemplating.

The reason I have gone into such detail about this issue is that Alexander's expansion of *metabolê* to cover the transition from not-contemplating to contemplating as well as coming-to-be in a strict sense, and his concurrent expansion of *teleiotês* to cover the possession of intelligible form as well as substantial form, provided much of the conceptual raw material for later Neoplatonic ideas about perfection. As I shall show in Chapters 3 and 4, the Neoplatonists held that during the act of self-intellection, the identity of two of Alexander's types of *teleiotês* (*teleiotês qua* intelligible form of "intellect", and *teleiotês qua* substantial form of "intellect") with the third type of *teleiotês* (*teleiotês qua* good of "human") was so strong, that this last type of *teleiotês* came to be seen more as the *existential* good of "human" and less as the *moral* good of a human. In other words, self-intellection came to be seen as the primary mechanism of reversion, of ascending to the next higher level of being, partly because during self-intellection so many types of perfection are attained. I shall also explain in Chapters 3 and 4 how the Neoplatonists used the concept of the specific difference to make the move from seeing *teleiotês* as a moral good to seeing it as an existential good.

For my present purpose what is important is once again pointing out Alexander's use of *eidos* ("species") instead of Aristotle's *genos* ("genus") in commenting on L4. Aristotle's definition of *to teleion* as that which has achieved excellence or superiority in a *genus* is now understood by Alexander as referring instead to that which has achieved excellence or superiority in a *species*. Achieving excellence or superiority in a genus can be interpreted as referring to the full and complete inherence of a substantial form in the thing in which it inheres. When related to the genus, the substantial form "human" fully and completely inheres as long as the human is alive.

Achieving excellence or superiority in a species, on the other hand, can be interpreted as referring not to the full and complete inherence of the substantial form "human", but rather to the full and complete exercise of the specific difference, the essential characteristic which makes the species "human" what it is: rationality, or the capability to think. When I am actively contemplating, I am not achieving excellence or superiority in my genus, "animal". I achieve excellence or superiority in my genus, "animal", when I am actively moving or sensing, because I am using the two capabilities which are the essential differentiating characteristics of the genus "animal". But when I actively contemplate I *am* achieving excellence or superiority in my species, because I am using my capability to think, which is the essential differentiating characteristic of the species "human".

Another respect in which Alexander's terminology prefigures that of the Neoplatonists can be detected in his assertion that the transition from intellectual inactivity to intellectual activity is not so much a transition from *dunamis* to *energeia* as it is a transition from disposition (*epitêdeiotês*) to perfection (*teleiotês*). This is because the transition is from one thing to itself, and not from one thing to another.[8]

Most importantly, of course, the result of Alexander's broadened understanding of *metabolê* is that *teleiotês* can now serve in all but one of the roles Aristotle appears to demand of *entelekheia*. As the end-state following a *metabolê*, *teleiotês* can serve as the complete *entelekheia* implied in *Physics* 3.1 and 3.2, because *metabolê* covers the *genesis* of a substantial form as well as the three *kinêseis*: *kinêsis* with respect to quantity, *kinêsis* with respect to quality and *kinêsis* with respect to place. Moreover, as the end-state following a *metabolê*, *teleiotês* can now serve as the second *entelekheia* of *De Anima* 2.1, because *metabolê* now covers the *genesis* of an intelligible form as well as the *genesis* of a substantial form. Finally, as we saw above, Alexander uses *teleiotês* to gloss the first *entelekheia* of *De Anima* 2.1, indicating that he saw *teleiotês* as referring to the substantial form in and of itself, that is, to form as substance (*ousia*) or essence (*to ti ên einai*), and not merely to form as that which comes-to-be as the result of a *metabolê*.[9]

But what about change itself? In *Physics* 3.1 Aristotle defined *kinêsis*, not the end-state following a *kinêsis*, as an *entelekheia*. Replacing *kinêsis* with a more encompassing *metabolê* won't solve this problem. This is because Alexander

[8] See *Quaest.* 3.2, 81,7-82,17 and 3.3, 84,2-27.

[9] Other places where *teleiotês* seems to refer to substantial form *qua* essence are Alexander, *DA* 6,30-7,8; 9,11; and 10,8; *Quaest.* 2.3, 50,19; and *in Metaph.* 3.2 (*ad* 996a20-21), 181,22; 5.1 (*ad* 1013a20), 347,15-18; and 5.4 (*ad* 1014b16), 359,13-25.

has expanded the notion of *metabolê* to allow *teleiotês* to serve as its end-result, and not to allow *teleiotês* to serve as the *metabolê* itself. Yet Alexander seems to have meant for *teleiotês* to include within its range of referents the first or initial *entelekheia* implied in *Physics* 3.1 and 3.2, given that he sometimes uses *teleiotês* interchangeably with *energeia*.[10]

Inasmuch as we are able to reconstruct his views from Simplicius' and Philoponus' citations, Alexander was aware of this problem, and says that in relation to the actual X which is a potential Y, the *energeia* of the actual X *qua* potential Y is a *teleiotês*. In other words, when I place a log on the fire, the *energeia* that is the wood's *kinêsis* from potential fire to actual fire is, in relation to the actual wood's being a potential fire, a *teleiotês*. This conflation of *entelekheia* as *teleiotês* and *energeia* as *teleiotês* is something Simplicius takes Alexander to task for, but Philoponus approves of.[11]

Simplicius' criticism seems to be based on Aristotle's assertion in L3 that change is an incomplete *energeia*. Since Alexander says that change is the *energeia* which takes place when an actual X changes to an actual Y, and that change as *energeia* is the *teleiotês* of the actual X *qua* potential Y, we will be forced to conclude that, given Aristotle's description of change in L3 as an incomplete *energeia*, change is an incomplete completeness. And this rather meaningless conclusion, as discussed in Chapter 1, is one of the positions we wanted to avoid being forced into.

According to Simplicius, Alexander's canonical position is that *kinêsis* is the first or initial transformation (*metabolê prôtê*) or the first or initial actuality (*entelekheia prôtê*) of what is in potentiality, the last or final (*hustatê*) being the *metabolê* at the point of *teleiotês*, completion. He calls the initial *metabolê* or *entelekheia* the "route" or "path" (*hodos*) to the final.[12] In other words, Alexander avoids using *teleiotês* to describe change because doing so would make him vulnerable to the criticism that he held change to be an incomplete completeness; and as a result he is forced to see change as a process, as the route or path from potentiality to actuality.

So despite his desire to use *teleiotês* in the sense of both *energeia* as well as *entelekheia* – to refer to the change itself as well as the end-point that is the culmination of a change – Alexander seems resigned to giving up on that goal. In short, Alexander is torn between this:

[10] See, for example, *Quaest.* 3.2, 81,7-82,17 and 3.3, 84,2-27; *ap.* Simplicium, *in Phys.* 3.1 (*ad* 201a9), 414,15-416,6.

[11] *ap.* Simplicium, *in Phys.* 3.1, 415,29-416,2; and *ap.* Philoponum, *in DA* 2.1 (*ad* 412a16), 216,9-22; and 2.4 (*ad* 415a16), 264,15-19 and (*ad* 416a34), 284,3.

[12] *ap.* Simplicium, *in Phys.* 3.1 (*ad* 201a11), 416,27-31.

2b[ii]´´

Phys. 1st: *entelekheia atelês* = *teleiotês qua* "state of being completed" = state of incompleteness (e.g., "being constructed")
DA 1st: *entelekheia teleia* = *teleiotês qua* "state of having been completed" = state of completeness (e.g., "having come to know")

Phys. 2nd: *entelekheia teleia* = *teleiotês qua* "state of having been completed" = state of completeness (e.g., "having been constructed")
DA 2nd: *entelekheia teleia* = *teleiotês qua* "state of having been completed" = state of completeness (e.g., "having come to contemplate")

which is unsatisfactory because change will now be held to be an incomplete completeness; and this:

2b[ii]´

Phys. 1st: *entelekheia atelês* = *teleiôsis qua* "process of completion" = incomplete process (e.g., "construction")
DA 1st: *entelekheia teleia* = *teleiotês qua* "state of having been completed" = state of completeness (e.g., "having come to know")

Phys. 2nd: *entelekheia teleia* = *teleiotês qua* "state of having been completed" = state of completeness (e.g., "having been constructed")
DA 2nd: *entelekheia teleia* = *teleiotês qua* "state of having been completed" = state of completeness (e.g., "having come to contemplate")

which is unsatisfactory because change will now be seen as a process above and beyond the changing thing rather than as a state possessed by the changing thing.

Regardless of Alexander's inability to solve this dilemma, his use of *prôtê* ("first" or "initial") and *hustatê* ("last" or "final") to distinguish between *entelekheia* as *energeia* and *entelekheia* as *teleiotês* is historically significant. Assuming that Simplicius is quoting Alexander accurately, the source of a long tradition among the commentators – including Avicenna and continuing into the Latin Middle Ages – of asserting that change is a *first* or *initial* perfection, has been detected in the fragments of Alexander's lost commentary on the *Physics*. It would also appear that in his frustration at being unable to decide between position 2b[ii]´´ and position 2b[ii]´, Alexander falls back on position 2b[i], namely, construing the first/second distinction broadly enough as to make it apply to change as well as to transitions such as intellection, that is, the transition from knowing to contemplating.

On the other hand Simplicius may not be reporting Alexander's views correctly, but imposing a later articulation of the distinction backwards to Alexander. My own guess is that when Simplicius quotes Alexander as saying that *kinêsis* is a *prôtên metabolên ê prôtên entelekheian* (*ap*. Simplicium *in Phys.* 3.1, 416,28-29), the *ê prôtên entelekheian* is probably a scribe's or Simplicius' own gloss. This is because Alexander nowhere else calls motion a first *entelekheia*, although he clearly implies that motion is a first *metabolê*. If this is in fact the case, Themistius will then deserve the honor of being the first commentator to describe *kinêsis* as a "first" *entelekheia*.

Themistius (fl. 365 AD) says in his *Paraphrase* of *Physics* 3.1 that in each instance of change the *entelekheia* is twofold. One type of *entelekheia*, which Themistius calls *entelekheia prôtê*, "first" or "initial" actuality, refers to the actuality possessed by the potential thing while it is still changing; while, in other words, the changing thing retains some part of its potentiality. The other type of *entelekheia*, which Themistius calls *entelekheia hustatê*, "last" or "final" actuality, refers to the actuality possessed by the fully changed thing; to the actuality, in other words, of the formerly potential but now actual thing, which retains none of the potentiality it possessed while it was still changing.[13]

By Themistius' reckoning, *kinêsis* is a first, or initial, actuality, and consists in the potential thing's passage (*poreia*) to the form which lies at the end of the change. Last or final *entelekheia*, by contrast, refers to the change (here Themistius uses *metabolê*) when it is at the point of full inherence of the form (*eis to eidos*). Themistius corrects Aristotle by saying that since *entelekheia* properly speaking, and in an absolute sense, is form (*all' epeidê kai to eidos entelekheian legomen tên kuriôs te kai haplôs*), *kinêsis* is really a passage *to* an *entelekheia*, rather than an *entelekheia* itself. The conclusion one has to draw, Themistius says, is that *kinêsis* is an *entelekheia* only in an incomplete or imperfect sense (*houtôs oun hê entelekheia oukh hôs kuriôs oude haplôs all'hôs atelês*). And in an apparent slap at Aristotle in L3, Themistius asserts that change can be correctly called an incomplete actuality, and it can be correctly called a complete activity, but it is not correct to call change an incomplete activity. Themistius' careful distinction between *entelekheia* and *energeia* seems (again, if Simplicius is reporting accurately) to have been taken from Porphyry.[14]

But because he also follows Alexander in using *teleiotês* to gloss *entelekheia*, Themistius is faced with the possible problem that, having described change as an *energeia teleia*, *teleiotês* now appears as a gloss of both *entelekheia* and *energeia*.[15] Another problem is that Themistius seems to have felt obliged somehow to accommodate Aristotle's bald assertion in L3 that

[13] Themistius, *in Phys.* 3.1 (*ad* 201a7-16), 69,6-20 and (*ad* 201a16-27), 70,5-13.

[14] *ap.* Simplicium, *in Phys.* 3.1 (*ad* 201a9), 415,6-8.

[15] Themistius pairs *teleiotês* with *entelekheia* at *in Phys.* 3.6 (*ad* 206a20-31), 92,9-12 (in a discussion of the infinite), and pairs *teleiotês* with *energeia* at *in Phys.* 8.4 (*ad* 254b32-255a32), 218,27-29 (in a discussion of locomotion). The only time Themistius uses *teleiôsis* in the *in Phys.* is when he is quoting Aristotle's assertion in *Phys.* 7.3, that *aretai* are *teleiôseis*.

kinêsis is an incomplete activity (*energeia atelês*). Themistius says in his comments on *Physics* 3.2 that one type of *energeia* is complete, the other incomplete, and that it is possible to speak of *energeia* properly and in an absolute sense, yet for it still to be incomplete.[16] What can Themistius mean by upholding, in his comments on *Physics* 3.2, precisely what he attacked in his comments on *Physics* 3.1?

It is in response to these problems that Themistius appeals to two distinctions. The first distinction is that between the two different ways in which *teleiotês* can be understood to refer to endedness: *being directed towards an end* as opposed to *serving as an end*. I have already described this first endedness distinction in Chapter 1.

But Themistius adds a second distinction to the mix, differentiating between two other modes of endedness, which I shall call "allotelic" endedness and "autotelic" endedness. Themistius says that in one sense an *energeia* is *teleia* when it is static, or at rest, and when the *energeia* consists in, for example, the functioning of an organ. When the eye makes the transition from not-seeing to seeing, there is no *kinêsis*, and the eye remains static. The *energeia* in this case is *teleia* not in the sense that it is complete or terminated, but rather in the sense that the activity of seeing is autotelic, that is, in the sense that this *energeia* is an end in itself. When the eye rotates, on the other hand, the *energeia* of the eye is a *kinêsis*, and is *atelês* in the sense that for the eye, the activity of rotation is allotelic, not autotelic. That is to say, the rotation of the eye is not an end in itself but only a means to another end, namely, the end-state following the *kinêsis kata topon* (i.e., locomotion) of rotation.[17]

What evidence might Themistius have adduced from the Aristotelian corpus in order to support his new distinction between autotelic and allotelic endedness? Answering this question will require me to leave Themistius aside for a while and return to Aristotle. To my mind the main sources of the distinction between autotelic and allotelic endedness can be found in the *Nicomachean Ethics*. At the very beginning of that work, in *EN* 1.1, 1094a3-5, Aristotle says that some ends are nothing more than activities (*energeiai*), while other ends are products (*erga*) which are above and beyond (*para*) activities. A commentator could infer from this that some activities serve as their own ends, that is, that some activities are ends in themselves. Other activities, by contrast, are directed at ends which are produced as a result of those activities. In short, activities are either autotelic or allotelic.

Reinforcing this inference are a number of assertions and arguments Aristotle makes later on in the *Nicomachean Ethics*. At *EN* 1.7, 1097a25-b6, Aristotle expands on the distinction he made in *EN* 1.1, saying now that some ends are means to other ends, while other ends are ends in themselves. Wealth is an end

[16] Themistius, *in Phys.* 3.2 (*ad* 202a3-7), 75,13-14.
[17] Themistius, *in Phys.* 3.2 (*ad* 201b29-202a3), 74,11-23.

in the former, allotelic sense, while happiness is an end in the latter, autotelic sense. Aristotle then goes on to claim that the *more* a thing is an end in itself and not sought or chosen for the sake of something else, the more *teleion* that thing will be.

The result is that instead of a twofold distinction we now seem to be presented with a threefold distinction, between what one scholar has recently termed "subservient", "subordinate" and "ultimate" senses in which something may be said to be *teleion*.[18] To apply this threefold distinction once again to *energeiai*, a subservient *energeia* will be chosen or sought *only* for the sake of some product that comes into being as a result of the *energeia*. In other words, a subservient *energeia* is entirely allotelic. For example, a surgeon's act of cutting is never an end in itself, but only ever a means to a further end, namely, the patient's health. A subordinate *energeia* will serve as an end in itself in one respect, but in another respect be chosen or sought for the sake of an end which is above and beyond it. In other words, a subordinate *energeia* is *both* autotelic and allotelic. In one respect health is an end in itself, since a surgeon's act of cutting is directed at nothing above and beyond health; and in another respect health is sought not for its own sake but rather for the sake of something above and beyond health, namely, happiness. An ultimate *energeia* will *only* ever be sought or chosen for its own sake, and never as a means to a further end. In other words, an ultimate *energeia* is entirely autotelic. Happiness is only ever sought for its own sake, and never for the sake of something above and beyond it.

Given Aristotle's claim that the more a thing is chosen or sought for its own sake and not for the sake of something which is above and beyond it, the more *teleion* it will be; and given his claim later in the chapter (*EN* 1.7, 1097b6-21) that happiness is not simply the thing which is most *teleion* but also the thing which is most *autarkes* ("independent" or "self-sufficient"); a commentator could fairly infer that what being *teleion* and being *autarkes* had in common was the fact that it is in virtue of satisfying these two criteria that happiness enjoys the characteristic of being to the greatest degree *uncaused*. This is because happiness, being entirely autotelic, will never be the effect of a final cause which is above and beyond it; that is to say, happiness is uncaused because it never depends upon a further final cause to bring it into being.[19]

It is true that Aristotle describes *to autarkes* in this chapter (*EN* 1.7, 1097b14-15) merely as "that which makes a life uniquely worthy of choice and *lacking in nothing*", a description that would seem to support an understanding of *teleion* as quantitatively complete rather than autotelically ended. But when

[18] Keyt 1978.

[19] Here our commentator would disagree with Heinaman 1988, who takes *teleion* in the *Nicomachean Ethics* to refer to supremacy in a genus, i.e., the second sense of *teleion* which Aristotle offers in L4. This position is modified by Santas 1989, who argues that this sense of *teleion* fits best when Aristotle is articulating his own *conception* of the good from *EN* 1.7 onwards (as opposed up to *EN* 1.7, when Aristotle is merely talking about the *concept* of the good).

Aristotle revisits the question of happiness in *EN* 10.6-8, he articulates a position which supports an understanding of *to autarkes* as uncaused.[20]

I hesitate to put my oar into these choppy waters, since it bears upon a fundamental disagreement between Aristotle scholars who think that Aristotle held an "inclusivist" or "comprehensive" view of happiness, and those who think that Aristotle held an "exclusivist" or "dominant" view of happiness. According to the inclusivist view, happiness consists in the *sum* of all activities which are in accordance with the virtues; this view seems to govern Aristotle's discussions of happiness in *EN* 1. According to the exclusivist view, happiness consists in the *one* activity – contemplation – which is in accordance with the highest virtue; this view seems to govern Aristotle's discussions of happiness in *EN* 10.

The suggestion that *to teleion* should in many instances be understood as that which is *ended* – and that *to teleiôtaton*, by extension, should be understood as that which is ended to the highest degree, namely, that which is most autotelic – is more in accordance with the exclusivist view of happiness. This is because understanding *to teleiôtaton* as that which is most autotelic – and hence as that which is most *uncaused* by any final cause which is above and beyond it – derives from the sense of *teleion* which is most reconcilable with *autarkes*, understood as that which is *causally* self-sufficient and thus uncaused. In other words, an exclusivist could argue that happiness consists solely in contemplation, by appealing to the fact that contemplation is the most autotelic human activity. That is, given the fact that contemplation is never the effect of a final cause which is above and beyond it, contemplation is the human activity which is to the greatest degree causally self-sufficient.[21] By contrast, an inclusivist will tend to understand *teleion* as "quantitatively complete", since an inclusivist argues that happiness consists in the sum of all activities which are in accordance with virtue. In other words, happiness is *teleion* in the sense that happiness can be viewed as a whole none of whose parts is missing.

Regardless of whether the inclusivist or exclusivist view more accurately reflects what Aristotle really thought happiness was, the fact remains that the Neoplatonists gravitated towards the exclusivist view, for reasons I shall discuss in Chapters 3, 4 and 6. For the moment, I should just mention Aristotle's claim (*EN* 10.7, 1177b26-78a2) that contemplation, the epitome of the completely happy life, is the most divine of all human activities and is thus the one activity that makes us humans in some sense immortal. This assertion provided the Neoplatonists with a clear piece of Aristotelian evidence in support of their

[20] I agree with Curzer 1990 that Aristotle's description of being *autarkes* and being *teleion* – the two main criteria for happiness – in *EN* 10.6-8 is a reconsideration, rather than a continuation, of his description of *to autarkes* and *to teleion* in *EN* 1.7.

[21] Aristotle says as much at *EN* 10.7, 1177b16-20. Surprisingly, exlusivists such as Heinaman 1988 fail to appeal to the notion of autotelic endedness to support their own attack against the inclusivists.

notion of reversion (*epistrophê*), according to which all things have a irreducible tendency upwards along the chain of being.

Once a commentator felt justified in construing *teleion* as "autotelically ended" – being an end in itself – he could be confident in also construing *ateles* as "allotelically ended". He could support this move by appealing to Aristotle's assertion (*EN* 10.4, 1174a14-23) that pleasure, like seeing, is an autotelic (*teleion*) activity. This is in contrast to *kinêseis*, which always appear to be allotelic (*ateles*), given the fact that *kinêseis* – e.g., housebuilding – are directed towards an end – shelter – which is above and beyond the activity of the *kinêsis* itself. I admit that this is not the sense of *teleion* and *ateles* which Aristotle himself had in mind in this passage. In fact Aristotle is quite clear that he is thinking in terms of completeness and incompleteness rather than in terms of autotelic endedness and allotelic endedness. Nevertheless a commentator who, like Themistius, had committed himself to construing *teleion* and *ateles* – at least in some cases – in terms of autotelic and allotelic endedness, could easily apply that new understanding to the difference between *energeiai* such as seeing, which is an autotelic activity (though not the *most* autotelic activity), and *kinêseis* such as the eye's rotation, which is entirely allotelic.

How did adding autotelic and allotelic endedness to his quiver of distinctions help Themistius integrate the *entelekheiai* of *Physics* 3.1 and 3.2 with those of *De Anima* 2.1? In his synopsis of *De Anima* 2.1, Themistius starts by saying that in contrast to matter, which is pure disposition, form (*eidos*) is a *teleiotês*, in the sense that it is form which represents the fulfillment (*anaplêrôsis*) of a thing's innate disposition, and it is form which represents the "leading-on" (*proagôgê*) of a thing towards its end. Themistius goes on to say that *qua* fulfillment, the *eidos* is the thing's substantial form, and *qua* "leading-on", the *eidos* is the thing's structure or shape. A thing composed of form and matter, Themistius says, is said to be complete (*teleion einai*) in view of its substantial form (*para tou eidous*), and to have "end-in-itself-ness" (*entelôs ekhein*) in view of its structure or shape (*para tês morphês*).

I take this to mean that a thing may be said to be *teleion* in the sense of "completed" when its substantial form has fully inhered in its subject. This is what Themistius had in mind in his *Physics* paraphrase when he said that the end-state following a *metabolê* is an *entelekheia* in the proper sense. A thing may also be said to be *teleion* in the sense of "ended". It is in view of its structure or shape that a thing's function becomes apparent. The shape or structure of the eye is ended in the sense that the matter of the eye is arranged in the way it is in view of the function – seeing – which the eye performs. To sum up: when the form of a thing is seen as its substance or essence, it is a *teleiotês* because it refers to the state of completeness following a change; when the form of a thing is seen as its shape, on the other hand, it is a *teleiotês* because it refers to the endedness of the potentiality or capability represented by possessing that shape.

In both of these senses, the soul is an *entelekheia*, which Themistius takes to mean "the state of completeness-and-endedness" (*tên hexin tês teleiotêtos* = [*fa-laysa yadullu qawluhu anṭalākhiyā fī lisāni l-Yūnāniyyīn ʿalā shayʾin ghayri*] *malakati l-kamāl*).[22] The soul is the substantial form of the body and in that sense is the end-state of the *metabolê* by which the matter of the body came to be informed by the soul. The soul is also a structure of faculties or capabilities which is ended in the sense that these faculties or capabilities are either allotelic, in that their activities are directed towards the coming-to-be of new actualities (as with the faculty of reproduction, whose activity is directed towards the coming-to-be of offspring); or autotelic, in that their activities are ends in themselves (as with the faculty of intellection, whose activity is directed at no end other than itself).

In other words, Themistius has combined the idea of completeness with the idea of endedness (both in the sense of being directed at an end and in the sense of serving as an end), and then added the allotelic/autotelic distinction, to create a new matrix of all the different ways of being a *teleiotês*. With the autotelic/allotelic distinction in hand, Themistius thinks he is better able than Alexander to construct a scheme flexible enough to accommodate all the senses in which an *entelekheia* can be understood as a *teleiotês*.

In particular, applying the allotelic/autotelic distinction to the directed-at-an-end half of the directed-at-an-end/serving-as-an-end distinction allows Themistius to hold that change is in one sense *teleion* – meaning "directed at an end" – and in another sense *ateles* – meaning allotelic, i.e., "directed at an end other than itself". This move allowed Themistius to skirt the major roadblock – reconciling Aristotle's assertion in L2 that change was an *entelekheia* with his assertion in L3 that change was *ateles* – that had stood in the way of Alexander's idea of appealing to *teleiotês* to effect the larger reconciliation of Aristotle's use of *entelekheia* in L1 and his use of *entelekheia* in L2. Now, Themistius can hold that change is a *teleiotês atelês* without making a fool of himself. This is because that phrase need no longer be understood – and ridiculed – as some paradoxical "incomplete completeness", but can now be construed as referring instead to allotelic endedness, to the quality of being directed at an end other than itself.

What is more, by applying the autotelic/allotelic distinction to the serving-as-an-end half of the directed-at-an-end/serving-as-an-end distinction, Themistius is able to accommodate *entelekheiai* such as post-change end-states, which serve as an end for the changes that produced them; and he is also able to accommodate *entelekheiai* such as intellection which serve as their own end. Thus:

[22] Themistius, *in DA* 2.1 (*ad* 412a2-19), 39,3-22 at 39,20 (= Thāmasṭiyūs, *Sharḥ Kitāb an-nafs li-Arisṭūṭālīs*, 42,9-44,4 at 44,1).

2b[ii]´´

Phys. 1st:

1. *entelekheia atelês* = *teleiotês qua* "state of being completed" = state of incompleteness (e.g., "being constructed")
2. *energeia atelês* = *teleiotês qua* "state of being directed towards an end other than itself" = state of allotelic endedness (e.g., "being constructed into a house")

DA 1st:

1a. *entelekheia teleia* = *teleiotês qua* "state of having been completed" = state of completeness (e.g., "having been born") [identical to *Phys.* 2nd (1)]

1b. *entelekheia atelês* = *teleiotês qua* "state of being directed towards an end other than itself" = state of allotelic endedess (e.g., "capable of reproducing another")

2a. *entelekheia teleia* = *teleiotês qua* "state of having been completed" = state of completeness (e.g., "having come to know")

2b. *entelekheia teleia* = *teleiotês qua* "state of being directed towards an end which is nothing other than its own exercise" = state of autotelic endedess (e.g., "capable of contemplating")

Phys. 2nd:

1. *entelekheia teleia* = *teleiotês qua* "state of having been completed" = state of completeness (e.g., "having been constructed")
2. *entelekheia atelês* = *teleiotês qua* "state of serving as an end for something other than itself" = state of allotelic endedness (e.g., "having been constructed into a house")

DA 2nd:

1. *entelekheia atelês* = *teleiotês qua* "state of being directed towards an end other than itself" = state of allotelic endedness (e.g., "reproducing")
2. *entelekheia teleia* = *teleiotês qua* "state of serving as its own end" = state of autotelic endedness (e.g., "contemplating")

The fly in the ointment is Themistius' uncertainty over how interchangeable *entelekheia* and *energeia* are in the definition of *kinêsis*. Nevertheless, the upshot is that when *teleiotês* is interpreted – as Themistius seems to have done – as referring to completeness *as well as* to the various types of endedness (endedness in the sense of *being directed towards an end* as opposed to endedness in the sense of *serving as an end*, and *autotelic* endedness as opposed to *allotelic* endedness), that very elastic term can serve in all the roles Aristotle demands of an *entelekheia*.

One objection which could be raised to Themistius' interpretation is that the fundamental idea of endedness is based on an incorrect reading of Aristotle. This is because when Aristotle used the term *telos* in L4 it is pretty clear that he meant for it to be understood as referring to limit or terminus rather than purpose or that-for-the-sake-of-which. I would argue in Themistius' defense that the passage in question (*Metaph.* 5.16, 1021b23-30) can be read as two distinct sentences. The first (*Metaph.* 5.16, 1021b23-25) is neutral as to the sense of *telos* (either *qua to hou heneka* or *qua peras* is appropriate), while the second (*Metaph.* 5.16, 1021b25-30), it is true, does foreground the "limit" sense of *telos*. To repeat what I said in Chapter 1, a commentator could understand "Those things in which their worthwhile end exists are also said to be complete, for they are complete by virtue of the end which they possess (*eti hois huparkhei to telos, spoudaion on, tauta legetai teleia· kata gar to ekhein to telos teleia* = *wa-ayḍan tuqālu tāmmatan allatī lahā tamāmun fāḍilun fa-innahā tāmmatun bi-tamāmihā lladhī huwa lahā*)" (*Metaph.* 5.16, 1021b23-25 = *Mā ba*ᶜ*da ṭ-ṭabī*ᶜ*a II*, 622,2-3), as referring to *telos* in the sense of purpose or that-for-the-sake-of-which (*to hou heneka*), with just as much reason as he could understand it as referring to *telos* in the sense of limit or terminus (*peras*).

3. Proclus, Ammonius and Asclepius
The Neoplatonic Turn to Causation

In trying to speak clearly about a very complex and opaque topic I may have given the impression that Themistius' expanded understanding of endedness represents a full-fledged theory. It does not. But however patchy it may in fact have been, the ways in which Themistius understood endedness nevertheless provide evidence of a subtle but important shift in ancient discussions of *entelekheia*. This is because Themistius' new use of *teleiotês* to glue together Aristotle's problematic applications of *entelekheia* to both *psukhê* and *kinêsis*, is one of the first indications that *teleiotês* had begun to have causal significance. Specifically, Themistius' appeal to the various senses in which *teleiotês* refers to endedness – both in the sense of *serving as an end* and *being directed towards an end*, and in the sense of *autotelically* and *allotelically* – is a sign that Aristotle's concepts of actuality and activity were on their way to being viewed less as *states of being* and more as *causes of being*, and particularly as *final causes of being*. Themistius' move towards viewing *teleiotês* (and hence *entelekheia*) in causal terms, shows the influence of Plotinus and especially Porphyry, whose distinction between a complete *energeia* and an incomplete *entelekheia* I have already mentioned.[1] The precise nature of this turn from actuality and activity to causation is the topic to be examined in this chapter.

To be sure, I am not proposing that the Neoplatonists made the move to causation simply for its own sake. The move to causation seems instead to have been a surface tremor arising from a deeper, tectonic shift; to have been little more, in fact, than a new use of a couple of Aristotelian and Alexandrian terms – *teleion* and *teleiotês* – as part of a larger effort to reconcile Platonic and Aristotelian cosmologies and theories of the soul. In particular, Neoplatonists applied *teleion* and *teleiotês* in their new, causal sense in order to blur the sharp distinctions between the Platonic (as understood by Plotinus) core doctrines of the *separability* of the soul and God's efficient and final causation of the world's *existence*, and the Aristotelian (as understood by Alexander) core doctrines of the *inseparability* of the soul and God's final causation of the world's *motion*.

As far as the issue of the separability of the soul is concerned Plotinus is well known for having devoted a section of his *Enneads* to attacking Aristotle's application of *entelekheia* to the soul. The reason was that the definition of

[1] Another hint in Themistius of Neoplatonic influence (and one which comes into full bloom in Proclus) is the idea that the contraries between which change takes place can be distinguished into better (*ameinon*) and worse (*phauloteron*): the better contraries are *to eidos*, in the case of substantial change; *to teleion*, in the case of quantitative change; *to melan*, in the case of qualitative change; and *to anô*, in the case of locomotion. Their base counterparts are, respectively, *hê sterêsis*, *to ateles*, *to leukon*, and *to katô*.

soul as *entelekheia* did seem to commit Aristotle – at least in the eyes of interpreters such as Alexander – to an openly anti-Platonic position, namely, that the soul is inseparable from the body just as form is inseparable from matter. This of course is at odds with Platonic psychology, which held that the soul pre-exists the body and survives its death.

Here is Plotinus' attack on Aristotle's *entelekheia*, as expressed in its Arabic paraphrase, the *Theology of Aristotle*:

L 7

(Ps.-)Arisṭūṭālīs, *Uthūlūjiyā* 3, 54,7-55,19
corr. Plotinus, *Enneads* IV.7.8(5),1-18[2]

If they say: The principal philosophers agree that the soul is the perfection of the body [*tamāmu l-badani*], and perfection is not a substance, and therefore the soul is not a substance, since the perfection of a thing is from the substance of the thing, we reply: *We must investigate their argument that the soul is a perfection, and in what sense they call her "entelekheia"* [*innahu yanbaghī an nafḥasa ᶜan qawlihim inna n-nafsa tamāmun mā wa-bi-ayyi l-maᶜānī sammawhā anṭalāshiyā*]. We say that *the principal philosophers have mentioned that soul is to body as a form whereby the body becomes ensouled, just as matter* by means of form becomes body: but though the soul is form to the body, yet *she is not a form to every body qua body but is a form only to the body that is alive in potentiality.* If the soul is a perfection after this description she is not of the class of bodies, for if she were a form to the body *like the form that is in a brazen idol, then if the body were divided and split up she too would be divided and split up, and if one of the members of the body were cut off part of her would be cut off too,* and this is not so. Therefore the soul is not a perfecting form [*laysati n-nafsu idhan bi-ṣūratin tamāmiyyatin*] like the natural and the artificial form; no, she is a perfection because it is she that perfects the body so that it comes to possess perception and mind. We say: *If the soul is a form, adhering and not separating, like the natural form* [*in kānati n-nafsu ṣūratan lāzimatan ghayra mufāraqatin*[3] *ka-ṣ-ṣūrati ṭ-ṭabīᶜiyyati*], *then how does she withdraw in sleep* and separate from the body without quitting it? Similar too is her action in the waking state when she returns to herself – for she often returns to herself – and casts off bodily affairs, though that is apparent from her activity only by night because of the quiescence of the senses and the cessation of their activities.

If the soul were a perfection of the body *qua* body, she would not separate from it [*law kānati n-nafsu tamāman li-l-badani bi-annahu*

[2] The translation, with minor changes, is that of Lewis 1959, 209-211. The italicized lines are those bits of the *Uthūlūjiyā* which Lewis saw as corresponding directly to words, phrases and sentences in the *Enneads*.

[3] I have transliterated Lewis' "separating" (it should really be "separable" or "separated") as the passive participle *mufāraqa* rather than the active participle *mufāriqa* because in general the term translates the Greek *exêirêmenon*, which is the passive participle of *exairein*.

> *badanun la-mā fāraqathu*] and would not know the remote, but would know only things present, like the cognition of the senses; then she and the senses would be one thing, and that is not so because *the soul recognizes a thing although it be remote from her, and recognizes the impressions* that the senses receive, and distinguishes them, as we have often said. The function of the senses is merely to receive the impressions of things, while recognition and discrimination belong to the soul.
>
> *We say that if the soul were a natural perfecting form* [*law kānati n-nafsu ṣūratan tamāmiyyatan ṭabīʿiyyatan*], *she would not oppose the body in its desires* and many of its activities, indeed she would not oppose it in anything at all, and, if any affection were impressed on the body, that affection would be in the soul too, and *man would have sense-perception only,* because the province of the body is sense-perception; *knowledge, thought and reflection are not within its province. The Materialists recognized that, and consequently they are compelled to acknowledge a second soul and a second mind that does not die.* Now we say that there is no second soul other than *this rational soul* which is in the body at the moment, and she it is of whom the philosophers say that she is the "*entelekheia*" of the body [*anṭalāshiyā l-badani*], though they speak of her as "*entelekheia*" and a perfecting form *in a way different from that* in which the Materialists speak [*ghayra annahum inna-mā dhakarū annahā anṭalāshiyā wa-ṣūratun tamāmiyyatun bi-nawʿin ākhara ghayri n-nawʿi lladhī dhakarū l-jirmiyyūna*]. I mean that she is not a perfection like the natural perfection, which is passive, but is an active perfection, that is, she makes perfection. In this sense do they say that she is the perfection of the natural organic body, potentially ensouled.

Others have analyzed Plotinus' attack.[4] For my present purpose, what is interesting is that in the Greek original from which this passage of the *Uthūlūjiyā* is derived, Plotinus himself does not use the term *teleiotês* to describe the soul as an alternative to the despised *entelekheia*. This is perhaps because, as we saw, Alexander had tied the two terms so closely in his own works on the soul, works in which Alexander upheld the soul's inseparability from the body even more adamantly than Aristotle himself had. Yet in the Arabic version, the term *tamām* – the standard early translation of *teleiotês* – is used extensively. As I shall show, this is because in the six centuries between Plotinus and the Arabic translation movement, *teleiotês* had become such a standard way for Neoplatonists to describe the soul while avoiding the use of the troublesome *entelekheia*, that the Arabic term *tamām*, which was used to translate both *teleiotês* and *entelekheia* during the early period of translation, when the *Uthūlūjiyā* was being put together, appears everywhere in that text. If I am right, it is one of the ironies of the history of philosophy that the term *teleiotês*, first introduced and promoted by the arch-Peripatetic Alexander – a

[4] See Bruni 1960; Hager 1964; Verbeke 1971; and Emilsson 1991.

philosopher fully committed to the idea that the soul was inseparable from the body – was seized on by later Neoplatonists as a way to introduce and promote Platonic-Plotinian ideas about the separability of the soul.

As I mentioned, the Neoplatonic turn consisted in a move from Aristotle's more natural-philosophical uses – in the context of motion and the soul – of *entelekheia* and *energeia*, terms indicative primarily of *states* of being (viz., actuality and activity); to the Neoplatonists' more metaphysical uses of both *teleiotês*, a term which came to be used to express the idea of the *final cause* of being, and of *teleion*, a term which came to be used to express the idea of the *efficient cause* of being. This turn to causation took place over several generations of Neoplatonist philosophers. These include Syrianus (d. ca. 437); his student Proclus (d. ca. 485); Proclus' student Ammonius (d. ca. 514); and Ammonius' students Asclepius (fl. 525) and Philoponus (d. ca. 570), through whose *apo phônês* ("lecture-note") commentaries on the *Metaphysics* and *De Anima*, respectively, we can reconstruct Ammonius' own philosophy.

The transformation that occurs during this period is a complex and profound story, and I do not want to give the impression that what I shall present here is an exhaustive description of how and why it happened; that is a task for specialists in Greek Neoplatonism. For now, what is important about this move – a manifestation of what I referred to in the Introduction as the "Ammonian synthesis", by which I mean the project of the Aristotle-commentator Ammonius and his students to integrate the greater *sumphônia* of reconciling Aristotle and Plato into the lesser *sumphônia* of reconciling Aristotle and Aristotle – is that it is crucial but unappreciated background both to the word choices made by the various Greco-Arabic translators, and, partly for that reason, to the theories of the soul and of causation of the Arabic philosophers al-Fārābī and Avicenna.

The gradual subsuming of *entelekheia* under *teleiotês* occurred because a Neoplatonist's use of *entelekheia* could be attacked as committing him to two unsavory theories (unsavory to a Neoplatonist, that is): to an ontology of the soul according to which the soul is understood as being inseparable from the body, and to a cosmology according to which God's causation of the world is understood as an instance of the final causation of motion or change, rather than as an instance of the efficient and final causation of existence. By contrast, using *teleiotês* rather than *entelekheia* allowed a Neoplatonist – as I shall show – to advocate the separability of the soul from the body, and the causation of existence rather than of motion; but it also left a number of loose ends, which the later Neoplatonists, including Avicenna, tried to tie up.

The turn to causation begins with the identification of being in a state of activity (*kat' energeian* or *energeiâi*) or being in a state of actuality (*kat' entelekheian* or *entelekheiâi*) and being perfect (*teleion*). Now "that which is in a state of activity" or "that which is in a state of actuality" are not included among the meanings of *to teleion* offered by Aristotle in L4. Nevertheless it is not too much of a stretch to connect *to teleion* with those two senses, for the following reasons.

First of all, if – as Alexander tells us – Aristotle thought that an *entelekheia* such as the soul was nothing other than a *teleiotês*, and if *to teleion* is the substantive adjective whose abstract noun is *teleiotês*, then that which is *kat' entelekheian* or *kat' energeian* will similarly be *to teleion*. Second, and more importantly, a characteristic of something which is *kat' entelekheian* or *kat' energeian* is that it stands as a cause to the thing which it is in contact with and which is changing from being *kata dunamin* to being itself *kat' entelekheian* or *kat' energeian*. That is perfectly Aristotelian: an actual or active fire is the cause of the potential fire's changing into actual or active fire.

But does a perfect thing likewise stand as a cause to something which is imperfect? Again, even though standing as a cause to something which is *ateles* is not one of the meanings of *teleion* offered by Aristotle in L4, connecting the two concepts is quite straightforward. As was discussed above, one of the meanings of *teleiôsis* is the process of concoction by which an immature living thing (an embryo or a child) becomes fully developed or mature (a fetus or an adolescent). The *teleiotês*, or state of complete development, possessed by a fetus which is at the point of being born refers mainly to its possession of all its component parts, a numerical wholeness accommodated in Aristotle's list of meanings in L4. The *teleiotês* of an adolescent, however, refers not to its possession of all its parts – it has precisely as many parts as the fully developed fetus – but rather to its sexual maturity. That is, *teleiotês* in this instance refers to the sexually mature thing's ability to reproduce, to bring something like it into existence; and hence *teleiotês* refers to its causality.

The Neoplatonists reckoned that if *teleiotês* can be seen to refer to *causality* in this way, it follows that something possessing *teleiotês* – namely, *to teleion* – can be seen to refer to *cause*.[5] In fact, it is a Neoplatonic cliché to speak of

[5] The perfect's necessary causation of other things is alluded to by Plotinus, *Enneads*, V.1.6,37-38 (*kai panta de hosa êdê teleia gennâi*); V.4.1,23-39 (esp. 26-28: *ho ti d'an tôn allôn* [viz., other than the First] *eis teleiôsin iêi, horômen gennôn kai ouk anekhomenon eph' heautou menein, all' heteron poioun*) (the entire passage is compressed into *al-fāʿilu l-awwalu yabqā ʿalā ḥālihi sākinan qāʾiman tāmman fa-yaḥduthu min tamāmihi fiʿlun*: *R. fī l-ʿilm al-ilāhī*, 179,22); and V.9.4,3-12 (*ou gar dê, hôs oiontai, psukhê noun teleôtheisa gennâi; pothen gar to dunamei energeiâi estai, mê tou eis energeian agontos aitiou ontos? .... Dio dei ta prôta energeiâi tithesthai kai aprosdea kai teleia; ta de atelê hustera ap' ekeinôn, teleioumena de par' autôn tôn gegennêkotôn dikên paterôn teleiountôn, ha kat' arkhas atelê egennêsan ....*) (the beginning of the passage corresponds to *wa-laysa ka-mā ẓanna nāsun anna n-nafsa idhā tammat wa-kamilat waladati l-ʿaqla*: *R. fī l-ʿilm al-ilāhī*, 168,17). Syrianus introduces the causality of the perfect into an Aristotelian context by explicitly equating the perfect's causality of the imperfect with the causality enjoyed by what is *entelekheiâi* towards what is *dunamei*: *in Metaph.* 14.5 (*ad* 1092a11), 185,29-186,14. The two concepts are further integrated by Proclus: *Theol. Plat.*, Vol. 1.6, 27,15-17; 5.20, 73,14-15; *Inst. Theol.*, Prop. 24, 28,8-13; 25, 28,21-30,4; 27, 30,25-32,2; 77, 72,20-74,7; *in Alc. I*, 235,10-12; *in Parm.*, 797,35-38; and *in Tim.*, Vol. 1, 297,2-18; 2, 56,12-68,5; 3, 22,20-28. Asclepius lists productivity as one of the criteria of the perfect in his commentary on L4: *in Metaph.* 5.16 (*ad* 1021b12), 338,14-339,7

how the perfect is "fecund" or "fertile" (*gonimon*).[6] By contrast, something imperfect, which does not possess *teleiotês* but which has a disposition or suitability (*epitêdeiotês*) to attain that *teleiotês*, can be seen to refer to *effect*.[7] While connecting actuality or activity with perfection via their common causality may have been a nifty move, it raised many questions, the answers to which had profound ramifications. Analyzing how late-antique and early-Arabic philosophers up to Avicenna tidied up the messy after-effects of this move, and dealt with the further implications of their answers to those questions, is the subject of the rest of Part I.

Perhaps the first and most obvious question raised by connecting the perfect and perfection to causality is, what kind of cause is the perfect, and what kind of cause is perfection? In other words, how exactly can what is perfect be described as producing its effect; and how exactly can perfection be described as producing its effect? Before trying to answer that question, it would be a good idea to say a few words about the term "cause". Recently, the trend among scholars of ancient philosophy has been to emphasize the fact that the Greek terms *aitia* and *aition* ought not to be seen solely as referring to a cause which produces its effect, but should sometimes be seen as referring to an *explanans* or explanatory factor which explains its *explanandum* or thing to be explained.[8] In other words, instead of asking how the perfect and perfection produce their effects, we should perhaps be asking how the perfect and perfection explain their *explananda*. But it is unclear whether our understanding of late-antique discussions of causation should automatically be revised in light of the recent work done on classical theories of causation and explanation.

On the one hand, the more general Neoplatonic discussions of the fecundity and productivity of the perfect seem to indicate that what the Neoplatonists are primarily focused on is how the cause produces its effect in the real world. On the other hand, Neoplatonic talk about perfection's acting as a final cause, as something which stands as a goal or object of desire in relation to its effect (in contrast with the perfect, which stands as a generator or producer in relation to its effect), will sound less counterintuitive to us if we imagine the Neoplatonists to be thinking of perfection as an *explanans* rather than as a cause. In this respect the debates about whether Aristotle, in particular, thought in terms of causes or explanations can also be applied to the Neoplatonic discussions. This is because those Aristotle scholars who today find his theory of final causality

(*theôria*) and 340,32-341,25 (*lexis*); at 339,3-7, Asclepius says that we call "perfect" that which is capable of perfecting another (*to dunamenon allo teleioun*).

[6] On the fecundity of the perfect see Proclus, *Theol. Plat.*, Vol. 2.7, 50,3-51,6; 4.3, 16,3; 5.5, 24,17; and *in Tim.*, Vol. 1, 25,14-18.

[7] See Proclus, *in Remp.*, Vol. 1, 218,3-4; *Inst. Theol.*, Prop. 79, 74,18-26; *in Parm.*, 668,4-19.

[8] Hocutt, 1974; Mure 1975; Moravcsik 1975; Frede 1980; Sorabji 1980, 3-69; Schofield 1991; Moravcsik 1992; and Freeland 1992.

philosophically incoherent, metaphorical, or superfluous, tend to assume the correctness of the "cause" view.

By contrast, those Aristotle scholars interested in defending the coherence of teleology, its essential role in Aristotle's thought, and its complementarity with efficient causality, tend to advocate the "explanation" view. There is nothing surprising in this, of course, since in a competition between the efficient cause and the final cause over which is more cause-like, the efficient will always be judged the winner by those with modern intuitions that what a cause causes is an *event*. Because the cause of an event must exist before the event, and because the efficient cause is temporally prior to its effect, while the final cause is either simultaneous with or temporally posterior to its effect, the efficient cause will appear the more cause-like to modern eyes. We are forced in the end to conclude, rather spinelessly, that the Neoplatonists are inconsistent on whether "cause" or "explanation" is at issue: sometimes they seem to be referring to causation, particularly when speaking of the fecund efficient causation of the perfect; and other times they seem to be referring to explanation, particularly when speaking of the complementarity between the way that the perfect operates and the way perfection operates. What I shall do, then, is begin by referring to the perfect and perfection as causes, and then later turn to describing the complementary ways they explain their respective *explananda*.

What does seem clear is that Neoplatonists such as Syrianus, Proclus, Ammonius and his students, interested not only in Platonizing Aristotle but also in Aristotelianizing Plato, worked very hard to apply Aristotle's four-cause theory to the cosmology they inherited from Plotinus and which derived many of its basic principles from Platonic works such as the *Phaedo*, *Phaedrus*, *Philebus*, *Timaeus* and *Parmenides*, the last two of which served as the culmination of the Neoplatonic curriculum. I have mentioned above that the Neoplatonists thought that the perfect operated as an efficient cause and that perfection operated as a final cause. What prompted them to choose the efficient cause for the perfect and the final cause for perfection? Why were the other two Aristotelian causes – the material and the formal – not in the running?

Answering that question is complicated by three corollary factors. The first factor is that later Neoplatonists actually had two extra causes to choose from apart from the four Aristotelian causes. One was the paradigmatic or exemplary cause, invented to accommodate the separate Ideas, which – unlike the inseparable formal cause – transcended their effects. The other extra cause was the instrumental cause, inherited from the Middle Platonists and designed to serve in the role of efficient cause in the sublunary world.[9]

The second factor is that according to the scheme which appears to have been invented by Syrianus and which was expanded upon by Proclus, the final,

[9] On the history of the paradigmatic cause, see Hankinson 1998, 326-327 and 351; on the instrumental cause, see 342 and 380-381.

paradigmatic and efficient causes were causes in a proper or strict sense (*kuriôs*) and inhabited – in the order just listed, from highest to lowest – the superlunary world of eternal existence. The formal, instrumental and material causes, by contrast, were not really causes at all but rather conjoint causes or causal factors (*sunaitia*) and inhabited the sublunary world of coming-to-be and passing-away.[10]

The third factor is that among the Neoplatonic commentators on Aristotle such as Syrianus, Ammonius and his students, the rigid assignment of cosmic roles to each of the causes came to take the form of a general law whenever it was applied in interpreting Aristotelian discussions of the four causes. The law held that final and efficient causes are *transcendent of* or *extrinsic to* their effects, while formal and material causes were *immanent in* or *intrinsic to* their effects. Applying this law to Aristotle's texts required less effort than might be expected. For though Aristotle nowhere makes such a canonical distinction between transcendent and immanent causes, in *Physics* 2.3 he contrasts the material cause and the efficient cause, saying that the material cause is a "constituent" (*enuparkhon*) of its effect.[11] This is repeated in *Metaphysics* 5.1, where Aristotle takes the next step and actually makes a distinction between principles that constitute (*enuparkhon*) their effects and those that are not constituent of (*mê enuparkhon*) and outside (*ektos*) their effects.[12] In *Metaphysics* 12.4, Aristotle contrasts the matter and form, which he calls the constituent causes, with the extrinsic efficient cause.[13]

In his comments on *Metaphysics* 5.1, Alexander extended the category of *mê enuparkhon* to cover ends as well as agents.[14] Syrianus, Proclus and Asclepius then took the next step in systematizing the distinction, saying that the formal and material causes are constituents of their effects, while the final and efficient causes are outside their effects.[15]

[10] Syrianus, *in Metaph.* 13.1 (*ad* 1076a10), 82,2-13; Proclus, *in Parm.*, 983,1-3 (following Westerink's suggestion of *telika* for Cousin's *teleia kai*); *in Tim.*, Vol. 1, 2,1-4,5; 4,26-28; 17,15-30; 263,19-264,3; and 3, 126,11-13.

[11] *enuparkhôn* at *Phys.* 2.3, 194b23 (= *wa-huwa fīhi, aṭ-Ṭabīʿa*, 101,1). Philoponus (*in Phys.* [*ad loc.*], 243,30-244,3) concludes that the efficient cause is therefore extrinsic to its effect.

[12] *enuparkhontos* at *Metaph.* 5.1, 1013a4 (= *wa-huwa fī sh-shayʾi* at *Mā baʿda ṭ-ṭabīʿa II*, 473,8), and *mê enuparkhontos* at 1013a7 (= *wa-laysa huwa fīhi* at *Mā baʿda ṭ-ṭabīʿa II*, 474,3); *toutôn de hai men enuparkhousai eisin hai de ektos* at *Metaph.* 5.1, 1013a19-20 (= *wa-baʿḍu l-ibtidāʾāti fī l-ashyāʾi wa-baʿḍuhā hiya khārija* at *Mā baʿda ṭ-ṭabīʿa II*, 474,11-12).

[13] cf. *ta enuparkhonta aitia* at *Metaph.* 12.4, 1070b22 (= *al-asbābu hiya l-mawjūdatu ... fī llatī takūnu* at *Mā baʿda ṭ-ṭabīʿa III*, 1522,10).

[14] Alexander, *in Metaph.* 5.1 (*ad* 1012b34), 345,37-346,16.

[15] See Syrianus, *in Metaph.* 3.1 (*ad* 995b27), 7,8-10 (where he cites Alexander as the source of the distinction); and 3.2 (*ad* 996a21), 13,30-14,38; Proclus, *Inst. Theol.*, Prop. 75, 70,28-72,4; *in Tim.*, Vol. 1, 237,9-11 and 239,24-240,1; 3, 4,17-18; 196,14-16; and 202,13-14; Asclepius, *in Metaph.* 1.9 (*ad* 991a8), 84,7-33 and (*ad* 991a19), 87,29-30; 5.1 (*ad* 1013a17), 305,2-17 (where the distinction is stated most canonically: some principles – the formal and material – are constituents of the effect [*hai men enuparkhousi*], while others – the final and efficient – are extrinsic to the effect [*hai de ektos*]). As I shall show in Chapters 6 and 11, Avicenna inherited this

With these three extra factors at play – the addition of the paradigmatic and instrumental causes to Aristotle's final, efficient, formal and material; the assigning of each of the six causes to a place in the cosmic hierarchy; and the distinction between final and efficient causes, which transcend their effects, and formal and material causes, which are immanent in their effects – determining which type of cause the perfect is and which type perfection is had ramifications beyond that simple act of identification.

The less complicated identification seems to be what kind of cause the perfect is. As mentioned above, since the perfect is called "fecund", and therefore seems to be productive of its effect's coming-to-be (*genesis*) in the way a father is productive of his son, it fits most comfortably in the role of efficient cause. But if the perfect produces its effects as an efficient cause, and if, strictly speaking, an efficient cause transcends its effect and belongs to the superlunary world of eternal existence, it will follow that the perfect similarly transcends its effects and belongs to the superlunary world of eternal existence. Does that mean that nothing down here in the sublunary world can be correctly described as being perfect? If it does, then we are left with two alternatives: either the perfect will fail to serve in the sublunary role of the actual or the active, namely, causing the potential to change into the actual or the active; or the actual or the active will be held to exist in the sublunary world only in a metaphorical sense, with true actuality and activity reserved for superlunary beings.

Which alternative I chose depended partly on the extent to which I, as a Neoplatonist, was committed to integrating Aristotelian four-cause theory into my cosmology. If my commitment is mild, then I shall tend to assign the four Aristotelian and two Neoplatonic causes to various stations in the hierarchy – final cause at the top of the superlunary world, then paradigmatic, then efficient, then formal at the top of the sublunary world, then instrumental, and then material – and not worry too much about how that might complicate my attempts to account for sublunary change. This is the impression Proclus usually gives. Proclus sees the perfect as belonging, strictly speaking, to the superlunary world of real efficient causation, and as applying specifically to the Demiurge, the lowest of the three major inhabitants of the intelligible world and the one responsible for causing the coming-to-be of sublunary entities. (Sometimes the One is spoken of as if it were an efficient cause, other times as if it were above any type of causation.)

Proclus derives the distinction between causes which are transcendent of their effects and causes which are immanent in their effects, from the fact that the final, paradigmatic and efficient causes inhabit the superlunary world and are thus transcendent of their effects in the sense of being *separate from matter*, whereas the formal, instrumental and material causes inhabited the sublunary world and

distinction and used it in his own work. I discuss the history of this distinction at greater length in Wisnovsky 2003a.

are thus immanent in their effects in the sense of being *inseparable from matter*. This seems to indicate that it was usually more important to Proclus to assign to each element of the cosmic hierarchy a station and a type of causation appropriate to that station – and then maintain, if forced, that the transcendent/immanent distinction applied in an equivocal way to sublunary causes and effects – than it was to apply the transcendent-immanent distinction univocally, that is, to hold that the distinction applies to causes down here in the sublunary world just as it applies to causes up there in the superlunary world.

If, on the other hand, integrating Aristotle's four-cause theory into the Neoplatonic cosmos is my main goal, then I shall tend to apply the transcendent-immanent distinction univocally, to sublunary entities as well as to superlunary ones, at the cost of losing the rigid identification of each element of the cosmic hierarchy with a particular type of cause. The upshot is that if the efficient cause operates univocally in both the superlunary and sublunary realms, and if the perfect is nothing more than the state of being which is enjoyed by an efficient cause relative to its effect, then – assuming that there are no efficient causes which are not perfect – the perfect will operate univocally in both the superlunary and sublunary worlds.

Regardless of what a Neoplatonist would say if forced to choose between an equivocal or a univocal understanding of the perfect, it is clear that the procession (*proödos*) of being from the One, at the very top of the superlunary hierarchy, through the Demiurge, at the bottom of the superlunary hierarchy, through the world of coming-to-be and passing-away, and all the way down to matter – the procession, that is, from things which are more perfect in their existence to things which are less perfect in their existence – was generally seen by the Neoplatonists as a procession from *efficient* causes to their effects.[16]

Now that the perfect has been shown to produce its effect as an efficient cause, albeit with some problematic implications, what kind of cause will perfection be? On the one hand, perfection can be understood simply as the abstract noun corresponding to the adjective *teleion*. Since something *teleion* operates, as we have seen, as an efficient cause, then *teleiotês* will simply mean efficient causality. On the other hand, *teleiotês* is spoken of by the Neoplatonists as something to be attained by means of imitation (*homoiotês*) and participation (*methexis*), and therefore seems to operate on its effects the way a final cause does. In other words, when a perfect X encounters an imperfect X and the imperfect X becomes a perfect X, the perfect X stands as an efficient cause to the imperfect X, while the perfection of X – the state of perfect X-ness in which the perfect X participates – stands as a final cause relative to the imperfect X.[17]

[16] Proclus, *Theol. Plat.*, Vol. 2.6, 40,9-27; 3.2, 7,21-27; Asclepius, *in Metaph.* 4.1 (*ad* 1003a21), 223,34-36. Ammonius' theory of procession and reversion, as reported in Asclepius' *apo phônês* commentary, is helpfully discussed by Verrycken 1990.

[17] e.g., Proclus, *Inst. Theol.*, Prop. 32, 36,3-4; and 153, 134,23-35.

Of course it is possible that efficient causation – the state or quality of being an efficient cause – is itself something to be striven for, and that it therefore causes its effects as a final cause. But strictly speaking this is incorrect, according to the Neoplatonists. On the contrary, *teleiotês* can be divided into two types. The first type of *teleiotês* refers to a thing's perfection taken in and of itself. A perfect X strives to maintain its own *teleiotês* in the sense that it strives constantly to fulfill the characteristic of X-ness, and thereby ascend to the cusp of the next level up in the cosmic hierarchy. In this first sense *teleiotês* seems to refer most directly to one of the original Aristotelian senses of *teleion* articulated in L4: the sense in which a thing which is *teleion* possesses a superiority or "unsurpassedness" in its genus or species. A first *teleiotês* will thus act on its effect as a final cause by serving as a goal: in this case, the goal of self-perfection. The second type of *teleiotês* refers to a thing's perfection in relation to things other than itself, and specifically in relation to things which are inferior to it in the hierarchy of beings. A perfect X which is also an imperfect Y strives to attain the state of perfect Y-ness in which a perfect Y participates. Again, this type of *teleiotês* – perfect Y-ness – acts on its effects as a final cause, by serving as the goal of change.

Proclus helps us out by illustrating what he means. In his commentary on the *Republic,* Proclus says that examples of a thing taken in itself are "human" or "soul", and examples of a thing taken in relation to others are "human master of slaves (*despotês*)" and "soul master of body".[18] Elsewhere, making an allusion to *Phaedrus* 247E4-6, Proclus claims that the distinction between the two types of perfection is analogous to the distinction between the solidity of ambrosia (*teleiotês* in relation to self) and the liquidity of nectar (*teleiotês* in relation to others).[19]

I shall discuss in Chapter 4 how Proclus' distinction between first *teleiotês* and second *teleiotês* caused Philoponus to rework Alexander's and Themistius' *entelekheia* schemes. For the moment, I shall focus on the role *teleiotês* plays in Neoplatonic cosmology. For just as the procession from the One, through the Demiurge, through the world of coming-to-be and passing-away, all the way down to matter – the procession, that is, from higher things which are perfect in their existence to lower things which are imperfect in their existence – was seen by the Neoplatonists as a procession from *efficient* causes to their effects, so the reversion or turning upwards (*epistrophê*) from matter, through the world of coming-to-be and passing-away, through soul, through Intellect, through the Ideas contained in the paradigmatic cause, all the way to the Good – the reversion, that is, from things which are imperfect in their existence towards

[18] Proclus, *in Remp.*, Vol. 1, 207,14-208,2; see also 2, 74,7-9; and *Inst. Theol.*, Prop. 153, 134,23-35.

[19] Proclus, *Theol. Plat.*, Vol. 4.15, 47,7-48,9; 4.16, 49,1.

their own perfection – was seen as a reversion from effects towards their *final* causes.[20]

A number of interrelated clusters of questions immediately arises. First, how does procession relate to reversion? Are they symmetrical, in the sense that what happens during reversion is simply the reverse of procession? Or is reversion something other than the mirror image of procession, and if so, what does each refer to? Second, in what sense do the One and the Good refer to the same entity? If they are different, is the Good superior to the One, or vice versa? If the One and the Good are the same, how can They – or It – operate *both* as an efficient cause and as a final cause, yet remain utterly simple and unitary? And third, how does all this relate to the sense in which the perfect and perfection are causes? Specifically, has the move to causation forced so many new meanings on perfect and perfection that they no longer refer to anything coherent?

The short answer to the first cluster of questions is that the Neoplatonists regarded procession and reversion as different but complementary, rather than as symmetrical. Sometimes, when referring to the two aspects of a single entity – when referring, that is, to its status as an element of procession and to its status as an element of reversion – its *ousia* ("being") was contrasted with its *teleiotês* ("perfection").[21] Other times, when describing what was passed down during procession, the term *to einai* ("existence") was used, and contrasted with *to eu einai* ("well-being"), which is what is attained during reversion. The distinction between *to einai* and *to eu einai* appears to have originated with Alexander, and the Neoplatonists seized upon it with much the same enthusiasm as they seized upon Alexander's promotion of *teleiotês*.[22]

[20] Plotinus, *Enneads* I.8.2,2-4 (*esti de touto* [viz., the Good] *eis ho panta anêrêtai kai 'ou panta ta onta ephietai'* [quoting Aristotle, *EN* 1.1, 1094a3] *arkhên ekhonta auto ka'keinou deomena*); Syrianus, *in Metaph.* 13.5 (*ad* 1079b24), 117,28-32; Proclus, *in Remp.*, Vol. 1, 286,11-287,10 (citing *Laws* X, 903C8); *Theol. Plat.*, Vol. 1.22, 104,3-12; 2.2, 20,17-25 (like Plotinus, citing *EN* 1.1, 1094a3 and 10.2, 1172b14-15); 2.8, 55,10-14 (citing *Letters* II, 312E); *Inst. Theol.*, Prop. 8, 8,29-10,13 (citing *Philebus* 20D); 12, 14,1-23; *in Alc. I*, 61,3-5; *in Parm.*, 621,3-7; 810,2-3.8-10.24-31; 845,19-25; 1124,16-20 (citing *Laws* IV, 716C); *in Tim.*, Vol. 1, 281,27-29; 285,21-286,3 (*ad* 28B8 and citing *Resp. VI*, 509B9); 355,28-357,23; 360,5-362,16 (*ad* 29D6-E4); 368,15-369,9 (*ad* 29E4-30A1); 370,19-21; Ammonius, *in Isag.*, 24,2-5; Asclepius, *in Metaph.*, 1.1 (*ad* 982a1), 15,7-10; 1.6 (*ad* 987b9), 47,9-10; 1.6 (*ad* 988a8), 51,31-52,7; 1.9 (*ad* 992a24), 103,9-11; 1.9 (*ad* 992b9), 106,33-107,4; 1.9 (*ad* 992b18), 108,23-26; 2.2 (*ad* 994a19), 123,7-17; 3.2 (*ad* 996a18), 151,22-32; 7.17 (*ad* 1041a9), 450,25-7.

[21] Plotinus, *Enneads*, III.4.1,8-17; Syrianus, *in Metaph.* 3.4 (*ad* 1001a29), 46,27-34; 13.5 (*ad* 1079b24), 117,28-32; Proclus, *in Remp.*, Vol. 1, 37,28-29; 98,23-25; 206,6-26; 236,19-237,3; 252,29-31; 270,13-272,7; 275,29-276,22; *Theol. Plat.*, Vol. 1.15, 70,5-6; 1.25, 109,8-9; 3.6, 21,16-17; 3.27, 94,15-16; *Inst. Theol.*, Prop. 31, 34,28-36,2; 35, 38,9-18; 36, 38,30-32; 37, 40,7-9; 38, 40,25-26; 43, 44,29-31; *in Alc. I*, 1,7-4,5; *in Parm.*, 831,25-28 and 1210,3-11; *in Tim.*, Vol. 1, 404,16-18 and 412,30-413,3; 3, 4,17-18 and 213,31-214,6; Asclepius, *in Metaph.* 3.2 (*ad* 996a18), 151,29-32; Philoponus, *in DA* (Proem.), 17,29-30; 1.1 (*ad* 403a29), 56,33-34; 2.2 (*ad* 413a11), 228,22-26; 2.8 (*ad* 420b16), 380,27-381,14; (Ps.-)Philoponus, *in DA* 3.12 (*ad* 434b8), 602,21-32; 3.13 (*ad* 435b19-22), 606,25-607,14; (Ps.-?)Simplicius, *in DA* 2.8 (*ad* 420b22); 3.1 (*ad* 425a10), 181,14-16; 3.12 (*ad* 434a27), 317,19-22; 3.13 (*ad* 435b19), 329,24-26.

[22] At *in Metaph.* 1.9 (ad 992a24), 121,19-20, Alexander argues that the Ideas cannot be final causes because the Ideas are held by Platonists to be the causes not of well-being (*tou eu einai*) but

The second cluster of questions posed more of a problem. As mentioned above, Proclus sometimes speaks as if the superlunary world were rigidly stratified according to causality: the final causality of the Good is at the top, then the paradigmatic causality of the Ideas, then the efficient causality of the Demiurge. If the efficient causation of the universe springs from the Demiurge, and if the final causation of the universe culminates in the Good, then there will be no identity between the ultimate final cause and the initial efficient cause in the superlunary world, and the final cause's status will be superior to that of the efficient cause.[23] But the complementarity I referred to in the last paragraph was not between the *coming-to-be* which the Demiurge causes here in the sublunary world, and the well-being which the Good causes in everything; but rather between *existence* and well-being. If efficient causation is to apply to eternal, superlunary existence as well as to sublunary coming-to-be, and if procession is to begin with the One and not with the Demiurge, then the One will have to be regarded as an efficient cause in some sense. And if a duality in the supreme

of being in a general or absolute sense (*tou holôs einai*): since the cause of something's being in a general sense must precede its effect, and since a final cause cannot precede its effect, the Ideas cannot act as final causes. (Asclepius also appeals to the distinction between *to einai* and *to eu einai* in his attempt to soften Alexander's criticism: *in Metaph.* 1.9 [*ad* 992a24], 103,6-104,9.) In his *DA* (3.3, 81,15-20), Alexander contrasts a man's faculties of nutrition and touch, which are inseparable from that man, and a man's faculty of intellection, which comes to the person only when he is mature: the former are responsible for the man's existence (*pros to einai*), the latter for the man's well-being (*pros to eu einai*). Themistius follows Alexander by saying that touch is the only one of the five senses necessary for an animal's being, the other four being necessary for the animal's well-being (*in DA* 3.12, 124,17-21 and 3.13, 126,13-15). These two Alexander passages are discussed briefly by Dooley 1993, 12n.5 and 163n.358. At *Quaest.* 2.19, devoted to the problem of whether Providence extends to the whole universe or just to the edge of sublunary world, Alexander appears to identify the idea of a thing's well-being (*to eu einai*) with its proper being (*hê oikeia ousia*) (63,13-14.16); and Alexander even seems to anticipate one of the ways Avicenna would later describe the difference between 1st and 2nd perfections when he distinguishes between *teleiotês* with respect to being and *teleiotês* with respect to well-being (63,22). As I shall discuss in Chapter 11, Alexander also applies the *to einai/to eu einai* distinction to Aristotle's division (*Metaph.* 5.5, 1015a20-26 [= *Mā baʿda ṭ-ṭabīʿa II*, 515,7-14]; see also *Phys.* 2.9, 199b33-15 and 200a31-b8 [= *aṭ-Ṭabīʿa*, 158,4-160,7 and 163,9-164,7]) between a thing's absolute necessity, in virtue of which the thing exists *baldly*, and a thing's hypothetical necessity, in virtue of which the thing exists *well* (Alexander, *in Metaph.* 5.5, [*ad* 1015a20], 360,19-28 and 361,11-13.24-29). Aristotle does use *to eu* to describe organs (e.g., the larynx) which are not necessary in the sense that they contribute not to being but only to well-being. But a hard distinction between *to einai* and *to eu einai* is nowhere found in Aristotle (apart from the definitely spurious *Econ.* [1343b18-19] and the probably spurious *MM* [2.11, 44,5-6 and 47,6]). Plato, *Crit.* 48b5-6, contrasts *to zên* and *to eu zên*; and mentions *to eu* in what appears to be a causal context at *Timaeus* 68E5-6. Plotinus seems to follow Alexander's *DA* comments when at *Enneads*, II.1.5,20-21 he makes a distinction between a lower type of soul, associated with the formation of our bodies, and which is responsible for our existence; and a higher, celestial soul, associated with our reason, and which is the cause of our well-being (*hê gar allê psukhê, kath' hên hêmeis, tou eu einai, ou tou einai aitia*).

[23] Proclus, *in Tim.*, Vol. 1, 294,9-296,12 (alluding to *Meteor.* 1.2, 339a26); *Theol. Plat.*, Vol. 2.9, 57,25-58,10; 59,13-21; 61,2-9; *in Parm.*, 887,36-888,35 and 1168,16-1169,11; *in Tim.*, Vol. 1, 260,19-262,2 and 305,6-16 (alluding to *Resp.* 509B6-9 and *Philebus* 27A1-B2); 355,28-357,23; 360,5-362,16; 368,15-369,9; 370,19-21.

principle is to be avoided, the final causality of the Good cannot be seen as being superior to the efficient causality of the One, but as identical to it.[24] At the level of the other inhabitants of the intelligible realm – Gods, Intellects, Demiurges – the final causality that leads upwards to the Good and the efficient causality that proceeds downwards from the One are not identical but complementary, in the way alluded to above: final causality refers to the respect in which an *explanans* explains the "well-being" (*to eu einai*) of an *explanandum*, and efficient causality refers to the respect in which an *explanans* explains the "existence" (*to einai*) of an *explanandum*.[25]

The third question then arises, how do all these different elements fit together in a way which allows us to construct a coherent theory of perfection and the perfect? The One and the Demiurge in the superlunary realm, and active things here in the sublunary realm, are all efficient causes of different types; do those different types of efficient causation correspond to different senses in which something may be said to be perfect? Or is "perfect" a univocal term which applies in exactly the same way to superlunary and sublunary things? Similarly, the Good in the superlunary realm, and actuality in the sublunary realm, are final causes of different types; do these different types of final causation correspond to different senses in which something may be said to be a perfection? Or is "perfection" a univocal term which applies in exactly the same way to superlunary and sublunary things?

In fact, all the different things to which the perfect and perfection have been applied can, with a little effort, be accommodated under Proclus' distinction between first and second perfections. Remember that a thing's perfection can be considered in relation to the thing itself, in which case it is a first perfection; and considered in relation to something else, in which case it is a second perfection. I shall focus on second perfection first. The "something else" in relation to which a thing is trying to attain its perfection in the second sense, is clearly the thing's effect. I am trying to attain my second perfection, to be perfect in the second sense, when I am being a good father; that is, when I am trying to attain perfection in my relation to others who stand below me in the cosmic hierarchy as my effects, namely my children, by means of my passing existence down to them, as well as by means of my serving as a goal for them to imitate. In short, I attain my second perfection by perfecting my efficient causation of others

[24] Proclus, *Inst. Theol.*, Prop. 13, 14,24-16,8; 33, 36,11-16; 113, 100,11-12; *in Parm.*, 788,12-28 and 1109,4-14 (citing *Letters* II, 312E); *in Alc. I*, 181,11-182,11; Asclepius, *in Metaph.* 1.4 (*ad* 985b4), 33,34-5; 3.2 (*ad* 996a18), 151,18-20.26-28; Simplicius, *in Cael.* 1.8 (*ad* 277b9), 271,4-21; and *in Phys.* 2.7 (*ad* 198a22), 365,20-21 and 367,24-29; and 8.10 (*ad* 267b17), 1360,24-1363,24. The extent to which Asclepius, Simplicius and Philoponus paint a coherent picture of Ammonius' theology is discussed in Verrycken 1990.

[25] Syrianus, *in Metaph.* 13.4 (*ad* 1078b32), 107,38-108,7; Proclus, *Theol. Plat.*, Vol. 6.15, 75,1-2; *in Parm.*, 826,30-35 and 842,26-28; *in Tim.*, Vol. 3, 226,10-18; Asclepius, *in Metaph.* 1.3 (*ad* 984b20), 28,18-29,8; 1.6 (*ad* 988a11), 52,21-25; and 3.2 (*ad* 996a18), 151,9-12; Damascius, *Treatise on First Principles* 3, 117,4-118,18.

(*teleiotês* here understood as the quality of being *teleion qua* actual and active) *and* by serving as a final cause for others to imitate (*teleiotês* here understood as the quality of being *teleion qua* superior in a genus or species).

The first perfection, by contrast, is related solely to the thing itself. I am trying to attain my first perfection, to be perfect in the first sense, when I am being a good human; that is, when I am trying to attain perfection as an individual member of my species – rational animal – by being as rational as I can be, by thinking about philosophy or, even better, by thinking about myself thinking about philosophy. As an element of the procession of existence, I am trying to attain my second perfection in the sense that I am trying to attain perfection as an efficient cause in relation to things below me in the hierarchy, just as the Demiurge does in relation to the world as a whole. As an element of the reversion towards well-being, I am both trying to attain my second perfection by serving as a final cause for things below me in the hierarchy to imitate; as well as trying to attain my first perfection by thinking about myself thinking about myself and thereby moving upwards in the hierarchy, just as the Demiurge does by contemplating the Ideas contained in the paradigmatic cause, according to whose model He continually creates the world.

These two senses of perfection – a first perfection which is relative to what is above and upwards, and a second perfection which is relative to what is below – are, I believe, part of Proclus' attempt to explain the dynamic tension between procession and reversion, and they derive from the new, Neoplatonic tying together of causality and being perfect. Does the distinction between first and second perfections also apply univocally to the One and the Good (or perhaps better, the One-Good, since they are held by Neoplatonists to be distinguishable only conceptually)? As the ultimate cause of the rest of the superlunary world and of the entire sublunary world, the One-Good could, it seems, be described as being in a state of second perfection, given that the One-Good can be related – as cause – to something other than itself. The One-Good could also be described as being in a state of first perfection, if we assume its primary activity to be the self-intellection, the turning inwards (though in this case not upwards, since there is nothing above it), that first perfection consists in, at least in the case of rational beings. It seems appropriate then to apply the scheme of first and second perfection to the One-Good, with the proviso that its first perfection is only a turning inwards and not upwards.[26]

Yet for many Neoplatonists the causal sense of first and second perfection – actualizing oneself and actualizing things below one – implied too much involvement in the messiness and multiplicity of both the superlunary and sublunary worlds to be properly applicable to the One-Good. Rather, the sense in which the One-Good is perfect and possesses perfection appears, on the surface,

[26] For an example of the first perfection/second perfection distinction applied to God, see Asclepius, *in Metaph.* 2.4 (*ad* 1000a5), 195,37-196,10.

to derive more from one of the original, primitive Aristotelian notions of *to teleion*, namely, that which is quantitatively complete (i.e., whole, not missing anything, not lacking anything) than it does from the Neoplatonists' new causal sense of *teleiotês*. Under the surface, however, the turn to causation can be detected, the only difference being that in the case of the One-Good's perfection the turn to causation consists in a turn from quantitative completeness to *causal self-sufficiency*, that is, to immunity from causedness; whereas in the case of perfection in procession and reversion, the turn to causation consists in a turn from actuality and activity to *causal productivity* and *self-actualization*.

What I mean is that the sense in which a thing is quantitatively complete in the old Aristotelian sense could not really be applicable to the One-Good, since it seemed too similar to the idea of wholeness, and wholeness implied having parts – having all of them, to be sure, but still having parts – a quality which clearly infringed on the One-Good's utter simplicity. Instead, the One-Good's *teleiotês* signified an absence of lack or need understood as causal independence rather than as quantitative completeness, as referring to the quality of *not requiring a cause*, and not to the quality of *being in possession of all one's parts*.

As a result the terms "perfect" (*teleion*) and "self-sufficient" (*autarkes*), and "perfection" (*teleiotês*) and "self-sufficiency" (*autarkeia*), came to be seen as mutually implicative, if not actually synonymous.[27] The connection between the two ideas was held by the Neoplatonists to spring from a passage in the *Philebus*, where the three elements of the Good are said to be the desirable, the sufficient and the perfect (*to epheton, to hikanon, to teleion*). These terms were understood by the Neoplatonists as referring, respectively, to the Good's final causality, self-sufficiency and perfection, and the sense one gets from Proclus at least is that each of the three terms was thought to imply the other two.[28] Finally, Neoplatonists could always cite *EN* 1.7, 1097b7-8 (*to gar teleion agathon autarkes einai dokei*), which I discussed in Chapter 2 – and, more ambiguously, *Metaph.* 14.4, 1091b16-19 – as evidence that Aristotle followed Plato in tying perfection (or at least goodness) to self-sufficiency.

Yet holding that the One-Good was perfect and self-sufficient raised its own problems. While being perfect and self-sufficient might be the qualities which best insured the One-Good's transcendence, they were less useful in explaining its productivity. Something self-sufficient is certainly eternal, and it may even act as a final cause by serving as a model for lower things which seek to attain

[27] Plotinus, *Enneads*, VI.7.2,48-49 (*ei oun teleion, ouk estin eipein hotôi elleipei, oude dia ti touto ou paresti*) (although this was rendered into Arabic as the more innocuous *fa-in kāna l-ʿaqlu tāmman kāmilan fa-innahu lam yaqdir qāʾilun an yaqūla inna-hu nāqiṣun fī shayʾin min ḥālātihi*: *Uthūlūjiyā* 5, 73,7-8); Proclus, *Theol. Plat.*, Vol. 4.25, 74,6-75; 5.7, 28,3; *Inst. Theol.*, Prop. 9, 10,14-16. cf. (Ps.-)Plato, *Definitiones*, 412b3: "Self-sufficiency: completeness in the possession of goods (*autarkeia teleiotês ktêseôs agathôn*)".

[28] Proclus, *Theol. Plat.*, Vol. 1.22, 101,14-19; 3.22, 79,9-22; *in Alc. I*, 153,10-15; Olympiodorus, *in Phaedonem*, 30,14-20; and *in Alc. I*, 42,18-43,3.

its quality of perfection and self-sufficiency; but it will only be productive of an effect below it if it passes some of the existence it does not need down to something which is not perfect and self-sufficient, and which does need some existence.

As a result the One-Good was held to be "the most self-sufficient" (*autarkestaton*) or even "above self-sufficiency" (*huperautarkes*), with the other inhabitants of the superlunary world now being described as being self-sufficient.[29] The tying of perfection to self-sufficiency also applied to the universe as a whole, which was described as being *teleion* and *autarkes*.[30] When referring to the self-sufficiency of superlunary beings other than the One-Good, however, the term *authupostaton* was often used instead of *autarkes*. *Authupostaton* seems to have meant "self-substantiating" or "self-constituted" as opposed to "self-sufficient", and the distinction, though obscure, was held to be meaningful. The basic difference seems to be that *autarkes* is a negation while *authupostaton* is an affirmation. In something *autarkes*, self-causation is denied, since it is held to be above all types of causation, even self-causation; in something *authupostaton*, however, self-causation is affirmed. Another way of distinguishing them is that *authupostaton* refers to the self-sufficiency of something like the universe as a whole, which has parts and which therefore is complete or perfect in the sense of not lacking any of its parts. By contrast, *autarkes*, strictly speaking, referred to the self-sufficiency of the One-Good, which is utterly simple and which is complete or perfect in the sense of not needing anything else to cause it.[31]

As will become clear in Chapter 10, Avicenna wrestled with a number of issues left unresolved by the Neoplatonists' application of the concepts of the perfect and perfection to problems of cosmology. The Neoplatonists' tying together of the Good's final causality, self-sufficiency and perfection, came into conflict with their desire to see the One as somehow productive – and hence as the efficient cause – of the world's existence. This is because the Good's final causality, self-sufficiency and perfection were attributes that best guaranteed its transcendence of the world, while the One's productivity and efficient causality were attributes that best guaranteed its involvement in the world. In addition, the Neoplatonists bequeathed to Avicenna an ambivalence about the univocity or equivocity of perfection and the perfect: were these terms applicable to superlunary and sublunary entities in different or identical ways? For now, however, I shall stick with the Neoplatonists and examine how this new way of looking at perfection and the perfect influenced the ways in which the soul – the

[29] Syrianus, *in Metaph.* 14.4 (*ad* 1091b16), 183,10; Proclus, *Inst. Theol.*, Prop. 10, 10,31-32; 127, 112,25-34.

[30] Proclus, *in Tim.*, Vol. 1, 289,17; 2, 89,31-90,2.

[31] Proclus, *Inst. Theol.*, Prop. 42, 44,11-24; 43, 44,25-32; 45, 46,12-19; *in Parm.*, 1145,31-1146,35. Also see Whittaker 1975.

most interesting and problematic example of a perfection – was integrated into a new, Neoplatonic *entelekheia* scheme.

4. Proclus, Ammonius and Philoponus
Neoplatonic Perfection and Aristotelian Soul

I have just shown how the Neoplatonists transformed the concepts of perfection and the perfect from referring, respectively, to a state of being (being in actuality or being in activity) and to a thing which possesses that state of being (the actual or the active), to referring, respectively, to a state which acts as a final cause and to a thing which acts as an efficient cause. The Aristotelian rationale for this transformation was that something which is in a state of actuality or activity is in some sense productive of the thing which is in a state of potentiality and which is changing, as a result of its contact with the actual or active thing, into something actual or active itself. Thus the actual or active stands as a cause – and specifically as an efficient cause – relative to the potential thing. The state of actuality, on the other hand, stands as a final cause – as a state to be attained – relative to the potential thing. Keeping a safe distance between themselves and the term *entelekheia* (and its adverbial forms *entelekheiâi* and *kat' entelekheian*) as a result of Plotinus' attacks on that term, the Neoplatonists used *teleiotês* – a term Alexander of Aphrodisias had promoted as a gloss of *entelekheia* – and *teleion*. One of the advantages of understanding *teleion* and *teleiotês* as causes was that the two terms could be applied quite neatly to the complementary cosmic forces of, respectively, procession and reversion, the former expressing the downward direction of the efficient causation of existence, the latter expressing the upward direction of the final causation of well-being.

The Neoplatonists went further and divided *teleiotês* into first and second perfections. The first refers to the type of perfection that obtains when a thing is related only to itself, and which serves as the goal of that thing's constant striving to attain or maintain its self-perfection and thereby ascend to the next level up in the cosmic hierarchy. The second refers to the type of perfection that obtains when a thing is related to something other than itself, that is, to the imperfect things that are below it in the cosmic hierarchy. A thing strives to attain its second perfection both in the sense that it strives to perfect its efficient causation of the things below it, and in the sense that it strives to serve as a goal for lower things to imitate in their own attempts at reversion. In the case of first and second perfection, the *teleiotês* operates on its effect as a final cause.

Given the contortions which commentators such as Alexander and Themistius subjected themselves to in their efforts to square Aristotle's use of *entelekheia* in his definition of soul (where the distinction between first and second *entelekheiai* is most clearly articulated) and his use of *entelekheia* in his definition of motion (where the distinction between initial and ultimate *entelekheiai* is only implied), the following question arises: how does the

Neoplatonists' distinction between first and second *teleiotêtes* square with the *entelekheia* schemes proposed by Alexander and Themistius? For the sake of clarity, this question ought to be split into three subsidiary questions: (1) Is the Neoplatonic distinction nothing other than a new formulation of the *De Anima*'s distinction between first and second *entelekheiai*? (2) Is it instead another attempt, in the tradition of Alexander and Themistius, to create a basis for reconciling the *De Anima*'s explicit distinction between 1st and 2nd *entelekheiai* and the *Physics*' implicit distinction between complete and incomplete *entelekheiai*? (3) Or is it a new distinction, formulated by Neoplatonist thinkers whose overriding interest may not have been soothing Peripatetic anxieties about Aristotle's seemingly inconsistent uses of *entelekheia*?

I shall begin answering the first question ("Is the Neoplatonic distinction nothing other than a new formulation of the *De Anima*'s distinction between first and second *entelekheiai*?") by recalling that the *De Anima's* distinction between first and second *entelekheiai* is most plausibly interpreted as referring to a distinction between an inactive possession (*hexis*) of a capability to perform a certain function, and the active exercise (*energeia*) of that capability. Proclus occasionally refers to both knowledge and contemplation as *teleiotêtes*, which might lead us to believe that he is following Aristotle's *De Anima* examples in some way; but Proclus does not identify the former as a first and the latter as a second perfection, and he seems to have Plato in mind as much as Aristotle.[1]

Other times Proclus contrasts the static quality of first perfection with the active quality of second perfection, saying at one point that just as the perfection of the gods is of two sorts – the first intellective, the second providential, the first at rest and the second in motion (*dittês gar ousês tês theias teleiotêtos, tês men noeras, tês de pronoêtikês, kai tês men en stasei, tês d'en kinêsei*) – so human souls have two perfections: one which consists in the contemplation of the eternal, divine things which the gods possess, the other which consists in a providential concern for things in the world of coming-to-be and passing-away.[2]

Commenting on Plato's definition of philosophy – becoming as much like a god as is humanly possible – Ammonius seems to be referring to Proclus' distinction between first and second perfections when he claims that just as gods have both cognitive (*gnôstikas*) activities and providential (*pronoêtikas*) activities, so philosophers must similarly contemplate all things and look after inferior things. Although Ammonius asserts that the difference between an activity which is self-related and one which is related to others consists in the difference between striving to fulfill one's *differentia* in respect of substance and striving to fulfill one's *differentia* in respect of perfection, Ammonius'

[1] Proclus, *Theol. Plat.*, Vol. 4.13, 43,19-20 (alluding to *Phaedrus* 247C8); *in Alc. I*, 187,8-18; *in Tim.*, Vol. 1, 79,9-13.
[2] Proclus, *in Tim.*, Vol. 3, 324,6-12.

distinction can in fact be reduced to the difference between Proclus' first and second perfections: the perfection of human is to live rationally (first perfection) and with *phronêsis* (second perfection); the perfection of horse is to run quickly (first perfection) and to be useful in war (second perfection).[3]

On the surface, then, it seems that the Neoplatonists' second *teleiotês* and the *De Anima's* second *entelekheia* might have something in common, in that they both express the quality of being active rather than being at rest: my mind is in a state of second *entelekheia* when it is actively contemplating, and it is in a state of first *entelekheia* when it is inactive. Certainly, if a second *teleiotês* referred to nothing other than the quality of productivity and efficient causality possessed by something which is *teleion*, then the *De Anima's* second *entelekheia* and the Neoplatonists' second *teleiotês* would indeed have something in common. A perfect thing is related to an imperfect thing as an efficient cause – that is, a perfect thing is productive of an imperfect thing's emergence into perfection – only when the perfect thing is active. This is an Aristotelian axiom which the Neoplatonists take for granted, and as we saw above it serves as one of the bases for their linking of *to teleion* to the efficient cause.

But as was also discussed above, when the Neoplatonists made their distinction between first and second *teleiotêtes*, they meant for the second *teleiotês* to refer to something more than just the quality of efficient causality possessed by what is *teleion*. What is also meant by the second *teleiotês* is the quality or state of perfect X-ness – that is, the quality of unsurpassedness in a species or genus – which a perfect X possesses and which an imperfect X strives to attain. And in fact, the sense in which the second perfection is understood to refer to the goal of serving as a final cause for others to imitate, as opposed to the sense in which it is understood to refer to the goal of acting on others as an efficient cause, was held to be the more basic sense of second perfection. In other words, I am striving to attain my second perfection not so much to possess the quality of efficient causality, as to possess, or to come as close as possible to possessing, the more important qualities associated with perfection: causal self-sufficiency and eternality.

The reason for this is that if a second *teleiotês* were nothing other than the quality of efficient causality which a perfect thing possesses, procession and reversion would be symmetrical rather than complementary. The efficient cause responsible for procession and the final cause responsible for reversion would compete over the same effect or *explanandum*, with reversion losing out to procession since reversion will refer to nothing more than the attaining of efficient causality. In other words, reversion would consist simply in gaining the ability to proceed. On the contrary, the efficient causation of procession and the final causation of reversion complement each other in the sense that the efficient cause and the final cause each explain a different type of effect or *explanandum*.

[3] Ammonius, *in Isag.*, 3,24-4,4.

The efficient cause involved in procession explains pure existence or existence in an absolute sense, while the final cause involved in reversion explains well-being, that is, special existence, X-ness as opposed to Y-ness. If the efficient causation of procession and the final causation of reversion are to be complementary in a meaningful way, therefore, a Neoplatonist's second *teleiotês* will have to refer to something more than simply the efficient causality or activity which *to teleion* possesses.

What about Proclus' comment that the first perfection is static and the second active? Since activity is what allowed the Neoplatonists to make their move from Aristotelian *energeia* and *entelekheia* to their new concept of *to teleion* as efficient cause, Proclus' assertion that the second perfection is active while the first is static would seem to support the idea that second perfection is nothing more than efficient causality, or at least that efficient causality was the essential characteristic of second perfection.

The fact of the matter is that Proclus is inconsistent in his application of the idea of activity to perfection and the perfect. More often than not, in fact, it is the first *teleiotês* – the turning inwards and upwards that occurs during self-intellection – which seems to involve more activity than the second *teleiotês*.[4] Even though my body may be still, my soul is very active when I think about myself thinking about myself, in my attempt to pull myself up to the next level of the cosmic hierarchy, however temporarily I may reside there. By contrast, I may be asleep or watching television when my graduate student is hard at work using my intellectual *teleiotês* as a goal to model himself after.

The classic example of this type of relationship is, unsurprisingly, the relationship between Socrates and his protégé Alcibiades. Socrates' intellectual perfection (*teleiotês*) serves as the goal of Alcibiades' *teleiôsis*, his journey towards his own intellectual perfection; but it is never clear whether Socrates needs to be actively using his capability to think in order to serve in the role of model. As long as Alcibiades keeps Socrates' intellectual *teleiotês* in mind as a goal to attain through imitation, it seems possible that Socrates can lie back and relax, or be actively engaged in some other activity.[5] Certainly, it is a condition of serving as a second *teleiotês* relative to something else that at some point in the past one actively sought one's own *teleiotês*. At some point in the past Socrates needed to have been active in attaining his own *teleiotês* before his *teleiotês* can then serve as a model for Alcibiades to imitate. But Socrates' active pursuit of his own perfection was a first *teleiotês*, not a second *teleiotês*. When Socrates is engaged in a dialogue with Alcibiades, teasing out the truth and impelling his protégé to think hard and behave more philosophically, Socrates may well be actively using his own capability to think. But Socrates'

[4] Proclus, *in Remp.*, Vol. 1, 21,18-21 and 212,2-8; *in Tim.*, Vol. 1, 243,26-246,9; 2, 117,28-29;

[5] Proclus, *Theol. Plat.*, Vol. 4.16, 49,2-3; 4.37, 109,1-13; *in Alc. I*, 121,1-123,20 (*teleiôsis* is also seen as something bestowed at 129,16; 132,4; 140,8; and 141,11).

active engagement in contemplation during the dialogue is more easily interpretable as a first *teleiotês* than it is as a second *teleiotês*, since Socrates' goal is always first and foremost attaining or maintaining his own self-perfection, not bestowing perfection on others; and this is why, I believe, Proclus calls self-perfection the first, or primary, *teleiotês*.

By contrast, serving as a goal for imperfect beings like Alcibiades will only ever be a second perfection for Socrates, that is, it will only ever be a perfection in a secondary sense, a mere by-product of the more important goal of self-perfection. The upshot is that the criterion of inactivity or activity, which could be useful in distinguishing the *De Anima*'s first and second *entelekheiai*, is inapplicable to the Neoplatonists' distinction between first and second *teleiotêtes*, since the Neoplatonists' distinction rests more on the difference between the primary goal of attaining one's self-perfection, and the secondary goal of serving as a goal for lower things to imitate.

The two pairs of perfections – the *De Anima*'s first and second *entelekheiai*, and the Neoplatonists' first and second *teleiotêtes* – cannot therefore be held to be strictly identical, so the first question mentioned above ("Is the Neoplatonic distinction nothing other than a new formulation of the *De Anima*'s distinction between first and second *entelekheiai*?") can be answered with a no. In fact the two pairs of distinctions now appear sufficiently incompatible that the second question mentioned above ("Is the Neoplatonic distinction another attempt, in the tradition of Alexander and Themistius, to create a basis for reconciling the *De Anima*'s explicit distinction between 1st and 2nd *entelekheiai* and the *Physics*' implicit distinction between complete and incomplete *entelekheiai*?") is hardly worth pursuing, since even if it could be shown that the Neoplatonic distinction squares more easily with the *Physics*' implicit distinction than it does with the *De Anima*'s explicit distinction, the Neoplatonic distinction will still be so different from the *De Anima* distinction that it becomes implausible to suppose that it was ever meant to serve as a new means of reconciling the *Physics* and *De Anima* distinctions.

My answer to the third question ("Is the Neoplatonic distinction a new distinction, formulated by Neoplatonist thinkers whose overriding interest may not have been soothing Peripatetic anxieties about Aristotle's seemingly inconsistent uses of *entelekheia*") is therefore a yes. But despite the incompatibility of the Neoplatonic distinction between first and second *teleiotêtes*, and the *De Anima*'s distinction between first and second *entelekheiai*, the term *teleiotês* came to be used by the Aristotle-commentator Philoponus, the student of Proclus' student Ammonius, in his discussions of the soul. Only now, as we shall see, *teleiotês* was promoted in order to underscore the sense in which the soul acted as a final cause, a move that was to have important ramifications on the issue of the soul's separability.

In spite of his hostility, inherited from Plotinus, towards Aristotle's definition of the soul as an *entelekheia*, and in spite of the fact that his distinction between first and second *teleiotêtes* differed from Aristotle's *De Anima* distinction between first and second *entelekheiai*, Proclus shows a little flexibility – perhaps ambivalence is a better term – towards Aristotelian psychology at certain points in his work.[6] Philoponus, involved in setting down his teacher Ammonius' lecture-notes on the very text of the *De Anima*, was forced, in a way that Proclus was not, to show even greater flexibility in order to reconcile Proclus' new understanding of *teleiotês* with the *De Anima*'s use of *entelekheia*.

The way this happened took several steps. The first step was to follow Alexander's lead in simply glossing *entelekheia* with *teleiotês*. Philoponus claims that when the soul is defined as an *entelekheia*, it means that the soul is a *teleiotês* and a form *(eidos)*.[7] But Philoponus makes a distinction between *entelekheia* and *teleiotês*, saying that *teleiotês* signifies something more elevated than what is signified by *entelekheia*. This is because *entelekheia* can refer to form (*eidos*) in both of form's guises – that is, both *qua* essence or formula (*kata ton logon*) and *qua* shape or structure (*kata tên morphên*) – whereas *teleiotês* only ever refers to form as essence, and never to form as shape.

As Philoponus points out, Aristotle himself sometimes speaks of the shape of something – of a statue, for example – as being its *entelekheia*. But while being snub-nosed and paunchy (*einai simon progastera*) may be the form *qua* shape of Socrates, and hence an *entelekheia* in that sense, being snub-nosed and paunchy is not Socrates' *teleiotês*, but rather something merely accidental.[8] Philoponus reckons that the reason why *teleiotês* is a particularly appropriate term with which to describe the soul, is that a *teleiotês*, understood as referring only to the substantial form or essence, is always the *cause* of the coming-to-perfection (*teleiôsis*) of the matter (in this case, the body) whose *teleiotês* it is.[9] *Entelekheia*, by contrast, can refer to both shape and essence; and because shape

[6] Sometimes (e.g., *in Tim.*, Vol. 2, 285,23-31) Proclus even allows that there is a sense in which the soul, as an *entelekheia*, is inseparable from the body which it animates, while in itself remaining separate. Other times he appears unsure of why precisely Aristotle's definition is unsatisfactory. At *Theol. Plat.*, Vol. 4.24, 71,10-72,11 and *in Tim.*, Vol. 3, 254,10-31, Proclus attacks Aristotle for assuming as self-evident the distinction between "living" and "ensouled" (*to zôion kai to empsukhon*) in his definition of soul in the *De Anima*, when in Proclus' opinion the two amount to the same thing. Yet at *in Tim.*, Vol. 1, 412,11, Proclus himself clearly advocates making such a distinction.

[7] Soul as *entelekheia* and soul as *teleiotês* and *eidos* are identified at Philoponus, *in DA* (Preface), 9,26-27; 1.5 (*ad* 411a26), 193,34-35; 2.1 (*ad* 412a3), 203,14; 2.1 (*ad* 412b6), 218,25-26.

[8] Philoponus, *in DA* 2.1 (*ad* 412a9), 211,11-26.

[9] Philoponus, *in DA* 2.1 (*ad* 412a3), 208,36-209,4. Asclepius, however, asserts that *morphê* is an end (*telos*), thereby implying that not just form *qua* essence but also form *qua* shape can serve as a cause: *in Metaph.* 5.24 (*ad* 1023a34), 349,10.

is not the cause of the coming-to-perfection of matter, *entelekheia* will not always refer to the soul's causation of the body's coming-to-perfection.

Philoponus' use of *teleiotês* in this way is important. Not only does it reflect the Neoplatonic move to causation in the understanding of perfection, it also frees him to analyze the soul-body relationship as *first and foremost* a relationship between cause and effect. This is in contrast to Aristotle's view that the relationship between soul and body is fundamentally a relationship between two types of substance (substance-as-form and substance-as-matter), and hence a relationship between two states of being (being-in-actuality and being-in-potentiality). In other words, Philoponus has, like Alexander, used *teleiotês* to gloss *entelekheia* in describing the soul; but what Philoponus meant by *teleiotês* is different from what Alexander meant. This is because Philoponus uses *teleiotês* in the Neoplatonic way, understanding *teleiotês* as referring not merely to a type of being – actuality as opposed to potentiality – but to a way of causing. As discussed above, the way a *teleiotês* causes its effect, or explains its *explanandum*, is as a final cause.

If the soul is a *teleiotês*, and if a *teleiotês* acts on its effect (or explains its *explanandum*) as a final cause, it follows that the soul acts on the body either exclusively, or at least primarily, as a final cause. But what does that really mean? I believe that what Philoponus has in mind is the idea that when we call the soul a *teleiotês*, we are asserting that the soul is the *explanans* and that the body is the *explanandum* insofar as the body is viewed in terms of its upward reversion. As mentioned above, Philoponus has said that when we speak of the soul as a *teleiotês*, what the *teleiotês* causes or explains is the *teleiôsis* of its effect or *explanandum*. I have already discussed Proclus' use of *teleiôsis* in his discussions of the causal relationship between Socrates and Alcibiades: Socrates' *teleiotês* serves as the goal, or final cause, of Alcibiades' *teleiôsis*, or upward journey towards intellectual perfection. Unsurprisingly the distinction between *teleiotês* and *teleiôsis* is most explicitly articulated in Proclus' comments on the *First Alcibiades*, even though Syrianus may have been the first to promote the idea that the distinction between *teleiôsis* and *teleiotês* was somehow basic; the distinction appears in Asclepius as well.[10]

[10] The evidence for the distinction between *teleiotês* and *teleiôsis* in Syrianus is ambiguous: at *in Metaph.* 38,21, *teleiôsis* corresponds to *energeia*, yet at 40,7, *teleiotês* corresponds to *energeia*. In Proclus the distinction is clearer though not held to be basic: *teleiôsis* is clearly meant to be understood as a temporal process at *Theol. Plat.*, Vol. 1.6, 30,10 and 4.34, 102,1-3 (alluding to *Timaeus* 37C6-D7); yet at *in Parm.*, 1237,3-17, Proclus qualifies that claim by saying that while *teleiôsis* may be a temporal process, it must be understood as one that is completed, not as one that is open-ended. As I mentioned in the text, the distinction between *teleiôsis* and *teleiotês* is used most often in the *Commentary on the First Alcibiades*, where Alcibiades is said to be at the starting point of the process of self-perfection (*teleiôsis*), the culmination of which is the attainment of the state of perfection (*teleiotês*): *in Alc. I*, 4,19-5,12; 6,17-7,3; 10,14-11,3. In more general terms, *teleiôsis* is simply a process which is undergone (*in Alc. I*, 172,19 and 224,13-228,20; *in Parm.*, 667,26-32; 988,6-10; 997,16-33; *in Tim.*, Vol. 2, 16,18-20 and 3, 24,1); whereas *teleiotês* is simply a state which is attained (*in Alc. I*, 174,6 and *in Alc. I*, 177,14; *in Parm.*, 988,6-10; and *in Tim.*, Vol. 3,

Philoponus also uses *teleiôsis* more generally, as a synonym of *genesis*, with *teleiotês* understood as the substantial form that inheres following the *genesis* of the composite.[11] It should be said, however, that when commenting on the *Physics* Philoponus employs both *teleiotês* and *teleiôsis* to define *kinêsis*. In his explanation of Aristotle's *Physics* 3.1 definition of *kinêsis* as an *entelekheia* Philoponus glosses *entelekheia* with *teleiotês*, not *teleiôsis*, saying that change is a first *entelekheia* in the sense that it is the *teleiotês* of the potentiality *itself*, in contrast to the second *entelekheia*, which refers to the *teleiotês* of the *thing* in which the potentiality used to exist before and during the change.[12] In this respect Philoponus anticipates the instinct of modern commentators to put to one side the question of what exactly Aristotle thinks an *entelekheia* might be, and concentrate instead on what Aristotle thinks change might be an *entelekheia of*.

Later on in his *Physics* commentary, however, Philoponus uses *teleiôsis* when he describes change as a "leading-on" (*proagôgê*).[13] The upshot is that just as with his understanding of *teleiotês*, Philoponus' understanding of *teleiôsis* seems to have been shaped more by Proclus' use of that term than by Aristotle's or Alexander's: as referring to a thing's upward reversion towards its *teleiotês*, be the *teleiotês* an intellectual form or a natural substantial form. The soul is the *teleiotês* of the body, and hence acts on the body as a final cause acts on its effects, by impelling the body's *teleiôsis* or upward reversion.[14]

24,12). When Asclepius uses *teleiotês* and *teleiôsis* in commenting on the first line of the *Metaphysics* ("All men by nature desire to know"), and explains that the state of having attained *gnôsis* is the soul's *teleiotês* and its good, while the soul's *teleiôsis* is the process of getting to that point, he very probably had in mind both Proclus' use of *teleiotês* and *teleiôsis* in discussing the causal relationship between Socrates and Alcibiades, as well as Alexander's use of *teleiotês* to explicate that very same line: Asclepius, *in Metaph.* 1.1 (*ad* 980a21), 5,35-6,2; and Alexander, *in Metaph.* 1.1 (*ad* 980a21), 1,4-9.

[11] Philoponus, *in DA* 1.1 (*ad* 402a9), 27,12-13; 1.3 (*ad* 406a12), 100,24-30; 2.4 (*ad* 415b21), 275,2-9; and 2.5 (*ad* 417b2), 303,13-15; but see also *in DA* 2.5 (*ad* 417b2), 301,9-12, where *genesis* seems to be understood as a *teleiotês* rather than a *teleiôsis*.

[12] Philoponus, *in Phys.* 3.1 (*ad* 200b12), 342,10-343,12 (*aṭ-Ṭabīʿa*, 171,8-13). Philoponus had read Themistius' *Paraphrase* of the *Physics* and even quotes Themistius' distinction between *entelekheia prôtê* and *entelekheia hustatê* at Philoponus, *in Phys.* 3.1 (*ad* 201a16), 351,8-15 (= *aṭ-Ṭabīʿa*, 176,6-9).

[13] Philoponus, *in Phys.* 3.3 (*ad* 202b21), 385,2-4.

[14] One difference between Philoponus and Proclus is that Proclus was very reluctant to see the soul as a *hexis* of the body, presumably because a *hexis* is inseparable from that whose *hexis* it is. At *in Tim.*, Vol. 1, 406,14-22 (*ad* 30B4-6), Proclus argues that because the soul is the final cause of the body just as the intellect is the final cause of the soul, and because a *hexis* cannot be a final cause, the soul cannot therefore be a *hexis*. Of course what Proclus means is that in no sublunary thing is the *teleiotês* ever really a *possession* (*hexis*); on the contrary, the most that can be said of the sublunary thing's relation to the *teleiotês* it constantly strives to attain is that it is a "participation" (*methexis*) in the *teleiotês*. Here Philoponus would disagree with Proclus, given Philoponus' identification of *teleiotêtes* such as *gnôsis* as *hexeis*. Nevertheless Philoponus would still hold, with Proclus, that perfection acts on its effect as a final cause; at *in DA* 2.4 (*ad* 415a16), 264,15-19 (repeated at *in DA* 2.4 [*ad* 416a34], 284,3), Philoponus cites Alexander's authority in holding that perfection is the final cause of the potential thing. Simplicius also seems to understand

As mentioned above, seeing the soul-body relationship as first and foremost a relationship between a cause and an effect, rather than as a relationship between one type of being and another type of being, freed commentators such as Philoponus to exploit the whole range of different ways that Aristotle and the Neoplatonists discussed the final cause, in support of the larger Neoplatonic project of reconciling Aristotelian and Platonic psychology. What advantages would a Neoplatonic commentator gain by seeing the soul primarily as a final cause? First, given the apparent irreconcilability between Proclus' distinction between first and second *teleiotêtes* and Aristotle's *De Anima* distinction between first and second *entelekheiai*, there might be some way to appeal to an Aristotelian distinction between the different ways a final cause is spoken of in order to create a new *teleiotês*-distinction which could then be reconciled with Aristotle's *De Anima* distinction. What I mean is this: if the *De Anima* distinction between first and second *entelekheiai* cannot be reconciled with Proclus' distinction between first and second *teleiotêtes*, there might be an advantage, given that a *teleiotês* acts as a final cause, to seeing whether a distinction between different types of final cause could be reconciled with the *De Anima* distinction.

The second advantage a Neoplatonic commentator would gain by seeing the soul primarily as a final cause has to do with the sticky problem of the soul's separability from the body. A Neoplatonic commentator on the *De Anima* faced a big challenge when reconciling the Platonic doctrine of the soul's separability and immortality, with Alexander's interpretation of Aristotle's psychology, which holds that the soul is as inseparable from the body as form is from matter. But given the Neoplatonic distinction between the efficient and final causes, which transcend their effects, and the formal and material causes, which are immanent in their effects, there might be some way to use the soul's being a *teleiotês*, and hence its acting as a final cause, to advocate the position that the soul is separate from the body.

Before reaping those benefits, the Neoplatonic commentators will first have to deal with the fact that even though Proclus' *teleiotês* was clearly understood as acting on its effect like a final cause, it is not so clear that Aristotle meant for the soul to be seen as a final cause. If anything, given his insistence that defining the soul as an *entelekheia* pointed to its being substance as form, Aristotle probably meant for the soul to be viewed first and foremost as the *formal* rather than the *final* cause of the body, and this was how Alexander understood things. But a Neoplatonic commentator could point out that when Aristotle starts talking, in *De Anima* 2.4, about the ways in which the soul is the cause of the body, he maintains that the soul is the cause of the body not only as form, but also as agent and end. There Aristotle says:

teleiotês as acting first and foremost as a final cause at (Ps.-?)Simplicius, *in DA* 1.1 (*ad* 402a4), 8,19-21 and *in DA* 3.4 (*ad* 429b10), 231,21-24.

L8

Arisṭūṭālīs, *Fī n-nafs*, 38,3-5
Aristotle, *DA* 2.4, 415b9-13

> [This is] because soul is a cause in the three ways we have mentioned above; that is, it is a cause as the origin of motion, and as that for the sake of which the body exists [*wa-min ajli dhālika kāna l-jirmu* = *kai hou heneka*], and it is [a cause as] the being [*jawhar* = *ousia*] of bodies possessing souls.

In this passage Aristotle is not simply covering all his bases, for he is consistent in maintaining that form, agent and end often coincide in natural things. For example, in *Physics* 2.7 he says:

L9

Arisṭūṭālīs, *aṭ-Ṭabīʿa*, 137,15-138,3
Aristotle, *Phys.* 2.7, 198a22-28

> It is clear that the causes are these, and that this is the extent of their number. Since the causes are four, the natural philosopher should know about each of them, and the question "On account of what?" should be reduced to them such that the response to it is in accordance with the doctrine of natural philosophy; I mean the matter, the form, the mover, and that for the sake of which. Often three of them devolve into one: for what the thing is, is sometimes also that for the sake of which the thing is [*fa-inna mā sh-shayʾu qad yakūnu ayḍan mā min ajlihi sh-shayʾu* = *to men gar ti esti kai to hou heneka hen esti*], and the thing from which the motion first comes, and that in a single sense.

This passage was interpreted by the commentators as implying that form and end were identical in more profound ways than form and agent were.[15] I shall try to explain, by way of an example, what the commentators seem to have had in mind here. The formal cause and final cause of my son's coming-to-be are identical in number because the very same form of humanity instantiated in my son's body at conception serves *both* as a formal cause - as his essence, in other words - *and* as a final cause - as that in view of which the matter that made up his body was set in motion. I, however, am the efficient cause of my son's coming-to-be, with the result that my son and I are identical only in the weak sense that we are both subsumed under the species "human" (that is, we both possess the form of humanity), and not in the strong (numerical) sense of identity, according to which the instantiation of the form of humanity in my son is the very same instantiation of the form of humanity in me.

The notion that the formal and final causes are identical to each other in a stronger sense than they are to the efficient cause, is supported in other passages where Aristotle simply collapses the end into the form. For example, in a

[15] See, for example, Philoponus, *in Phys.* 2.7 (*ad* 198a14), 297,30-298,6 and (*ad* 198a24), 301,7-302,3; and Simplicius, *in Phys.* 2.7 (*ad* 198a22), 363,32-364,15 and 265,14-18.

passage intended to encourage philosophers to search for the nearest or most immediate cause of a thing, Aristotle appeals to his four-cause scheme to explain the coming-to-be of a human being:

L10

Arisṭāṭālīs, *Mā ba^c^da ṭ-ṭabī^c^a II*, 1073,15-1074,2
Aristotle, *Metaph.* 8.4, 1044a32-b1

> When it is asked, "What is the cause?", it is necessary, since "cause" is spoken of in many ways, that all of the ways in which a cause can be, be spoken of. For example, "What is the cause as matter of man?" It is the menstrual fluid. The cause as mover? The semen. The cause as form? It is the essence [*to ti ên einai* = *mā huwa bi-l-anniyyati*]. The cause as that for the sake of which? It is the end [*wa-l-^c^illatu llatī ka-lladhī min ajlihi fa-hiya t-tamāmu* = *ti d'hôs hou heneka; to telos*]. (It is likely that these two are one thing.)

But while this passage clearly supports a strong identification of the formal and final causes, it seems to undermine the claim that the efficient cause is identical to the formal and final causes in only a weak sense. This is because the example of the efficient cause in this passage is not the father, but the father's semen. In fact, Aristotle implies that strictly speaking, it is not even the father's semen – viewed as a composite of matter and form – which is the efficient cause of the son's coming-to-be, but only the form of humanity contained in the father's semen. This is because the matter of the father's semen is not transferred at conception to the son, but dissolves and evaporates at conception; the form of humanity contained in the father's semen, by contrast, is transferred to the son (*Generation of Animals* 2.3, 737a8-16 = *Fī kawn al-ḥayawān*, 64,13-19).

The result is that the form of humanity which was contained in my semen and transferred at conception to my son *is* the very same form of humanity which was instantiated in my son's body at conception and which served as that in view of which the matter that made up his body was set in motion. It turns out, therefore, that the efficient cause is numerically identical - that is, identical in a strong sense - to the formal and final causes. I suppose it could be argued that although the very same form of humanity contained in my semen came to be instantiated in my son's body at conception, that form of humanity acted as an efficient cause only while it was contained in my semen. Once the form of humanity was transferred from my semen and came to be instantiated in my son's body at conception, it no longer served as his efficient cause, but started to serve as his formal and final cause.

This argument is not really cogent, however, for the most one could hope to conclude is that the efficient cause and the formal and final causes are not numerically identical at the same time: before the moment of my son's conception, the form was contained in my semen; after the moment of conception, the form was contained in him. And once employed, the criterion of temporality could just as easily divide the formal cause from the final cause. The final cause - the form of humanity in view of which the matter that made up my son's body was set in motion - operated only during the process of formation. Once that process of formation was completed, the form of humanity, now fully instantiated in my son's body, operated only as a formal cause.

Partly in response to this confusion, Aristotle holds that some efficient causes are intrinsic to their effects, others extrinsic (*tôn de toioutôn eniôn men en autois hê arkhê tês kinêseôs estin ... eniôn d'exô = wa-min hādhihi l-anwāʿi mā btidāʾu l-ḥarakati fīhi ... [wa-]min khārijin*).[16] And in other passages Aristotle implies that the semen is not so much an efficient cause as something which the efficient cause (i.e. the father) uses as an instrument (*hôs organôi = mithla ālatin*).[17] To sum up, then, while Aristotle holds that the formal, final and efficient causes may sometimes be reduced to the same thing, it is unclear whether the formal cause can be identified in a stronger way with the final cause than either can with the efficient cause. It seems that this is true if the efficient cause is something extrinsic to the effect, as a father is to his son; but false if the efficient cause is something intrinsic to the effect, as the form of humanity contained in the father's semen and transferred at conception is to the son.

Even the strong identification of the formal and final causes can be undermined. For in one very important case, the final cause cannot be held to be identical to the formal cause: the Unmoved Mover is the final cause of celestial activity, but It is not the formal cause or essence of the spheres. Because the Unmoved Mover is not confined to a material body, and because form, by Aristotle's reckoning (*Physics* 2.1, 193b4-5), is never separable from matter in the real world, but only when speaking in purely logical terms (*kata ton logon*), the Unmoved Mover cannot be a formal cause. In other words, because Aristotle holds that the Unmoved Mover acts on Its effects as a final cause, and because the Unmoved Mover is separate from matter, there must therefore be *some* final causes which are separate from matter and hence not collapsible into formal causes.

To the commentators, however, it still seemed that of form, agent and end, form and end were most closely identifiable. It also seemed that when push came to shove – as in L10, the *Metaphysics* passage – Aristotle was willing to collapse end into form, but not vice versa, at least in the case of sublunary causation. In other words, assuming form and essence are the same, Aristotle would be prepared to say that end was subsumable under essence, but not that essence was subsumable under end. There were some indications, therefore, that of form and end, form was more basic. So despite Aristotle's claim in *De Anima* 2.4 that the soul is the cause of the body as form, end and agent together, his discussions elsewhere of how form, agent and end coincide implied that form was

[16] *GA* 1.18, 724a31-35 = *Fī kawn al-ḥayawān*, 29,13-16.
[17] *GA* 1.22, 730b20 = *Fī kawn al-ḥayawān*, 47,7.

still somehow the most basic of these three non-material causes. The perception that the form was *primus inter pares* was reinforced, of course, by Aristotle's assertion in *De Anima* 2.1 that the soul is substance as form.

Nevertheless, Aristotle's willingness to see the soul as a final cause – however subsumable final causality may be under formal causality – gave the commentators at least some flexibility to interpret the soul's being a *teleiotês* as referring to its being a final cause. In order to explain more precisely how the soul served as a final cause, and thereby reinforce the connection between the soul and the Neoplatonic understanding of *teleiotês*, the commentators turned to another Aristotelian distinction, that between two types of "that for the sake of which": *to hou* ("that in view of which") and *to hôi* ("that for the benefit of which").

Aristotle articulates the distinction in *De Anima* 2.4 and *Metaphysics* 12.7, and alludes to it in *Physics* 2.2 and *Eudemian Ethics* 8.3. He asserts that *to hou heneka*, that for the sake of which, may be spoken of in two ways: in the genitive, as *to hou* (or *tinos*), "that in view of which"; and in the dative, as *to hôi* (or *tini*), "that for the benefit of which".[18] Aristotle's distinction is very compressed and far from transparent.[19] It was also translated variously into Arabic: in the *De Anima* translation edited by Badawī, it appears as *wa-maᶜnā min ajli ᶜalā wijhatayni iḥdāhuma lahu wa-l-ukhrā fīhi*; in the Arabic version of Themistius' *Paraphrase of the De Anima*, it appears as *wa-lladhī bi-sababihi yuqālu ᶜalā ḍarbayni aḥaduhumā lladhī min qibalihi wa-l-ākharu lladhī lahu*; and in the *Metaphysics* translation it appears as *wa-dhālika anna mā min ajlihi yūjadu li-shayʾin wa-li-dhī shayʾin* (reading *li-dhī* for Bouyges' *li-dhā*).[20]

The contexts in which Aristotle introduces this distinction are quite different. In the *Physics*, the distinction is meant to show that nature is similar to art in that the form – *that in view of which* an artifact is created, such as the shape of an axe – must be taken into account by the natural philosopher, and not just the matter. Nature is also like art because the matter the artisan uses in creating the artifact is determined by the use which the "customer" or "end user" – *that for the benefit of which* – makes of the artifact, given its form. Thus an axe is made of iron and not clay, given the function – cutting – which the form "axe" represents to the person who benefits from using it.[21]

[18] *to men hou, to de hôi*: *DA* 2.4, 415b2 and *esti gar tini to hou heneka [kai] tinos*: *Metaph.* 12.7, 1072b2-3; cf. *Phys.* 2.2, 194a35-36 and *EE* 8.3, 1249b9-19.

[19] The fullest treatment of Aristotle's distinction between *to hou* and *to hôi* is that of Gaiser 1969.

[20] Arisṭūṭālīs, *Fī n-nafs*, 37,15-16; Themistius, *in DA* 2.4 (*ad* 415b2-3), 50,11 (= Thāmasṭiyūs, *Sharḥ Kitāb an-nafs li-Arisṭūṭālīs*, 68,12-13); Arisṭāṭālīs, *Mā baᶜda ṭ-ṭabīᶜa III*, 1599,3.

[21] The example Philoponus uses is that of a door: "Now 'end' is two-sided: 'that in view of which' and 'that for the benefit of which'. For example, the form of a door is a 'that in view of which' end, since the artisan strives for this, being what people call an 'aim' [*skopon*]. As for 'that for the benefit of which', well, the door is not on account of itself, in order that its form should

So far so good. But how exactly is the distinction useful in explaining the final causation of natural things, such as souls, as opposed to artifacts, such as doors or boats? When, in the *De Anima* passage, Aristotle applies the distinction between the final cause *qua to hou* and the final cause *qua to hôi* to living things, the distinction seems to be based not so much on the difference between, respectively, form and user, but rather on the difference between what is eternal and divine and what is mortal.[22] There seem to have been two ways to reconcile the *Physics*' form/user criterion with the *De Anima*'s eternal/mortal criterion, depending on whether one understands the "that for the benefit of which" in the *De Anima* to be referring to the soul-body composite, or to the soul alone.

The first interpretation, advocated by Themistius, runs along the following lines: *that in view of which* nature creates living bodies is the form of divine immortality which nature directs them to attain as a species, through the faculty of reproduction in their souls. *That for the benefit of which* nature creates living bodies, on the other hand, are the ensouled bodies themselves – that is, the soul/body composites – which attain the form of immortality through reproduction.[23] The second interpretation, which strikes me as more sensible, is advocated by Philoponus, and goes like this: as with the first interpretation, *that in view of which* nature creates living bodies is the form of divine immortality which nature directs them to attain as a species, through the faculty of reproduction in their souls. But in contrast to the first interpretation, *that for the benefit of which* nature creates living bodies are the souls that use the bodies as instruments in order to attain immortality as a species. Philoponus also expresses the stipulation that *that for the benefit of which* does not apply to things – such as metals and rocks – which possess no souls to use their bodies as instruments; instead, only *that in view of which* applies to inanimate things.[24] What is more, commenting on the issue of formal-final-efficient identity discussed in L9, Philoponus says that substantial form is identical with end only in the "in view of which" sense (i.e., *qua to hou*), and not in the "for the benefit of which" sense (i.e., *qua to hôi*).[25]

come into being, but rather in order that it serve a function for man; thus the door comes into being for the benefit of man, being in some sense an end, so that it [i.e., the door] may protect the house"; Philoponus, *in Phys.* 2.2 (*ad* 194a12), 230,5-10. Olympiodorus follows Philoponus at Olympiodorus, *in Meteor.* 4.2 (*ad* 379b8-10), 284,7-19.

[22] In the comments to his edition of the *De Anima*, Ross says "In ll. 1-2 A. says that eternity and divinity are the *hou heneka* in the sense of being that at which all things aim [*to hou*]; in ll. 20-21 he says that soul is the *hou heneka* in the sense of being that in whose interests [*to hôi*] the bodies of animals and plants exist" (Ross 1961, 228).

[23] Themistius, *in DA* 2.4 (*ad* 415b3-7), 50,15-26 (= Thāmasṭiyūs, *Sharḥ Kitāb an-nafs li-Arisṭūṭālīs*, 69,2-12).

[24] Philoponus, *in DA* 2.4 (*ad* 415b2 and 15), 269,25-270,32 and 274,1-23. See also (Ps.-?) Simplicius, *in DA* 2.4 (*ad* 415b2), 110,31-36 and (*ad* 415b17 and 20), 111,22-112,2.

[25] Philoponus, *in Phys.* 2.7 (*ad* 198a14), 297,30-298,6 and 301,18-302,2. Proclus claims that divine souls can only be final causes *qua to hou* because divine souls are separate from bodies and hence are not tied to material instruments; Proclus, *in Tim.*, Vol. 3, 254,10-31 (*ad* 41D7).

In any case, the distinction between *to hou* and *to hôi* was useful in helping Philoponus understand more precisely the ways in which the soul could be seen to be a final cause, and thereby reinforced the sense in which the soul could be seen as a Neoplatonic *teleiotês*. Thus:

2b[ii]´

Phys. 1st:
1. *entelekheia* = *teleiotês qua* "state of being completed" = (the potential X's) state of completeness (e.g., "[the bricks' and mortar's] being constructed")
2. *entelekheia* = *teleiôsis qua* "process of being completed" = process of completion (e.g., "construction")

DA 1st:
1a. *entelekheia* = *teleiotês qua* "state of having been completed" = state of completeness (e.g., "having been born")
1b. *entelekheia* = *teleiotês qua* "resulting substantial form" = essence (e.g., "humanity")
1c. *entelekheia* = *teleiotês qua* "final cause *qua to hou*" = state in view of which *teleiôsis* occurred (e.g., "being a perfect human")
2a. *entelekheia* = *teleiotês qua* "state of having been completed" = state of completeness (e.g., "having come to know")
2b. *entelekheia* = *teleiotês qua* "resulting substantial form" = essence (e.g., "knowledge")
2c. *entelekheia* = *teleiotês qua* "final cause *qua to hou*" = state in view of which *teleiôsis* occurred (e.g., "being perfectly knowledgeable")
3. *entelekheia* = *teleiotês qua* "final cause *qua to hôi*" = user (e.g., "the soul [uses the bodily organs, in view of being perfectly knowledgeable, to cause the *teleiôsis* of coming-to-know]")

Phys. 2nd:
1. *entelekheia* = *teleiotês qua* "state of having been completed" = state of completeness (e.g., "having been constructed")
2. *entelekheia* = *teleiotês qua* "resulting substantial form" = essence (e.g., "houseness")
3. *entelekheia* = *teleiotês qua* "final cause *qua to hou*" = state in view of which *teleiôsis* occurred (e.g., "being a perfect house")

DA 2nd:
1. *entelekheia* = *teleiotês qua* "state of being completed" = (the potential X's) state of completeness (e.g., "[the intellect's] contemplating")
2. *entelekheia* = *teleiôsis qua* "process of being completed" = process of completion (e.g., "contemplation")

The major difference between Themistius' and Philoponus' schemes is that as a result of the new, Proclan understanding of *teleiotês*, Philoponus can now see *teleiotês* as referring simply to "final cause" and not, as Themistius had, as referring to all the different senses of endedness. In other words, Philoponus now replaces "endedness" with "end" in the semantic field of *teleiotês*. By this choice, however, Philoponus is forced to forfeit the very handy notion of endedness, which provided Themistius with four new senses of *teleiotês* with which to reconcile Aristotle's seemingly incompatible uses of *entelekheia* in *De Anima* 2 and *Physics* 3: allotelic endedness, which can mean both the "state of being directed towards an end other than itself" and the "state of serving as an end for something other than itself"; and autotelic endedness, which can mean both the "state of being directed towards an end which is nothing other than its own exercise" and the "state of serving as its own end".

On the other hand, by understanding *teleiotês* in the Proclan rather than Themistian way, as end rather than endedness, Philoponus gains two new senses of *teleiotês*, the final cause *qua to hou* and the final cause *qua to hôi*. Still, the deal seems hardly fair. Philoponus has lost four senses of *teleiotês* and gained only two, and therefore he must surely be less able to reconcile Aristotle's seemingly incompatible uses of *entelekheia* than Themistius was. I believe this is true. What Philoponus' move does show, I think, is that he was more worried about reconciling Platonic and Aristotelian doctrines about the separability of the soul than he was with reconciling Aristotle's seemingly incompatible uses of *entelekheia*. In other words, Philoponus had integrated the greater *sumphônia* of harmonizing Plato's and Aristotle's psychologies, into the lesser *sumphônia* of sorting out what Aristotle means when, for example, he distinguishes between final causes which are *to hou* and those which are *to hôi*. But how exactly does understanding *teleiotês* as end help Philoponus create a compromise between Plato and Aristotle on the issue of the soul's separability?

The first thing to be stressed is that Aristotle's position on the soul's separability – or at least the intellect's separability – is sufficiently underdetermined that Neoplatonic commentators such as Philoponus (and, as we shall see, Avicenna as well) could point to a number of passages in Aristotle's works where Aristotle allows for the possibility of, while not expressly advocating, some version of separability. The following are the most prominent of those Aristotelian passages:

L11

Arisṭūṭālīs, *Fī n-nafs*, 20,10
Aristotle, *DA* 1.4, 408b18-19

As for the intellect, it seems to come into being [*ya<ta>kawwinu* = *enginesthai*] as a cause of the soul, permanent and never passing away [*ghayra fāsidin* = *kai ou phtheiresthai*].

L12

Arisṭūṭālīs, *Fī n-nafs*, 31,13-15
Aristotle, *DA* 2.1, 413a3-9

It has become clear that neither the soul nor any of its parts is separable from the body, because the *entelechy* of some living things belongs only to their parts. But it is not yet clear if the soul is the *entelechy* of the body as the pilot [is] of the ship [*rākibi s-safīnati = plôtêr ploiou*].

L13

Arisṭūṭālīs, *Fī n-nafs*, 72,19-21
Aristotle, *DA* 3.4, 429a22-25

It is doubtless the case that the intellectual [part] of the soul, called "intellect" (namely, that by which it reasons and holds opinions) does not actually exist in anything before it apprehends the thing by means of its comprehension. For this reason it does not follow that it is intermingled with the body [*li-dhālika lā yajibu an yakūna mukhālaṭan li-l-jirmi = dio oude memikhthai eulogon auton tôi sômati*].

L14

Arisṭūṭālīs, *Fī a*ʿ*ḍā*ʾ *al-ḥayawān*, 10,24-11,8
Aristotle, *PA* 1.1, 641a32-641b10

When someone considers what has just been said, a difficulty arises, because it is difficult [to decide] whether the natural philosopher should wish to speak about all soul or about one [particular type or part of] soul. If it is about all soul, then there will be no difference at all between that person and the natural philosopher. For the philosopher's intellect has as its object intelligible things. Natural philosophy would have as its object knowledge of all things; because all correlatives are the object of the same study (as is the case with sensation and sensible things), it will belong to the same science to study intellect and intelligible things, given the fact that they are correlative. Yet neither all soul nor all its parts is an origin of movement: the principle of growth is what is found in trees; the principle of alteration is what is found in the [faculty of] sensation; and the principle of locomotion is [found in yet] another thing, which is not what the intellect is found in. This is because locomotion is also found in other types of animal, but intellect is found in none of them [i.e., in none of the other types of animal]. It is therefore clear to us that the discussion is <not> about all soul, because not all soul is nature, but instead about only some part of it, since the soul contains many parts.

L15

Arisṭūṭālīs, *Fī kawn al-ḥayawān*, 63,22-23
Aristotle, *GA* 2.3, 736b28-30

It follows from our discussion that we should say the intellect alone enters from outside [i.e., the body], and that only it is divine, on account of the fact that its activity is not at all associated with any bodily activity.

L16

Arisṭāṭālīs, *Mā baᶜda ṭ-ṭabīᶜa II*, 706,6-7
Aristotle, *Metaph.* 6.1, 1026a5-6

[It is clear] that it belongs to the natural philosopher, in [his branch of] knowledge, to investigate a certain type of soul, namely, the one which is not without matter [*fa-anna li-ṭ-ṭabīᶜiyyi fī l-ᶜilmi an yanẓura fī nafsin mā wa-hiya llatī lā takūnu min ghayri ᶜunṣurin = kai dioti kai peri psukhês enias theôrêsai tou phusikou, hosê mê aneu tês hulês estin*]

L17

Arisṭāṭālīs, *Mā baᶜda ṭ-ṭabīᶜa III*, 1486,13-1487,2
Aristotle, *Metaph.* 12.3, 1070a24-26

Now whether anything [viz., any form] remains afterwards [viz., after its effect] requires investigation, because there is nothing preventing certain things [from remaining after their effects]. An example is whether the soul is this way; not all of it, though, but the intellect, since not all of it [viz., not all of the soul] can possibly [remain after its effect].

Most modern commentators would argue that the balance of evidence still tips towards inseparability, given the heavy weight of Aristotle's tying of *entelekheia* to form in *DA* 2.1. Nevertheless, Aristotle's position will, I hope, seem more underdetermined than has generally been supposed.[26] It is easy to imagine that for a Neoplatonic commentator, the scale could be tipped back towards separability given that since Alexander's time the soul was held to be a *teleiotês*; given that since Proclus' time a *teleiotês* was held to cause its effect as a final cause; and given that since Syrianus' time final causes were held to transcend their effects.

As seen above, moderate Neoplatonic commentators such as Philoponus – commentators who sought concessions not only from Aristotle and Alexander but from Plato and Plotinus as well – argued that the soul uses the body as an instrument and that in this sense the soul is a final cause *qua to hôi* (as user and beneficiary, that is) of the body. As a final cause *qua to hôi,* the soul can be seen to be immanent in its effect in order to accommodate Aristotle and Alexander. In order to accommodate Plato and Plotinus, however, the intellect or human rational soul – the type of soul which is eternal and divine and which acts as a final cause *qua to hou* – will be held to be separate. The fact that the final cause *qua to hôi* seems to be immanent in its effect while the final cause *qua to*

[26] An example of the tendency among some scholars of ancient philosophy to see Aristotle's theory of the soul-body relationship as more consistent than I am presenting it as being, and to blame the Neoplatonists for willfully corrupting it, is Blumenthal 1990. For a recent defense of the idea that Aristotle allowed for the possibility of the soul's – or at least the intellect's – separability, see Bolton 1978.

hou seems to transcend its effect is reflected in Philoponus' reluctance to commit himself to holding that a *teleiotês* in and of itself will imply *either* separability *or* inseparability.[27]

How does a separate *teleiotês* act as a final cause, drawing its effect up to its higher ontological level? First we must be precise about what a *teleiotês* is a final cause *of*. I have already discussed the fact that to Neoplatonists such as Philoponus what a *teleiotês* causes or explains is a thing's coming-to-perfection, its *teleiôsis*. So strictly speaking, it would be incorrect to say that the soul is the *teleiotês* of the body; rather, the soul is the *teleiotês* of the body's coming-to-perfection. Even more precisely, the soul is the final cause of the body insofar as the body is seen as an element of reversion, as something striving upwards towards self-perfection. The point is that not only the body but also the soul and even the human intellect can be regarded as each undergoing comings-to-perfection (*teleiôseis*) whose ultimate end is a separate *teleiotês*. This separate *teleiotês* is apprehended during self-intellection, the activity which the Neoplatonists regarded as the final step in a human's reversion to a higher level.

I have already spoken in Chapter 2 about why the specific difference, rather than the species, should be seen as corresponding to the *teleiotês* in this context. Neoplatonists such as Ammonius agreed, arguing that only the specific difference can be seen to be truly perfective (*teleiôtikê*), that is, cause-like.[28] In short, what seems to happen during self-intellection is that my species changes from "rational animal" to "active intellect". In other words, once the specific difference ("*noêtikos*") of my original species ("*anthrôpos*") has been attained as a *teleiotês*, my former specific difference ("*noêtikos*") becomes my new genus ("*nous*"). The new specific differences which set one species of the genus "*nous*" apart from another species of the genus "*nous*", are "active" (*energeiâi*) and "potential" (*dunamei*).

The reversion carries on upwards in the sense that the specific difference "active" then becomes its own genus – (intellectual) activity – with the specific difference now being "eternal" or "intermittent". The highest a human can attain in life is intermittent (i.e., non-eternal) intellectual activity. In death (according to Avicenna, as we shall see) or following the completion of a certain number of transmigrations (according to Proclus and some other Neoplatonists), eternal intellectual activity can be attained.

[27] At *in DA* 2.2 (*ad* 412b9), 219,9-10, Philoponus says that taken in and of itself, the *teleiotês* of a thing will be inseparable from that thing; but at *in DA* 2.1 (*ad* 412a3), 206,18-23, he says that taken as the thing's perfecting activity (*tên heautou energeian teleiôtikên*) – taken as a cause, that is – the *teleiotês* will be separable from the thing.

[28] Ammonius, *in Int.*, 71,5-11; Proclus was slightly less certain, sometimes (e.g., *Inst. Theol.*, Prop. 108, 96,9-22) maintaining that one can become perfect through imitating either a genus or a specific difference, other times (e.g., *in Alc. I*, 18,4-7; 247,10-11; 248,2-4; 278,3-13) implying that it is only during self-intellection – that is, during intellection of the specific difference "rational" – that a thing reverts in a proper sense.

In any case the notion that self-intellection is the primary mechanism of reversion, and that this reversion consists more generally of an ascension to *teleiotêtes* – to final causes, that is – by means of imitation, is present in virtually all Neoplatonic thinkers.[29] Self-intellection is the only truly divine activity since it is the only truly self-sufficient, and hence perfect, activity, a precept which appears to have come from Aristotle (*EN* 10.7, 1177b15-26), as I mentioned in Chapter 2.[30] The view that because self-intellection requires nothing else to bring it about, it is complete and perfect in the sense of self-sufficient, will, as I shall show in Chapters 6 and 11, prove influential on Avicenna's theories of perfection and the perfect. For now, I shall discuss how all these Greek terms were rendered into Arabic by the translators of the eighth, ninth and tenth centuries.

[29] Plotinus, *Enneads*, I.8.1,7-10; Proclus, *Theol. Plat.*, Vol. 1.14, 66,3-5 (where he quotes Parmenides' famous – and variously interpreted – dictum in Fr. 3 that being is a necessary precondition of, or perhaps even identical to, thinking [*to gar auto noein estin te kai einai*], and also alludes to *Laws* X 897B); *Inst. Theol.*, Prop. 32, 36,3-4 and 186, 162,13-23; *in Alc. I*, 291,3-5 and 308,4-5; *in Parm.*, 627,12-14; 771,26-30; 789,31-790,4; 1148,1-17; Philoponus, *in DA* 1.3 (*ad* 407b9), 138,25-139,2 (citing the beginning of Plotinus, *Enneads* II.2); and (Ps.-?)Simplicius, *in DA* 2.1 (*ad* 412a10), 84,13-22 and 2.1 (*ad* 412a22), 88,13-89,12.

[30] See also Proclus, *Theol. Plat.*, Vol. 3.6, 22,3-6; *Inst. Theol.*, Prop. 114, 100,16-27.

5. Greek into Arabic
The Greco-Arabic Translations and the Early Arabic Philosophers

In this chapter I shall show that the philosophical tendencies of the Ammonian synthesis, which I have just described at length, had an impact on the choices made by the Greco-Arabic translators when rendering into Arabic Greek words relating to the idea of perfection and the perfect, as well as on the ways in which the early Arabic philosophers such as al-Kindī and al-Fārābī formulated their own ideas about perfection and the perfect. I hope it will become clear that the translation movement was less a transparent, lexicographical process, than it was part and parcel of the Ammonian synthesis described in the previous chapter. What I mean is that the Greco-Arabic translators chose words based on certain current philosophical presuppositions, namely, those of Ammonius and his successors in the sixth century.

Scholars such as Walzer, Frank, Endress, Gätje, Daiber and Arnzen have each briefly discussed the translation into Arabic of the terms *entelekheia*, *teleion* and *teleiotês*, some in the form of glosses to their editions of the Arabic translations of Greek works, others in the form of footnotes to their studies of the translation history of individual texts; none pretends to offer the reader a diachronic analysis.[1] My objective for this chapter is to propose – very tentatively, because the evidence is still sketchy – a narrative of the Arabic *fortuna* of an interrelated cluster of Greek terms, those just mentioned as well as the terms *telos*, *telikos* and *teleiôtikos*.

According to Gutas' useful summary, the Greco-Arabic translation movement can be divided into five stages: (1) the first and earliest period, in which Euclid's *Elements* and Aristotle's *Rhetoric* were translated; (2) the period of the circle of translators surrounding the philosopher al-Kindī (d. 875); (3) the period of Ḥunayn b. Isḥāq (d. 873) and his school; (4) the period of Qusṭā b. Lūqā (d. ca. 912); and (5) the period which Gutas calls the "stage of scholarly emendation, i.e., on the basis of contents rather than original texts".[2] Based on the evidence I will present here, the only modification to Gutas' scheme I would suggest is incorporating the retranslating efforts of Isḥāq b. Ḥunayn (d. 910), which seem to bridge the fourth and fifth periods: though chronologically they fall in fourth period, Isḥāq's efforts are distinct from Qusṭā's; and though their aim of emendation was that of the fifth and final period, Isḥāq seems to have had access to new texts, at least in the case of the *De Anima*.

[1] Walzer 1953, 95-96; Frank 1958-59, 242n.2 and 249; Endress 1966, 121; Gätje 1971, 34, 39 and 43; Daiber 1980, 5, 157, 369 and 456-7 (who also mentions the Syriac intermediary renderings of *entelekheia*); and Arnzen 1998, 375-7.

[2] Gutas 1998.

Inevitably, the borders between any such periodization are fuzzy, and one can detect transitions in word choice even within the work of a single translator. One overall conclusion I am inclined to draw is that much of the effort of the fourth and fifth stages – and particularly that of Isḥāq b. Ḥunayn – was devoted to cleaning the mess left by the disparate and sometimes conflicting efforts of the translators of the al-Kindī circle. The mopping up was undertaken with a view to creating a more systematic Greco-Arabic lexicon, one which superseded the old, al-Kindī-circle terminology because the new one could be used consistently in more than one translated text.

This effort at standardization did succeed, in the sense that philosophers such as Avicenna came to use the revised Aristotelian terminology in much of his work, particularly in canonical passages such as his definitions of important concepts such as motion (*al-ḥaraka*) and the soul (*an-nafs*). Nevertheless, enough of the al-Kindī-circle vocabulary not only remained in some of the unrevised translations, but had infiltrated the work of earlier philosophers (I am thinking of al-Kindī himself but most of all al-Fārābī), that many of the earlier terms and the ideas expressed by those terms came to be present in Avicenna's work, though often in less prominent passages than the ones containing the standardized vocabulary of the later periods. Some of the most important of these vestigial, early-period terms are those that express the concepts of perfection and the perfect.

The first translation which required a standard rendering of any of the Greek terms I have been discussing was that of Euclid's *Elements*, which used the Arabic *tāmm* to translate the Greek *teleios* in Euclid's discussions of perfect number (*arithmos teleios*).[3] This very early use of *tāmm* to translate Euclid's *teleios* may have prompted Usṭāt, a member of the al-Kindī circle and – to the best of our knowledge – the translator of most of the version of the *Metaphysics* contained in the lemmata of Averroes' *Tafsīr Mā baᶜda ṭ-ṭabīᶜa* (*Great Commentary on the Metaphysics*) and edited by Bouyges, to render *to*

[3] According to De Young 1981 (Vol. 1, Pt. 1, 1-3), there were three translations of the arithmetical sections of Euclid's *Elements*, the first two by al-Ḥajjāj b. Yūsuf b. Maṭar, which are not extant, and the last by Isḥāq b. Ḥunayn and revised by Thābit b. Qurra, which is the translation edited and translated into English by De Young. There are two versions of this last translation, of which one (*majmūᶜ* "a") lists the definition as Bk 7, Def. 24, and reads *al-ᶜadadu t-tāmmu* (De Young 1981, Vol. 1. Pt 1, 5,9); and the other (*majmūᶜ* "b") lists the definition as Bk 7, Def. 23, and reads *al-ᶜadadu lladhī yuqālu t-tāmmu lahu* (De Young 1981, Vol. 1. Pt 2, 321,6). We can surmise, however, that *tāmm* was the translation of *teleios* in the earlier versions by al-Ḥajjāj, because *tāmm* was also used in the Leningrad MS Akademia Nauk C2145, which is a more literal translation than the Isḥāq/Thābit version and which therefore fits Ibn al-Nadīm's description of al-Ḥajjāj's translation; see De Young 1981, Vol. 1, Pt 1, 28. Also see the translation by Thābit b. Qurra (d. 901) of Nicomachus of Gerasa's *Introduction to Arithmetic*, where *teleios* is again rendered into Arabic by *tāmm*: Nīqūmākhis al-Jārāsīnī, *K. al-madkhal ilā ᶜilm al-ᶜadad*, 36,6-40,23; *teleios* is rendered into Arabic as *at-tāmm* at 36,10; 37,5.15; 39,6.19; 40,15.16.21; "superabundant" is translated as *zāyid (= zā'id) ᶜalā t-tamāmi*, and "deficient" is translated as *nāqiṣ ᶜani t-tamāmi*. Avicenna himself discusses perfect (*tāmm*), superabundant (*zā'id*) and deficient (*nāqiṣ*) numbers in *K. ash-shifā'/Riyāḍiyyāt* 2: *al-Ḥisāb*, 30,21-23 and 32,7-33,22.

teleion of *Metaphysics* 5.16 as *at-tāmm*, as is apparent in L4. The same translator may also have reasoned that just as *teleion* was the adjective deriving from the noun *telos*, so *telos* should be rendered into Arabic by the noun *tamām* from which the adjective *tāmm* is derived; this is made clear in Table 1 in Appendix I.

More specifically, Table 1 shows that *telos* was rendered as *ghāya* in Book 2 (which is probably just an artifact of Averroes' use of Isḥāq b. Ḥunayn's later translation of Book 2 in addition to Usṭāt's); then, in Book 3, as *ghāya* and as *tamām*, and also as *ghāya wa-tamām*, a hendiadys that also turns up in the Arabic version of the *Parts of Animals*;[4] and then Usṭāt used only *tamām* in the rest of the *Metaphysics*. As Table 2 shows, Usṭāt also rendered *entelekheia* (mainly in its adverbial use in the dative case) as *fiᶜl* in Books 1-8; and as *tamām* in Book 9 onwards, except for once in Book 12, where an instance of *entelekheia* in the dative is rendered as *fī l-kamāl* (which is probably just an artifact of Averroes' use of Abū Bishr Mattā's later translation of Book 12 up to 1072b16). My guess is that Usṭāt began by rendering *entelekheia* as *fiᶜl*, believing it to be virtually interchangeable with *energeia*. But when confronted with Aristotle's attempt in *Metaphysics* 9 – his longest sustained discussion of potentiality and actuality – to distinguish between *energeia* and *entelekheia*, Usṭāt changed tack and began rendering *entelekheia* as *tamām*.

The result of Usṭāt's switch was that an attentive but Greekless reader of the Arabic *Metaphysics* such as Avicenna (who, after all, claimed in his autobiography to have read the *Metaphysics* 40 times), turned to canonical passages on the four causes in *Metaphysics* 5.2, and found *telos*, or final cause, rendered as *tamām*, and contrasted with the form, the matter and the agent; and then turned to canonical passages on substance and actuality in *Metaphysics* 9 and found *entelekheia*, or actuality, also rendered as *tamām*, and contrasted with potentiality.

My point is that in the translation of Aristotle's *Metaphysics* itself there existed a lexical momentum pushing close readers such as Avicenna to assume that the ideas of actuality and final cause fell together naturally. This conflation of *telos* and *entelekheia* could be nothing more than an accidental result of a translator's word choice. But to my mind, the fact that Usṭāt seems not to have felt it necessary to revise his translation in order to separate the two concepts is a sign that he was influenced by the profound philosophical shift that had occurred among the Neoplatonists who glossed *entelekheia* with *teleiotês*, and then spoke of the *teleiotês* as operating like a *telos*; and that in this sense Usṭāt, like other early Greco-Arabic translators, cannot be extracted from the philosophical continuum of the Ammonian synthesis.

[4] *PA* 2.3, 650a27 = *Fī aᶜḍāʾ al-ḥayawān*, 32,23; 3.6, 669a13 = 80,3; 3.9, 672a5 = 87,12; and 3.14, 675a16 = 96,6; cf. also 1.1, 641b25 = 11,21.

The philosophical shift from *entelekheia* to *teleiotês* is also evident in the word choices of other translators in the al-Kindī circle, another of whose members was the compiler of the *Uthūlūjiyā*, al-Ḥimṣī.[5] It seems from L7 that given al-Ḥimṣī's use of the transliteration *anṭalāshiyā* to render the *entelekheia* of the *Enneads*, his use of *tamām* probably rendered a term other than *entelekheia* – *teleiotês* seems the obvious candidate – in whichever bits and pieces of Greek Neoplatonic source-text the non-*Enneads* material in the *Uthūlūjiyā* is a translation of. Of course al-Ḥimṣī's use of *tamām* in this context may not have been a direct translation from some ghostly Greek original at all, but rather his own importation into the *Uthūlūjiyā* of the Arabic version of a Greek term – again, presumably *teleiotês* – that he had seen as a gloss of *entelekheia* in another text circulating among al-Kindī's team of translators.

It does seem that the point of the L7 passage is that the soul may be called the *tamām* of the body, as long as it is clear that a *tamām* can be separable or inseparable, unlike a nasty *anṭalāshiyā*, which is usually understood as being inseparable. To my mind this shows that al-Ḥimṣī was aware of Proclus' and the Ammonian commentators' use of *teleiotês* in the context of the soul, as opposed to Alexander's use of *teleiotês*; for even though Alexander used *teleiotês* to gloss *entelekheia*, he was clear that the soul was inseparable from the body just as form was inseparable from matter.

Another interesting feature of L7 is the use of the term *tamāmiyya*, as in *ṣūra tamāmiyya*, meaning "perfecting form". This almost certainly rendered, or echoed, *eidos teleiôtikon* (or perhaps *eidos telesiourgon*), rather than *eidos telikon*, "final form", which makes no sense there, or anywhere for that matter. What the compiler seems to have wanted to do first in L7, is to distinguish between form *qua* shape (*eidos qua morphê*) and form *qua* essence or substance (*eidos qua ousia*), a distinction which appears, as I mentioned in Chapter 4, in Philoponus' commentary on the *De Anima*. Though an *entelekheia* can refer to either type of *eidos*, a *teleiotês* will refer only to *eidos* as substance, and not to *eidos* as shape. The soul is an *entelekheia* only in the sense that it refers to *eidos* as substance, not in the sense that it refers to *eidos* as shape; therefore, it is fine to call the soul a *tamām-teleiotês* because it refers only to the substantial sense of *eidos*.

In the third paragraph of L7 the compiler then argues that even though the Materialist philosophers – perhaps Alexander is in the frame here – sometimes spoke of this latter type of form – i.e., *eidos qua ousia* – as "perfecting", what they really had in mind was in fact a passive, natural perfecting form, one which is inseparable from the body in which it inheres. Their "perfecting form" is therefore not truly perfecting in a Neoplatonic sense, since the Neoplatonists consistently used *eidos teleiôtikon* to refer to something separable, with

[5] On the very murky history of this work see Zimmermann 1986, in tandem with the review by Rowson 1992.

genuine agency: to separate Forms, not to inseparable forms.[6] If the soul is to be spoken of as a perfecting form, it must be so in that truly active, productive sense, the sense in which the Forms are active and productive, and not in the natural, passive sense which the Materialists have in mind. Again, the influence of the Neoplatonic turn to causation is clear: the soul is a perfection in the sense that it is a cause of the body just as a separate Form is the cause of its effect, and not in the sense that it is an inseparable form, be it a *morphê* or even a natural *ousia*.

The renderings of the relevant Greek terms into Arabic in the Arabic versions of Proclus' writings, mainly from Proclus' *Elements of Theology* and often disguised as essays by Alexander of Aphrodisias, are listed by Endress in his *Proclus Arabus*.[7] They generally follow the pattern described above, using *tāmm* to translate *teleion*, and either transliterating *entelekheia* as *anṭalāshiyā* or rendering it as *tamām*. But the most innovative and important feature of these translations is the introduction of the hendiadys *tāmm kāmil* (sometimes *tāmm wa-kāmil*) as a translation of *teleion*, and, less often, *tamām wa-kamāl* as a translation of *entelekheia* and *teleiotês*. To the passages listed by Endress I can add the following other instances where *k-m-l* has been introduced into the picture. In one "Alexander" translation, which Hasnawi has argued is in fact an excerpt from Philoponus' *De aeternitate mundi contra Proclum*, the Aristotelian definition of motion is cited, and *kamāl* is used once, and *tamām* used four times, to render *entelekheia*.[8] In the Arabic version of what is genuinely Alexander's *Quaestio* 3.3 (*De sensu* = *Fī l-ḥiss*), we find the hendiadys *mutammima mukmila* and *ilā tamāmihi wa-kamālihi*.[9] The hendiadys also appears as a translation of *teleiôsis*, and of verbs stemming from *teleiôsis*, in the Arabic versions of Aristotle's *Generation of Animals* and *History of Animals*.[10] The use of this hendiadys added the Arabic root *k-m-l* to the quiver of terms used by the translators, who in the fourth and fifth stages of the translation movement tended, as I shall soon show, to discard *t-m-m* almost entirely and use *k-m-l* instead.

The final important text which appears to be from this early period, but about which there has been much discussion among scholars, is the text edited by Badawī and thought by him to have been the final, revised translation of Isḥāq b.

[6] Syrianus, *in Metaph.* 13.4 (*ad* 1078b32), 107,38-108,8; Proclus, *Inst. Theol.*, Prop. 45, 46,12-19; and *in Remp.*, Vol. 1, 270,13-272,7 and 286,11-287,10; and Philoponus, *in DA* 2.1 (*ad* 412a3), 206,18-23.

[7] Endress 1973, 67 and 115-117.

[8] *Maqālat Aliskandar fī anna l-fiʿl aʿammu mina l-ḥaraka ʿalā raʾy Arisṭū*, 293,8 (*kamāl*) and 294,9.11.13.14 (*tamām*). For the arguments that its attribution to Alexander is wrong and that it is in fact a translation of excerpts from Philoponus' *De aeternitate mundi contra Proclum*, see Hasnawi 1994, 68-75, and Zimmermann 1994, 22-27.

[9] *Maqālat Aliskandar fī l-ḥiss*, 176,68-69; 178,90; 190,185; and 192,194 (*Quaest.* 3.3, 83,37; 84,28; 86,22.24).

[10] *GA* 1.8, 718b7 = *Fī kawn al-ḥayawān*, 11,16; 4.1, 763b22 = 134,5; 4.4, 773a14 = 159,6; 4.7, 776a4 = 166,19; and 5.10, 777b27 = 171,6; *HA* 6.3, 561a6 = *Ṭibāʿ al-ḥayawān*, 249,2.

Ḥunayn, which the *Fihrist* mentions in its compressed and cryptic description of the Arabic reception of the *De Anima*. As Frank has convincingly argued, the version edited by Badawī cannot be, as Badawī thought, Isḥāq's later, revised edition.[11]

Above and beyond the arguments offered by Frank and others, it is clear that Isḥāq used an entirely different vocabulary to render terms such as *entelekheia* and *teleiotês* – particularly the terms *kamāl* and *istikmāl* – than the translator of the Badawī text had. For example, as Table 3 makes clear, Badawī's *Fī n-nafs* either renders *entelekheia* (mainly in the dative case, that is, in its adverbial sense) as *fiᶜl* or simply transliterates it as *anṭalāshiyā* (and once as *anṭalākhiyā*), occasionally glossing it with *tamām*. The rendering of *entelekheia* as *fiᶜl* is just as Usṭāt had done in the first eight books of his *Metaphysics* translation, and the transliteration of *entelekheia* as *anṭalāshiyā* is just as al-Ḥimsī had done in his compilation of the *Uthūlūjiyā*. The Badawī-text's translator's use of *tamām* to gloss *anṭalāshiyā* in L1 not only echoes the Greek commentators' gloss of *entelekheia* with *teleiotês*, it is also a sign of the second period of translation, as manifest in the use of *tamām* in L7, the *Uthūlūjiyā*'s discussion of the soul's definition. A similar use of *tamām* to render *entelekheia* is found in the translation of a short, late-antique paraphrase of the *De Anima* and in a commentary on that paraphrase, both of which have recently been re-edited by Arnzen, who ascribes them to Ibn al-Biṭrīq (fl. ca. 835) and dates them to around 820-845, that is, to the second stage of the translation movement.[12]

In contrast to the Badawī text, it is obvious from Tables 4 and 5 that in his *Physics* translation Isḥāq viewed the root *k-m-l*, introduced during the second stage alongside *t-m-m* in the aforementioned hendiadys, as the best Arabic term for *entelekheia*, since that way it could be more easily distinguished from *telos*, which Isḥāq now rendered with *ghāya*. In other words, Isḥāq's purpose in using *k-m-l* and *ghāya*, respectively, for *entelekheia* and *telos*, while reserving *t-m-m* for *teleiotês*, was to prevent the Greekless reader of the Arabic *Physics* from conflating two distinct Aristotelian concepts, *entelekheia* and *telos*, each of which – as I just showed – had commonly been rendered as *tamām* by his predecessors.[13]

[11] Frank 1958-59.

[12] Anonymous, *Paraphrase of the De Anima*, 183,18-22 (= [Ps.-]Isḥāq b. Ḥunayn, *K. an-nafs*, 129,13-16); Anonymous, *Commentary on the De Anima*, 213,15-217,16 (= [Ps.-]Isḥāq b. Ḥunayn, *K. an-nafs*, 139,20-1140,23) and 219,7-16 (=[Ps.-]Isḥāq b. Ḥunayn, *K. an-nafs*, 141,3-10).

[13] More specifically, as Tables 4 and 5 make clear, Isḥāq's *Physics* renders *entelekheia* as *istikmāl* in Books 1, 2 and 8, and as *kamāl* elsewhere in the *Physics*, most notably in the discussion of motion in *Phys.* 3.1 and 3.2; by contrast *telos* is rendered as *ghāya* in Books 1 and 2; as *tamām* and *ākhir* in Books 3 and 4; and as *ākhir*, *intihāʾ*, *ghāya* and *inqiḍāʾ* in Books 5-8. The Arabic paraphrases of Philoponus' commentary on the *Physics* seem to show that Isḥāq wanted to reserve *kamāl* for *entelekheia*, *tamām* for *teleiotês*, and *ghāya* for *telos*. Philoponus' views are paraphrased in Arabic and attributed to "ḥ" (which the editor, Badawī, takes to be shorthand for Yaḥyā al-Naḥwī, i.e., John Philoponus) at *aṭ-Ṭabīᶜa*, 171,8-13: "He (i.e., Aristotle) means by *kamāl*

The upshot is that given Isḥāq's preference for *istikmāl*, *kamāl*, and *ghāya* in his *Physics* translation; given the use of *istikmāl* for *entelekheia* and *kamāl* for *teleiotês* in the Arabic version of Themistius' *Paraphrase of the De Anima*, as can be seen in Table 3; and finally, given the appearance of *istikmāl* and *kamāl* in the lemmata contained in Avicenna's *Marginal Notes on Aristotle's De Anima*, which can also be seen in Table 3; the evidence supports either a strong hypothesis or a weak hypothesis regarding Isḥāq's revised version of the *De Anima*. The strong hypothesis is that Isḥāq's final, revised version of the *De Anima* is nothing other than the Arabic version of Themistius' *Paraphrase*. The weak hypothesis is that Isḥāq's final, revised version is not the Arabic version of Themistius' *Paraphrase*, but the one which exists in the majority of Avicenna's lemmata, the similarity in terminology between it and the Arabic Themistius being nothing other than a manifestation of the new way *entelekheia* was being translated during the fourth and fifth stages.

Other pieces of evidence suggest that the progression from *tamām* to *istikmāl* in the translation of *entelekheia* may have had a number of intermediate stages, or, perhaps better, may have had an intermediate period of uncertainty, lasting from the end of the second stage to the beginning of the fourth stage, from about 850 to 900, during which a number of possible alternative translations of *entelekheia* contended with each other, with *istikmāl* eventually emerging as the victor. The great translator Ḥunayn ibn Isḥāq, responsible above all for the many translations of Galen's works into Arabic, provides some circumstantial evidence of this shift: in his own work, the *Masā'il*, Ḥunayn used the hendiadys *tāmm kāmil* as well as the new *istikmāl*.[14]

The move from *t-m-m* to *k-m-l* can also be detected in the *Essay on the Definitions and Descriptions of Things*, attributed to al-Kindī, where two versions of the Aristotelian definition of the soul are offered, with the term *tamāmiyya* used to render *entelekheia* in the first and *istikmāl* in the second.[15] Assuming that al-Kindī was in fact the author of that work, one translator in al-Kindī's circle may have suggested, with *teleiotês* in mind, that al-Kindī use

in this sense the passage from what is potential to what is actual, not the state of completeness (*lā t-tamām*) .... *Kamāl* is of two types: initial and final. The final consists of the termination of what is potential [once it has arrived] at the [state of being] actual. The first consists in the procession towards (*at-taṭarruq ilā*) the final perfection, potentiality being preserved with it; this [first *kamāl*] is motion"; and at 187,2-3: "Because perfection (*al-kamāl*) applies to the end (*al-ghāya*) as well as to the passage to it (i.e., to the end, *as-sulūk ilayhā*)". Alternatively, the *Fihrist* claims that it was Qusṭā, not Isḥāq, who translated the first four books of Philoponus' *Physics* commentary, so the quotations above could be Qusṭā's own work, or perhaps even Yaḥyā b. ᶜAdī's revision of Qusṭā's translation of Philoponus. In any case, the quotations above do seem to show an early-tenth-century desire to avoid conflating the ideas of *entelekheia*, *telos* and *teleiotês*.

14 *mithla l-afāᶜili t-tāmmati l-kāmilati ... al-fiᶜlu l-mustakmilu*: Ḥunayn ibn Isḥāq, *al-Masā'il fī ṭ-ṭibb li-l-mutaᶜallimīn*, 65,1-2. cf. also Muḥammad b. Zakariyā ar-Rāzī's (d. ca. 930) pairing of *tāmm* and *kāmil* in his description of how the fetus leaves the womb when it is *tāmm aṣ-ṣūra* and *kāmil al-maᶜnā*: *Maqāla fī-mā baᶜda ṭ-ṭabīᶜa*, 127,5-6.

15 (Ps.-?)al-Kindī, *R. fī ḥudūd al-ashyā' wa-rusūmihā*, 113,7-8. On al-Kindī's debt to the *Uthūlūjiyā*, see now Adamson 2000.

tamāmiyya to define the soul, the idea being that the adjective *tāmm* could be derived from the abstract noun *tamāmiyya* just as easily as it could be derived from *tamām*, in the same way that *teleion* could be derived from *teleiotês* as well as from *telos*. Another translator in al-Kindī's circle may then have suggested that he use the new term *istikmāl* as an alternative.

The shift from *t-m-m* to *k-m-l* is also apparent in Qusṭā b. Lūqā's translation of Ps.-Plutarch's *Opinions About Natural Philosophy Which Philosophers Agree On*, where change is defined in the Aristotelian way with *entelekheia* again appearing as *tamāmiyya*; yet in his rendering of the Aristotelian definition of the soul, Qusṭā used *kamāl*.[16] Qusṭā's use of *kamāl* to render *entelekheia* in the Aristotelian definition of the soul is mirrored in a contemporaneous source from the Jābirean corpus (ca. 900), the *Kitāb al-ḥudūd*.[17] Qusṭā's translation also seems to have been the source for Saᶜdiyā (d. 942) and al-Masᶜūdī (d. ca. 953), who list the Aristotelian definition of the soul and use *kamāl*.[18] A final piece of evidence supports the hypothesis that Isḥāq's *istikmāl* supplanted Qusṭā's *kamāl* in the first quarter of the tenth century as the standard translation of *entelekheia*, as a result of its presence in what appears to be the final, revised translation of the *De Anima* by Isḥāq b. Ḥunayn: in his *Essay in Response to Questions Asked*, al-Fārābī defines the soul in the Aristotelian manner but uses the term *istikmāl*, not *kamāl*.[19] The related uncertainty over whether *tamām* or *ghāya* was a better translation of *telos* (and, correspondingly, whether *al-ᶜillatu t-tamāmiyyatu/as-sababu t-tamāmiyyu* or *al-ᶜillatu l-ghāʾiyyatu/as-sababu l-ghāʾiyyu* was a better translation of *to aition telikon*, "final cause"), can be seen as early as Ibn al-Biṭrīq's second-stage translation of the late-antique *De Anima* paraphrase mentioned earlier.[20]

The result of all this is that in his *Physics* translation, and in what appears to be his later *De Anima* translation, Isḥāq used *kamāl* or *istikmāl* to render *entelekheia*, and *ghāya* to render *telos*, in an attempt to avoid his predecessors' overuse of *tamām*. Despite Isḥāq's best efforts, however, a number of the Greek philosophical texts which were to have the greatest impact on Avicenna's

[16] motion is a *tamāmiyya*: (Ps.-)Plutarch, *Fī l-ārāʾ aṭ-ṭabīᶜiyya allatī tarḍā bihā l-falāsifa*, 120,6-7 (= Daiber, *Aetius Arabus*, 21,4); the soul is a *kamāl*: (Ps.-)Plutarch, *Fī l-ārāʾ*, 157,2-4 (= Daiber, *Aetius Arabus*, 50,12-13).

[17] Jābir, *K. al-ḥudūd*, 113,3-7.

[18] Saᶜdiyā, *K. al-āmānāt wa-l-iᶜtiqādāt*, 189,11; al-Masᶜūdī, *Murūj adh-dhahab wa-maᶜādin al-jawhar*, 52, 362,10.

[19] *ḥadda Arisṭū n-nafsa fa-qāla innahā istikmālun awwalu li-jismin ṭabīᶜiyyin āliyyin dhī ḥayātin bi-l-quwwati*: al-Fārābī, *R. fī jawāb masāʾil suʾila ᶜanhā*, 99,1-2.

[20] At Anonymous, *Paraphrase of the De Anima*, 185,7-8 (= [Ps.-]Isḥāq b. Ḥunayn, *K. an-nafs*, 129,23-24), Aristotle investigates what *al-ᶜillatu l-ghāʾiyya* of nourishment is. Yet at Anonymous, *Paraphrase of the De Anima*, 193,3-4 (= [Ps.-]Isḥāq b. Ḥunayn, *K. an-nafs*, 132,12-13), the final cause of locomotion is listed as [*al-ᶜillatu t-*]*tamāmiyya*. In the *Commentary* (*ad* 415b8), Ibn al-Biṭrīq uses *ᶜillatun tamāmiyyatun* and *ᶜillatun ghāʾiyyatun* within three lines of each other: Anonymous, *Commentary on the De Anima* 225,1-10 (= [Ps.-]Isḥāq b. Ḥunayn, *K. an-nafs*, 142,12-19).

philosophy – the Arabic version of Aristotle's *Metaphysics* above all – fit squarely in the second-stage tendency to conflate the concepts of actuality and final causation by using *t-m-m* to render Aristotle's *entelekheia* and *telos* as well as the commentators' *telikon*. What is more, as a result of the third- and fourth-stage attempts to restrict the use of *t-m-m* to the instances of *teleiotês* in the commentaries on the *Physics* and the *De Anima*, the Neoplatonic concept of *teleiotês* as final cause came into circulation and appeared to be consistent with the earlier translators' use of *t-m-m* to render both *entelekheia* and *telos*. And given that Avicenna's main discussions of causality in general, and final causality in particular, are contained in his metaphysical rather than natural-philosophical works – unlike Aristotle's canonical discussions of causation, which are more prominent in the *Physics* than in the *Metaphysics* – the Arabic *Metaphysics*' use of *t-m-m* to render both *entelekheia* and *telos* provided even greater momentum pushing Avicenna in the direction of seeing actuality or perfection as being related to its effect as a final cause.

Just as important is the fact that the early translators' uses of *t-m-m* had infiltrated many of the discussions of causation and cosmology of Avicenna's predecessors al-Kindī, the Ikhwān aṣ-Ṣafā᾿ and al-Fārābī, the last of whom played an important role in shaping Avicenna's thought on this subject. In discussions of causation, for example, al-Kindī lists the final cause as *al-ᶜillatu t-tamāmiyyatu* in his *On First Philosophy*, a practice echoed in the *Epistles* of the Ikhwān aṣ-Ṣafā and in the Jābirean text *The Book of Research*.[21] In discussions of cosmology, al-Kindī describes God in the title of one work as the perfect agent (*al-fāᶜilu t-tāmmu*), though in that same work he uses *ghāya* rather than *tamām* to assert that God is the end of every other cause (*huwa ghāyatu kulli ᶜillatin*); and in his *On First Philosophy* al-Kindī argues that the eternal – which by his reckoning referred only to God – is necessarily perfect (*fa-l-azaliyyu tāmmun iḍṭirāran*), an echo of which can again be found in the Jābirean text *The Book of Research*.[22] Al-Kindī also uses *naqṣ* and *tamām* to label the contraries between which an *istiḥāla* (*alloiôsis*) or *taghayyur* (*metabolê*) occurs, in contrast to the more Peripatetic *quwwa* and *fiᶜl*, a sign that thinkers such as al-Kindī were beginning to investigate the nature of the parallelism between the Aristotelian potentiality/actuality distinction and the deficiency/perfection distinction, an Arabic variant of the disposition/perfection distinction introduced by Alexander and promoted by the Neoplatonists.[23]

[21] al-Kindī, *Fī l-falsafat al-ūlā*, 11,8.11 (the final cause is also listed at 11,4 as *mutammima*, which seems to be a sign of the second-stage "Alexander" translations); Ikhwān aṣ-Ṣafā᾿, *Rasā᾿il*, Vol. 2, 79,15-17; 89,9-10; 115,23-24; 155,6-7; 3, 358,18 and 359,4-6 (the Ikhwān also seem to use *tāmm* and *kāmil* interchangeably at Vol. 3, 371,2 and 379,6.11-12); Jābir, *K. al-baḥth*, 525,10.

[22] al-Kindī, *Risālat al-Kindī fī l-fāᶜil al-ḥaqq al-awwal at-tāmm wa-l-fāᶜil an-nāqiṣ alladhī huwa bi-l-majāz*, 169,6-7; and *Fī l-falsafat al-ūlā*, 29,4. Jābir, *K. al-baḥth*, 524,16-525,7 (admittedly, this passage is a bit murky).

[23] al-Kindī, *K. fī l-falsafat al-ūlā*, 27,24-29,4; and *Risālat al-Kindī ilā Aḥmad b. al-Muᶜtaṣim fī l-ibāna ᶜan sujūd al-jirm al-aqṣā wa-ṭāᶜatihi li-llāh ᶜazza wa-jalla*, 179,11-23.

Although al-Fārābī uses Qusṭā's *kamāl* and Isḥāq's *istikmāl* and *ghāya*, and is clearly the product of the more purely Aristotelian fourth and fifth stages of the translation movement, the influence of the more Neoplatonic second-stage translations of the al-Kindī circle is also obvious in his writings, particularly in his use of *tāmm* and *nāqiṣ* to describe two contrary types of existence. As far as his influence on Avicenna is concerned, the most important instance of al-Fārābī's use of *tāmm* in this metaphysical way occurs in al-Fārābī's *On the Philosopher's* (i.e., Aristotle's) *Aims* [lit., *Scopes*] *in Each Book of the Treatise Designated by Letters* (i.e., the *Metaphysics*), the little book which – according to Avicenna's autobiography – helped Avicenna move to a higher stage of understanding what Aristotle's *Metaphysics* was all about. In his book al-Fārābī says that metaphysics, or universal science, examines things which are common to all beings, such as existence (*al-wujūd*) and oneness (*al-waḥda*), as well as the different types (*anwā*ᶜ) and concomitant properties (*lawāḥiq*) of existence and oneness, such as priority and posteriority (*at-taqaddum wa-t-ta*ᵓ*akhkhur*), potentiality and actuality (*al-quwwa wa-l-fi*ᶜ*l*), and the perfect and the deficient (*wa-t-tāmm wa-n-nāqiṣ*).[24]

It is slightly confusing that al-Fārābī should use the substantive adjectives *tāmm* and *nāqiṣ*, and not *tamām* and *naqṣ* (or *naqṣān*), the nouns most parallel to *taqaddum* and *ta*ᵓ*akhkhur*, *quwwa* and *fi*ᶜ*l*; perhaps those last four substantives were understood as *lawāḥiq*, "concomitant properties" of *existence*, while the substantive adjectives *at-tāmm* and *an-nāqiṣ* were meant to be understood as *anwā*ᶜ, "types" or "species" of *existent*. An awareness of the problem of delineating the precise nature of the parallelism between the actuality (*al-fi*ᶜ*l*)/potentiality (*al-quwwa*) distinction on the one hand, and the perfect (*at-tāmm*)/deficient (*an-nāqiṣ*) distinction on the other, is more apparent in al-Fārābī than it was in al-Kindī. In a sense, al-Fārābī's efforts to reconcile the two pairs of concepts, the former Aristotelian and the latter Neoplatonic, are very much in the tradition of the Ammonian synthesis.[25]

In view of the fact that actuality (*al-fi*ᶜ*l*) is tied to form (*aṣ-ṣūra*) (since a thing is in actuality only when it possesses its form), while potentiality (*al-quwwa*) is tied to matter (*al-mādda*) (since a thing is in potentiality when it only possesses its matter), al-Fārābī asserts that being in actuality is more perfect in respect of existence (*akmalu wujūdan*) than being in potentiality.[26] Al-Fārābī appeals to the criterion of causation to defend this assertion: the matter

[24] al-Fārābī, *Maqāla ... fī aghrāḍ al-ḥakīm fī kulli maqālatin min al-kitāb al-mawsūm bi-l-ḥurūf*, 35,8-11.

[25] That al-Fārābī saw himself as part of the tradition of the Ammonian synthesis is evident throughout his treatise *On the Harmony between the Opinions of the Two Philosophers, Plato the Divine and Aristotle*, but particularly in his claim that Ammonius' arguments about God's being both an efficient and final cause were so well known that they did not require citation: *K. al-jam*ᶜ *bayna ra*ᵓ*yay al-ḥakīmayni Aflāṭūn al-ilāhī wa-Arisṭūṭālīs*, 24,24-25,1.

[26] al-Fārābī, *K. ārā*ᵓ *ahl al-madīnat al-fāḍila*, 12, 64,9-13; *K. as-siyāsat al-madaniyyat al-mulaqqab bi-Mabādi*ᵓ *al-mawjūdāt*, 38,10 and 39,1-3; and *R. fī al-*ᶜ*aql*, 23,1-8.

exists only in order that the form which inheres in it may exist, but in no sense is the form for the sake of the matter.[27] In other words, the actual is a more perfect type of existent than the potential because a thing which is in actuality is a cause, while a thing which is in potentiality is not; and because causes are better than effects, a thing which is in actuality is more perfect and more excellent than a thing which is in potentiality. Al-Fārābī's use of causality as the distinguishing feature of perfection and the perfect is of course a familiar Neoplatonic move. But al-Fārābī not only follows the Neoplatonists' move to causation here. He pushes the Ammonian synthesis forward by attempting to incorporate more fully the Neoplatonists' distinction between first and second perfections into Aristotle's distinction between first and second actualities.

Al-Fārābī's distinction between first and second perfections – actually, the terms he uses are Themistius', "initial" (*awwal*) and "ultimate" (*akhīr*) – rests on the criterion of causation, just as Proclus' distinction had done. And in one passage in his *Siyāsa madaniyya* al-Fārābī clearly echoes Proclus' distinction, saying that terms signifying perfection (*kamāl*) and excellence (*faḍīla*) are divided into those that point to some characteristic which the thing in question has in and of itself, such as "existent" and "one"; while others point to some characteristic which the thing has in relation to something else other than it, such as "just" and "generous".[28]

However, al-Fārābī seems to have Aristotle's distinction between first and second *entelekheiai* in mind when in other passages he departs subtly from Proclus' distinction. Proclus had said that a first perfection referred to a thing's perfection when the thing was viewed in and of itself, and that a second perfection referred to a thing's perfection when the thing was viewed as a cause of something else. Al-Fārābī asserts, however, that a thing's initial perfection refers to the state something is in when what normally would issue as an effect from it *does not do so*. The ultimate perfection, on the other hand, refers to the state the thing is in when what normally would issue from it as an effect in fact *does so*.

The criterion of causation is present in both distinctions, but it is applied differently in each. For Proclus, something to which the term "first perfection" is correctly applied may well be a cause – in fact, it is certainly a cause – but it is not viewed *qua* cause. Only something to which the term "second perfection" is correctly applied is viewed *qua* cause. Al-Fārābī, on the other hand, asserts that something which is in a state of first perfection is not, in fact, a cause at all: no effect issues from it. By contrast, something which is in a state of second perfection is a cause: the effects that normally issue from it cannot help but issue from it. In short, both distinctions rest on the criterion of causation, but whereas for Proclus the criterion of causation is understood as referring to

[27] al-Fārābī, *K. as-siyāsat al-madaniyya*, 36,11-12; 38,12; and 39,5.
[28] al-Fārābī, *K. as-siyāsat al-madaniyya*, 49,12-15.

whether or not a thing *is viewed as the cause of some effect*, al-Fārābī held that the criterion of causation referred to whether or not a thing *is in fact the cause of some effect*. That al-Fārābī had Aristotle's distinction between first and second *entelekheiai* in mind seems clear from the fact that he uses one of Aristotle's *De Anima* examples – being asleep and being awake – to illustrate what he means. That he also had the *Physics* distinction in mind seems clear from the fact that in his distinction he uses the terms that Themistius invented – *prôtê/awwal* and *hustatê/akhīr* – in order to distinguish between the state of change and the state of having changed.[29]

What I am getting at is that al-Fārābī's distinction between first and second perfections, based on the criterion of not-being-a-cause/being-a-cause, seems intended to reconcile not only the Aristotelian distinction with the Neoplatonic distinction, but also to reconcile the *Physics* distinction with the *De Anima* distinction. Al-Fārābī's reasoning seems to proceed along the following lines. The state of being changed into something actual (the first *entelekheia* of the *Physics* commentators) retains some potentiality, and is therefore not the cause of anything; possessing the capability to perform a function (the *De Anima*'s first *entelekheia*) is an inactive state, and is therefore not the cause of anything; a thing taken in and of itself (Proclus' first *teleiotês*) is not (viewed as) the cause of anything. Second perfections are slightly trickier. The state of having changed into something actual (the second *entelekheia* of the *Physics* commentators) is the final cause of the change; contemplating (the *De Anima*'s second *entelekheia*) is the final cause of the acquisition of knowledge; and a thing's perfection taken in relation to a lower thing (Proclus' second *teleiotês*) is the final cause of that lower thing, at least when both cause and effect are viewed as elements of reversion.

Al-Fārābī's attempt to merge the three distinctions into one is interesting, and it certainly earns him a place of honor in the Ammonian synthesis, but what interests me more is the cosmological implication of his attempted reconciliation, an implication which throws into stark relief the underlying difference between his distinction and that of Proclus. According to al-Fārābī's way of distinguishing first and second perfections, the eternal things above the sphere of the moon will only ever be in a state of second perfection: they are always actual, and as a result they cannot help but cause their effects.[30] By contrast, sublunary things down here in the world of generation and destruction are sometimes in a state of second perfection, when they are actual and thus are causes; while at other times they are in a state of first perfection, when they are potential and thus are not causes.

[29] al-Fārābī, *K. ārā' ahl al-madīnat al-fāḍila*, 5, 49,5-8; 23, 105,9-11; 24, 108,7-8; *K. as-siyāsat al-madaniyya*, 64,15-66,8.
[30] al-Fārābī, *R. fī al-ʿaql*, 32,8-33,3.

For Proclus, however, it was a thing's first perfection – its active turning inwards and (thereby) upwards towards self-perfection – which made it a cause of other things; which created the causality, in other words, of its second perfection. Proclus' superlunary beings were *primarily* engaged in seeking their first perfection, in pursuing their inward and upward *epistrophê*, which is why, of course, Proclus referred to it as a first, or primary, perfection. Their second perfection, consisting in their providence towards things below them – their causation of them, in fact – is almost a by-product of their more primary act of reversion. Al-Fārābī seems to have this Neoplatonic axiom in mind when he insists that superlunary things – and particularly God – do not derive any perfection from their causation of things below them.[31] But if this is the case, in what sense will superlunary entities be in a state of perfection? Either they will be in a state of first perfection, which according to al-Fārābī means that they will not in fact be causing their effects, which is impossible; or they will be in a state of second perfection, in which case they will in fact be causing their effects. But their being in a state of second perfection derives from their being causes of effects, which in turn contradicts al-Fārābī's assertion that the higher derives no perfection from its causation of the lower. Al-Fārābī is forced to conclude that God's act of self-substantiation – Proclus' first perfection – is what earns Him the attribution of perfection; and that His causation of things below Him is nothing more than a consequence and concomitant (*tābiᶜatan wa-lāḥiqatan*) of His own, self-substantiating perfection.[32]

Despite its problems, al-Fārābī's distinction had some influence on Avicenna's cosmology, as I shall show in Chapters 6 and 11. For now, what is important is al-Fārābī's inference that because contingent, sublunary things are sometimes in a state of first perfection and other times in a state of second perfection, since they are sometimes not causing and other times causing, their existence is less perfect than that of superlunary things, which are always in a state of second perfection and thus are always causing. Al-Fārābī's clear implication is that all eternal things – spheres, souls, intellects and God – can be characterized as being in a state of perfection, and particularly second perfection, an implication which, as discussed immediately above, involved him in a serious contradiction.[33]

Leaving that problem aside, however, how is one supposed to solve the further problem of distinguishing between the various eternal things? For al-Kindī this was not a problem, since there were no eternal things other than God. Al-Fārābī, on the other hand, faced a dilemma; most of the time he said simply that God is the most perfect with respect of existence, that the intellects were existentially less perfect than God, that the souls were existentially less perfect than the

[31] al-Fārābī, *K. ārāʾ ahl al-madīnat al-fāḍila*, 7, 55,1-56,8 (and implied at 1, 38,12-13).
[32] al-Fārābī, *K. as-siyāsat al-madaniyya*, 47,14-50,7.
[33] al-Fārābī, *Sharḥ li-kitāb Arisṭūṭālīs fī al-ᶜibāra*, 193,13-15 (*ad* 23a21-26); *K. ārāʾ ahl al-madīnat al-fāḍila*, 2, 40,2-10; *K. as-siyāsat al-madaniyya*, 64,15-66,8.

intellects, and so on.[34] But if all superlunary things satisfy the criterion of necessary causation; if all superlunary things cannot help but cause their effects; and if causation is the distinguishing mark of existential perfection; how then will God be *more* perfect than an intellect or a soul or a sphere? God is a cause, an intellect is a cause, a soul is a cause and a sphere is a cause; things which are causes are perfect; therefore God, the intellects, the souls and the spheres are perfect. Again, how is God *more* perfect than an intellect?

Sometimes al-Fārābī says that the answer lies in God's lack of any potentiality and causedness whatsoever.[35] But if this is the case, and the intellects, souls and spheres possess some potentiality or causedness, they will not satisfy al-Fārābī's own criterion of being in a state of perfection. Other times, again appealing to Proclus' concept of first *teleiotês*, al-Fārābī explains that God's self-causation or self-substantiation (*tajawhur*) is more perfect than his causation of others, and hence primary to Him. Al-Fārābī's implication is that since only in God is self-causation prior to the causation of others, God's existence is more perfect – in the sense of more self-sufficient – than other existences.[36]

Ultimately al-Fārābī was stumped by the problem of degrees of perfection. Should perfection be understood univocally, as referring to a single attribute which sublunary things, superlunary things and God all possess? Or should perfection be understood equivocally, as referring to different attributes, one of which sublunary things possess, another of which superlunary things possess, and a final one which God only possesses? As I shall show in Chapter 10, Avicenna grew so frustrated by the problem, and was so dissatisfied with his attempted solution, that he ended up deciding to side-step perfection entirely.

[34] *K. ārā' ahl al-madīnat al-fāḍila*, 5, 48,4-5; and 9, 59,3-11; *K. as-siyāsat al-madaniyya*, 34,1-2; 40,3-8; 42,15; 49,15-50,7; 50,8-11; 51,7-52,4; 53,1-10.

[35] al-Fārābī, *K. ārā' ahl al-madīnat al-fāḍila*, 1, 37,6-38,13.

[36] al-Fārābī, *K. as-siyāsat al-madaniyya*, 47,11-49,11.

6. Avicenna on Perfection and the Soul
The Issue of Separability

In this and subsequent chapters I shall show how several of the most important elements of Avicenna's psychology and cosmology can be better understood when they are seen to be shaped by the doctrinal presuppositions of the Ammonian synthesis as well as by the word choices of the early Greco-Arabic translators. In other words, the Ammonian synthesis provided the philosophical momentum, and the early Greco-Arabic translations provided the lexical momentum, which together propelled Avicenna towards holding that the ideas of actuality and perfection on the one hand, and of the final cause on the other, were at least mutually implicative, if not identical.

Like earlier philosophers of the Ammonian synthesis, Avicenna struggled to find the best way to reconcile Aristotle's use of perfection in his definition of the soul with the Neoplatonists' broader understanding of perfection as signifying superiority in the hierarchy of being, and hence causation. And like earlier philosophers of the Ammonian synthesis, Avicenna aggressively interpreted a number of other Aristotelian concepts and distinctions in order to use them as tools to fashion a new synthesis. But unlike late-antique Greek thinkers such as Ammonius and Philoponus, Avicenna was helped along by the early Greco-Arabic translations, and particularly by the translations of the *Metaphysics* and the *Uthūlūjiyā*, which, by using the same Arabic root – *t-m-m* – to render the Greek *entelekheia*, *teleiotês* and *telos*, did part of the job for him.

One of the lessons which I hope will be drawn from the preceding chapters is that the passage of Neoplatonic ideas from Greek into Arabic seems to have been diffuse rather than concentrated, sieve-like rather than funnel-like. What I mean is that important Neoplatonic ideas found their way to thinkers such as Avicenna on board a large number of different vehicles, particularly the Aristotle-commentaries by philosophers such as Syrianus, Ammonius, Philoponus, Simplicius and Olympiodorus (the Arabic translations of which – though only a few now appear to be extant – are attested to in the catalogues of Ibn an-Nadīm, Ibn al-Qiftī and Ibn Abī Uṣaybiʿa); and that these Neoplatonic ideas were not all stuffed into the two or three mislabeled vehicles which we do have at hand: the Plotinian *Theology of Aristotle*, the Proclan *Liber de causis* and the works of pseudo-Alexander. The fact that Avicenna received important elements of Aristotelianism already Neoplatonized in the commentaries, is particularly important given how uncomfortable he seems to have been with many of the ideas expressed in the *Uthūlūjiyā*.[1] This will become most apparent later on in

[1] In fact, there is some evidence, based on a sentence in a letter to one of his disciples, Kiyā, in which Avicenna describes the scope of his *K. al-inṣāf* (*wa-awḍaḥtu sharḥa l-mawāḍiʿi l-mushkilati fī l-fuṣūṣi ilā ākhiri Uthūlūjiyā ʿalā mā fī Uthūlūjiyā mina l-maṭʿani*: *R. ilā Kiyā*, 121,19-20), that

this chapter, where I shall show that Avicenna's position on the soul and its relationship with the body owes much more to the Aristotle-commentator Philoponus than it does to Plotinus or Proclus. In Chapter 10, Avicenna will also be shown to owe a great deal to the Aristotle-commentators Syrianus, Ammonius and Asclepius, particularly with regard to the issue of God's being both an efficient and final cause. Where Avicenna does appear to borrow directly from the Arabic Plotinus and Proclus is in his use of the phrase "above perfection" (*fawqa t-tamām*) to describe God.

How does Avicenna use perfection to define the soul? Somewhat surprisingly, Avicenna does not use *istikmāl*, the term cited in the lemmata of his *Marginal Notes on Aristotle's De Anima* – and which, as I discussed above, is probably the term Isḥāq b. Ḥunayn employed to render *entelekheia* in his revised translation of the *De Anima* – opting instead for Qusṭā's *kamāl*. Avicenna uses *kamāl* to define the soul in two ways, the first as part of the standard Aristotelian definition, the second as part of his own modified definition, in which the various types of soul or faculties of soul are defined in a series. The standard Aristotelian definition appears in the *On the Soul* (*Fī n-nafs*) section of the *Natural Philosophy* (*Ṭabīʿiyyāt*) part of his great *summa*, the *Book of Healing* (*Kitāb ash-shifāʾ*):

L18

Ibn Sīnā, *Kitāb ash-shifāʾ/Ṭabīʿiyyāt (6): Fī n-nafs* 1.1, 12,6-8
Avicenna, *Liber de anima seu sextus de naturalibus I-III*, 29,61-63
So the soul which we are defining is a first perfection of a natural instrumental body [which the soul uses] to perform the activities of living [*fa-n-nafsu llatī naḥudduhā hiya kamālun awwalu li-jismin ṭabīʿiyyin āliyyin lahu an yafʿala afʿāla l-ḥayāti* = *Ideo anima quam invenimus in animali et in vegetabili est perfectio prima corporis naturalis instrumentalis habentis opera vitae*].[2]

This definition is repeated almost exactly in Avicenna's *Investigation of the Soul's Faculties* (*Mabḥath ʿani l-quwā n-nafsāniyya*), in his *Essay on the Soul, its Survival and its Reversion* (*Risāla fī n-nafs wa-baqāʾihā wa-*

Avicenna may have realized that the *Uthūlūjiyā* was wrongly attributed to Aristotle. Gutas 1988, 63-64 (following Kraus 1942, 272-73, n.3), translates *ʿalā mā fī Uthūlūjiyā mina l-maṭʿani* as "despite the fact that the *Theologia* is somewhat suspect", thus giving Avicenna credit for sensing its false provenance. Zimmermann 1986, 184, translates the sentence "for all one may find to object to in the *Uthūlūjiyā*", maintaining that the sentence only refers to what he calls the "chaotic scattiness" of the work, not its hazy provenance. In any case it seems absolutely clear that Avicenna was uncomfortable philosophically, if not philologically, with parts of the *Uthūlūjiyā*, so the question of its influence on him must be answered on a case-by-case basis.

[2] On the reception of Avicenna's definition of the soul by medieval Latin thinkers see now Hasse 2000, 236. Apart from my detailed discussion in Chapter 8 of the Latin translation of L36, Latinists can consult van Riet's notes for explanations of the Latin translation's divergences from the Arabic in this and other passages.

ma^cādihā), in his *Book of Definitions* (*Kitāb al-ḥudūd*), and in his *Discussions* (*al-Mubāḥathāt*); and in an abbreviated and less formal way, in the *Demonstration* (*al-Burhān*) section of the *Logic* (*Manṭiq*) part of his *Shifā*ʾ.[3]

Avicenna's slightly modified version appears in a later chapter of the *Fī n-nafs* of the *Shifā*ʾ, in the *Risāla fī n-nafs wa-baqā*ʾ*ihā wa-ma*ʿ*ādihā*, and in the *Salvation* (*Kitāb an-najāt*):

L19

Ibn Sīnā, *Kitāb an-najāt*, 258,2-10

> The soul is, as it were, a single genus divisible into three parts. The first part is the vegetative soul; it is the first perfection of a natural body possessing organs in so far as it reproduces, grows, and nourishes itself .... The second part is the animal soul; it is the first perfection of a natural body possessing organs in so far as it perceives particular things and moves intentionally. The third part is the human soul; it is the first perfection of a natural body possessing organs in so far as it performs activities that come about as a result of deliberate choice and rational inference, and in so far as it perceives universal things.[4]

Two questions immediately arise. First, why did Avicenna use *kamāl* instead of *istikmāl*, which was the term contained in the Arabic text of Aristotle which he commented on? Second, how does the first way of defining the soul, as articulated in L18, relate to the second, as articulated in L19?

To answer the first question, two possibilities present themselves. The first is that Avicenna wanted to use the same term – *kamāl* – which appeared in Isḥāq's translation of the definition of change in *Physics* 3.1. But given that it is unlikely that Avicenna knew that the same Greek term – *entelekheia* – was used in the *Physics* 3.1 definition of change and in the *De Anima* 2.1 definition of the soul, there is no reason why Avicenna should want to give himself the same headache – using the same term to define change and the soul – which had so plagued the Greek commentators Alexander and Themistius. It seems instead that in his uses of *kamāl* and *istikmāl* Avicenna was trying to make a distinction between the type of perfection – *istikmāl* – which resulted from non-kinetic transitions such as sensation and intellection (that is, transitions that involve the presence or absence of a relation); and the type of perfection – *kamāl* – which either resulted from kinetic changes and alterations (the soul, for example) or

[3] Ibn Sīnā, *Mabḥath* ʿ*ani l-quwā n-nafsāniyya*, 2, 153,13; *R. fī n-nafs wa-baqā*ʾ*ihā wa-ma*ʿ*ādihā*, 1, 56,4; *K. al-ḥudūd*, 14,2-3; *al-Mubāḥathāt*, 129,11 (= *Mubāḥatha* 5, #343); *K. ash-shifā*ʾ*/Manṭiq (5): al-Burhān* 2.9, 181,11-12.

[4] Ibn Sīnā, *K. ash-shifā*ʾ*/Ṭabī*ʿ*iyyāt (6): Fī n-nafs* 1.5, 39,13-40,7; *R. fī n-nafs wa-baqā*ʾ*ihā wa-ma*ʿ*ādihā* 2, 57,3-9.

which described the kinetic change or alteration itself (change, for example).[5] And indeed, Avicenna also uses *kamāl*, not *istikmāl*, to define motion:

L20

Ibn Sīnā, *Kitāb ash-shifāʾ/Ṭabīʿiyyāt (1): as-Samāʿ aṭ-ṭabīʿī* 2.1, 83,5

> So motion is a first perfection of what is potential in so far as it is what is potential [*fa-l-ḥarakatu hiya kamālun awwalu li-mā huwa bi-l-quwwati min jihati mā huwa bi-l-quwwati*].[6]

In trying to reserve *istikmāl* for non-kinetic transitions such as sensation and intellection Avicenna follows the lead of the Arabic version of Alexander's *De Intellectu,* which employs *istikmāl* in this way.[7]

The second question ("How does the first way of defining the soul, as articulated in L18, relate to the second, as articulated in L19?") will take a little longer to answer. I believe that Avicenna's use of perfection in both his standard, Aristotelian definition of the soul as well as in one that appealed to the different capacities or faculties represented by each type of soul – vegetative, animal or human – is a sign of the tectonic shift that had taken place as a result of the new, Neoplatonic conception of perfection. What I mean is that Avicenna is pulled in two directions: by Aristotle's use of perfection to define the soul, and by the Neoplatonists' use of perfection to describe how beings which are higher in the cosmic hierarchy relate to beings which are lower in the manner that causes relate to effects.

Avicenna wants to use the more general Neoplatonic concept of perfection to describe how the higher faculties of the soul relate as causes to the lower ones, while at the same time retaining the more specific Aristotelian use of perfection to describe the relation of the soul as a whole to the body. The tension in Avicenna's work between these two competing tendencies becomes more apparent in two further clusters of discussions: one on the problem of how form and perfection are related, the other on how first and second perfections are

[5] Ibn Sīnā, *K. ash-shifāʾ/Ṭabīʿiyyāt (6): Fī n-nafs* 2.2, 66,15-17. In the *Metaphysics* (*Ilāhiyyāt*) of the *Shifāʾ*, Avicenna allows that *istikmāl* can cover changes as well as non-kinetic transitions when he takes Aristotle to task for not having made clear enough that an *istikmāl* can either be instantaneous (*dufʿatan*), as is the case with non-kinetic transitions such as "not-knowing to knowing", or can proceed over time (*sālikan*), as is the case with the transition from "boy to man": *K. ash-shifāʾ/Ilāhiyyāt (2)* 8.1, 332,15-18 and 333,1-11.

[6] This formulation is repeated, with minor variations, at *K. an-najāt 2: Ṭabīʿiyyāt*, 170,7-14, and *K. al-hidāya* 2.1, 138,1. On Avicenna's definition of motion see Haschmi 1956; Hasnawi 1998; and now Hasnawi 2001. On the medieval Latin translations of Avicenna's (and Aristotle's) definitions of motion see the classic treatment of Maier 1958a (Avicenna's theory is treated at 12-20). The "Marinus" Latin translation of this passage reads *unde motus est perfectio prima eius quod est in potentia secundum quod est in potentia*, according to Jules Janssens, who is currently preparing an edition of that text. Maier appears to follow a later translation.

[7] Alexander, *R. fī al-ʿaql ʿalā raʾy Arisṭūṭālīs*, 33,18-20; 38,2-3 (where *kamila* is used for the exercise of the capability to walk, and *istakmala* is used for the exercise of the capability to think); and 39,15-17.

distinguished. Once those problems have been dealt with, the question of how the soul relates to the body as cause to effect can be treated properly; and once we answer that question, we can better understand Avicenna's position on the thorny issue of the separability or inseparability of the soul.

In some respects Avicenna follows earlier philosophers of the Ammonian synthesis in his attempts to delineate the precise relationship between form and perfection. Philoponus, as I showed above, held that while *entelekheia* and *eidos* may be identical in the sense that both refer to form as shape as well as form as substance, *teleiotês* refers only to the type of form – form as substance, not form as shape – which could be correctly applied to the soul. Avicenna, by contrast, understands *kamāl* ("perfection") to be a far more broadly applicable term than *ṣūra*, "form".[8] For example, in his *Marginal Notes on Aristotle's De Anima*, Avicenna makes a clear distinction between form and perfection:

L21

Ibn Sīnā, *at-Ta*ᶜ*līqāt* ᶜ*alā ḥawāshī Kitāb an-nafs li-Arisṭū* (*ad DA* 2.4, 415b2), 91,3-16

The Easterners say that it [i.e., the soul's being the form of the body] is not distinct from [its being] a "perfection", but is rather identical to [its being] a perfection [*al-istikmāl*]; and then they leave it at that ....

It seems that he [Aristotle] means by "perfection" [*bi-l-istikmāli*] something other that what he means by "form", even though it [perfection] is a logical consequence of it [what he means by form], for a thing is called a form only relative to its substrate, while it is called a perfection relative to all that is perfected by it [*ilā kulli mā yukmalu bihi*]. The substrate and the matter are sometimes perfected by it [the perfection] though not in the sense that it [the perfection] is a part of it [the substrate]; and the composite which is given the nature of a species is sometimes perfected by it [the perfection]. It is known that it [the perfection] is the part from which its [the composite's] actions issue, such that the perfection has an influence on the form, because the perfection is the perfection of a species while the form is the form of a matter. The matter is what is formed – not perfected – by form ....

Because "form" implies "being impressed upon" [*al-inṭibā*ᶜ] he [Aristotle] casts it aside for another term which applies to what is separable as well as to what is inseparable. Even though his present aim with "form" is what covers both of them [i.e., that which covers what is separable and what is inseparable], he drops it in favor of a new term which does not have any discernible implication [i.e., of having to be impressed on matter].

[8] Avicenna also maintains that when we predicate the term "perfection" of something, we are not making any claim about whether that thing is a substance or not; on this see now Sebti 1999.

I should explain that Avicenna's method in his *Kitāb al-inṣāf*, a kind of problem-by-problem commentary on the entire Arabic Aristotelian corpus, was for him first to articulate the positions of "Easterners" (i.e., Khurāsānīs and Transoxanians) and "Westerners" (i.e., Baghdādīs) on issues of interpretation that arose as a result of ambiguities in Aristotle's works, and then to "judge fairly" (*inṣāf*) between them.[9] His *Marginal Notes on Aristotle's De Anima* probably represents a working draft of the section of the *Kitāb al-inṣāf* devoted to problems arising from Aristotle's *De Anima*, and position (2) in the passage above is either the Westerners' position – a position which, as we shall see, Avicenna sides with – or a draft of Avicenna's "fair judgment", the Westerners' position having been lost or unreported in what is available to us now.

The philosophical reasons Avicenna gives in his *Marginal Notes on Aristotle's De Anima* for rejecting the Easterners' simple identification of form and perfection are similar to those offered in L7, the *Uthūlūjiyā* passage, in which the term used for perfection is *tamām* rather than *kamāl* or *istikmāl*. These reasons are reiterated in Avicenna's *Fī n-nafs*:

L22

Ibn Sīnā, *Kitāb ash-shifāʾ/Ṭabīʿiyyāt (6): Fī n-nafs*
1.1, 6,13-7,2 and 7,8-10
Avicenna, *Liber de anima seu sextus de naturalibus I-III*,
19,27-20,37 and 20,44-21,3

Now while every form is a perfection, not every perfection is a form [*thumma kullu ṣūratin kamālun wa-laysa kullu kamālin ṣūratan = Deinde dicimus quod omnis forma est perfectio, sed non omnis perfectio forma*]. For the king is the perfection of the state and the captain is the perfection of the ship [*fa-inna l-malika kamālu l-madīnati wa-r-rubbāna kamālu s-safīnati = magister enim fabricandi perfectio est civitatis et carpentarius lignorum perfectio est navis*], yet neither is the form of the state or the ship. The kind of perfection which is itself separable [from that whose perfection it is] will not really be a form possessed by matter and contained in matter [*fa-mā kāna mina l-kamāli mufāraqata dh-dhāti lam yakun bi-l-ḥaqīqati ṣūratan li-l-māddati wa-fī l-māddati = Et cuiuscumque perfectionis est essentia per se separata, ipsa certe non est forma materiae nec in materia*]. The form that is contained in matter is a form which is impressed upon it and which subsists through it, except on the rare occasion when it is used technically and the perfection of a species is spoken of as the form of a species – though in fact it has been settled that technical usage dictates that something be a form relative to matter; an end and perfection relative to the whole [*wa-bi-l-qiyāsi ilā l-jumlati ghāyatan wa-kamālan = comparatione vero totius collectionis sit finis et perfectio*]; and an efficient principle and moving power relative to setting-in-motion ....

[9] See Gutas 1988, 130-140.

> Therefore it is clear that when, in the course of defining the soul, we say that it is a perfection [*kamāl* = *perfectio*], it will be the most indicative of its meaning. What is more, it [i.e., "perfection"] encompasses all the types of souls in all their aspects, with the soul that is separable from matter not being an exception to it [i.e., to being a perfection].

What precisely Avicenna means when he links together the ideas of perfection and species is not immediately clear. Elsewhere in the *Fī n-nafs* of his *Shifā'* and in a long passage from his *Risāla fī n-nafs* Avicenna helps us a bit by explaining that the soul is a *potentiality* (*quwwa*) relative to its activity; a *form* (*ṣūra*) relative to the matter it inheres in, if it happens to be an enmattered soul; and a *perfection* (*kamāl*) relative to the species "animal" or "human". But, Avicenna argues, perfection is the most complete (*atamm*) and the most generally applicable (*a^camm*) of the three terms.

That perfection is more complete and more broadly applicable than *potentiality* needs no argument, Avicenna says. Presumably this is simply because the soul can be described not only as being in a state of first *entelekheia* (i.e., as a potentiality or capability), but also as being in a state of second *entelekheia* (i.e., as an activity or an exercise of that capability).

Showing that perfection is more complete and more broadly applicable than *form* is trickier, however. Perfection is more complete than form because, Avicenna argues, perfection is more closely related to the nature (*ṭabī^ca*) of the thing in question than form is. The nature of "human", for example, refers more to a human in actuality – a human that is both matter and form, that is – than it does to a human in potentiality, which is just the matter. Since perfection is related to the matter/form composite, while form is related to matter alone, perfection will be related more closely to the nature of the thing than form will.

As far as the breadth of its applicability is concerned, Avicenna's motivation is clearer: to find a way for the term "perfection" to be understood in a way which is broad enough to cover separable entities – captains of ships, generals of armies, kings of countries, and rational souls – as well as inseparable entities, such as vegetative and animal souls, and more generally, the forms of natural things. Since form, strictly speaking, is immanent in the thing in which it inheres, while perfection can either transcend or be immanent in the thing whose perfection it is, perfection will be more broadly applicable than form, and therefore perfection is a better term than form with which to define the soul. As Avicenna says, the rational soul is not imprinted on matter as form is.[10] In fact, in his *Book of Definitions* (*Kitāb al-ḥudūd*), just as in L22, Avicenna recognizes that "form" is spoken of so loosely that it might appear to be extensionally identical with perfection, and thus to include in its range of

[10] Ibn Sīnā, *R. fī n-nafs wa-baqā'ihā wa-ma^cādihā* 1, 50,11-53,2 and 54,12-55,2.

referents not only inseparable perfections but separate perfections as well.[11] What the passages above and the *Risāla fī n-nafs* passages are meant to show is that technically speaking, this is incorrect.

Now I shall examine the second problem mentioned above, namely, how Avicenna distinguishes between first and second perfections. Generally speaking, Avicenna has three methods of distinguishing first from second perfections. The first (1) is cause of activity vs. activity itself; the second (2) is form vs. function; and the third is split into two further subdivisions, (3a) necessary for existence vs. necessary for well-being, and (3b) necessary for existence vs. not necessary for existence.

The first way that Avicenna splits first and second perfections (1) can be found in his *Mabḥath ᶜani l-quwā n-nafsāniyya* and in his *Risāla fī n-nafs*. In those texts Avicenna bases the distinction between first and second perfections on the difference between the cause or principle of an activity, and the activity which follows upon that principle. In the *Mabḥath* Avicenna says:

L23

Ibn Sīnā, *Mabḥath ᶜani l-quwā n-nafsāniyya* 2, 153,11-13

> Perfections are divisible into two types: [they are] either the principles of activities and effects [*mabādiʾu l-afāᶜīli wa-l-āthāri*], or [they are] the activities and effects themselves, the one being "first" and the other being "second". The first is the principle [*al-mabdaʾu*], and the second is the activity and effect. The soul is a first perfection [*kamālun awwalu*] because it is a principle, and not originating from a principle.

This is very close to what Avicenna says in the *Risāla fī n-nafs*:

L24

Ibn Sīnā, *Risāla fī n-nafs wa-baqāʾihā wa-maᶜādihā* 1, 55,12-56,1

> Now a body's perfection may be a principle, or it may follow upon a principle [*qad yakūnu mabdaʾan wa-qad yakūnu baᶜda l-mabdaʾi*], for sensation and locomotion are also a perfection of the animal body. Now the soul is a principle of these [activities], and for this reason we say that the soul is a body's first perfection.

Although defining the first perfection in terms of its causation of the second perfection may smack of the Neoplatonists' *teleiotês*, this would, I think, be a superficial reading. Avicenna's distinction seems rather to be a slightly modified version of Aristotle's. Avicenna's second *kamāl* and Aristotle's second *entelekheia* are identical in that they both refer to activity. But whereas Aristotle's activity follows after a first *entelekheia* understood as *capability*, Avicenna's activity follows after a first *kamāl* understood as *cause*.

[11] Ibn Sīnā, *K. al-ḥudūd*, 16,6-13 and 17,7-8.

An example of the second method of distinguishing first and second perfections (2) occurs in the *Fī n-nafs* section of the *Shifāʾ*:

L25

Ibn Sīnā, *Kitāb ash-shifāʾ/Ṭabīʿiyyāt (6): Fī n-nafs* 1.1, 11,7-11
Avicenna, *Liber de anima seu sextus de naturalibus I-III*, 27,40-28,45

"Perfection" [*al-kamāl* = *perfectio*] has two aspects: a first perfection and a second perfection. The first perfection is that by which a species becomes a species in actuality [*bi-l-fiʿli* = *in effectu*], such as the shape [*ka-sh-shakli* = *sicut figura*] that "sword" has. The second perfection is a kind of acting or being-acted-upon that attaches as a consequence to the thing's species, such as the cutting that "sword" has, and such as the distinction-making, deliberating, sensing and moving that "human" has.[12]

Although Avicenna's distinction between first and second *kamāls* in this passage seems quite close to Aristotle's in L1, there is a subtle difference. Avicenna's distinction appears to derive from a slightly later *De Anima* passage (*DA* 2.1, 412b11-413a3), where Aristotle says that cutting is to the power of an axe just as seeing is to the power of an eye. But whereas Aristotle clearly meant for the example in this later passage to be understood as illustrating the distinction between the capability to perform a function and the function itself – and hence to be understood as a refinement of the capability/exercise distinction introduced earlier, in L1 – it seems to have been interpreted by Avicenna instead as referring to a distinction between *form* and function.

Avicenna might have reasoned along the following lines: given that Aristotle says at the very beginning of L1 that the soul is *entelekheia* in the sense of substantial form; given that Aristotle goes on to say later in L1 that the soul is a first *entelekheia*; and given that in L1 and in the later passage (412b11-413a3) Aristotle illustrates what first *entelekheia* means by using an example that is most easily interpreted as referring to a capability to perform a function; form and capability to perform a function are therefore equivalent. The problem with this line of reasoning is that when Avicenna gives an example of first *kamāl*, he says that it should be understood as "shape" (*shakl* = *morphê*). The implication is that soul is form *not* in the sense of substantial form, but in the sense of shape, and this is clearly not what Aristotle meant, given that in L1 he linked the soul to form as *substance*.

Avicenna's third method of distinguishing between first and second perfections is itself divided into two versions. The first version (3a) bases the distinction on the difference between what is necessary for a thing to exist, and what is

[12] As with its definition of the soul, the *Fī n-nafs* distinction between form and function in L25 is repeated in somewhat compressed form in the *Burhān*: Ibn Sīnā, *K. ash-shifāʾ/Manṭiq (5): al-Burhān* 2.9, 182,16-23. On the Latin *fortuna* of L25 see Hasse 2000, 235.

necessary for its well-being, or for it to exist well. This is articulated in a passage in the *Najāt*:

L26

Ibn Sīnā, *Kitāb an-najāt*, 161,6-14

> As a result of the separate principle, natural bodies seek their own perpetuity as well as that of their perfections [*istibqāʾun li-dhawātihā wa-stibqāʾun li-kamālātihā*]. Now their perfections are either first perfections, upon whose disappearance the things whose perfections they are cease to exist; or second perfections, whose disappearance does not lead to the ceasing-to-exist of the things whose perfections they are, but instead leads to the thing's ceasing to be in a state of well-being (*ilā rtifāʿi ṣalāḥi ḥālātihi*). The separate principle does not itself go about seeking the perpetuity of these second perfections, but [does so] instead by means of placing powers in the [natural] bodies; for it is the first perfections and principles from which these second perfections issue. The activities of natural bodies derive from their second perfections, given that their activities come about through these powers.

The distinction here in the *Najāt* is clearly informed by the Neoplatonic distinction between *to einai*, the existence that is passed along in the downward course of procession, and *to eu einai*, the well-being that is striven for in the upward course of reversion. This distinction also seems to be in line with a distinction Avicenna makes in several of his biological works, where he splits the final cause (*al-ʿillatu t-tamāmī*, in this case) into a necessity and a benefit (*ḍarūra wa-manfaʿa*), a distinction which itself derives from the Aristotelian distinction between *anankê* and *ôpheleia*.[13]

The second version of Avicenna's third method (3b) of distinguishing between first and second perfections is found in his *Notes* (*Taʿlīqāt*) and in the *Metaphysics* of his *Book of Science for ʿAlāʾ ad-Dawla* (*Ilāhiyyāt-i Dānishnāma-yi ʿAlāʾī*). In these two works Avicenna bases the distinction not on the difference between what is necessary for a thing's being and what is necessary for its well-being, as with (3a), but rather on what is necessary for a thing's being and what is extra, or a bonus. Avicenna puts it this way in the *Taʿlīqāt*:

[13] e.g., *K. ash-shifāʾ/Ṭabīʿiyyāt (8): al-Ḥayawān* 12.5, 207,5 = *al-Qānūn fī ṭ-ṭibb (1)* I.4.2, 35,23. Avicenna's formulation may derive from Aristotle's statement at *GA* 1.4, 717a16-17 (= *Fī kawn al-ḥayawān*, 7,3-4), that the final cause of a thing is either "by necessity" (*dia to anankaion* = *li-lladhī huwa lāzimun bi-ḍṭirārin*) or "for the better" (*dia to beltion* = *li-lladhī huwa amthalu wa-ajwadu*).

L27

Ibn Sīnā, *at-Taᶜlīqāt*

21,16-19: Just as He [i.e., God] bestows upon everything what it needs as far as its existence and perpetuating [its existence] are concerned, so He also bestows upon it something above and beyond its need for these. An example is the fact that He bestows upon man philosophy and astronomy, since no man needs astronomy as far as his existence and perpetuating [his existence] are concerned. What is required as far as his existence is concerned is the first perfection [*fa-mā lā budda minhu fī wujūdihi huwa l-kamālu l-awwalu*], while that other is the second perfection.

21,22-22,2: The Necessary of Existence is also the cause of every existent, and has bestowed upon every existent its existence's perfection, which is what it needs as far as its existence and perpetuating [its existence] are concerned; and He has also added to these two what it [the existent] does not need. The Qur'ān hints at this concept when it says [20:50]: "He [i.e., Moses] said: 'Our Lord is He Who gives to everything its creation, then guides [it]'". The guidance is what he [man] does not need as far as his existence or the perpetuation [of his existence] are concerned, while the creation is what he needs as far as his existence or the perpetuation [of his existence] are concerned. Also when it says [quoting Abraham] [26:78]: "Who created me [i.e., Abraham], then guided me". Philosophers call what something needs as far as its existence or the perpetuation of its existence are concerned the first perfection, and what it does not need as far as its existence or the perpetuation [of its existence] are concerned the second perfection.[14]

It seems that just as we were faced with the challenge of reconciling the various ways Aristotle explicitly (as in *De Anima* 2) and implicitly (as in *Physics* 3) distinguished first from second *entelekheiai*, so we must try to make some sense of all the different ways – (1), (2) and (3a) and (3b) – Avicenna has divided first and second perfections. One question I should try to answer first is whether these different ways of distinguishing first and second perfections might reflect a progression or development in Avicenna's thought.

The question of development arises because each of the different ways of dividing first and second perfections comes in a cluster of texts – (1) in the *Mabḥath* and the *Risāla fī n-nafs*; (2) in the *Fī n-nafs* and *Burhān* of the *Shifā'*; (3a) and (3b) in the *Najāt*, *Taᶜlīqāt* and *Dānishnāma-yi ᶜAlā'ī* – and because each text coincides chronologically with the other texts in its cluster. The first cluster of texts (1) appears to date from Avicenna's earliest period of

[14] The terms used in the *Dānishnāma-yi ᶜAlā'ī* are *āfirīnish-i farīḍa* and *āfirīnish-i ziyādat*, referring to God's creation of what is required for an existent to exist (i.e., existence), and God's creation of something extra which is not required for an existent to exist (e.g., philosophy or astronomy): *Dānishnāma-yi ᶜAlā'ī: Ilāhiyyāt*, 100,9-11 (cf. also 109,1). The Qur'ānic quotations cited in the *Taᶜlīqāt* passage are also cited in the *Dānishnāma* passage at 100,7-9.

philosophical activity, from 1000-1014.[15] The second cluster of texts (2), taken from the *Kitāb ash-shifāʾ*, dates from what Gutas has referred to as Avicenna's "Middle Period", between 1020 and 1027.[16] The third cluster of texts, (3a) and (3b), date from the very end of the middle period, around 1027 (3a); and from the period immediately following, which Gutas has called the "Period of Eastern Philosophy", between 1027 and 1030 (3b).[17]

Despite the close correspondence of texts within each cluster, it would be a mistake, in my opinion, to argue that a development took place in Avicenna's thought. Apart from anything else, someone arguing for a developmentalist interpretation of Avicenna's theory of perfection would have to confront the fact that the *Najāt* passage (L26) turns out to be identical to, and hence was copied and pasted from, *Ḥikma ʿArūḍiyya*, 51v5-10, and therefore dates from around 1001, during Avicenna's early period.[18]

I think instead that it would be more accurate to argue that the difference between the ways the distinction between first and second *kamāl*s is expressed in cluster (1) and cluster (2) can be attributed instead to the *type of work* Avicenna was writing. The texts in cluster (1) are independent, stand-alone essays, works in which Avicenna felt able to modify Aristotle's distinction in a more dramatic way than he would have done in cluster (2). This is because the texts in cluster (2) are taken from the *Shifāʾ*, Avicenna's most Aristotelian work, in which Avicenna wanted to veil his modifications by using examples, such as the axe and cutting, which were drawn from the Aristotelian texts themselves.

By contrast, the difference between the way Avicenna expresses the first *kamāl*/second *kamāl* distinction in clusters (1) and (2), and the way he expresses the distinction in clusters (3a) and (3b), is attributable not so much to a difference between *types of work* as it is to a difference between *subject-matter*. In clusters (3a) and (3b), Avicenna is not writing about the soul in particular but about natural philosophy (3a) and cosmology (3b) more generally. And whereas the ways he expressed the distinction in clusters (1) and (2) are obviously derived – though with modifications – from Aristotelian psychology, the ways he expressed the distinction in clusters (3a) and (3b) are clearly inspired – again,

[15] Gutas 1988, 82-87, argues for a very early dating (ca. 1000) of the *Mabḥath ʿani l-quwā n-nafsāniyya* (which he refers to, following Landauer, its first editor, as *Maqāla fī n-nafs ʿalā sunnat al-ikhtiṣār, The Compendium on the Soul*). He dates the *R. fī n-nafs wa-baqāʾihā wa-maʿādihā* (which he refers to as *Ḥāl an-nafs al-insāniyya*) at around 1014 (Gutas 1988, 99-100). For an argument against Gutas and in favor of a later dating of this work see Michot 1997a, 240n.6.

[16] Gutas 1988, 101-112.

[17] On the dating of the *Najāt* to around 1027, see Gutas 1988, 112-114. Gutas (Gutas 1988, 141-144) actually dates the *Taʿlīqāt* to the last period of Avicenna's life, that is, to around 1035-1037. But I believe that Janssens 1986 and 1997 has shown enough of a textual correspondence between the *Taʿlīqāt* and the *Dānishnāma-yi ʿAlāʾī* – verified by the correspondence I just demonstrated between L27 and the corresponding *Dānishnāma* passage – to throw the burden of proof on those who would deny that they came from the same period, namely, 1027-1032.

[18] Gutas 1988, 87-93 and 112-114, discusses the *Najāt*'s borrowings from Avicenna's earliest works.

with slight modifications – by Neoplatonic cosmology, and particularly by the Neoplatonists' application of the distinction between *to einai* and *to eu einai* to their cosmology of procession and return.

In other words, just because each cluster might – with some rough edges – be distinguished from the others chronologically, a doctrinal progression from one cluster to the next need not be postulated. I cannot see that the way Avicenna distinguished between first and second *kamāl*s in clusters (3a) and (3b) is somehow a response to, or more coherent than, the ways he distinguished between first and second *kamāl*s in clusters (1) and (2). On the other hand, I do see that there is a sense in which the ways the distinction is articulated in clusters (1) and (2) can be reduced to the ways the first *kamāl*/second *kamāl* distinction is articulated in (3a) and (3b), and that in this sense the (3a) and (3b) cluster is the most philosophically basic articulation of the distinction. To be more precise, I believe (3a) to be the most basic articulation of the distinction. This is because the way the distinction is articulated in (3b) seems to be nothing more than (3a) with some religious terminology (*khalq* and *āfirīnish*) and a couple of Qur'ānic quotations (20:50 and 26:78) thrown in for good measure.

How can the distinction expressed in cluster (1), namely, the principle of an activity as opposed to the activity that follows from that principle; and the distinction expressed in cluster (2), namely, a form as opposed to the function associated with possessing that form; be reduced to the distinction expressed in cluster (3a), namely, what is necessary for existence as opposed to what is necessary for well-being? Well, an activity that follows from a principle and a function such as "cutting" are quite obviously reconcilable. Just as "activity" in general will either be allotelic, in which case it leads to an end outside itself, or autotelic, in which case it leads to no end other than itself, so "function" – which means nothing more than an activity whose endedness is being stressed – will either be allotelic (e.g., reproduction) or autotelic (e.g., intellection).

What about "principle" in cluster (1) and "form" in cluster (2)? I think that what they share becomes more obvious if the term *mabda'* in (1), which I have translated as "principle", is understood as referring more to the idea of "starting-point" than to the idea of "cause". Let us also assume that when Avicenna said in cluster (2) that the first *kamāl* is form as shape, what he was doing was simply emphasizing the endedness of the soul. What I mean is that the soul is not simply the substantial form that results from a previous activity – reproduction – it is also the springboard for future activities. In the sense that it is the springboard for future activities, the soul is more like a form as shape – the arrangement of matter structured with a view to performing some function – than it is like a form as substance. With this in mind, the form can be seen as the springboard from which there arise activities associated with possessing that form. My soul is the springboard from which there arise the activities or functions associated with my soul, such as moving, perceiving, deliberating and so on. Similarly, the form of an axe is the starting-point from which the activities associated with that form, such as chopping, derive. That is to say, just as without the axe's form, the axe's activity of chopping could never take place, so without the human soul's form (i.e., its complex structure of capabilities), the human soul's activities of nourishing, growing, reproducing, moving, sensing, acting and thinking could never take place.

Both (1) and (2) can be reduced to (3a), then, because the "starting-point" in (1) and the "form" in (2) are both required for a thing – a form/matter composite, that is – to exist. By contrast, the thing does not have to perform the activity or function that springs from possession of that form in order to exist. An axe that sits in the garage and is never used for chopping is still an axe, because it possesses its form. A human who watches television all day and never exercises his intellectual capability is still a human, because he possesses his soul. But an axe that is often used for chopping, and a human who thinks constantly about philosophy, not only exist but exist well, since well-being results from the full and repeated exercise of a thing's capabilities.

Now that I have reduced the ways in which the distinction between first and second *kamāl*s is expressed in the other clusters to the way it is expressed in cluster (3a), the question arises, how does motion or change, which Avicenna defines in L20 as a first perfection, fit into the picture? I have to admit that I am stumped by this question. I cannot see that motion or change is a starting point as opposed to the activity that springs from that starting-point; if anything, change is itself an activity, the second *kamāl* as articulated in cluster (1). I also cannot see that change is a form as opposed to a function, since again, change is surely closer to function than it is to form, and hence change ought to be seen as a second *kamāl*, at least as it is articulated in cluster (2). And as I just discussed, a thing need not be active – in a state of change, that is – in order to exist, so change fails to fulfill the requirement of being a first *kamāl* according to clusters (3a) and (3b). My guess is that Avicenna's calling change a first *kamāl* is nothing other than a vestigial remain of the *Physics* 3 commentary tradition he inherited from Philoponus, Themistius and perhaps Alexander, if Simplicius is quoting him accurately. In other words, in the context of his *Physics*, Avicenna is happy to apply the Arabic version of the commentators' distinction between *entelekheia prôtê* and *entelekheia hustatê* to, respectively, the state of change which the changing thing possesses and the resulting state of actuality which the changed thing possesses, *without* feeling the need to reconcile that distinction with the numerous articulations of the first *kamāl*/second *kamāl* distinction found elsewhere in his work.

I believe that the reason for this is that like Philoponus but unlike Themistius and Alexander, Avicenna was a part of the Ammonian synthesis. That is to say, Avicenna was heir to the effort, begun by Ammonius, to fuse together the greater *sumphônia* (reconciling Plato and Aristotle) and the lesser *sumphônia* (reconciling Aristotle with Aristotle). What that meant in practical terms is that Philoponus' appeals to Aristotle's distinction between final causes which are *to*

Elsewhere, though less often, Avicenna uses *al-ʿillatu l-kamāliyya* and *as-sababu l-kamālī*.[22]

As was the case with Neoplatonic commentators such as Philoponus, Avicenna's views about the final cause in general had important ramifications on the particular issue of the soul's separability and inseparability. In the introduction to the section on causes in the *Ilāhiyyāt* of his *Kitāb ash-shifāʾ*, Avicenna claims that the four causes can be divided into two subsets: one subset is the matter and the form, which are *intrinsic to* or *immanent in* their effect; the other subset is the agent and the end, which are *extrinsic to* or *transcend* their effect:

L30

Ibn Sīnā, *Kitāb ash-shifāʾ/Ilāhiyyāt (2)* 6.1, 258,1-8
Avicenna, *Liber de philosophia prima sive scientia divina V-X*, 292,27-36

We say that a thing's cause must either be intrinsic to its constitution and a part of its existence, or not [*immā an yakūna dākhilan fī qiwāmihi wa-juzʾan min wujūdihi aw lā yakūna* = *vel est intra essentiam rei et pars esse eius vel non*]. If it is intrinsic to [the thing's] constitution and a part of its existence, then either it is the part on account of whose existence alone it is not necessary that [the thing] be in actuality, but rather only in potentiality, and is called "*hylê*"; or it is the part whose existence is identical to the [thing's] coming to be in actuality, and is "form". If it is not a part of [the thing's] existence, then either it is that for whose sake [the thing] is, or it is not. If it is that for whose sake [the thing] is, it is the "end". If it is not that for whose sake [the thing] is, then either [the thing's] existence comes from it without its being contained in [the thing] except in an accidental way - and is the "agent" - or [the thing's] existence comes from it with it being contained in [the thing], and is also the "element" or "substrate".

I already discussed – in Chapters 3 and 4 – the Neoplatonic distinction between immanent and transcendent causes, as well as the history of its incorporation into Aristotelian philosophy, a history which appears to have begun with

shifāʾ/Ṭabīʿiyyāt (8): al-Ḥayawān 12.5, 207,2.5 and 12.13, 256,17; *al-Qānūn fī ṭ-ṭibb* (1), I.4.2, 35,23; *R. fī n-nafs wa-baqāʾihā wa-maʿādihā* 1, 53,13-54,2; *K. ash-shifāʾ/Manṭiq (5): al-Burhān* 2.9, 182,5; 4.4, 295,9 and 297,4.14; *Dānishnāma-yi ʿAlāʾī: Ilāhiyyāt*, 54,7; and *ar-Risālat al-ʿarshiyya fī ḥaqāʾiq at-tawḥīd wa-ithbāt an-nubuwwa*, 18,2-3.

22 Instances where Avicenna calls the final cause *al-ʿillatu l-kamāliyya* and *as-sababu l-kamālī* are *K. ash-shifāʾ/Ṭabīʿiyyāt (6): Fī n-nafs* 5.4, 228,7; *R. fī n-nafs wa-baqāʾihā wa-maʿādihā* 9, 100,2.10; *K. ash-shifāʾ/Manṭiq (5): al-Burhān* 2.9, 182,12; and *ar-Risālat al-ʿarshiyya fī ḥaqāʾiq at-tawḥīd wa-ithbāt an-nubuwwa*, 22,18-20 and 29,3-4. In using *al-ʿillatu l-kamāliyya* Avicenna could be following Ibn Miskawayh, who also cites Aristotle as the source of the view that the final is the noblest of the causes (*wa-hādhihi l-ʿillatu l-akhīratu llatī tusammā l-kamāliyyata wa-hiya ashrafu l-ʿilali*); *ap.* at-Tawḥīdī, *al-Ḥawāmil wa-sh-shawāmil*, #159, 342,17-343,2.

Syrianus.[23] We are given a hint that Avicenna probably viewed his distinction between immanent and transcendent causes as being in line with a tradition of interpreting *Metaphysics* 5.1, Aristotle's discussion of *arkhê*, "origin" or "principle". In his earliest *summa*, the *Ḥikma ʿArūḍiyya*, Avicenna introduces the same distinction between immanent and transcendent causes that he would expand upon later in the *Ilāhiyyāt* of the *Kitāb ash-shifāʾ*; but in the *Ḥikma ʿArūḍiyya* – much of whose metaphysics section seems to be an abridgement of the "philosophical lexicon" Aristotle offers in *Metaphysics* 5 – Avicenna uses *mabdaʾ*, the Arabic term that corresponds to the Greek *arkhê*, instead of *ʿilla*, the Arabic term that corresponds to the Greek *aition*, which Aristotle discusses in *Metaphysics* 5.2.[24] Avicenna says:

L31

Ibn Sīnā, *al-Ḥikmat al-ʿArūḍiyya*, 4v16-5r5

> "Origin" [*al-mabdaʾ*] is that upon which a thing's existence depends, either its matter, if it is material; or its form, if it is composed of matter and form; or its end, if it exists for some end; whereas that which facilitates and particularizes, and the instrument, attach as concomitants to the agent; and the paradigm [exists] because of that very agent's imperfection with respect to the act's issuing and existing from it. A composite substance has two conjoint causes [*sababāni muqāranāni*] - its matter and its form - and two transcendent causes [*sababāni mufāraqāni*] - its agent and its end. An accident has three causes, of which form is not one. Form and the separate [substances] have two causes: agent and end.[25]

[23] See Wisnovsky 2003a.

[24] There is in fact a striking correspondence between the metaphysics section of Avicenna's *Ḥikma ʿArūḍiyya* and *Metaphysics* 5. In addition to *mabdaʾ/arkhê*, Avicenna discusses Aristotelian terms such as "potentiality" (*quwwa/dunamis* = *Ḥikma ʿArūḍiyya* 3r6-17/*Metaph.* 5.12), "necessary" (*wājib/anankaion* = *Ḥikma ʿArūḍiyya* 4v16-5r5/*Metaph.* 5.5), "perfect" (*tāmm/teleion* = *Ḥikma ʿArūḍiyya* 4v14-16/*Metaph.* 5.16), "universal" (*kullī/holon* = 4v6-12/*Metaph.* 5.26) and "prior and posterior" (*qabla* + *mutaqaddim/proteron* and *baʿda* + *mutaʾakhkhir/husteron* = *Ḥikma ʿArūḍiyya* 5r7-5v15/*Metaph.* 5.11).

[25] Unlike many other sections of the *Ḥikma ʿArūḍiyya*, this passage is not copied in *an-Najāt*. Other passages where Avicenna makes the distinction between immanent (formal and material) and transcendent (efficient and final) causes are *K. al-hidāya*, 243,5-244,3 (and implied at 237,4-5); *ʿUyūn al-ḥikma*, 52,3-11; *K. an-najāt*, 344,2-14; *Dānishnāma-yi ʿAlāʾī: Ilāhiyyāt*, 53,9-54,9 (where the distinction is between causes which are inside the effect itself [*andar dhāt-i maʿlūl*] and those which are outside the effect itself [*bīrūn az dhāt-i maʿlūl*]); and *ar-Risālat al-ʿarshiyya fī ḥaqāʾiq at-tawḥīd wa-ithbāt an-nubuwwa*, 18,5-11. Jolivet 1991 was the first to notice the distinction in Avicenna, though he seems unaware of its Neoplatonic pedigree, nor of the apparent evolution in Avicenna's views and uses of the distinction, both of which I describe at greater length in Wisnovsky 2003a. Although the distinction between intrinsic and extrinsic causes originates in the Neoplatonists, Avicenna's immediate source may have been al-Fārābī, in whose epitome of the *Physics* (preserved only in Latin) the distinction appears; cf. *materia et forma (que due sunt intra rem) et agens et finis (que due sunt extra rem)*: *Epitome of Aristotle's Physics*, 475,7-8.

But if final causes transcend their effects; if perfection acts on its effect – the body – as a final cause; and if the soul is a perfection; then the soul will *always* transcend the body. But this is not quite what Avicenna wants to prove, since he thinks that vegetative and animal souls, at least, are immanent in their bodies. How does Avicenna avoid the dilemma of being forced on the one hand into holding that all souls transcend their effects just as ends do, and being forced on the other hand into holding that all souls are immanent in their effects just as forms are?

Part of the job was done for him by the Arabic translators' conflation of two distinct ideas in Greek philosophy. The result of the use of the phrases *al-ᶜillatu t-tamāmī* and *as-sababu t-tamāmī* to render *to aition telikon* ("final cause") as well as *to aition teleiôtikon* ("perfecting cause") in the commentaries, was that the difference between the two types of cause – the former an end, the latter a Form which operated as an agent and an end – was lost in the Arabic, which collapsed the latter into the former. The result was that Arabic philosophers such as Avicenna allowed the final cause an even greater spectrum of causality than the Neoplatonic philosophers had. For example, in the section of *Ilāhiyyāt* 6.5 of his *Kitāb ash-shifā'* where he discusses whether "end" and "good" are identical, Avicenna says:

L32

Ibn Sīnā, *Kitāb ash-shifā'/Ilāhiyyāt (2)* 6.5, 294,6-9; 294,12-295,12; and 296,3-5
Avicenna, *Liber de philosophia prima sive scientia divina V-X*, 339,33-37; 339,41-341,71; and 341,84-86

As for the question subsequent to this [viz. are the end and the good identical?], it will be resolved through our saying that an end which occurs in an agent's act is divisible into two categories: [1] an end which is a form or accident in a patient receiving the act, and [2] an end which is not in any way a form or accident in a receiving patient, and is thus inevitably contained in the agent ....

An example of the first [category] is the form of humanity in human matter: [the form of humanity] is an end of the active potential for formation in the matter of man. It is toward [this end] that its act and its setting-in-motion are directed. An example of the second [category] is seeking shelter, for it is an end of the person seeking to build the house and is thus the principle of motion of his being [a builder], and is not in any way a form contained in the house. It appears that the end of the proximate agent (the one who is in closest contact with the setting-in-motion of the matter) is a form contained in the matter, and that that whose end is not a form in the matter is [conversely] not a proximate principle of the setting-in-motion as such. So if it happens that that whose end is a form contained in the utilized matter, and that whose end is something other than a form in this matter, were one thing, then its oneness would be accidental. [Say] for example, that a man is building a house therein to take shelter:

> in so far as he is a seeker of shelter, he is a motivator and a first cause of the act of building. [But] in so far as he is a builder, he is an effect of the seeker of shelter. Hence the end of the seeker of shelter is different from the end of the builder. This being so, in the case of the one man who is both a seeker of shelter and a builder, his end in so far as he is seeker of shelter will be different from his end in so far as he is builder.
>
> Now that this has been settled, we say: as for the first category, the end has a relationship to many things which are prior to it in terms of actual occurrence [in time] as well as in terms of existence. [This is so] because [the end] has: [1] a relationship to the agent; [2] a relationship to the receiving patient when [the receiving patient] is potentially [a receiving patient]; [3] a relationship to the receiving patient when [the receiving patient] is actually a receiving patient; and [4] a relationship to the motion. With regard to [1] the agent, [the end] is an end, and with regard to [4] the motion it is a terminus and not an end. This is because the end [is that] on account of which the thing exists, and toward which the thing is directed; the thing will not cease to exist once [the end] exists, but will instead be perfected by [the end]. The motion, by contrast, ceases to exist once it reaches its terminus. With regard to [2] the potentially perfected receiving patient, [the end] is a good which sets [the receiving patient] in its proper state. [This is] because evil consists in the non-existence of [the receiving patient's] perfection, whereas good, by contrast, consists in [the receiving patient's] actual existence and occurrence [in time]. And with regard to the actualized receiving patient, [the end] is a form ....
>
> Therefore, every end is on the one hand an end, and on the other hand a good, either supposed or real. And this is the situation concerning the good and the final cause [*ḥālu l-khayri wa-l-ᶜillati t-tamāmiyyati* = *causae perfectivae*].

Let me summarize Avicenna's new taxonomy of final causes as outlined in the passage above. First of all, Avicenna makes a distinction between ends that are contained in the patient – that is, ends that are immanent in the effect that is acted upon by the cause – and ends that are contained in the agent – that is, ends that are immanent in the cause that acts upon the effect. He claims that ends that are immanent in the patient are forms contained *in matter*: that is to say, they are natures, essences, and quiddities, such as "humanity" and "house-ness". Those ends that are immanent in the agent, on the other hand, are the purposes or ends the agent has *in mind* – seeking shelter, for example – and not the form of the structure he is building.

Avicenna expands his taxonomy to cover not only actual agents and patients but also potential patients and motion. Strictly speaking, Avicenna says, the final cause may be related to several things: (1) when it is related to the actual patient, the final cause is a *form*; (2) when it is related to the agent, the final cause is an *end*; (3) when it is related to motion, the final cause is a *terminus*;

and (4) when it is related to the potential patient, the final cause is a *good*. Final causes of types (1), (2) and (3) are immanent in their effects; whereas final causes of type (4) transcend their effects.

The upshot is that because Avicenna holds that the final cause is identifiable with perfection, perfection will subsume form (i.e., number 1), not be identical to it, as the standard interpretation of Aristotle holds. When viewed as a final cause, therefore, perfection can perform the immanent/transcendent double-duty demanded of sublunary souls more plausibly than form can. That Avicenna should have seen his expansion of final causality to subsume formal causality, as being entirely in line with Aristotelian thought should not surprise us, given Aristotle's general implication that the end is superior to the other causes, a position explicitly upheld by Avicenna.[26]

Avicenna's new understanding of perfection and the final cause allowed him to subsume formal causality under final causality. But what about the efficient cause, the third type of cause which Avicenna, following *De Anima* 2.4, says the soul can be seen to be? This question is particularly acute because, as I mentioned above, Avicenna's *ᶜilla tamāmiyya* seems at least partly to have been the product of the translators' conflation of the *aition telikon*, which (obviously) operates as a final cause, and the *aition teleiôtikon*, which operates as a final *and* as an efficient cause. I believe that Avicenna's attempt to create a concept of final causality broad enough to subsume not only the sense in which the soul is the form of the body but also the sense in which the soul is the efficient cause of the body forced him to appeal, as Philoponus had done, to the distinction between the two types of final cause: that in view of which (*to hou*) and that for the benefit of which (*to hôi*).

What does Avicenna himself have to say about the Aristotelian distinction between the type of final cause which is "that in view of which" (*to hou*) and the type of final cause which is "that for the benefit of which" (*to hôi*)? Avicenna treats the distinction most directly in his *Marginal Notes on Aristotle's De Anima*:

L33

Ibn Sīnā, *at-Taᶜlīqāt ᶜalā ḥawāshī Kitāb an-nafs li-Arisṭū* (*ad DA* 2.4, 415b2), 94,18-23

... i.e., "that for the sake of which" [*alladhī min ajlihi*] is of two types: one is "that in view of which" [*alladhī min qibalihi*], such as pleasure, the good, health and so on; and the second is "that for the benefit of which" [*alladhī lahu*], it being that which strives for the end, such as that which strives for pleasure or health. Among things which are subject to passing-away the end is that they imitate – as much as is possible for them – the eternal, divine things, namely the divine thing which is perpetuity. The end "for

[26] See for example *Metaph.* 1.2, 982b5-11. For Avicenna's view that the end is superior to the other causes, see *K. ash-shifāʾ/Ilāhiyyāt (2)*, 300,7-9.

> the benefit of which" consists in the things which are subject to change. Since the thing which is subject to passing-away cannot persist forever and attain this imitation (this being sought by it as an object of desire and [through] an act of will) as an individual, it strives for it in its species.[27]

I ought to remind readers that Aristotle's distinction between *to hou* and *to hôi* appeared most prominently in two contexts. In *Physics* 2.2, the distinction is meant to differentiate between a thing's form – that in view of which – and a thing's user – that for the benefit of which. The form of a door is a *that in view of which*; the user of a door is a *that for the benefit of which*. In *De Anima* 2.4, the distinction is meant to differentiate between eternality (or divinity) – the *form* striven for by individual, mortal members of a species – and the individual, mortal thing which *uses* its body to attain immortality through its species.

Although as far as I can tell Avicenna nowhere else articulates the *to hou/to hôi* distinction as explicitly as he does in L33, the language he uses in discussions of how the soul is related to the body, and of how the higher faculties of the soul, such as the intellect, are related to the lower ones, make it quite clear that he had Aristotle's distinction between *to hou* and *to hôi* in mind. What I mean is that Avicenna felt that a single thing – the soul – could be viewed as an efficient cause and as a final cause, though from different angles, or more precisely, as two different ways of explaining two different *explananda*.

In the sense that the soul is a mover, in the sense that it causes the body to move, the soul is an efficient cause. The soul as efficient cause is the *explanans* of the existence of the body's motion. In the sense that the soul uses or benefits from the body's motion, the soul is a final cause *qua to hôi*: the soul as final cause *qua to hôi* is the *explanans* of the fact that the body's motion is intended to attain some end, namely, the final cause *qua to hou*. But since the soul as efficient cause of the body is numerically identical to the soul as final cause *qua to hôi* of the body, Avicenna can subsume efficient causation under final causation, in order to reconcile his implication that the soul's being the perfection of the body is equivalent to its being the final cause of the body, with his explicit assertion that the soul is the formal and efficient cause of the body as well as its final cause. What Avicenna seems to mean, therefore, is that when we use the term "perfection" to describe the soul, we are saying that the soul is first and foremost a final cause, and that the other ways in which it is a cause – as formal cause and as efficient cause – can in fact be subsumed under its being a final cause. Viewed as the formal cause of the body, the soul is inseparable, since formal causes are immanent in their effects. Viewed as the efficient cause

[27] The fact that both the Arabic Themistius and L33 use *alladhī min qibalihi* and *alladhī lahu* for *to hou* and *to hôi*, respectively, is yet more evidence linking the Arabic Themistius to Isḥāq's revised translation of the *De Anima*: Themistius, *in DA* 2.4 (*ad* 415b3-7), 50,15-26 (= Thāmasṭiyūs, *Sharḥ K. an-nafs li-Arisṭūṭālīs*, 69,2-12).

and final cause *qua to hôi* of the body, however, the soul transcends the body, since efficient and final causes transcend their effects.

This is all well and good. But is Avicenna not forced into a contradiction, given that he is well known to have thought that vegetative and animal souls are immanent in their bodies, while human rational souls transcend their bodies; given that vegetative and animal souls are efficient causes and final causes *qua to hôi*, since vegetative and animal souls both move and use their bodies in view of attaining a final cause *qua to hou*, namely, species-eternality; and given that efficient and final causes transcend their effects?

The difference between vegetative and animal souls on the one hand, and human rational souls on the other, is that human rational souls are the only souls in which a faculty – the theoretical intellect – is both a final cause *qua to hôi* and a final cause *qua to hou*. What do I mean by this? Avicenna says in the *Ta^{c}līqāt* that the soul both *is* an end and *has* an end; and says in the *Mubāḥathāt* that the soul both *is* a perfection and *has* a perfection.[28] In other words, it is important to think of perfection not only in the way that Aristotle did in the *De Anima*, where the soul *as a whole* was viewed as a perfection; but also to think of perfection as the Neoplatonists did, where perfection was viewed as a universal principle which described the way all things – not just souls – revert upwards towards their well-being, towards being what they are as best they can.[29]

As far as the soul is concerned, the perfection it *has* will of course be something higher than it. When discussing how the faculties of the human soul relate to each other, Avicenna employs terms – "using", "serving" and "instrument" as well as "attaining" and "end" – that make it clear that he saw each faculty's relationship with the one below it as the relationship between a final cause *qua to hôi* (higher faculty) and the effect of a final cause *qua to hôi* (lower faculty); and each faculty's relationship with the one above it as the relationship between the effect of a final cause *qua to hou* and a final cause *qua to hou*. In other words, faculty (Y) uses lower faculty (X), which in turn uses the body, in view of attaining a final cause *qua to hou*. My theoretical intellect *uses* my practical intellect, which in turn *uses* my animal faculty of locomotion, to move my body to the library, *in view of* my theoretical intellect's attaining peace and quiet, which is itself *in view of* its thinking about philosophy, which is itself *in view of* its attaining conjunction with the Active Intellect, which is itself *in view of* its attaining immortality.

[28] Ibn Sīnā, *at-Ta^{c}līqāt*, 63,3-64,4; and *al-Mubāḥathāt*, 232,15-233,4 (= *Mubāḥatha* 6, #693) – the question – and 233,12-19 (= *Mubāḥatha* 6, #694) – Avicenna's response.

[29] The expansion of the *to hou* sense of the final cause to cover causal relations between the intellect and the soul – in other words, the doctrine that just as the body is *min qibali* or *min ajli* the soul, so the soul is *min qibali* or *min ajli* the intellect – can be found in compressed form in the treatise on the soul by (Ps.-?)Porphyry; see Kutsch 1954, 268,5-6 (Arabic text).

In other words, just as individual animal souls use their vegetative faculty of reproduction, which in turn uses their bodies, in view of attaining the form of immortality through the species, so human rational souls use their animal faculties of locomotion and sensation in view of attaining individual immortality.[30] The only difference is that *each* human rational soul can attain the immortality which the Active Intellect possesses and which serves as the final cause *qua to hou* of the activities of the theoretical intellect and its lower faculties. Once the theoretical intellect has attained that immortality, it becomes identical in species, rather than numerically identical, with the Active Intellect, thus allowing the theoretical intellect to retain its individuality. At the point when the theoretical intellect becomes identical in species with the Active Intellect, the theoretical intellect ceases to be a final cause *qua to hôi* and becomes a final cause *qua to hou.*[31]

The upshot is that even though vegetative and animal souls may act as efficient causes and as final causes *qua to hôi*, moving and using their bodies, they never act as final causes *qua to hou*, as goals in view of which their bodies or lower faculties are employed. On the contrary, the final cause *qua to hou* of vegetative and animal souls transcends them: it is the immortality which they cannot attain as individuals but which they can attain through reproduction. Human rational souls, by contrast, do contain within themselves a final cause *qua to hou*: the theoretical intellect, and particularly the "acquired intellect" (*al-ᶜaqlu l-mustafād*) in view of which all lower faculties of the intellect and of the soul as a whole are employed. For it is when the theoretical intellect is fully activated, when it is in the state of acquired intellect and hence in conjunction with the superlunary Active Intellect, that the goal of individual immortality is attained. Avicenna's position seems to be that it is when perfection is understood not as an efficient and formal cause but first and foremost as a final cause – and further, when perfection is understood not as any final cause but primarily as a final cause *qua to hou* – that the transcendence of the human rational soul is best guaranteed.

How does Avicenna's tying of perfection to the two types of final causality, as well as to efficient and formal causality, square with his distinction, articulated in cluster (3a), between first perfections and second perfections? I said previously that when Avicenna made his distinction between first and second perfections, as articulated in cluster (3a), he had in mind the Neoplatonic distinction between procession and reversion. The first perfection, "what is necessary for a thing to exist", clearly corresponds to the substantial form possessed by a thing

[30] Ibn Sīnā, *K. an-najāt*, Cairo, 1913, 274,3-8; *K. ash-shifāᵓ/Ṭabīᶜiyyāt (6): Fī n-nafs* 1.5, 50,13-15; *R. fī l-kalām ᶜalā n-nafs al-nāṭiqa*, 198,8-12 (reading *li-l-mutaṣarrif* for al-Ahwānī's *li-t-taṣarruf*); *K. al-ishārāt wa-t-tanbīhāt*, 160,8-9; and *at-Taᶜlīqāt*, 176,8-11.

[31] In addition to the passages cited in note 139, see Ibn Sīnā, *K. al-ishārāt wa-t-tanbīhāt* 3, 125,16-18 and 126,12-17; *K. al-hidāya*, 302,9-305,7; and *R. fī n-nafs wa-baqāᵓihā wa-maᶜādihā* 2, 66,1-13

composed of form and matter. Without the substantial form, the composite would not exist as an actual, concrete thing. Here the substantial form will be seen to act on its effect, or explain its *explanandum*, as a formal cause. The reason why the substantial form – and hence the formal cause – is tied to procession is because the inherence of substantial forms in the sublunary world is the effect of an efficient cause: the Active Intellect, in its role as "Giver of Forms" (*wāhibu ṣ-ṣuwar*). Thus the first perfection, as articulated in cluster (3a), corresponds to the formal cause, and is itself the effect of an efficient cause.

The second perfection, as articulated in cluster (3a), "what is necessary for a thing to exist well", clearly refers to the exercise of the capability associated with that form. Which cause does that correspond to? I would like to say that it corresponds directly to the final cause *qua to hôi*. But because, strictly speaking, a second perfection ought to refer to an *activity* and not to an *active thing*, and because a cause is more likely to be an active thing than an activity, it is difficult to see how there will be a strict correspondence between the second perfection and the final cause *qua to hôi*.[32]

In a way this is the old question we saw in Philoponus: does *teleiotês* refer to "endedness", in which case it would refer to an activity (in this case, *serving as an end*); or to "end"; in which case it would refer to an active thing? Because of the lexical momentum in Arabic tying *kamāl* and *tamām* more closely to "end" than to "endedness", the problem is perhaps slightly less acute, and the second perfection, "what is necessary for a thing to exist well", can be understood both as an active thing and as an activity, and thus be seen to correspond to the final cause *qua to hôi*. Without actively striving to attain its goal, a thing would not be able to exist well. Here the active thing will be seen to act on its effect, or explain its *explanandum*, as a final cause *qua to hôi*, since by being an active user of what is below it, it succeeds in existing well.

In other words, the reason why the final cause *qua to hôi* is tied to reversion now appears to be because the final cause *qua to hôi* refers to the composite when it is actively using, and thus benefiting from, something below it in the cosmic hierarchy, in view of – that is, while striving to attain – something higher than it in the cosmic hierarchy. Thus the second perfection, as articulated in cluster (3a), corresponds to the final cause *qua to hôi*.

What about the final cause *qua to hou* and the efficient cause? How do they fit into the scheme of procession and reversion? Answering this question will require me to qualify my position that there is a direct correspondence between the first perfection and procession, and the second perfection and reversion. Instead, I should make the obvious point that procession and reversion are dynamic rather than static. A single thing cannot be extracted from procession or reversion and then held to be an element *only* in procession or *only* in reversion.

[32] *pace* Lettinck 1994, 167-171, who views the *to hou/to hôi* distinction as the straightforward equivalent (and antecedent) of Avicenna's distinction between first and second perfections.

A single thing is always playing two roles: one role is as an element of procession, and the other role is as an element of reversion.

As discussed above, when the substantial form is seen as an element of procession, it will act on its effect, or explain its *explanandum*, as a formal cause. When, on the other hand, the substantial form is seen as an element of reversion, it will act on its effect, or explain its *explanandum*, as a final cause *qua to hou*. This is because the substantial form acts on its effects not only as a formal cause, giving actual, concrete existence to the composite in which it inheres; but also as a final cause *qua to hou*, serving as the goal in view of which a lower being exercises the capability associated with its own (lower) substantial form.

I shall try to explain what I mean. Let Y be higher and X lower. Y's substantial form will serve in two roles, both as an element of procession and as an element of reversion. Seen as an element of procession, Y's substantial form operates as Y's own formal cause: it is by virtue of Y's possession of the substantial form "Y-ness" that it can be said to *exist* as a Y. Seen as an element of reversion, on the other hand, Y's substantial form operates as a final cause *qua to hou*, namely, as the final cause *qua to hou* of X. This is because X, being in possession of a lower substantial form (viz., "X-ness"), constantly strives to revert upwards by imitating Y and thereby coming to possess Y's substantial form (viz., "Y-ness").

Similarly, the efficient cause, like the final cause *qua to hôi*, corresponds to the composite when it is in a state of activity. Like the final cause *qua to hôi*, an efficient cause can only be a cause when it is active. This is because the active thing acts on its effect not only as a final cause *qua to hôi*, using what is beneath it in the cosmic hierarchy as a means of attaining some higher goal; but also as an efficient cause, moving what is beneath it in the cosmic hierarchy just as the soul moves the body, or giving existence to what is beneath it within its own species just as the father gives existence to the son.

Again, let Y be higher and X lower. Y will once more serve in two roles, both as an element of procession and as an element of reversion. Seen as an element of procession, Y operates as an efficient cause, by coming into contact with X, passing existence down to X and making X so actual and perfect and full of existence that X comes to possess Y's own substantial form (viz., "Y-ness"). Seen as an element of reversion, on the other hand, Y operates as a final cause *qua to hôi*. This is because Y uses X in view of an even higher element in the reversion – Z – whose substantial form (viz., "Z-ness") in turn operates as the final cause *qua to hou* of Y.

With this scheme in mind, we can begin to answer our question, namely, how does Avicenna's tying of perfection to the two types of final causality, as well as to efficient and formal causality, square with his distinction, articulated in cluster (3a), between first perfections and second perfections? The answer is that the formal cause and the efficient cause are, respectively, the *effect* of a first perfection and the first perfection *itself*. Y's first perfection is its efficient causality, an efficient causality which causes X's substantial form – X's formal cause, in other words – to come into existence.

Moreover, the final cause *qua to hôi* and the final cause *qua to hou* are, respectively, the *effect* of a second perfection and the second perfection itself. The second perfection for which Y strives is Y's final cause *qua to hou*, namely, the substantial form which Z possesses (viz., "Z-ness") and which Y imitates and strives to attain. Y's final causality *qua to hôi* – its use of X in order to imitate and attain "Z-ness", is therefore the effect of Y's second perfection.

What does all this X, Y and Z-ness tells us about Avicenna's theory of the separability of the human rational soul? It tells us that Avicenna's conception of the human rational soul was one which requires us to view the soul as dynamic rather than static, relative rather than absolute, and complex rather than simple. In other words, the human rational soul is constantly switching between activities of one sort or another – thinking, moving, using – each of which stands in a cause-and-effect relationship with the faculties of the soul below it and above it.

Simply put, the criterion of activity vs. inactivity will determine whether at any given moment the soul is separate or not. Avicenna's view, of course, is that in itself the human rational soul is *mufāraqa*, which means both *separable* as well as *separated*. *In itself*, then, the human rational soul is separable; but the human rational soul is *in fact* separated only when it is using its lower faculties, and its lower faculties are using the bodily organs they are associated with, in order to think. The human rational soul is in fact separated, in other words, only when it is operating as the final cause *qua to hôi* of its lower faculties and of the bodily organs those lower faculties are associated with, in view of its own, true, higher final cause *qua to hou*, namely, the immortality of the Active Intellect.

When it is asleep, however, or when it is using its lower faculties merely to reproduce or to nourish, the human rational soul is *not* in fact separated, only separable; when, in other words, the human rational soul is operating as the final cause *qua to hôi* of its lower faculties and of the bodily organs those lower faculties are associated with, in view of a false, lower final cause *qua to hou*, such as sensory gratification. And since sensory gratification is not the true and real final cause *qua to hou* of the human rational soul, nor, likewise, will the human rational soul be truly operating as a final cause *qua to hôi* of its lower faculties and of the bodily organs those lower faculties are associated with. The general rule to be drawn is that whenever the human rational soul is not operating as a true and real final cause *qua to hôi*, the human rational soul will not in fact be separated. This is because it is only when the human rational soul is operating as a real and true final cause *qua to hôi* – that is, whenever the human rational soul is using its lower faculties and the bodily organs those lower faculties are associated with, in view of its own, true final cause *qua to hou* – that the human rational soul will in fact be separated.

Why have I gone into such detail in analyzing how Avicenna's theory of perfection is related to his ideas about causality, and particularly final causality, and in explaining what that relationship tells us about his views concerning the soul's immanence or transcendence? There are two reasons. First of all, some scholars have presented Avicenna's ideas about the human rational soul's separability or separatedness as nothing but thinly veiled Platonism. For example, in an article first published in 1981, Muḥammad al-Miṣbāḥī suggested that Avicenna's use of the idea of "separable" or "separated" perfection (*al-kamālu l-mufāraq*) represented a dramatic turn away from Aristotle's psychology and towards Plato's.[33] Other scholars, such as Fazlur Rahman, call Avicenna's doctrine of the separability or separatedness of the human rational soul "entirely non-Aristotelian", claiming that a passage from the *Enneads* should be seen as its source.[34]

But given Avicenna's rejection of the Platonic/Plotinian doctrine of the soul's pre-existence and descent into the body; given the fact that Aristotle's position on the soul's, or at least the intellect's, separability or separatedness is more underdetermined than most modern scholars have allowed; given the radical conceptual transformation which the concept of perfection underwent as a result of the activities of Greek commentators and Greco-Arabic translators; and finally, given Avicenna's inheritance of an increasingly hardened distinction between the formal and material causes, which are intrinsic to or immanent in their effect, and the final and efficient causes, which are extrinsic to or transcend their effect; Avicenna's position on the soul's separability or separatedness should, I believe, be seen as a sophisticated and justifiable reading of Aristotle by a philosopher who stands as the culmination of the Ammonian synthesis, rather than as a symptom of his being in thrall to some caricature of Platonism or Neoplatonism.

[33] al-Miṣbāḥī 1980-81.

[34] Rahman 1952, 108, citing *Enneads* IV.7.12. In fact the Arabic version of the Plotinian chapter immediately following the passage which Rahman cites in support of his claim (*Uthūlūjiyā* 1, 18,13-16) expounds the doctrine of the soul's pre-existence and descent from the world of mind into the body, a position Avicenna is crystal-clear in rejecting. By Avicenna's reckoning the soul comes into existence (*ḥudūth*) at the same time as the body. Avicenna does maintain that it is not the body which is the essential cause of the soul's coming into existence, but rather the superlunary separate causes; but this in no way commits him to the Platonic/Plotinian position that the soul pre-exists the body and then descends into the body. For Avicenna's position that the soul does not pre-exist the body see, for example, the chapter entitled *Faṣlun fī ithbāti ḥudūthi n-nafsi* in *K. an-najāt 2: Ṭabīʿiyyāt*, 300,2-302,8, esp. 300,6 (*fa-muḥālun an takūna qad wujidat* [i.e., *an-nufūs*] *qabla l-badani*) and 301,12-13 (*fa-qad ṣaḥḥa idhan anna n-nafsa taḥduth kullamā yaḥduthi l-badanu ṣ-ṣāliḥu li-stiʿmālihā iyyāhu*); see also *K. ash-shifāʾ/Ṭabīʿiyyāt (6): Fī n-nafs* 5.4, 228,19-229,2. For a criticism of Avicenna's account of how the body is responsible for the soul's individuation, see now Druart 2000.

The second reason is that by describing as precisely as I can how Avicenna thought the soul was related to the body I hope to have shown how crucial an appreciation of the complex and dynamic cosmology of procession and reversion is to understanding what Gutas has named Avicenna's "metaphysics of the human rational soul". The next four chapters explain how Avicenna tries to integrate that cosmology of procession and return, a cosmology which he inherited from earlier thinkers of the Ammonian synthesis, with the ontology of the Muslim doctrinal theologians, or *mutakallimūn*, in order to lay the foundation for a new, Avicennian synthesis.

Part II

The Beginnings of the Avicennian Synthesis

7. Essence and Existence (A)
Materials from the Kalām and al-Fārābī

As shown above, when Avicenna distinguishes between first and second perfections on the basis of the difference between what is necessary for a thing's existence, and what is necessary for a thing's well-being, he has in mind a broader distinction, that between the downward procession of existence and the upward reversion towards well-being. Avicenna, like Proclus and Ammonius, maintained that the final cause was the Aristotelian cause best suited to explaining the upward reversion of each thing towards its well-being, and that the efficient cause was the Aristotelian cause best suited to explaining the downward procession of existence from one thing to another. I have just shown how the tension between procession and reversion plays out in the case of Avicenna's position on the issue of the ontology of the soul. But how are procession and reversion reflected in Avicenna's metaphysics and cosmology in general? Specifically, what does linking the final cause to reversion tell us about Avicenna's metaphysics of essence and existence, and about the ways in which God is the cause of the world? Chapters 7 through 11 will be devoted to answering those questions.[1]

In an article published in 1984, Jean Jolivet suggested that the origins of Avicenna's distinction between essence and existence lay not in ancient Greek philosophy, as has generally been supposed, but in early Islamic doctrinal theology (*kalām*), and specifically in the ninth- and tenth-century debates between Muslim dogmatists (*mutakallimūn*) over how the terms "thing" (*shayʾ*) and "existent" (*mawjūd*) relate to each other.[2] In the next four chapters I shall argue that Jolivet is correct in highlighting the *kalām* background to Avicenna's essence/existence distinction. I shall also argue, however, that an important and previously overlooked testing-ground for the essence/existence distinction – Avicenna's analysis of the relation between efficient and final causes – arose from his efforts to solve a problem of Aristotelian exegesis by appealing to Neoplatonic notions of procession and reversion.

Chapter 7 is an introduction to the problem. I shall survey early *kalām* discussions of things and existents, as well as al-Fārābī's discussions, and present evidence supporting Jolivet's hypothesis that these *kalām* discussions were the backdrop against which Avicenna made his distinction between essence (*māhiyya*, literally "whatness", and often Latinized as "quiddity") and existence

[1] Chapters 7 through 9 derive from Wisnovsky 2000, though with alterations, some minor, others significant.

[2] Jolivet 1984.

(*wujūd*).[3] While it is easy to imagine a progression from the *mutakallimūn*'s use of *mawjūd* ("existent") to Avicenna's use of *wujūd* ("existence"), the route from *shay*ᵓ ("thing") to *māhiyya* ("essence") seems less direct. I explore the possibility that the concept of "thingness", *shay*ᵓ*iyya*, served to link the *mutakallimūn*'s use of *shay*ᵓ and Avicenna's use of *māhiyya*. In Chapters 8 and 9, I discuss some previously unexamined passages where Avicenna uses the term *shay*ᵓ*iyya* to explain how the final cause can be seen to be prior to the efficient cause. More particularly, Chapter 8 addresses a philological problem: whether or not these passages should be emended to read *sababiyya*, "causality", instead of *shay*ᵓ*iyya*, "thingness". I argue that *shay*ᵓ*iyya* should be retained. In Chapter 9, I discuss what *shay*ᵓ*iyya* means in the context of Avicenna's attempt to unpack a rather compressed assertion which Aristotle makes about how efficient and final causes relate to each other. In so doing I hope to cast some light on how exactly the concept of thingness bridges the *mutakallimūn*'s discussions of things and existents, and Avicenna's distinction between essence and existence. Chapter 10 is devoted to showing how Avicenna's tying together of essence and final causality on the one hand, and existence and efficient causality on the other hand, can be better understood in the context of his inheritance of the Ammonian cosmology of procession and reversion.

Given the opaque and scattered nature of most of the early sources available to us, we cannot know for sure when and where thinkers writing in Arabic first used the terms *shay*ᵓ and *mawjūd*. It is fairly certain, however, that the *mutakallimūn*'s first discussions of things and existents arose not out of some general and spontaneous interest in ontology, but out of a desire to marshal Qurᵓānic evidence in favor of their own positions and against their opponents' on two basic theological topics: God's attributes (in this case, whether or not God could be correctly spoken of as a *thing*, and if so, how) and God's creative power (in this case, whether or not it is *things* which God causes to come into existence and pass out of existence, and if so, how). In order to buttress their arguments the *mutakallimūn* had to address the question of what *shay*ᵓ, "thing", means when it is used in the Qurᵓān.

The term *shay*ᵓ appears in many places in the Qurᵓān, and mainly refers, in a general and undifferentiated sense, to the objects of God's attributes. God is all-powerful (*qadīr*); over what is God all-powerful? Things, or, more precisely, every thing. Similarly, things are the objects of God's knowing (*ᶜ-l-m*), creating

[3] It is true that *māhiyya*, "quiddity", is only one of several terms – including *ḥaqīqa, dhāt, ṣūra, ṭabīᶜa* and, as we shall see, *shay*ᵓ*iyya* – which, taken as a whole, constitute Avicenna's idea of "essence" (cf. Goichon 1937, 48). As will become clear, *māhiyya* is first among equals in this cluster of terms. Goichon sees *dhāt* as the essential term for essence, following the lead of its Latin translation as *essentia*; *māhiyya*, by contrast, was rendered as *quidditas*.

(*kh-l-q*), witnessing (*sh-h-d*), being in charge of (*w-k-l*), preserving (*ḥ-f-ẓ*), encompassing (*ḥ-y-ṭ*), reckoning (*ḥ-s-b*) and supervising (*r-q-b*).[4]

Despite the Qurʾān's straightforward, quasi-pronominal use of *shayʾ* (*ʾamr* is used as an all-purpose direct object in much the same way), early commentators and *mutakallimūn* nevertheless tried to determine what precisely it meant to be a thing. For example, it seems clear enough that because things are the objects of God's attributes, they are *other than* God. The distinction between thing and God is reinforced by the famous verse 42:11, *laysa ka-mithlihi shayʾ*, "No thing is [even] like a likeness of Him". Believers are also instructed not to verge towards polytheism by associating things with God (3:64; 4:36; 6:151; 12:38; 22:26; 60:12). Finally, the divine act of creation is described in two famous verses, 16:40 (*inna-mā qawlunā li-shayʾin idhā aradnāhu an naqūla lahu kun fa-yakūnu*) and 36:82 (*inna-mā amruhu idhā arāda shayʾan an yaqūla kun fa-yakūnu*), as consisting in God's saying "Be!" to a thing, at which point the thing then *is*.

But the strong suggestion that things are other than God weakens slightly when one takes into account a number of verses that seem to indicate that God Himself is a thing. For example, 6:19, "Say: Which thing is the greatest in terms of witnessing? Say: God is witness between you and me" (*qul ayyu shayʾin akbaru shahādatan qul Allāhu shahīdun baynī wa-baynaka*), implies that God is a thing, and 28:88, "Every thing will perish save His face" (*kullu shayʾin hālikun illā wajhahu*), implies that at least the divine countenance is a thing.

This ambiguity was reinforced by the early Arabic grammarians, who held that *shayʾ* was the most generally applicable of terms (*aʿammu l-ʿāmm*), applying to all that may be placed in relation to a predicate (*yaqaʿu ʿalā kulli mā ukhbira ʿanhu*).[5] That is, *shayʾ* refers to every *mubtadaʾ* (subject) in relation to which one could place a *khabar* (predicate). If we want to predicate any attributes of God, therefore, we will be forced to maintain that He is a thing. This grammatical consideration seems to have overridden the weight of Qurʾānic evidence, and apart from the very early arch-unitarian Jahm ibn Ṣafwān (d. 746), who – as we shall see – held to a strictly understood interpretation of thing (namely, that it was synonymous with *makhlūq*, "created", and that therefore

[4] *q-d-r*: 2:20, 2:26, 2:109, 2:148, 2:259, 2:284, 3:26, 3:29, 3:165, 3:189, 4:85, 5:17, 5:19, 5:40, 5:120, 6:17, 8:41, 9:39, 11:4, 16:77, 18:45, 22:6, 24:45, 29:20, 30:50, 33:27, 35:1, 41:39, 42:9, 46:33, 48:21, 57:2, 59:6, 64:1, 65:12; *ʿ-l-m*: 2:29, 2:231, 2:282, 4:32, 4:176, 5:97, 6:80, 6:101, 7:89, 8:75, 9:115, 20:98, 21:81, 24:35, 24:64, 29:42, 29:62, 33:40, 33:54, 40:7, 42:12, 48:26, 49:16, 57:3, 58:7, 64:11; *kh-l-q*: 6:101, 6:102, 13:16, 16:48, 20:50, 25:2, 27:88, 32:7, 39:62, 40:62, 51:49, 54:49; *sh-h-d*: 4:33, 5:117, 22:17, 33:55, 34:47, 41:53, 58:6 (and implied in 3:5, 14:38, 40:16); *w-k-l*: 6:102, 11:12, 39:62; *ḥ-f-ẓ*: 11:57, 34:21; *ḥ-y-ṭ*: 4:126, 41:54; *ḥ-s-b*: 4:86; and *r-q-b*: 33:52.

[5] Sībawayhi (d. ca. 796), *al-Kitāb I*, 47,7; and *ap.* az-Zabīdī, *Tāj al-ʿarūs min jawāhir al-qāmūs I*, 185a20-21.27-28. The formulation *ash-shayʾu huwa mā yajūzu an yukhbara ʿanhu* is also found in al-Khʷārazmī (d. 997), *Mafātiḥ al-ʿulūm*, 22,14-15; in that same work al-Khʷārazmī reports (199,14-200,1) that *shayʾ* is also used by the "Algebrists" as a kind of universal variable.

God was not a thing), consensus arose around the fence-straddling assertion that God was a *shayʾun lā ka-l-ashyāʾi*, "a thing not like [other] things".[6]

But whether or not it is right to call God a thing was not the only problem which the term *shayʾ* forced the early *mutakallimūn* to confront. More seriously, the *mutakallimūn* had to contend with the implication of verses 16:40 and 36:82 (mentioned above) that things were somehow there *before* God said "Be!" to them; for otherwise, what would God be saying "Be!" to?[7] It seemed perfectly sensible to draw the conclusion, as most Muᶜtazilites did, that thing applies not only to what exists (*al-mawjūd*) but also to what does not exist (*al-maᶜdūm*); and that what does not exist in turn applies not only to what did not exist and now exists, such as the world, but also to what does not now exist but will exist, such as the Day of Resurrection.

Other *mutakallimūn*, by contrast, held that *shayʾ* applies solely to what exists. This was partly because the Muᶜtazilite view could be seen as leading to two unsavory alternatives. The first arises from the premise that even before it exists one particular thing – my great-great-grandson – is and always has been distinct from another particular thing – my great-great-granddaughter. In 68 years God will say "Be!" to one non-existent thing, my great-great-grandson, and in 72 years God will say "Be!" to another non-existent thing, my great-great-granddaughter. The same premise can be applied to things that have existed but now do not. Thus my great-great grandfather, even though he is non-existent now, remains one thing, and my great-great-grandmother remains another thing, and both will remain distinct things up to, including and (presumably) beyond the Day of Judgment. The problem is that all these pre- and post-existent individual things must *be* or *subsist* somewhere before and after they exist. Let us say they are all located somewhere *outside* God's mind; in that case they will share the attribute of eternality with God, and the precept of *tawḥīd*, understood as divine uniqueness, will be violated. Let us then say that they are all located *within* God's mind; in that case they will introduce multiplicity into God, and the precept of *tawḥīd*, understood as divine simplicity, will be violated.

Alternatively, and just as problematically, the Muᶜtazilite conception could be understood as implying that before and after they exist, things were and will be undifferentiated, just one great eternal blob of Thing. In other words, when things are non-existent, they are undifferentiated; when things are existent, they are distinct one from the other. But this conception would expose the Muᶜtazilites to the charge that an eternal and undifferentiated non-existent Thing was, for all intents and purposes, equivalent to the eternal and (in itself)

[6] (Ps.-)Abū Ḥanīfa (ca. 950), *al-Fiqh al-akbar* (= Mullā ᶜAlī b. Sulṭān Muḥammad al-Qārī, *Sharḥ al-fiqh al-akbar*), 16,18.

[7] The term *amr* is used synonymously with *shayʾ* to refer to the things which God is saying "Be!" to, at 2:117, 3:47, 19:35, 36:82 and 40:68. In his *Tafsīr* (*ad* 2:117) aṭ-Ṭabarī (d. 923) describes the positions of various "interpreters" (*muʾawwilūn*) on this issue (*Tafsīr aṭ-Ṭabarī II*, 542,1-550,7).

undifferentiated prime matter of the Eternalists (*ad-dahriyya*). God's sole possession of eternality will be infringed upon, and the precept of *tawḥīd*, understood as divine uniqueness, will once again be violated.[8]

To some extent the arguments just articulated are conjecture, for as I mentioned above, contemporaneous evidence of early *kalām* discussions of things and existents is hard to come by. Al-Ashᶜarī's (d. 935) *Maqālāt al-islāmiyyīn* contains a few typically terse descriptions of the views held by early *mutakallimūn*:

(1) a thing is something created which has a likeness (Jahm ibn Ṣafwān and various Zaydī Shiᶜites);
(2) a thing is a body (Anthropomorphists – *al-mushabbiha*);
(3) a thing is what can be pointed to (Hishām al-Fuwaṭī [d. ca. 842]);
(4) a thing is a thing before it comes into being (ᶜAbbād b. Sulaymān [d. 864]; certain Baghdadi Muᶜtazilites); saying "X is a thing" is the same as affirming X; affirming X covers the time before X came into being as well as the time after it came into being (al-Khayyāṭ [d. ca. 913]); a thing is all that can be known, and all that can be called to mind and of which predication is possible; things are knowable as things before they come into being. Things can be called things before they come into being (al-Jubbāʾī [d. 915]);
(5) a thing is an existent (al-Ashᶜarī); a thing is a thing only when it exists (Abū l-Ḥusayn aṣ-Ṣāliḥī; Ibn ar-Rāwandī [d. ca. 950]).[9]

From the end of the ninth century to the end of the tenth – the period, that is, just before Avicenna started writing philosophy – the *mutakallimūn* holding positions 1, 2 and 3 became increasingly isolated, and the debate about things polarized into positions 4 and 5, with most Muᶜtazilites holding position 4 and virtually everyone else – Ashᶜarites and Māturīdites in particular, but also some Shiᶜites – holding position 5.[10] With God's uniqueness and simplicity at stake,

[8] On this see Wolfson 1946, reprised in Wolfson 1976, 359-372. The world-view of the eternalists was shaped partly by Aristotelian notions of potentiality (*quwwa*) and actuality (*fiᶜl*) then coming into circulation. See, for example, al-Kindī (d. ca. 870), *R. ilā Aḥmad b. al-Muᶜtaṣim fī l-ibāna ᶜan sujūd al-jirm al-aqṣā wa-ṭāᶜatihi li-llāh ᶜazza wa-jalla*, 187,3-19; as well as the evidence preserved in the Jābirean corpus (ca. 900), where one can detect the infiltration of notions of potentiality and actuality into the *shayʾ/mawjūd/maᶜdūm* paradigm: *K. ikhrāj mā fī l-quwwa ilā l-fiᶜl*, 2,14-3,1; *K. al-khawāṣṣ al-kabīr*, 357,1-2; *K. al-mīzān aṣ-ṣaghīr*, 427,3-5; 431,8-11; 445,13-14; 451,18.

[9] See al-Ashᶜarī, *Maqālāt al-islāmiyyīn I-II*, 158,1-163,8; 181,1-182,4; and 518,4-520,8. Perhaps our earliest source regarding the debate over things and existents is the Zaydī Shiᶜite al-Qāsim ibn Ibrāhīm (d. 860), *K. ad-dalīl al-kabīr*, 74,10-76,7.

[10] Muᶜtazilites: al-Khayyāṭ, *K. al-instiṣār*, 60,4-14; 107,6-108,8; 126,1-2; Saᶜdiyā al-Fayyūmī (i.e., Saadia Gaon, d. 942), *K. al-amānāt wa-l-iᶜtiqādāt*, 11,10-12 and 213,13-15; ᶜAbd al-Jabbār (d. 1025), *al-Mughnī IV* 247,12-13; *V* 202,8-203,9; 249,4-8; 251,3-4; 252,4-6; *VI/1* 79,17-80,15; *VI/2* 75,5-77,7 and 135,3-136,9; *VIII* 74,1-82,12; *XII* 20,1-3 and 48,5-6. Ashᶜarites: Ibn Fūrak (d. 1015), *Mujarrad maqālāt al-Ashᶜarī*, 42,7-18 and 252,4-256,22; and al-Bāqillānī (d. 1013), *K. at-tamhīd*, 193,17-194,6; 195,6-196,12; 266,4-9. (In fact, al-Ashᶜarī admitted in his *K. al-ᶜamad* that

not to mention the nature of His causation of the world, the original dogmatic formulae devised to encapsulate these two positions grew into fully articulated school doctrines. The *kalām* discussion of things and existents came to encompass general questions of ontology, and the metaphysical notions used in the debate became more sophisticated.

This increase in complexity went hand in hand with the intensifying philosophical activity of the period, activity that involved translating Greek philosophical texts into Arabic as well as composing original philosophical works in Arabic. In his *Kitāb fī l-falsafat al-ūlā*, al-Kindī uses *shay*ʾ in a brief discussion of essence, existents and non-existents, but for the latter three terms he uses *dhāt*, *ays* and *lays* respectively.[11] Al-Fārābī was the first *faylasūf* to incorporate the term *māhiyya* ("whatness", "quiddity" or simply "essence") – a term deriving primarily from the rendering of the Greek *to ti ên einai* as *mā huwa* in the Arabic translations of Aristotle's logical works – into the *kalām* problematic of things and existents.[12]

Al-Fārābī appears at first glance to come down fully on the side of the Muᶜtazilites on the issue of whether or not thing was a more overarching category than existent, but closer examination reveals that his view is more

he himself had originally held the Muᶜtazilite position: "We wrote a treatise on the topic of 'thing', to the effect that things are things even if they be non-existent. We have retreated from it [i.e., the position articulated in this book] and [now] contradict it, so whoever comes across it [the book], let him not place any store by it"; reported by Ibn ᶜAsākir, *Tabyīn kadhib al-muftarī fī-mā nusiba ilā l-Imām Abī l-Ḥasan al-Ashᶜarī*, 133,5-6.) Māturīdites: al-Māturīdī (d. ca. 944), *K. at-tawḥīd*, 39,20-43,21; 86,2-92,20; 104,8-106,18; 242,3-16; and Abū l-Layth as-Samarqandī (d. ca. 990), *Sharḥ al-fiqh al-absaṭ li-Abī Ḥanīfa*, 119,1-2 (= lines 426-7). Shiᶜites: ash-Shaykh al-Mufīd (d. 1022), *Awāʾil al-maqālāt fī l-madhāhib wa-l-mukhtārāt*, 42,14-19. See also Frank 1980 and now Frank 1999; Dhanani 1994, 27 n.4 and 29-30; McDermott 1978, 196-9; Klein-Franke 1994; Gimaret 1988, 142-150; and van Ess 1991-1997, *I* 357f.; *II* 481f. and 499-501; *IV* 45-49 and 432-435.

[11] al-Kindī, *K. fī l-falsafat al-ūlā*, 41,3-43,18.

[12] It is true that *to ti ên einai* (and its variants) was translated as *māhiyya* only rarely, and primarily in the context of distinguishing definition (*al-ḥadd*) from property (*al-khāṣṣa*): the former is a statement that "indicates the thing's essence" (*ad-dāllu ᶜalā māhiyyati sh-shayʾi*), the latter one that does not. See, for example, *Top.* 101b38-102a1 (= *Ṭūbīka*, 474,17); 102a21 (= 475,14); 103b10-11 (= 481,11); and 154a30 (= 685,12-13). In the *Organon to ti ên einai* was mostly translated as *mā huwa*. See, for example, *An. Post.* 83a21 (= *Taḥlīlāt thāniyya*, 375,6); 83b5 (= 376,14); 84a26 (= 380,8); 97a25 (= 448,5) and 97b2 (= 449,4); 102a32-33 (= 476,12); 103b21.30.34 (= 482,4.12.15); 120b21 (= 552,15); 122a5-6.12-19.21.32.36 (= 557,18, 558,6-11.13 and 559,4.8.9.10.11[*bis*]); 128a14.19 (= 581,15 and 582,1) and 148a1 (= 656,8). It is also translated as *mā huwa sh-shayʾ*: *An. Post.* 79a25.27.29 (= *Taḥlīlāt thāniyya*, 354,2.4.5) and *Top.* 101b22 (= *Ṭūbīka*, 474,1); and as *mā sh-shayʾ*: *An. Post.* 82b37 (= *Taḥlīlāt thāniyya*, 373,15); and *Top.* 101b21 (= *Ṭūbīka*, 473,17); *Top.* 103b24.26 (= *Ṭūbīka*, 482,8.9) and 148a1 (= 656,7). In the *Metaphysics*, *to ti ên einai* was translated as *mā huwa* at 994b17 (= *Mā baᶜda ṭ-ṭabīᶜa I*, 34,8) and 993a18 (= *I*, 161,13); as *mā hiya* and *mā sh-shayʾ* at 1016a33-34 (= *II*, 536,5-6); as *mā huwa sh-shay'* at 994a11 (= *I*, 17,3); as *mā anniyyatu sh-shay'* at 1024b29 (= *II*, 685,1); and as *mā kaynūnatu sh-shayʾ* at 1013b22 (= *II*, 487,14). Mostly, however, *to ti ên einai* in the *Metaphysics* was translated as *mā huwa bi-l-anniyya*: at 1025b29-29 (= *II* 705,8); 1030a6 (= *II* 795,10); 1030a17 (= *II* 798,6); 1030a29 (= *II* 802,6); 1031a9-10 (= *II* 818,10); 1031a18 (= *II* 821,16); 1031b30 (= *II* 831,7); 1033b7 (= *II* 860,15-16); 1035b16 (= *II* 903,8); 1037a21 (= *II* 936,8-9); 1037a33-b1 (= *II* 939,15); 1044a36 (= *II* 1074,1); 1045b3 (= *II* 1096,13); and 1075a2 (= *II* 1693,1).

nuanced. Al-Fārābī first establishes that his definition of *mawjūd* as "that which, outside the soul, is set apart by some essence, be it conceived of or not" (*mā huwa munḥāzun bi-māhiyyatin mā khārija n-nafsi tuṣuwwirat aw lam tutaṣawwar*), is broader and hence more basic than the other definitions of *mawjūd* he suggests.[13] Al-Fārābī defines *shayʾ*, on the other hand, as "all that possesses some essence, in whichever way, be it outside the soul or conceived of in any sense whatsoever, divided up or undivided" (*kullu mā lahu māhiyyatun mā kayfa kāna khārija n-nafsi aw kāna mutaṣawwaran ʿalā ayyi jihatin kāna munqasimatan aw ghayra munqasimatin*).[14] Thus defined, *mawjūd* is not as broadly applicable as *shayʾ*, because *shayʾ* covers essences both outside and inside the mind, whereas *mawjūd* covers merely those outside the mind. In this sense al-Fārābī appears to be echoing the Muʿtazilite position.

On the other hand, al-Fārābī again follows the Arabic translations of the Organon and argues that *mawjūd* has one technical use that *shayʾ* does not: as the copula (*rābiṭ*) that connects the subject (here the logical term *al-mawḍūʿ* as opposed to the grammatical term *al-mubtadaʾ*) to the predicate (*al-maḥmūl* as opposed to *al-khabar*) in categorical affirmative propositions (*fī l-aqāwīli l-jāzimati l-mūjibati*).[15] For example, al-Fārābī says, when we wish to state that Zayd is a just person, it might make sense to say "Zayd is existent as a just person" (*Zaydun mawjūdun ʿādilan*), while it makes no sense to say "Zayd is thing as a just person" (*Zaydun shayʾun ʿādilan*). In this technical, copulative sense, *mawjūd* is more broadly applicable than *shayʾ*, although al-Fārābī stresses that the first, non-copulative sense of *mawjūd* is more basic. As he did with *māhiyya*, al-Fārābī has tried to incorporate an Aristotelian notion – here the copulative or predicative sense of *to einai*, "to be" – into the *kalām* problematic of *shayʾ* vs. *mawjūd*.[16] To sum up al-Fārābī's position, then, *shayʾ* is more broadly applicable than *mawjūd* in the first, more basic sense, yet less broadly applicable than *mawjūd* in the second, more technical sense.[17]

The *kalām* discussions of things and existents and al-Fārābī's efforts to Aristotelianize them provide the backdrop for an important discussion in *Ilāhiyyāt* 1.5 of Avicenna's *Kitāb ash-shifāʾ*, where Avicenna takes some important steps towards constructing a distinction between essence and

[13] al-Fārābī, *K. al-ḥurūf*, 116,23-117,1.

[14] al-Fārābī, *K. al-ḥurūf*, 128,6-8.

[15] al-Fārābī, *K. al-ḥurūf*, 125,12-13.

[16] al-Fārābī, *K. al-ḥurūf*, 128,12-13. In *Metaph.* 4.2, 1003b10 (= *Mā baʿda ṭ-ṭabīʿa I*, 301,9-10) Aristotle claims that we can say that even something that is non-existent (*to mê on = alladhī laysa bi-huwiyyatin*) in some sense *is* non-existent (*einai mê on = fa-innahu laysa huwiyyatan*). Generally speaking, *to on* in the *Metaphysics* was translated into Arabic not as *al-mawjūd* but as *al-huwiyya* ("being"). Al-Fārābī's analysis is discussed by Jolivet 1984, 17; Abed 1991, 111-117; Zimmermann 1981, xliv-xlv, lx-lxiii and cxxx-cxxxiv; and Shehadi 1982, 45-69.

[17] In his *Introduction* (to Logic, that is), al-Fārābī is neutral about which term is more broadly applicable, saying simply that "Thing and existent are the most generally applicable [terms] by which an individual or species may be characterized (*fa-innā sh-shayʾa wa-l-mawjūda humā aʿammu mā yumkinu an yūṣafa bihi shakhṣun aw nawʿun*)": *K. īsāghūjī ay al-madkhal*, 122,7-8.

existence.[18] In *Ilāhiyyāt* 1.5 Avicenna attempts to make the following points. First (29,5-31,2), he argues that thing and existent are primitive, basic and immediately apprehensible concepts. Because there are no terms more broadly applicable than thing and existent, they are indefinable, in the Aristotelian sense of definition at least; that is, there is no genus under which they can be subsumed as species. Second (31,2-32,3), Avicenna shows that thing and existent have different meanings. "Thing" is associated with terms such as "inner reality" (*ḥaqīqa*) and "whatness" (*māhiyya*), and refers to an entity viewed in light of essence; "existent" is associated with terms such as "affirmed" (*muthbat*) and "realized" (*muḥaṣṣal*), and refers to an entity viewed in light of existence. Third (32,3-34,14), Avicenna explains that although they have different meanings, thing and existent are co-implied (*mutalāzimāni*). In this context, Avicenna's purpose in describing *shayʾ* and *mawjūd* as co-implied is to convey the idea that although they have different meanings, neither *shayʾ* nor *mawjūd* is more broadly applicable than the other: the domains of objects to which each term refers fully overlap. The reflexivity inherent in the sixth-form term *talāzum* has important connotations as far as Avicenna's distinction between essence and existence is concerned. For at least in this context, Avicenna is saying that neither *shayʾ* nor *mawjūd* is logically prior to the other. There is no hint here that being an existent is somehow subordinate to, or an accident of, being a thing.

To sum up, then, the debate in the tenth century came to turn on how things and existents relate to each other both *extensionally* (that is, whether or not the domain of things overlaps with the domain of existents) and *intensionally* (that is, whether or not thing and existent have the same meaning). Logically speaking, these were the options:

(1) *thing and existent are mutually exclusive both extensionally and intensionally*: "things are never existents and existents are never things; to be a thing and to be an existent have different meanings" (no one from this period seems to have held this view);

(2) *thing is subsumed extensionally but not intensionally under existent*: "things are always existents but existents are not always things; to be a thing and to be an existent have different meanings" (no one from this period seems to have held this view);

(3a) *existent is subsumed extensionally but not intensionally under thing*: "existents are always things but things are not always existents; to be a thing and to be an existent have different meanings" (most Muʿtazilites)

(3b) *existent is subsumed extensionally but not intensionally under thing**: "existents are always things but things are not always existents (*although

[18] Ibn Sīnā, *K. ash-shifāʾ/Ilāhiyyāt (1)*, 29,5-34,14.

mawjūd can be used as a copula whereas *shay*ᵓ cannot); to be a thing and to be an existent have different meanings" (al-Fārābī);

(4a) *thing and existent are identical both extensionally and intensionally*: "things are always existents, and existents are always things; to be a thing and to be an existent have the same meaning" (Ashᶜarites and Māturīdites);

(4b) *thing and existent are identical extensionally but different intensionally*: "things are always existents, and existents are always things; to be a thing and to be an existent have different meanings" (Avicenna).

The debt Avicenna owes to the *kalām* discussions of things and existents seems self-evident, given the similarity of his position to that of the Ashᶜarites and Māturīdites. In this regard Jolivet is surely correct. But more precisely, Avicenna's position in *Ilāhiyyāt* 1.5 is a compromise between the Ashᶜarites' and Māturīdites' position on the one hand, and the Muᶜtazilites' and al-Fārābī's position on the other. For although Avicenna advocates the extensional identity of thing and existent just as the Ashᶜarites and Māturīdites do, he also advocates the intensional difference between thing and existent just as the Muᶜtazilites and al-Fārābī do.

In any case, Jolivet reckons that the influence of the *mutakallimūn* was greater than that of the Aristotelian philosophers because no Greek antecedent can be found for *shay*ᵓ (*pragma* is the possibility Jolivet explores and rejects), in contrast to *mawjūd*, whose roots lie in the Greek term *to on* (and similarly *ta onta* for *mawjūdāt*, and *to einai* for *wujūd*).[19] Although Jolivet is correct in asserting that *to on* is the Greek equivalent of *mawjūd*, and that *pragma* is not the Greek equivalent of *shay*ᵓ, the fact remains that a Greek antecedent for *shay*ᵓ does exist: *ti* ("something"). In fact, the question of the ontological status of the non-existent – *to mê on* – and its relation to the something – *to ti* – has an ancient pedigree. The problem originates with some cryptic lines of Parmenides, is discussed at length by Plato in the *Sophist*, is analyzed by Aristotle in the *Metaphysics* and the *Physics*, and emerges as a coherent ontology among the Stoics, who – like the Muᶜtazilites and al-Fārābī – put "something" (*ti*) at the top of their ontological pyramid, above even "existent" (*to on*).[20]

[19] Jolivet 1984, 15-16. On this see also Hadot 1980.

[20] Parmenides, fr. VI, lines 1-2 (*esti gar einai, mêden d'ouk estin* – "It is [possible] to be, but there is no nothing") and VII,1 (*ou gar mêpote touto damêi einai mê eonta* – "That there are non-existent things will never be proven") (In fact, Parmenides comes across as a proto-Ashᶜarite when al-Fārābī – perhaps distilling Aristotle's refutation of Parmenides at *Phys.* 1.3, 186a22-b12 [= *aṭ-Ṭabīᶜa*, 21,1-14; 23,15-25,2 and 26,1-4], or, as appears more likely, simply lifting from Abū ᶜAlī ibn as-Samḥ's commentary on that passage [= *aṭ-Ṭabīᶜa*, 22,1-23,14; 25,3-22 and 26,5-8; see particularly *wa-mā laysa bi-mawjūdin laysa bi-shay*ᵓ*in* at 22,2] – quotes Parmenides as asserting that "All that is other than existent will not be a thing" – *wa-kullu mā huwa ghayru mawjūdin fa-laysa bi-shay*ᵓ*in*: al-Fārābī, *K. al-ḥurūf*, 128,19); Plato, *Sophist* 236E onwards; Aristotle, *Metaph.* 4.2, 1003b10 (= *Mā baᶜda ṭ-ṭabīᶜa I*, 301,9-10) (At *Metaph.* 14.2, 1089a5-28, Aristotle argues that Plato's conception of *to mê on* as "the false" – *to pseudos* – is useless in explaining coming-to-be and passing-away, and proposes that a better conception of *to mê on* is "the potential" – *to kata*

It would be tempting to assert a Stoic link here, but tracing Stoic influence on Arabic *kalām* and *falsafa* has always been a tricky business. Many scholars have tried, with varying degrees of success.[21] Less uncertain is the influence Stoicism had on the Greek Aristotle-commentators, whom the Arabic philosophers in turn read carefully. For example, in his commentary on Book 4, Chapter 1 of Aristotle's *Topics*, Alexander of Aphrodisias criticizes the Stoics for elevating "something" above "existent":

L34

Alexander, *in Top.* 4.1 (*ad* 121a10), 301,19-25

> Here is a way you can demonstrate how wrong the Stoics are in holding that "something" is the genus under which "existent" is subsumed: if it is a something, it will clearly be an existent as well; and if it is an existent it will be definable as existent. Now they wriggle out of this dilemma by holding that "existent" is said of bodies alone, and on this basis they speak about "something" being a higher genus than it, given that it ["something"] is predicable of incorporeal as well as corporeal entities.

Now any attempt to use this particular passage as evidence of a direct filiation between Stoic and Mu^c^tazilite ontology will be frustrated by the fact that only Alexander's comments on part of Book 1 and Books 5-8 of the *Topics* survive, at least according to Ibn an-Nadīm.[22] But elsewhere in Alexander's commentary on the *Topics*, as well as in Simplicius' commentary on the *Categories*, the Stoic ontology is articulated, although less starkly than in the *in Top.* 4.1 passage just translated.[23] To sum up: Jolivet is correct in asserting that the *kalām* discussions of things and existents were likely to have been the most important (and certainly the most immediate) influences on Avicenna, but wrong in reasoning that this was because ancient philosophers had no such discussions.

Having briefly dealt with the question of Greek antecedents, I can focus on the question of how exactly the *kalām* discussions of things and existents influenced Avicenna's distinction between essence and existence. For while it is easy enough to imagine his making the move from *mawjūd* to *wujūd*, less obvious is Avicenna's progression from *shay*ᵓ to *māhiyya*, the term he uses most consistently to describe essence when contrasting it with existence. To some

dunamin – a position followed explicitly by al-Fārābī, *K. al-ḥurūf*, 120,8-121,6 and 123,1-124,4; see also Aristotle's distinction between absolute and incidental non-existence in *Phys.* 1.8 and 1.9, 191a23-192b7 [= *aṭ-Ṭabī*ᶜ*a*, 66,1-76,4]). On the Stoic ontology, and on the way in which incorporeals are said to "subsist" rather than "exist", see Hadot 1969; Graeser 1971; Goldschmidt 1972; Pasquino 1978; Brunschwig 1988 and 1990; and now Caston 1999.

[21] e.g., Pines 1936, 116-117; van Ess 1966, 191-200; Jadaane 1968, 43-98; and Wolfson 1976, 355-372; these are reviewed briefly in Gutas 1994, 4959-4962.

[22] Ibn an-Nadīm, *K. al-fihrist*, 249,17-19.

[23] Alexander *in Top.* 1.5 (*ad* 101b38) 42,13-25, and 4.6 (*ad* 127a26), 359,12-16; Simplicius *in Cat.* 5 (*ad* 3b10-23), 105,7-20, and 8 (*ad* 8b26), 222,30-33.

extent Avicenna's progression from *shay'* to *māhiyya* can be reconstructed by analyzing the *Ilāhiyyāt* 1.5 passage devoted to showing how thing and existent have different meanings.

In that passage Avicenna starts by asserting that every thing (*shay'*) or entity (*amr*) has an inner reality (*ḥaqīqa*) by which it is what it is (31,5-6). This inner reality (e.g., triangularity) is sometimes called "existence that is specific" (*al-wujūd al-khāṣṣ*); specific, that is, to one class of things (triangles) as opposed to another class of things (cats). Existence that is specific is distinct from the more general type of existence which Avicenna calls "affirmative existence" (*al-wujūd al-ithbātī*) (31,7-8). To predicate affirmative existence of an entity is to assert *that* the entity is, not *what* the entity is. To predicate existence that is specific, on the other hand, is to assert *what* the entity is, not *that* the entity is. Since existence that is specific is identical to inner reality, and since inner reality is identical to whatness (*māhiyya*), it follows that existence that is specific is identical to whatness (31,10). Since existence that is specific is identical to whatness, and since existence that is specific is distinct from affirmative existence, it follows that whatness is distinct from affirmative existence. In other words, essence is distinct from existence.[24]

A brief remark later on in *Ilāhiyyāt* 1.5 raises the intriguing possibility that *shay'iyya*, thingness, served to link Avicenna's distinction between things and existents on the one hand and his distinction between essence and existence on the other:

L35

Ibn Sīnā, *Kitāb ash-shifā'/Ilāhiyyāt (1)* 1.5, 33,16-18
Avicenna, *Liber de philosophia prima sive scientia divina I-IV*, 38,20-23

> According to people who hold this view [that what is predicated can be a non-existent, i.e., the Muᶜtazilites], in and among all that is predicated and known are some entities [*'umūran* = *res*] that, when non-existent, possess no thingness [*lā shay'iyyata lahā* = *non habent similitudinem*]; let the person who is inclined to agree with that go back to whatever dogmatic formulae they babbled out unintelligibly, [formulae] which do not deserve any attention.[25]

In this passage Avicenna is attacking those who maintain that there is a class of non-existent entities that possess no thingness, and hence are not things. A later commentator on the *Ilāhiyyāt*, Mullā Mahdī Narāqī (d. 1764), advises us that Avicenna's target here was a group of Muᶜtazilites who, in maintaining that some non-existents (viz., those that are impossible, *al-mustaḥīlāt* or *al-*

[24] Avicenna's discussion of things and existents in *Ilāhiyyāt* 1.5 is related to similar treatments in Aquinas' work in Craemer-Ruegenberg 1991.
[25] I shall discuss in Chapter 8 the various mistranslations of *shay'iyya* into Latin.

*mumtani*ᶜ*āt*) had no thingness and hence were not things, deviated from the classical doctrine of their school.[26]

Despite Avicenna's use of the term *shay*ʾ*iyya* here, any attempt to prove that the term served to bridge the ninth- and tenth-century *kalām* discussions of things and existents on the one hand, and Avicenna's discussions of essence and existence on the other, will face two difficult challenges. The first challenge is that *shay*ʾ*iyya* would play a bridging role more convincingly if that term had appeared often and in a wide variety of ninth- and tenth-century *kalām* texts. It does not. In fact, I have not seen a single instance of *shay*ʾ*iyya* where I most expected to find it: in a text written by a Muᶜtazilite, a member of the school most infamous for affirming the thingness of the non-existent. Nor, to my knowledge, does *shay*ʾ*iyya* appear in an Ashᶜarite text until al-Juwaynī (d. 1085), that is, not until a generation after Avicenna's death.[27]

But *shay*ʾ*iyya* does make a few appearances in the tenth century. It turns up once (in a passage attributed to Jaᶜfar aṣ-Ṣādiq (d. 765) commenting on the credal formula *shay*ʾ*un lā ka-l-ashyā*ʾ*i*, "[God is] a thing not like [other] things") in the *Kāfī* of the Shiᶜite traditionist Abū Jaᶜfar al-Kulaynī (d. 940).[28] It is only in the *Kitāb at-tawḥīd* of al-Māturīdī (d. 944) that *shay*ʾ*iyya* is also used consistently to describe and attack the doctrine of the Muᶜtazilites.[29] Later in the tenth century, al-Māturīdī's use of *shay*ʾ*iyya* in the context of anti-Muᶜtazilite polemics was echoed in the *Sharḥ al-fiqh al-absaṭ li-Abī Ḥanīfa* of the Ḥanafite scholar Abū l-Layth as-Samarqandī (d. 990).[30]

Are these appearances of *shay*ʾ*iyya* the first uses of the term, or are they evidence of earlier Muᶜtazilite use? At this stage of research it is difficult to tell.

[26] Mullā Mahdī Narāqī, *Sharḥ al-ilāhiyyāt min kitāb ash-shifā*ʾ, 265,2. Marmura 1984a (revised slightly in Marmura 1991-92) argues that what troubled Avicenna specifically was the Muᶜtazilite Abū Hāshim's and his followers' application of their *shay*ʾ*/mawjūd/ma*ᶜ*dūm* paradigm to the problem of bodily resurrection. Also see Black 1997 for a discussion of the dilemmas that faced Avicenna in distinguishing between fictional entities such as phoenixes, which have some kind of mental existence even though they never exist as concrete objects in the outside world, and impossibilities such as a square circle, which have neither mental nor concrete existence.

[27] Strangely enough, Juwaynī devoted a long section of his *Shāmil* to reviewing the debate about things and existents, yet does not once use the term *shay*ʾ*iyya* there: *ash-Shāmil fī uṣūl ad-dīn*, 23,18-33,24; but see his use of the term in other contexts, at 113,2.4; 161,25.26.27; and 169,6.17. Ash-Shahrastānī (d. 1153) uses *shay*ʾ*iyya* in several places: *K. nihāyat al-iqdām fī* ᶜ*ilm al-kalām*, 33,20; 150,7.8.10; and 151,2.7. For an argument that ash-Shahrastānī is more properly described as an Ismāᶜīlī, rather than an Ashᶜarite, see Steigerwald 1997. Al-Ghazālī (d. 1111) himself mentions the Muᶜtazilite view without using *shay*ʾ*iyya*: *Tahāfut al-falāsifa*, 358,8-11.

[28] Abū Jaᶜfar Muḥammad b. Yaᶜqūb al-Kulaynī, *al-Uṣūl min al-kāfī*, 82,4-85,9 at 83,6-8. In Ibn Bābawayh's slightly later collection of Imāmī Shiᶜite sayings, *shay*ʾ*iyya* is also used in the context of affirming that God is a thing unlike other things, except this time in a passage attributed to Jaᶜfar aṣ-Ṣādiq's son, Mūsā al-Kāẓim: Abū Jaᶜfar Muḥammad ibn Bābawayh aṣ-Ṣadūq, *K. at-tawḥīd*, 94,9-95,1.

[29] al-Māturīdī, *K. at-tawḥīd*, 41,10(*bis*).15; 86,3.16; 104,10.11.12.15; 132,19; 238,9.10; 242,8.9.11.12.13.14(*bis*).18. See also the brief discussion of al-Māturīdī's use of *shay*ʾ*iyya* in Gimaret 1980, 182-184 and 203.

[30] Abū l-Layth as-Samarqandī, *Sharḥ al-fiqh al-absaṭ li-Abī Ḥanīfa*, 119,1.2 (= lines 426-7).

With such a tiny proportion of what was written by ninth- and tenth-century *mutakallimūn* now available to us, assertions about the term's history will inevitably suffer from tentativeness. But the fact that the term seems to be absent from the few Muᶜtazilite and Ashᶜarite sources we do have from this pre-Avicennian period indicates that al-Māturīdī might well deserve the honor of being called *Abū Shayʾiyya*.[31] What is interesting here is that because Avicenna grew up outside Bukhārā – that is, in Transoxania, an area where the Samarqandī Ḥanafism of al-Māturīdī was strong – and because he was taught jurisprudence by a Ḥanafite scholar called Ismāᶜīl az-Zāhid, Avicenna may well have come across the term *shayʾiyya* during his youthful *fiqh* studies, if not in al-Māturīdī's *Kitāb at-tawḥīd*, then perhaps in Abū l-Layth as-Samarqandī's commentary on Abū Ḥanīfa's *al-Fiqh al-absaṭ*. Even if Ismāᶜīl az-Zāhid himself was not a Māturīdite in *kalām* (Bukhāran Ḥanafites tended to be less rationalistic and speculative in *kalām* than those in Samarqand, and in any case there were Ḥanafites such as Ibn Fūrak who were Ashᶜarite in *kalām*), it is perfectly possible that Ismāᶜīl could have used a simple commentary such as Abū l-Layth's when teaching his young student the Ḥanafite creed.[32]

Of course it is also perfectly possible that Avicenna came up with the term *shayʾiyya* all by himself. Others have remarked on al-Māturīdī's predilection for abstract nouns ending in *-iyya*, an extreme example being his grafting of the Arabic *-iyya* (equivalent to the English suffixes "-ness" or the more Latin-sounding "-ity") onto the Persian *hast* ("is") to form *hastiyya* ("is-ness").[33] Al-Māturīdī's predilection for abstract nouns was a trait Avicenna certainly shared. But given the presence of the term *shayʾiyya* in a small number of tenth-century *kalām* texts as well as in Avicenna's *Ilāhiyyāt* 1.5, there is a possibility – nothing more – that the term played a bridging role between the earlier *kalām*

[31] My own guess is that the Muᶜtazilite al-Kaᶜbī al-Balkhī (d. 931), a student of al-Khayyāṭ and of al-Jubbāʾī, and an active participant in debates in Khurāsān and Transoxania during this period, may well be the missing link, since he is cited (and attacked) so extensively by his contemporary al-Māturīdī. But until al-Kaᶜbī al-Balkhī's *Maqālāt* is fully edited – at the moment it remains in manuscript in Yemen, apparently – this must remain only a tentative suggestion.

[32] On Avicenna's Ḥanafite education, see Gutas 1987-1988. On Ismāᶜīl az-Zāhid, see Ibn Sīnā, *Autobiography*, 20,4-7, and al-Khaṭīb al-Baghdādī, *Tārīkh Baghdād* 6, 310,17-311,18 (= #3355). On Māturīdism in Transoxania, see Madelung 1971 and 1991, and now Rudolph 1996. Other hints of Avicenna's Ḥanafite background can be detected in the fragments from Avicenna's *Lisān al-ᶜarab*, where Abū Ḥanīfa is mentioned by name and quoted at length in a discussion of the particulars of prayer (*Risāla fī l-lugha*, 15,2.10.13); none of the other founders of the Sunnī *madhāhib* is mentioned, let alone a Shiᶜite Imām. In fact Avicenna defines the Shiᶜites as those who incline towards ᶜAlī b. Abī Ṭālib to an excessive degree (*wa-lladhīna yamīlūna ilā jānibi ᶜAliyyi bni Abī Ṭālibin bi-akthara mina l-qadri l-muᶜtadili yusammūna anfusahum ash-Shīᶜata*): *Risāla fī l-lugha*, 16,7-9. What is more, at *Ḥikma ᶜArūḍiyya* 5r12-13, Avicenna offers, as an example of priority with respect to perfection, the sense in which Abū Bakr (r. 632-634), the first of the rightly guided caliphs, is prior in nobility to the second, ᶜUmar (r. 634-644) (*wa-yuqālu "qabla" fī l-kamāli ka-qawlinā innā Abā Bakrin mutaqaddimun ᶜalā ᶜUmara fī sh-sharafi*). It is hard to imagine a Shiᶜite 21-year-old using Abū Bakr, and not ᶜAlī, as an example of priority in respect of perfection or nobility.

[33] Rudolph 1996, 212-13; compare al-Fārābī, *K. al-ḥurūf*, 111,17-21.

discussions of things and existents and Avicenna's distinction between essence and existence.

The second challenge to my hypothesis still remains to be met. For even if future research is able to establish a firmer link between *kalām* uses of the *term shayʾiyya* and Avicenna's own use of it in *Ilāhiyyāt* 1.5, the fact remains that the *concept* of what it is to be a thing (of thingness, in other words) which Avicenna articulates in *Ilāhiyyāt* 1.5, appears to be inconsistent with his discussions of things elsewhere. More importantly, Avicenna's concept of thingness in *Ilāhiyyāt* 1.5 does not seem to mesh with his concept of *māhiyya*, or essence. Despite Avicenna's clear assertion in *Ilāhiyyāt* 1.5 that thing and existent are co-implied (*mutalāzimāni*) and extensionally identical, there are several discussions of essence and existence elsewhere in the *Ilāhiyyāt* and in other works from Avicenna's middle period, which suggest that *shayʾ* – and *māhiyya*, as we shall see – is at the very least logically prior to *mawjūd*, and perhaps even a broader category than *mawjūd*. If *shayʾ* is logically prior to *mawjūd*, then Avicenna's assertions about the reciprocal nature of the co-implication (*talāzum*) between thing and existent – so clearly articulated in *Ilāhiyyāt* 1.5 – will be undermined. Even more seriously, if *shayʾ* is a broader category than *mawjūd*, then their extensional identity will be repudiated.

The following are summaries of the relevant passages, including *Ilāhiyyāt* 1.5, in chronological order:

(1) *Ḥikma ʿArūḍiyya*, 2v8-10: "One" is a necessary accident of things (*mina l-aʿrāḍi l-lāzimati li-l-ashyāʾi*). Essence is a thing (*bal takūnu l-māhiyyatu shayʾan*), be it a man or a horse, an intellect or a soul; that thing is only subsequently characterized as being one or existent.[34]

(2) *Madkhal* 1.2: The essences of things (*māhiyyātu l-ashyāʾ*) are sometimes found in concrete objects in the outside world, and other times are conceived of in the mind. But essence has *three* aspects: as a concrete, external existent; as a mental, internal existent; and a third aspect, in which it is unrelated to either concrete or mental existence.[35]

(3) *Madkhal* 1.12: Genera and species may be divided into those which are *before* a state of multiplicity (that is, those contained in the Active Intellect), those which are *in* a state of multiplicity (that is, those contained individually in sublunary concrete existents), and those which are *after* a state of multiplicity (that is, those contained as abstracted universals in human intellects). Taken in itself a genus or a species is a thing. "Animal", taken in itself, is an intentional object (*maʿnan*), regardless of whether it is a concrete or a mental existent, or whether it is general or specific.[36]

[34] This passage is identical to *K. an-najāt*, 340,12-15.

[35] Ibn Sīnā, *K. ash-shifāʾ/Manṭiq (1): al-Madkhal* 1.2, 15,1-7.

[36] Ibn Sīnā, *K. ash-shifāʾ/Manṭiq (1): al-Madkhal* 1.12, 65,4-12. On this passage see Marmura 1979.

(4) *Ilāhiyyāt* 1.5 (discussed above): "Thing" and "existent" are primary, indefinable categories. Whatever is predicable of thing will also be predicable of existent, and whatever is predicable of existent will also be predicable of thing. Although they are co-implied, thing and existent have different meanings.

(5) *Ilāhiyyāt* 5.1: A universal (*kullī*) such as "horseness", taken in and of itself (*fī nafsihi*) – that is, without considering whether it is one or many (*lā wāḥida wa-lā kathīra*), a concrete existent in the outside world or a mental existent inside the soul (*lā mawjūda fī l-aᶜyāni wa-lā mawjūda fī n-nafsi*), in potentiality or in actuality (*lā bi-l-quwwati wa-lā bi-l-fiᶜli*) – is a thing (*shayʾ*).[37]

(6) *Ilāhiyyāt* 7.1: "One" (*al-wāḥid*) and "existent" (*al-mawjūd*) are equally predicable of things (*qad yatasāwayāni fī l-ḥamli ᶜalā l-ashyāʾ*); all that may be characterized by "one" may also be characterized by "existent", but the two terms do not have the same meaning as each other.[38]

From these passages a discrepancy seems to emerge over the issue of what exactly is it to be a thing; over the question, that is, of thingness. The message from the *Ilāhiyyāt* 1.5 passage discussed above at length is that thing and existent are extensionally identical yet intensionally different. In other words, while thingness and existence have different meanings, neither term applies to any entity that the other does not apply to. Yet in the *Ḥikma ᶜArūḍiyya* and in *Ilāhiyyāt* 7.1 Avicenna implies that thing is a universally applicable subject of which one and existent may be predicated. In other words it is *one* and existent, not *thing* and existent, which are extensionally identical yet intensionally different.[39] Thing therefore seems to be a category which is more basic than, and hence logically prior to, the categories one and existent.

This logical priority is reinforced by Avicenna's implication in *Ilāhiyyāt* 5.1 that properly speaking, thing should be elevated above considerations of existence. There Avicenna claims that a universal is a thing when taken in itself,

[37] Ibn Sīnā, *K. ash-shifāʾ/Ilāhiyyāt (1)* 5.1, 196,6-13.

[38] Ibn Sīnā, *K. ash-shifāʾ/Ilāhiyyāt (2)* 7.1, 303,6-12.

[39] Avicenna's assertion that *mawjūd* and *wāḥid* are extensionally identical but intensionally different almost certainly derives from Aristotle's discussions in *Metaph.* 4.2, 1003b22-1004a2 (= *Mā baᶜda ṭ-ṭabīᶜa I*, 310,1-311,4 and 316,9) where Aristotle discusses how "that which is" (*to on* = *al-huwiyya*) and "that which is one" (*to hen* = *al-wāḥid*) can be seen to be extensionally identical but intensionally different, in the sense that both are equally predicable of substance (*ousia*). See also "'That which is one' is said of [the same things] 'that which is' is said of" (*to hen legetai hôsper kai to on* = *yuqālu l-wāḥidu ka-mithli mā tuqālu l-huwiyyatu ayḍan*) at *Metaph.* 7.16, 1040b16-24 (= *MBṬ II*, 999,14-1000,5); and "'That which is' and 'that which is one' are the predicates spoken most universally of everything" (*to gar on kai to hen katholou katêgoreitai malista pantôn* = *fa-inna l-wāḥida wa-l-huwiyyata maqūlātun kulliyyatun aktharu dhālika tuqālu ᶜalā jamīᶜi l-ashyāʾi*) at *Metaph.* 10.2, 1053b16-21 (= *MBṬ III*, 1268,11-1269,3). The assertion is repeated by Themistius (*fa-inna l-mawjūda shayʾun wa-l-wāḥida shayʾun ākharu*) in his paraphrase of *Metaphysics* 12.7: Thāmasṭiyūs, *Sharḥ ḥarf al-Lām min Kitāb Mā baᶜda ṭ-ṭabīᶜa li-Arisṭū*, 15,13.

that is, when it is separated from any consideration of the mode of its existence: one or many, concrete or mental, potential or actual. Not only is a universal taken in itself a thing, but – we are told in *Madkhal* 1.12 – a genus or a species taken in itself is a thing. Even more importantly, Avicenna says in the *Ḥikma ^{c}Arūḍiyya* passage that an essence taken in itself is a thing, and that "one" – and, by implication, "existent" – is merely a necessary accident of essence taken in itself. Most starkly of all, Avicenna asserts in *Madkhal* 1.2 that essence has a third aspect, unrelated to any type of existence whatsoever.

The clear message given in *Ilāhiyyāt* 1.5 that thing and existent are co-implied, with neither being prior to the other, is therefore muffled by the many hints from the other passages that thing is logically prior to existent. More serious is the question of extension. For while all the passages are consistent in maintaining that thing and existent have different meanings, two in particular – *Ḥikma ^{c}Arūḍiyya* 2v8-10 and *Madkhal* 1.2 – imply that there is a separate category of things – essence taken in itself – to which existence need not apply. In these passages Avicenna seems to have forced himself into advocating the Mu^{c}tazilite position that existent is subsumed extensionally but not intensionally under thing; that is, that existents are always things but things are not always existents.[40]

Is there any other evidence in Avicenna's writings to help us understand his concept of thingness? Does that evidence allow us to reconcile Avicenna's various positions on things and essences? These questions will be addressed in Chapters 8 and 9.

[40] Much ink has been spilled trying to determine how Avicenna meant this extra aspect of essence to be understood. Some maintain that it should be understood simply in the context of a thought experiment, in which *māhiyya* can be isolated in a purely logical sense from its existence as a concrete individual in the outside world and from its existence as a universal concept in the mind. Others, citing remarks Avicenna makes in *Ilāhiyyāt* 5.2, believe that the passage provides evidence that he thought existence was attached to essence merely as an accident. Western interpreters in the Catholic tradition have generally understood Avicenna as implying the latter, but consensus is now emerging that the former is also a feasible interpretation. For a sampling of different views see Goichon 1937 *passim*; Gilson, 1948, 121-131; Rahman 1958; Morewedge 1972; Rahman 1981; Burrell 1986; Nasr 1989; and Marmura 1992.

8. Essence and Existence (B)
*Shay*ʾ*iyya or Sababiyya?*

To get a fuller picture of the subtle tension in Avicenna's thought between things and essences we must look for other instances of *shay*ʾ*iyya* in Avicenna's writings. After all, the isolated instance of thingness in *Ilāhiyyāt* 1.5 – the only instance of *shay*ʾ*iyya* that Jolivet cites – hardly constitutes a fully articulated concept in Avicenna's thought. Where else, if anywhere, does *shay*ʾ*iyya* appear in Avicenna's works? It turns out that the *Ilāhiyyāt* 1.5 passage, the one that so clearly echoes the earlier Muʿtazilite discussions of things and existents, is not the only time when Avicenna uses the term *shay*ʾ*iyya*.

Far more often than its lonely appearance there, where the *mutakallimūn* are hovering in the background, Avicenna uses *shay*ʾ*iyya* in a cluster of discussions which have nothing to do with early *kalām* debates and which are driven by a problem specific to Aristotelian philosophy: the relation between efficient and final causes. In *Ilāhiyyāt* 6.5 Avicenna writes:

L36

Ibn Sīnā, *Kitāb ash-shifā*ʾ*/Ilāhiyyāt (2)* 6.5, 292,1-294,5
Avicenna, *Liber de philosophia prima sive scientia divina V-X*, 335,84-339,32

The subsequent objection [to the reality of final causation, viz., "How can the end be anything but posterior to the other causes?"] will be solved by knowing that the end may be taken to be a thing as well as taken to be an existent. Although a thing cannot be other than an existent, the difference between thing and existent is just like the difference between some entity and its concomitant. You have already come to know and to verify this. Consider, once again, the case of man: man has an inner reality, consisting of his definition and his essence, which is not conditioned upon [his] existence's being particular or general, concrete or in the soul, or potential or actual.

[292,6] Each cause, insofar as it is that [particular] cause, has an inner reality and a THINGNESS. In its THINGNESS the final cause is the reason why the other causes actually exist as causes. In its existence the final cause is the effect of the other causes' actually [existing] as causes. It is as if the THINGNESS of the final cause were the cause of the cause of its [own] existence; conversely it is as if its existence were the effect of the effect of its [own] THINGNESS. However its THINGNESS does not become a cause unless it occurs as an image formed in the soul, or as something analogous to that. The only cause of the final cause in its THINGNESS is another cause which is different from the cause toward which one thing sets [another] in motion, or toward which something is set in motion.

Know that something can be caused in its THINGNESS, and caused in its existence. An example of what is caused in its THINGNESS is twoness: contained in the definition of its being twoness is its being caused by oneness. What is caused in its existence is so plainly knwon [as to require no explanation]. Similarly, one thing might possess another thing that occurs as an existent in its THINGNESS, as twoness possesses numberness; or else one thing might be additional to another thing that is added to its THINGNESS, as wood and stone contain quadrangularity. Natural bodies are causes of the THINGNESS of many forms and accidents (I mean of those [forms and accidents] which can only recur in them), as well as being causes of the existence of some of them [the forms and accidents] without [being a cause of] their [the forms' and accidents'] THINGNESS, as is sometimes thought to be the case in mathematics.

[293,4] It has thus become easy for you to understand [!] that the final cause, with regard to its THINGNESS, is prior to the efficient and receptive causes, and similarly, prior to form insofar as form is a formal cause leading toward it [the final cause]. In addition, the final cause is prior to the other causes in its existence in the soul. As for [the final cause's being prior to the other causes] in the agent's soul, this is because it [the final cause] comes to exist first and then agency, seeking out a receptive patient, and the quality of the form come to be represented as images. As for [the final cause's being prior to the other causes] in the souls of those other than the agent, one [cause] need not follow another in any kind of necessary order. Therefore, in terms of THINGNESS and in terms of existence in the intellect, there is no cause prior to the final [cause]; instead, it is a cause of the rest of the causes' becoming causes. However, the actual existence of the other causes as causes is [itself] a cause of its [the final cause's] existence. The final cause is a cause not insofar as it is an existent, but insofar as it is a thing. In the sense that it is a cause, it is the cause of the causes, while in the other sense it is the effect of the causes.

[293,12] This is [so] when the final cause is involved in coming-to-be; when, however, the final cause is not involved in coming-to-be but its existence is, instead, above coming-to-be (as will be explained in its place), then none of the other causes is a cause of it [the final cause], not even in the case of the One which is Itself occurrence and existence. [In the former sense] therefore the final cause will be caused by the rest of the causes not because it is a final cause but rather because it is subject to coming-to-be; and if it [the final cause] is not subject to coming-to-be it will not be caused at all. When you consider its [the final cause's] being a final cause, you will find it to be a cause of the rest of the causes' being causes (viz., being an efficient cause and a receptive cause and a formal cause) but not of their being entities and existents in themselves. So what is essential to the final cause insofar as it is a final cause is being a cause of the rest of the causes, while what is accidental to it (insofar as it [the final cause] is understood to be [actually] occurring in the world of generation) is being an effect

in the world of generation. It has thus been made clear to you [!] how something may be cause as well as effect, given that it is [both] an agent and an end, this being one of the Natural Philosophers' principles.

Avicenna also mentions thingness in the same context in *Najāt/Ilāhiyyāt* 1.11:

L37

Ibn Sīnā, *K. an-Najāt*, 345,1-11

In terms of coming into existence [*fī ḥuṣūli l-wujūdi*] the end is posterior to the effect, while it is prior to the rest of the causes in terms of THINGNESS. It is clear that THINGNESS is something other than existence in concrete reality [*ghayru l-wujūdi fī l-aᶜyāni*]. For an intentional object [*al-maᶜnā*] has an existence in concrete reality and an existence in the soul as well as something common [to both]: what is common [to both] is THINGNESS. The final [cause] insofar as it is a thing is prior to the other causes and is the cause of the causes in terms of their being causes. Insofar as it is an existent in concrete reality it [the final cause] is posterior. When the efficient cause is not itself the final cause, the agent is posterior to the end in terms of THINGNESS. This is because the other causes become actual causes only on account of the final, whereas it [the final cause] is not on account of anything else, but exists first in a kind of existence and then makes the [other] causes become actual causes. Once this distinction is made, the result, it seems, is that the primary agent and the primary mover in anything is the end.[1]

Before I try in to explain what Avicenna means when he uses *shay'iyya* in these very difficult passages, and to determine whether or not this helps us reconcile the apparent tension in his thought between thingness and essence, I must devote this chapter to resolving a textual problem. The problem is that there are some indications that *sababiyya*, "causality", and not *shay'iyya*, "thingness", was the word Avicenna used in the passages above. This is in spite of the overwhelming evidence provided by the manuscripts used to come up with the Cairo edition of the *Ilāhiyyāt*, which are unanimous in their reading of *shay'iyya*.[2] I shall argue that the balance of evidence compels us to retain *shay'iyya*.

The textual problem in the *Ilāhiyyāt* might never have come to light had it not been for the fact that the Latin translator Gundisallinus consistently rendered what appears as *shay'iyya* in L36 – the long *Ilāhiyyāt* 6.5 passage – not as

[1] The term *shay'iyya* occurs on 345,2(*bis*).4.7. Unlike the sections of the *Najāt* immediately surrounding L37, L37 itself is not identical to the analogous section in the *Ḥikma ᶜArūḍiyya* (4v16-5r5). Nor is there anything analogous to L37 in the *Mabda' wa-maᶜād*, the other early work from which Avicenna lifted passages into the *Najāt*. The conclusion must be that L37 was composed originally for the *Najāt*.

[2] The manuscripts examined for the Cairo edition are described in the introduction to Anawati 1978, 17-21. The use of *shay'iyya* in the *Najāt* is confirmed in the 1593 edition: *K. an-najāt mukhtaṣar ash-shifā' li-bn Sīnā*, 58,22-26.

realitas or *entitas*, as one would have expected, but as *causalitas*.[3] For example, Avicenna's assertion that "Each cause, insofar as it is that [particular] cause, has an inner reality and a THINGNESS", and which reads in Arabic:

> *wa-kullu ᶜillatin fa-innahā min ḥaythu hiya tilka l-ᶜillatu lahā ḥaqīqatun wa-SHAYᵓIYYATUN,*

was rendered into Latin as:

> *omnis autem causa, inquantum est ipsa causa, habet certitudine et CAUSALITATEM.*[4]

One explanation of this anomaly takes into account the fact that translating Avicenna's philosophical works into Latin appears to have been a two-step process. A first translator – the Jewish émigré Ibn Dāwūd, or Avendauth – would render the Arabic orally into the vernacular Spanish of twelfth-century Toledo; as he went along, a second translator – the Catholic cleric Gundissalinus – would render the vernacular Spanish into proper philosophical Latin.[5] Given this scenario, it is easy to imagine how the first translator might have tried faithfully to render *shayᵓiyya* into the vernacular Spanish as *cosità*. The second translator might then have confused *cosità*, "thingness", with *causità*, "causality", terms which were probably pronounced much the same.[6]

It appears more likely, however, that *taṣḥīf*, a scribal misplacement of diacritical marks, was the cause of the divergence between the Arabic and Latin texts. The *taṣḥīf* in this case would consist in a scribe's having mispointed *shayᵓiyya* as *sababiyya* ("causality"), a far less mysterious term. (I take it as obvious that *shayᵓiyya* is the *lectio difficilior* here.)

Confusing the pairs of terms is perfectly understandable. In a medieval Arabic manuscript, after all, many words would have been written down without diacritical marks. As a result, the skeleton (*rasm*):

[3] Avicenna, *Liber de philosophia prima sive scientia divina V-X*, 337,88.90.91.92.94.96.97.00.1. 3.5 and 338,11 (= *Ilāhiyyāt*, 292,6[*bis*].8.9[*bis*].10.12.14.16 and 293,2.3.4.8). On the translators, see van Riet's comments in her introduction to Avicenna, *Liber de philosophia prima sive scientia divina I-IV*, 123*.

[4] Avicenna, *Liber de philosophia prima sive scientia divina V-X*, 336,87-337,88 (= *Ilāhiyyāt*, 292,6). On the next page, Avicenna's assertion "that the final cause, with regard to its thingness, is prior to the efficient cause", and which reads in Arabic *anna l-ᶜillata l-ghāᵓiyyata fī SH-SHAYᵓIYYATI qabla l-ᶜillati l-fāᶜilati*, was rendered into Latin as *quod causa finalis in CAUSALITATE praecedit causas agentes*: Avicenna, *Liber de philosophia prima sive scientia divina V-X*, 337,5-6 (= *Ilāhiyyāt*, 293,4).

[5] On this see van Riet's comments in her introduction to Avicenna, *Liber de anima seu sextus de naturalibus I-III*, 95*-98*, and Burnett 1997, 12-14.

[6] This is the theory advanced by d'Alverny with regard to two instances where, as she understood it, *cosà* had been misunderstood as *causa*. These are mentioned (without references to the text) in d'Alverny 1951, 133, and repeated in d'Alverny 1952, 60. The instances of mistranslation she probably had in mind are Avicenna, *Liber de anima seu sextus de naturalibus I-III*, 192,20 (= *K. ash-shifāᵓ/Ṭabīᶜiyyāt (6): an-Nafs*, 103,11) and 273,11 (= 154,19).

سٮٮٮه

can just as easily be pointed as *sababiyya* ("causality"):

سببية

as it can be pointed as *shay'iyya* ("thingness"):

شيئية.

But given the lack of extant Arabic *Ilāhiyyāt* manuscripts from before 1284 (let alone from before the Arabic-Latin translation movement in the middle of the twelfth century), it is impossible to say whether a scribe mistranscribed *shay'iyya* as *sababiyya* before the manuscript reached Avendauth's hands and Avendauth then read the mispointed manuscript accurately; whether the manuscript reached Avendauth with these words pointed as *shay'iyya* and he then "corrected" the pointing to *sababiyya* before translating it; or whether the manuscript reached Avendauth with these words unpointed and he then pointed them incorrectly as *sababiyya* before translating them.

In any case, what inclines me towards attributing the divergence between the Arabic and Latin texts to *taṣḥīf* and not (as d'Alverny thought) to mishearing, is that what appears as *shay'iyya* in the *Ilāhiyyāt* 1.5 passage discussed earlier (i.e., L35) was also incorrectly rendered into Latin but this time as *similitudinem*, clearly the result of Avendauth's (or an earlier scribe's) mispointing – the skeleton:

سٮٮٮه

having been pointed as *shabīh* ("similitude"):

شبيه

instead of as *shay'iyya* ("thingness"):

شيئية

– rather than of Gundissalinus' mishearing.[7]

On the other hand, the specter of *taṣḥīf* raises the chilling possibility that the original Arabic texts – the ones written or dictated by Avicenna himself – should in fact be read with *sababiyya*, not *shay'iyya*. This concern is heightened by the fact that the oldest manuscript of the Latin translation of the *Ilāhiyyāt* dates from about 1240, while the oldest Arabic manuscript of the *Ilāhiyyāt* dates from 1284.[8]

However, I believe that the Latin translation does not, in itself, provide enough evidence to justify concluding that Avicenna wrote or dictated *sababiyya* rather than *shay'iyya*. First of all, if *causalitas* were an indication that the original Arabic should read *sababiyya*, not *shay'iyya*, then – by way of consistency – we would also expect to see the instances of *shay'* in the *Ilāhiyyāt* 6.5 passage to have been rendered into Latin as *causa*. This is not the case. The Arabic of the *Ilāhiyyāt* 6.5 passage immediately preceding the last quotation:

> *wa-ammā sh-shakku lladhī yalīhi fa-yanḥallu bi-an yuʿlama anna l-ghāyata tufraḍu SHAY'AN wa-tufraḍu mawjūdan,*

was rendered accurately into Latin as:

> *Sed dubitatio quae sequitur hic solvitur hoc modo: scilicet, iam scis quod finis ponitur RES et ponitur ens.*[9]

Second, *sabab* would clearly have been out of place in almost every instance where *shay'* was mistranslated into Latin as *causa* rather than *res*, so we can be quite certain that in *Ilāhiyyāt* 6.5, at least, the original Arabic text did not read *sabab*.[10]

[7] Avicenna, *Liber de philosophia prima sive scientia divina I-IV*, 38,21 (= *Ilāhiyyāt*, 33,17). Jolivet 1984 seems not to have noticed this mistranslation; Rahman 1958, 5n.2, mentions it, as does Khodeiri 1959-61, 316. Elsewhere in the Latin translation of the *Ilāhiyyāt*, *bi-sababihi* was mistranslated as *comparationis* – van Riet sees this as a result of misunderstanding it as *nisbatahu*: 188,80 (= *Ilāhiyyāt*, 166,4) – and *sababun* as *comparationes*: 493,96 (= *Ilāhiyyāt*, 413,12). This confusion also occurs in a passage of the *Fī n-nafs*, where *sabab* was translated into Latin as *comparatio* (Avicenna *Liber de anima seu sextus de naturalibus IV-V*, 20,79 = *K. ash-shifā'/Ṭabīʿiyyāt (6): an-Nafs*, 174,14).

[8] Introduction to Avicenna, *Liber de philosophia prima sive scientia divina I-IV*, 125*-138*.

[9] Avicenna, *Liber de philosophia prima V-X*, 336,84-85 (= *Ilāhiyyāt*, 292,1).

[10] In addition to the two instances alluded to by d'Alverny, *shay'* is mistranslated as *causa* elsewhere in the Latin version of the *Ilāhiyyāt*: *shay'ayni* becomes *duarum causarum* at 99,62 (= *Ilāhiyyāt*, 86,3), and *sā'ir al-ashyā'* becomes *ceterae causae* at 394,84 (= *Ilāhiyyāt*, 341,3). In the Latin translation of *al-Afʿāl wa-l-infiʿālāt*, the fourth book of the *Ṭabīʿiyyāt*, *shay'* was also occasionally mistranslated as *causa*: Avicenna, *Liber quartus naturalium de actionibus et passionibus qualitatum primarum*, 23,72 (= *K. ash-shifā'/Ṭabīʿiyyāt (4): al-Afʿāl wa-l-infiʿālāt*, 213,15); 28,54 (= *al-Afʿāl wa-l-infiʿālāt*, 217,3); and 79,73 (= *al-Afʿāl wa-l-infiʿālāt*, 256,6). Conversely, *asbāb* was mistranslated in the *Fī n-nafs* as *rebus* at 21,82 (=*K. ash-shifā'/Ṭabīʿiyyāt (6): an-Nafs*, 174,15), and *sabab* as *res* at 21,83 (= *K. ash-shifā'/Ṭabīʿiyyāt (6): an-Nafs*, 174,16).

All in all, the evidence provided by the Latin translation of the *Ilāhiyyāt* (and the parallels in the translation of the *Fī n-nafs*) allows us merely to hypothesize that *taṣḥīf* occurred in one or more of the manuscript lines that reached Andalusia. It is not conclusive with regard to the question of whether the original text should read *sababiyya* rather than *shayʾiyya*.

The Latin mistranslation of *shayʾiyya* in the *Ilāhiyyāt* – if it was in fact a mistranslation, as I believe – does, however, explain the absence of analogous concepts in discussions of final and efficient causes by later Latin philosophers, and the presence in those same discussions of *causalitas*.[11] Medieval European thinkers would probably not have been struck to find Avicenna's concept of thingness missing from their translations of the *Ilāhiyyāt*, since *shayʾiyya* does not appear in al-Ghazālī's (d. 1111) summary of Arabic philosophy, the *Maqāṣid al-falāsifa*, through which – as *Intentiones philosophorum* – many Latins were introduced to Avicenna's thought. The *Maqāṣid* was popular due to al-Ghazālī's fluency of style and liberality with examples, qualities which Avicenna painfully lacked. It is an irony of the history of medieval philosophy that during the period before Averroes' (d. 1198) *Tahāfut at-tahāfut* was translated into Latin – that is, before al-Ghazālī was exposed as a philosophy-basher – "Algazel" was seen by some Europeans as Avicenna's greatest disciple.[12]

The non-appearance of *shayʾiyya* in the *Maqāṣid* is, on the surface, evidence inclining us towards thinking that the *Ilāhiyyāt* 6.5 and *Najāt* passages should be emended to read *sababiyya*. But *shayʾiyya*'s absence in the *Maqāṣid* has a more straightforward explanation. Al-Ghazālī based the *Maqāṣid* primarily (though not entirely) on Avicenna's Persian *summa*, the *Dānishnāma-yi ʿAlāʾī*,

[11] The Latin Avicenna's "theory" that the final cause is prior to the efficient in terms of *causality* is cited explicitly by Henry of Ghent (d. 1293), *Quodlibet XIII*, 106,71-78; and by Duns Scotus (d. 1308), *Quaestiones super libros Metaphysicorum Aristotelis I-IX*, Bk. 5, Quest. 1, Para. 51. Avicenna's "theory" (or the gloss on it contained in the Latin translation of al-Ghazālī's *Maqāṣid* – see note 14 in this chapter) also seems to inform the opinions of Alexander of Hales (d. 1245), *in Metaph. 1*, 12rC (Avicenna's *Ilāhiyyāt* 6 is mentioned at 12vE and 104rD), *in Metaph. 3*, 54rD-55rD, and *in Metaph. 5*, 105rA-D; of Thomas Aquinas (d. 1274), *Scriptum super libros Sententiarum* 1.8, 52,5-6); *in Metaph.* 5 #775 and #782; *in Phys.* 2.3, #186; and *Summa contra gentiles* 3.17.9; of Siger of Brabant (d. 1283), *Quaestiones in metaphysicam* 5.9, 203-4; of John Buridan (d. 1358), *in Metaph. 5*, quaest. 1, Fols 26a-27a; of Albert of Saxony (d. 1390), *Expositio et quaestiones in Aristotelis Physicam*, 111,6-9; and of Francisco Suarez (d. 1617), *Disputationes metaphysicae* Disp. XXVII, Sect. 2, paras 7-14, (172-177). Maier 1955, 212-213 and 302-303, discusses Avicenna's "theory" and relates it to Buridan's; see also Biard 1997, 494-495. This is not to say that Avicenna's concept of thingness was lost forever to European thinkers. In 1907 Horten translated the instances of *shayʾiyya* in *Ilāhiyyāt* 6.5 correctly into German as *Dingheit* (Horten 1907, 428-9), and the instances of *shayʾiyya* in the *Najāt* passage were translated by Carame into Latin as *entitas*: Carame 1926, 34,21-35,19 (*shayʾiyya* is rendered as *entitas* at 34,23[*bis*] and 35,2.7).

[12] e.g., Giles of Rome, introducing the section on al-Ghazālī from his *Errores Philosophorum*, 38,4-5: *Algazel autem, ut plurimum Avicennam sequens et eius abbreviator existens ....*"

in which a Persianized equivalent of *shay'iyya* does not make an appearance.[13] Avicenna's Persian statements in the *Dānishnāma* that:

L38

Ibn Sīnā, *Ilāhiyyāt-i Dānishnāma-yi ᶜAlā'ī*, 54,9-10 and 55,2

The end is the cause of all the causes .... So when there is an end, it is the cause of all the causes.

were rendered into Arabic by al-Ghazālī in the *Maqāṣid* as:

L39

al-Ghazālī, *Maqāṣid al-falāsifa*, 190,10.13

Part of what is special about the final cause is the fact that the other causes become causes through it .... So when the final exists among all the causes, it is the cause of the causes.[14]

Since al-Ghazālī did not allow the straw-man philosopher of the *Maqāṣid* to apply the concept of *shay'iyya* to the question of how efficient and final causes relate to each other, he probably felt no need to criticize thingness in the polemical *Tahāfut al-falāsifa*. And perhaps as a consequence of *shay'iyya*'s absence in the *Tahāfut al-falāsifa*, Averroes may have felt no need to raise the topic in the *Tahāfut at-tahāfut*. Nor is Avicenna's distinction between thingness and existence cited by Averroes in the latter's long commentaries on any of the most canonical Aristotelian discussions of the four causes, *Physics* 2.3 and 2.7 and *Metaphysics* 5.1 and 5.2.[15] Therefore, *shay'iyya's* absence from al-Ghazālī's (and hence Averroes') discussions of efficient and final causes does not by itself constitute evidence in favor of either reading.

Some evidence that appears to favor *sababiyya* may be found in the writings of two other thinkers trained in the Ashᶜarite theological tradition. The Ashᶜarite *mutakallimūn* ash-Shahrastānī (d. 1153) and Fakhr ad-dīn ar-Rāzī (d. 1210) wrote extensively about Avicenna's metaphysics, among other topics. If *shay'iyya* were to appear in one of their summaries or critiques of Avicenna's discussions of causality, it might help confirm its inclusion in the *Ilāhiyyāt* 6.5 and *Najāt* passages.

[13] On the *Dānishnāma*'s relationship to al-Ghazālī's *Maqāṣid*, see Janssens 1986.

[14] Interestingly, the *Intentiones philosophorum* – the Latin translation of the *Maqāṣid al-falāsifa* – contains several extra lines which are in neither the *Dānishnāma* nor the Arabic edition of the *Maqāṣid*; these include the assertion "Indeed, the final cause is last in terms of existence, yet first and foremost in terms of intention" (*Causa vero finalis est ultima in esse, et est prima et precedens in intencione* = *Intentiones philosophorum*, 38,5-6). My guess is that the extra line is a gloss by Avendauth or Gundissalinus, given their intimate involvement in translating both al-Ghazālī's *Maqāṣid* and Avicenna's *Ilāhiyyāt* into Latin. Stern 1962 describes how this precept was applied to the arrangement of topics in philosophy books.

[15] Averroes *in Phys.* 2.3 and 2.7 (= *Aristotelis opera cum Averois commentariis IV*, 59D-63K) and Ibn Rushd, *Tafsīr Mā baᶜda ṭ-ṭabīᶜa II*, 475,1-481,8; 483,7-487,8; 490,1-497,6).

The opposite seems at first glance to be the case. One major piece of evidence tempting us to reject *shayʾiyya* in favor of *sababiyya* in the *Najāt* is the fact that in ash-Shahrastānī's doxography, the *Kitāb al-milal wa-n-niḥal*, ash-Shahrastānī paraphrases the *Najāt* passage on final and efficient causes (i.e., L37) but appears to read *sababiyya* instead of *shayʾiyya*. According to the editor's critical apparatus, however, most of the *Milal* manuscripts read *shayʾiyya*. The *Milal*'s importance as a piece of evidence one way or the other is therefore limited.[16]

More alarming is the evidence pointed to by ar-Rāzī. Ar-Rāzī wrote a very important commentary on as well as a shorter summary of Avicenna's *Kitāb al-ishārāt wa-t-tanbīhāt*, a late work of Avicenna that greatly influenced subsequent Islamic philosophy.[17] In the *Ishārāt* discussions of final and efficient causes *shayʾiyya* does not make an appearance. Instead, Avicenna uses *māhiyya* – not *shayʾiyya* – in the passage from the *Ishārāt*'s metaphysics section (*Namaṭ* 4: *Fī l-wujūd wa-ᶜilalihi*) which parallels the *Ilāhiyyāt* 6.5 and *Najāt* passages, as well as the term *ᶜilliyya* (causality):

L40

Ibn Sīnā, *Kitāb al-ishārāt wa-t-tanbīhāt*, 139,14-20

Something may be caused with reference to its essence and its inner reality, and it may be caused in terms of its existence .... The final ... is the efficient cause of the causality of the efficient cause [*li-<ᶜilliyyati> l-ᶜillati l-fāᶜiliyyati*].[18]

In another passage from *Ishārāt* 4, Avicenna says:

L41

Ibn Sīnā, *Kitāb al-ishārāt wa-t-tanbīhāt*, 140,6-9

The final cause – that on account of which the thing is – is a cause, through its essence [*bi-māhiyyatihi*] and its [being an] intentional object [*wa-maᶜnāhu*], of the causality of the efficient cause [*li-ᶜilliyyati l-ᶜillati l-fāᶜiliyyati*], while it is an effect of it in its existence. The efficient cause is a cause of its [the end's] existence if it is one of the ends that actually come into being, but it [the efficient cause] is not a cause of its [the end's] causality nor of its [being] an intentional object.

In his summary of the *Ishārāt*, entitled *Lubāb al-ishārāt*, ar-Rāzī has this to say about the *Ishārāt* passages:

[16] *K. al-milal wa-n-niḥal II*, 1092,6-1093,4.

[17] In Chapter 9, n. 8 I briefly discuss Michot's objections to giving the *Ishārāt* a late date.

[18] I supply *ᶜilliyya* with MS F, to concur with the phrasing in L41.

L42

ar-Rāzī, *Kitāb lubāb al-ishārāt*, 80,4-5

How clever the Shaykh was to say that the final cause is an efficient cause of the causality of the efficient cause [*li-ᶜilliyyati l-ᶜillati l-fāᶜilati*].[19]

To my mind Avicenna's use of *ᶜilliyya* in the *Ishārāt* passages devoted to efficient and final causality is simply evidence of what appears to be an almost universal preference for *ᶜilliyya* over *sababiyya* in his works.[20] But a counterargument might run like this. Given *shayᵓiyya*'s absence in the *Ishārāt* passages, and given instances elsewhere in Avicenna's works where he uses *ᶜilliyya* to describe priority in causality, we would be perfectly justified in emending the *Ilāhiyyāt* 6.5 passage (i.e., L36) and the *Najāt* passage (i.e., L37) to read *sababiyya* instead of *shayᵓiyya*.[21] In other words, Avicenna sometimes uses *ᶜilliyya* to describe priority in causality, and other times (e.g., in the *Ilāhiyyāt* 6.5 and *Najāt* passages) uses *sababiyya* to describe priority in causality; *shayᵓiyya* need not come into the picture at all.

As attractive as this counterargument might appear, I believe it suffers from flaws graver than those of my own argument. First of all, when Avicenna talks about priority in *ᶜilliyya* it is clear from the contexts in which the term appears that he is referring to the priority enjoyed by *any* cause – be it formal, material, final or efficient – to its effect. As far as I know, Avicenna nowhere says that the final cause in particular enjoys priority in *ᶜilliyya* to the efficient cause.

Second, Avicenna's assertion in the *Ishārāt* that the final cause is a cause *through* its essence (*bi-māhiyyatihā*) *of* the causality of the efficient cause (*li-ᶜilliyyati l-ᶜillati l-fāᶜiliyyati*), is perfectly reconcilable with his assertions in *Ilāhiyyāt* 6.5 that the final cause is both a cause *through* its own thingness and *of* the efficient cause's thingness. As for the first prepositional phrase (i.e., *bi-māhiyyatihā*), the *Ishārāt* passages are meant to show that the final cause's priority derives from its essence; and essence, as I have shown in Part 1, is conceptually very similar – though not, it seems, identical – to thingness. Because *māhiyya* is much closer in meaning to *shayᵓiyya* than it is to *sababiyya*, the *Ishārāt* passages can just as easily be understood as providing

[19] Ar-Rāzī echoes this in his fully fledged commentary, *Sharḥ al-ishārāt*, 193,36-194,20 (outside box) and in his *al-Mabāḥith al-mashriqiyya I*, 661,21-662,8.

[20] e.g., *Ilāhiyyāt* 16,3; 166,12; 169,10(*bis*); and 266,11. Goichon 1938, 150, says that *sababiyya* is "très rarement employé". In addition to the instance she cites (she refers to "*Qaḍāᵓ*, 57", but I have been unable to locate this), the only places where I have comes across *sababiyya* in Avicenna's works are *ar-Risālat al-ᶜarshiyya fī ḥaqāᵓiq at-tawḥīd wa-ithbāt an-nubuwwa*, 24,6; and *ᶜUyūn al-ḥikma*, 52,8. According to the editor's apparatus for the latter work, however, the manuscripts contain many variant readings of *sababiyya*, and in any case, the term is not applied either there or in the *Risāla ᶜarshiyya* to the final cause specifically but rather to the substrate (*mawḍūᶜ*), end and agent collectively.

[21] See *aqdam bi-l-ᶜilliyya* in *K. ash-shifāᵓ/Manṭiq (5): al-Burhān*, 297,10-11; *taqaddum fī l-ᶜilliyya* in *Avicenna's De Anima – Arabic Text*, 230,3, and in *K. al-hidāya*, 241,1; and *qabla fī l-ᶜilliyya* in *Ḥikma ᶜArūḍiyya*, 5r13.

evidence in favor of, rather than against, retaining *shay'iyya* in the *Najāt* and *Ilāhiyyat* 6.5 passages. As for the second prepositional phrase (i.e., *li-ᶜilliyyati l-ᶜillati l-fāᶜiliyyati*), the apparent discrepancy between the final cause's being the cause of the efficient cause's thingness and its being the cause of the efficient cause's causality, is resolved by recognizing that the thingness (*shay'iyya*) of any cause (*ᶜilla*) is precisely its causality (*ᶜilliyya*).

My confidence in *shay'iyya* is strengthened by turning from the evidence in later Ashᶜarism to that in later Shiᶜite Avicennism. For example, in aṭ-Ṭūsī's (d. 1274) commentary on the *Ishārāt* passages on final and efficient causes, he follows Avicenna's lead and uses *māhiyya* as well as *ᶜilliyya*:

L43

aṭ-Ṭūsī, *Sharḥ al-ishārāt*, 193,31-194,6

> The essence of the end and its [being an] intentional object – *I mean its being some particular thing or other* [*kawnahā shay'an mā*] – is different from its existence .... [The final cause's] causality [*ᶜilliyyatuhā*] consists in the fact that it makes the agent an actual agent and is thus a cause of the agency of the agent. The agent is a cause of the fact that that essence [of the final cause] becomes an existent. Thus the essence of the end is a cause of the cause of its existence not in an absolute sense, but in a certain respect, so no circularity need be implied by this.[22]

It seems clear from his gloss on *māhiyya* and *maᶜnā* – that they refer to the end's being some thing or other – that aṭ-Ṭūsī had read the *Ilāhiyyāt* 6.5 and *Najāt* passages carefully and was borrowing from them to flesh out the much terser *Ishārāt* passage. For it is the distinction between *essence* and existence, not one between *causality* and existence, that Ṭūsi (rightly) sees as underlying Avicenna's distinction between the final cause's causality and the efficient cause's causality.

Like aṭ-Ṭūsī, Mullā Ṣadrā (d. 1640) – in his commentary on the *Ilāhiyyāt* 6.5 passage – seems aware of the *Ishārāt* passage when he pairs *shay'iyya* with *māhiyya*, and uses *ᶜilliyya*:

L44

Mullā Ṣadrā, *at-Taᶜlīqāt ᶜalā Ilāhiyyāt ash-shifā'*, 258,3

> Therefore the final cause, *through its essence and its thingness*, is a cause of the causality of the rest of the causes [*li-ᶜilliyyati sā'iri l-ᶜilali*].[23]

[22] Compare similar uses of *māhiyya* by Avicenna's pupil Bahmanyār ibn al-Marzubān (d. 1067) (*at-Taḥṣīl*, 546,1-9), as well as Sabzawārī (d. 1878) (*Sharḥ ghurar al-farā'id* [also known as *Sharḥ-i manẓūmah*], 161,11-12).

[23] In his *K. al-mashāᶜir*, 7,13 and 20,19.20, Mullā Ṣadrā – in existentialist rather than commentator mode – chucks *shay'iyya* into the dustbin of terms denoting essence.

Even in his own philosophical treatises Mullā Ṣadrā occasionally retains *shayʾiyya*. In the *Kitāb al-asfār*, for example, he says:

L45

Mullā Ṣadrā, *al-Asfār al-arbaʿa* II, 347,4-5

> Although with respect to thingness [*bi-ḥasabi sh-shayʾiyyati*] the end is prior to the act, it follows nonetheless that with respect to existence it is posterior to the act and subsequent to it.

To summarize Chapter 8, then, pieces of evidence from the later Latin and Ashʿarite traditions tempt us to reject *shayʾiyya* and replace it with *sababiyya*. Nevertheless, I feel the burden of proof still lies with anyone who would advocate such an emendation, in view of the following factors: the apparent unanimity of the extant *Najāt* and *Ilāhiyyāt* manuscripts in reading *shayʾiyya*; the inconsistent and scattered mistranslations of *sabab*, *shayʾ* and *shabīh* in the Latin translations of the *Ilāhiyyāt* and the *Fī n-nafs*, which indicate *taṣḥīf* in the Latin translators' Arabic manuscripts but not necessarily in the originals those manuscripts were derived from; the principle of *lectio difficilior*, which clearly favors thingness over causality; Avicenna's use of *māhiyya* – a term that is far closer in meaning to *shayʾiyya* than *sababiyya* – in the parallel *Ishārāt* passages; Avicenna's clear preference for *ʿilliyya* over *sababiyya* when discussing causality; Mullā Ṣadrā's equation of *shayʾiyya* and *māhiyya*; and finally, *shayʾiyya*'s appearance in Avicenna's *Taʿlīqāt* and *Mubāḥathāt*, as we shall see in Chapter 9.

9. Essence and Existence (C)
The Question of Evolution

Now that I have argued in favor of retaining thingness in the *Ilāhiyyāt* 6.5 passage (i.e., L36) and in the *Najāt* passage (i.e., L37), albeit with a few qualms, I must try to explain what exactly the term means in the context of Avicenna's discussion of the relation between efficient and final causes. Once this is done it will be easier to determine how these discussions contribute to our understanding of Avicenna's concepts of thingness and essence, and of his progression from the *kalām* problematic of *shay*ʾ vs. *mawjūd* to his own problematic of *māhiyya* vs. *wujūd.*

I think that when Avicenna asserts in *Ilāhiyyāt* 6.5 that the final cause is prior in its *shay*ʾ*iyya* to the efficient cause, he is using the term in one of the two early *kalām* senses of thing: the notion that a thing (for example, the Day of Resurrection, or my great-great-granddaughter) can subsist mentally in God's – or anyone's – mind, before it exists in the real world. Here is an example of how thingness thus conceived works in final causation. I am thirsty and a bottle of soda is in the refrigerator. I want to quench my thirst by drinking that bottle of soda. Quenching my thirst exists in my mind as a final cause. My motion to the refrigerator – the efficient cause of my quenching my thirst – then comes into concrete existence in the outside world. But the quenching existed first in my mind – as a *thing* – before it existed concretely in the outside world. In this sense the final cause is prior in its thingness (prior as a thing, that is) to the efficient cause. This is why Avicenna asserts in *Ilāhiyyāt* 6.5 that "its [i.e., the final cause's] thingness does not become a cause *unless it occurs as an image formed in the soul*" (292,9) and "In terms of thingness and *in terms of existence in the intellect*, there is no cause prior to the final cause" (293,8-9).

Avicenna's assertions here are echoed in the *Ta*ᶜ*līqāt*:

L46

Ibn Sīnā, *at-Ta*ᶜ*līqāt*, 128,17-19

> The end is prior in its thingness to all the causes and posterior in the existence it derives from them. The end which is absolutely non-existent [*al-ghāyatu l-ma*ᶜ*dūmatu* ᶜ*alā l-iṭlāqi*] is not a cause. Instead, it must exist in the agent's mind [alternatively, "in the agent himself" – *fī nafsi l-fā*ᶜ*ili*] in order to perform its action.[1]

When *shay*ʾ*iyya* is used in this way, as the basis for the priority enjoyed by things which are in the mind but which have not yet come into being in the outside world, it helps Avicenna flesh out an Aristotelian assertion: that the

[1] Also see Ibn Sīnā, *at-Ta*ᶜ*līqāt*, 158,14.

efficient and final causes can be seen to be causes of each other. In *Physics* 2.3 Aristotle briefly discusses the reciprocity between efficient and final causes:

L47

Arisṭūṭālīs, *aṭ-Ṭabīʿa*, 103,8-13
Aristotle, *Phys.* 2.3, 195a8-11

> Sometimes things are causes one of the other [*wa-qad takūnu ashyāʾu baʿḍuhā sababun li-baʿḍihā* = *esti de tina kai allêlôn aitia*]. For example, hard work is the cause of the body's health and the body's health is the cause of hard work, though not in an identical way [*ghayra anna dhālika laysa min wajhin wāḥidin* = *all' ou ton auton tropon*]; the body's well-being is a cause in that it is an intended end, while hard work is a cause in that it is the origin of motion.[2]

The interpretive challenge facing Avicenna here was to uphold Aristotle's fairly straightforward idea – that the efficient can be seen as the cause of the final and the final can be seen as the cause of the efficient – without falling into the trap of circularity. For if the final cause is *simply* the cause of the efficient cause, and the efficient is *simply* the cause of the final, each will be the cause of the cause of itself, and circularity will result. Avicenna had to find some way to unpack (and defend) Aristotle's compressed assertion by providing a metaphysical basis for the distinction between the ways in which the final cause and the efficient cause operate.

This is where the *kalām* distinction between *shayʾ* and *mawjūd* came in handy. Understood as a thing, the final cause can have a *shayʾiyya* in the mind before it comes into existence concretely in the outside world. In terms of its being a *shayʾ* in the mind – in terms of its *shayʾiyya* in the mind, that is – the final cause can be seen to be the cause of the efficient cause. On the other hand, the efficient cause comes into concrete existence in the outside world before the final cause comes into concrete existence in the outside world. My motion to the refrigerator exists concretely before my quenching exists concretely. By distinguishing between the final cause's priority as thing and the efficient cause's priority as concrete existent, Avicenna has managed to wriggle out of the hole of circularity.

But while Avicenna's analysis in *Ilāhiyyāt* 6.5 helps him flesh out Aristotle's assertion about the reciprocity between efficient and final causes, it raises two serious problems. The first is this: let us assume, as Avicenna says, that all final causes are prior in their thingness to the efficient causes with which they are paired. It follows that nothing without priority in thingness will be a final cause; in other words, being prior in thingness will be a necessary condition of being a final cause. But this description of how the final cause works will

[2] This is echoed in *Metaph.* 5.2, 1013b9-12 (= *Mā baʿda ṭ-ṭabīʿa II*, 486,9-10). At *Metaph.* 1.3, 983a32, Aristotle asserts that the final cause is the "opposite" (*antikeimenê*) of the efficient.

exclude all natural phenomena from the domain of entities that occur for a final cause. This is because natural things – a tree, or a rock – possess no mind or consciousness in which the *shayʾiyya* of an intended end can exist before it exists in the outside world as a concrete existent. Thus natural processes – a tree's growth, or a rock's fall to the ground – will not operate according to final causation, and final causation will be restricted to intentional acts.[3]

Avicenna appears to be aware of the problematic implications of using *shayʾiyya* as the basis on which the priority of the final cause rests when he appeals – again in his *Taʿlīqāt* – to another Aristotelian assertion: that form and end are often identical, particularly in natural phenomena.[4] In other words, the completion of the natural process by which a form inheres in a properly disposed matter can itself be regarded as a final cause, with the result that there is no need to appeal to intentionality or consciousness:

L48

Ibn Sīnā, *at-Taʿlīqāt*, 128,17-25

> The form is sometimes the same as the end, as in the case of health: it is a form and it is the same as the end. The ends of natural entities are the same as the existence of the form in the matter, because an individual nature will move only in order for a form to inhere in a matter.

But why has Avicenna not felt free to restrict the final cause to intentional action and be done with it? Apart from violating a fundamental Aristotelian belief in natural teleology, restricting the final cause's causality to intentional action would also undermine almost universal Peripatetic assertions of the priority of the science of final causality. As I mentioned in Chapter 6, Aristotle is quite clear in holding that knowledge of the final cause is superior to that of the other causes.[5] Following him, Avicenna not only says that knowledge of the final cause is the most excellent part of metaphysics (*al-ḥikma*), but implies that teleology can be seen as its sum and substance.[6]

What is more, if final causation were restricted to intentional acts, Avicenna would face a second problem: that of unrealized ends. In intentional acts a final cause need not come into concrete existence for its effect to come into concrete existence. Let us say, for example, that unbeknown to me my son has drunk the

[3] For an example of this line of argument see ar-Rāzī, *Sharḥ al-ishārāt*, 194,1-6 (outside box). Alexander also confronts this objection: *ap.* Simplicium, *in Phys.* 2.3 (*ad* 194b26), 310,25-311,37, and 2.8 (*ad* 198b16), 372,11-15

[4] I have discussed the nature of the identity between form and end at length in Chapters 3 and 6; see *Phys.* 2.7, 198a25 (= *Ṭabīʿa* 137,20-138,1) (i.e., L9) and 198b3 (= 140,12-13); *Metaph.* 5.24, 1023a34 (= *Mā baʿda ṭ-ṭabīʿa II* 655,9-10) and 8.4, 1044a36-b1 (= *II* 1074,1-2); and *GC* 1.7, 324b13-18.

[5] *Metaph.* 1.2, 982b5-11. At the very least this is how Alexander of Aphrodisias understood the above passage: *in Metaph.* 1.2, 14,3-4; cp. *in Metaph.* 1.3 (*ad* 983a31-33), 22,7-14; 3.2 (*ad* 996b8), 184,21-4; 5.1 (*ad* 1013a7-8), 346,11-18; and 5.2 (*ad* 1013b3) 350,28-31.

[6] *Ilāhiyyāt*, 300,7-9.

bottle of soda in the refrigerator. My motion to the refrigerator will come into concrete existence even if the bottle of soda is not there, that is, despite the fact that my quenching will fail to come into concrete existence. In *Mubāḥatha* 5 Avicenna seems to be grappling with this problem:

L49

Ibn Sīnā, *al-Mubāḥathāt*, 116,15-117,2
[*Mubāḥatha* 5, #277]

> If it [the existence of the effect] were to come about as a result of the thingness of something else whose existence is conceived, it [what was conceived] would be a cause whether or not it existed [in the outside world]; yet a thing's existence will never be causally dependent upon that whose non-existence and whose existence is all the same to it. As long as the cause of existence does not exist, its effect will not exist. Were something to exist regardless of whether some other thing existed or not, [the latter] would have no effect in its existence in addition to the "effect" of straightforward simultaneity [*akthara min athari l-maᶜiyyati s-sādhijati*]; but causality is more than simultaneity, even though it goes hand in hand with simultaneity.[7]

In other words, if it makes no difference whether or not the final cause exists concretely for its effect to exist concretely, the final cause will not fulfill the basic criterion of causality: being that whose existence necessitates the effect's existence. At best the final cause will be a cause only metaphorically.

Now Avicenna is clear that mental existence fully warrants being called existence. So he could defend himself by saying that even in the case of unrealized ends the final cause *did* exist and its existence *did* necessitate the effect's existence; the final cause simply existed in the mind, not in concrete reality. Nevertheless, the fact remains that in Muᶜtazilite ontology the thing (*shayʾ*) which is in the mind alone qualifies as a non-existent (*maᶜdūm*), and not as an existent (*mawjūd*). Avicenna's use of *shayʾiyya* in *Ilāhiyyāt* 6.5 to describe how the final cause operates could therefore be *interpreted* as implying that an unrealized end – that is, a final cause which only ever "exists" in the mind – is a non-existent thing (*shayʾ maᶜdūm*). And given that only an existent, not a non-existent thing, can be properly spoken of as a cause, the final cause will fail to satisfy the basic criterion of causality.

Avicenna seems aware of this problem in the *Najāt* passage on final and efficient causes (i.e., L37). There he asserts that "an intentional object (*al-maᶜnā*) has an existence in concrete reality and an existence in the soul *as well as something common [to both]: what is common [to both] is thingness.*" Avicenna is implying that for thingness to serve as the basis on which the final

[7] cf. 93,5-8 (= *Mubāḥatha* 4, #177). Concern about how the final cause's possible non-existence affects its causality is also evident in Awḥad az-zamān Abū l-Barakāt al-Baghdādī, *K. al-muᶜtabar fī l-ḥikma* III, 52,12-53,5.

cause's priority rests, we will need to add the condition that the end must be realized concretely. Only then will thingness link the intentional object's existence in the mind with its concrete existence in the outside world. Things which have a mental existence but no corresponding concrete existence – unrealized ends, that is – will not be much use in pointing to the final cause's priority.

It is my view that Avicenna moved from *shayʾiyya* in *Ilāhiyyāt* 6.5 and in the *Najāt* to *māhiyya* in the *Ishārāt* precisely to skirt these various problems. Avicenna starts using *shayʾiyya* in order to pre-empt one Aristotelian problem – the possibility of circularity in the relation between efficient and final causes – and then later discards *shayʾiyya* in favor of *māhiyya* because using *shayʾiyya* created the two further problems just discussed, each of which undermined the primacy of the final cause.

Avicenna's chronological progression from *shayʾiyya* to *māhiyya* can be detected in his discussions of efficient and final causality, for his assertions about the basis on which the final cause's priority rests change from *shayʾiyya* and *ḥaqīqa* in the *Ilāhiyyāt* and the *Najāt* (middle period), to *ḥaqīqa* and *māhiyya* in the *Ishārāt* (late period).[8] This becomes even clearer when we look carefully at the progression of Avicenna's thought *within* the middle period. According to Gutas' careful reconstruction, Avicenna started writing the *Kitāb ash-shifāʾ* with *Ṭabīʿiyyāt* 1 (i.e., *as-Samāʿ aṭ-ṭabīʿī*) but stopped after finishing only twenty folios; then wrote *Manṭiq* 1 (i.e., *al-Madkhal*); then completed *Ṭabīʿiyyāt* 1; and then wrote the entire *Ilāhiyyāt*.[9] After completing the rest of the *Kitāb ash-shifāʾ* Avicenna wrote the *Najāt*.

The fact that Avicenna had already written the *Madkhal* but had not yet started the *Ilāhiyyāt* is clear from his discussion of the relationship between efficient and final causality in *Ṭabīʿiyyāt* 1:

L50

Ibn Sīnā, *Kitāb ash-shifāʾ/Ṭabīʿiyyāt (1): as-Samāʿ aṭ-ṭabīʿī* 1.11, 53,4-12

Avicenna, *Liber primus naturalium: Tractatus primus de causis et principiis naturalium*, 95,2-19

The agent is, in a way, a cause of the end; how could it not be so, when the agent is what makes the end occur as an existent? The end

[8] Michot 1997b has recently argued for an earlier dating of the *Ishārāt*, based on evidence contained in *Mubāḥatha* 3. Given our current uncertainty about the *Mubāḥathāt* – in particular, if they constitute a single work from a single period or are, as it seems to me, a grab-bag of many separate discussions recorded over Avicenna's lifetime – I feel Michot's conclusion remains highly tentative, and the traditional late dating of the *Ishārāt* should be retained. Avicenna does use the term *shayʾiyya* once in the *Manṭiq* of the *Ishārāt* (*K. al-ishārāt wa-t-tanbīhāt*, 15,6-8; *shayʾiyya* appears on line 8) but in the context of describing the function of the specific difference (*al-faṣl*), not in the context of final and efficient causality.

[9] Gutas 1988, 101-112. Compare al-Jūzjānī's Prologue to the *Shifāʾ* in *Manṭiq (1)*, 2,13-3,17 and his description of the composition of the *Shifāʾ* contained in his biography of Avicenna (Ibn Sīnā, *Autobiography*, 54,1-60,7).

> is, in a way, the cause of the agent; how could it not be so, when the agent acts only on account of it [the end]; otherwise, why would it be acting? For the end sets the agent in motion towards being an agent. For this reason, when it is said "Why do you exercise?", and it is said "In order to be healthy", that will be an answer; just as, when it is said "Why are you healthy?", and it is said "Because I exercised", it will be an answer. Exercise is the efficient cause of health, and health is the final cause of exercise .... The agent is not a cause of the end's becoming an end, nor of the end's essence in itself [*wa-lā li-māhiyyati l-ghāyati fī nafsihā = nec ut finis habeat esse in se*]; rather it is a cause of the existence of the end's essence in concrete reality. *The difference between essence and existence is as you already know.* The end is a cause of the agent's being an agent, for it [the end, reading *fa-hiya*] is the cause of [the agent's] being a cause, whereas the agent is not a cause of the end in terms of [the end's] being a cause. *This will be made clear in First Philosophy.*

Having taken into account all the new evidence from Chapters 8 and 9, I can make the following additions (in **bold**) to my earlier chart (i.e., from Chapter 7) of the progression in Avicenna's thought about thingness and essence:

(1) *Ḥikma ᶜArūḍiyya*, 2v8-10: "One" is a necessary accident of things (*mina l-aᶜrāḍi l-lāzimati li-l-ashyāʾi*). Essence is a thing (*bal takūnu l-māhiyyatu shayʾan*), be it a man or a horse, an intellect or a soul; that thing is only subsequently characterized as being one or existent.

(2) *Madkhal* 1.2: The essences of things (*māhiyyātu l-ashyāʾi*) are sometimes found in concrete objects in the outside world, and other times are conceived of in the mind. But essence has three aspects: as a concrete, external existent; as a mental, internal existent; and a third aspect, in which it is unrelated to either concrete or mental existence.

(3) *Madkhal* 1.12: Genera and species may be divided into those which are *before* a state of multiplicity (that is, those contained in the Active Intellect and the other celestial intellects), those which are *in* a state of multiplicity (that is, those contained individually in sublunary concrete existents), and those which are *after* a state of multiplicity (that is, those contained as abstracted universals in human intellects). Taken in itself a genus or a species is a thing. "Animal", taken in itself, is an intentional object (*maᶜnan*), regardless of whether it is a concrete or a mental existent, or whether it is general or specific (*wa-laysa fī nafsihi bi-ᶜāmmin wa-lā khāṣṣin*).

(4) *Ṭabīᶜiyyāt* 1.11: The efficient cause causes the final cause to exist in concrete reality, that is, to exist in an absolute or affirmative sense; the final cause causes the efficient cause to exist as an efficient cause, that is, to exist in a special sense.

(5) *Ilāhiyyāt* 1.5: "Thing" and "existent" are primary, indefinable categories. Whatever is predicable of thing will also be predicable of existent, and

whatever is predicable of existent will also be predicable of thing. Although they are co-implied, thing and existent have different meanings.

(6) *Ilāhiyyāt* 5.1: A universal (*kullī*) such as "horseness", taken in and of itself (*fī nafsihi*) – that is, without considering whether it is one or many (*lā wāḥida wa-lā kathīra*), a concrete existent in the outside world or a mental existent inside the soul (*lā mawjūda fī l-aᶜyāni wa-lā mawjūda fī n-nafsi*), in potentiality or in actuality (*lā bi-l-quwwati wa-lā bi-l-fiᶜli*) – is a thing (*shayʾ*).

(7) *Ilāhiyyāt* 6.5: The other causes are prior to the final cause in terms of existence; the final cause is prior to the other causes in terms of thingness. The other causes are the causes of the final cause's existence; the final cause is the cause of the other causes' thingness. Thing is logically prior to existent ("the difference between thing and existent is just like the difference between some entity and its concomitant" – 292,2-3); thingness is operative only when existent in the soul, i.e., in intentional action.

(8) *Ilāhiyyāt* 7.1: "One" (*al-wāḥid*) and "existent" (*al-mawjūd*) are equally predicable of things (*qad yatasāwayāni fī l-ḥamli ᶜalā l-ashyāʾi*); all that may be characterized by "one" may also be characterized by "existent", but the two terms do not have the same meaning as each other.

(9) *Najāt*: The other causes are prior to the final cause in terms of existence; the final cause is prior to the other causes in terms of thingness; thingness is what is common to both mental existence and concrete existence.

(10) *Ishārāt/Fī l-wujūd wa-ᶜilalihi*: The final cause is a cause, through its essence, of the causality (*ᶜilliyya*) of the efficient cause; the efficient cause is a cause of the existence of the final cause.

Avicenna's use of *māhiyya* when discussing the final cause's priority in the *Ishārāt* suffered from none of the obstacles strewn across the path of his earlier uses of *shayʾiyya*. Unlike *shayʾiyya*, *māhiyya* was clearly identified with form, so natural phenomena with forms but no intentionality could more easily be accommodated in a universal teleology. Unlike a *shayʾiyya* in the mind, which smacked of the Muᶜtazilites' non-existent thing, the mental existence of a *māhiyya* was explicitly allowed for, so unrealized ends with mental but no concrete existence could more easily satisfy the basic criterion of causality. And unlike *shayʾiyya*, *māhiyya* was clearly held to be logically prior to existence, so the primacy of final causation could be more easily upheld. For all these reasons Avicenna opted for *māhiyya*, and in so doing went some way to resolving the tension between his inconsistent uses of the term *shayʾ*, and by extension, between his concepts of thingness and essence.

Let me summarize what I have proven in Chapters 7, 8 and 9. I first argued that the discussions of things and existents by the *mutakallimūn* were the most important source of Avicenna's distinction between essence and existence. This is because Avicenna's position on how things and existents are related to each other – at least as articulated in *Ilāhiyyāt* 1.5 – is a slightly modified version of that propounded by the Sunnī *mutakallimūn*; the position of al-Fārābī, by contrast, is a slightly modified version of that propounded by the Muᶜtazilites. I then argued that the concept of "thingness" (*shayʾiyya*) served to link the early *kalām* concept of "thing" (*shayʾ*) with Avicenna's concept of "essence" (*māhiyya*). I showed that despite some textual indications otherwise Avicenna uses the term *shayʾiyya* to explain how the final cause is prior to the efficient cause. I then argued that Avicenna's statements in *Ilāhiyyāt* 6.5 and elsewhere that the final cause is prior to the efficient cause in terms of thingness or essence, while the efficient cause is prior to the final cause in terms of existence, should be understood as a way to avoid the circularity that loomed behind Aristotle's statement in *Physics* 2.3, 195a8-11, that sometimes the efficient cause is the cause of the final cause and the final cause is the cause of the efficient cause, as health is the cause of hard work and hard work is the cause of health. Finally, I argued that Avicenna's incompatible ideas about thingness and essence, in the course of their application to the problem of distinguishing final and efficient causality, approach resolution.

10. Causal Self-Sufficiency vs. Causal Productivity

To the arguments just presented I shall now suggest that Avicenna's distinction between essence and existence, and his assertions that the final cause is prior to the efficient cause in terms of essence or thingness while the efficient cause is prior to the final cause in terms of existence, should also be viewed as springing from yet another problematic. Just as I argued that *kalām* debates about the relationship between "thing" (*shay*ʾ) and "existent" (*mawjūd*) provided the *immediate* terminological and philosophical basis for Avicenna's distinction between essence and existence, so I shall now argue that the Neoplatonists' distinction between "well-being" (*to eu einai*) and "existence" (*to einai*) provided the *ultimate* basis for Avicenna's distinction between essence and existence. And just as I earlier argued that "thingness" served to link the early *kalām* concept of "thing" with Avicenna's concept of "essence", so I shall now also argue that the concept of "perfection" (*teleiotês* = *tamām*/*kamāl*) served to link the Neoplatonists' concept of "well-being" (*to eu einai*) with Avicenna's concept of "essence". And just as I earlier argued that Avicenna applied the distinction between essence and existence to the relationship between final and efficient causes in order to avoid the circularity that loomed behind Aristotle's statement that sometimes the efficient cause was the cause of the final cause and the final the cause of the efficient, so I shall now also argue that Avicenna applied the distinction between essence and existence to the relationship between final and efficient causes in order to avoid the circularity that loomed behind the Neoplatonists' scheme of procession and reversion.

Although it is easy enough to see the transition from *to einai* to *al-wujūd*, Avicenna's main term for existence, less obvious is the route from the Neoplatonists' *to eu einai* to *māhiyya*, Avicenna's main term for essence. As I mentioned, I would like to suggest that the missing link between the Neoplatonists' *to eu einai* and Avicenna's *māhiyya* was the concept of perfection. How is this so? In Chapter 6 I showed that a substantial form can be viewed as an element of procession, in which case it is both the formal cause of the composite in which it inheres, and the effect of a higher efficient cause which bestowed it on the composite. Alternatively, the substantial form can be viewed as an element of reversion, in which case it is the final cause *qua to hou* of the thing below it which is actively striving to attain it. The substantial form viewed as an element of reversion is clearly what Avicenna had in mind when, in his early treatise on (among other topics) procession and reversion, entitled *The Origin and the Destination* (*al-Mabda*ʾ *wa-l-ma*ʿ*ād*), he identifies forms (*ṣuwar*) with the perfections of bodies (*kamālāt al-ajsām*); when, in the *Burhān* of his *Shifā*ʾ, he equates the essence of a thing with a thing's perfect form; and when, towards the end of the *Ilāhiyyāt* of his *Shifā*ʾ, he asserts that reversion (*maᶜād*) consists in the coming about of a thing's perfection.[1] These pieces of evidence place Avicenna squarely in the Neoplatonic tradition described above.

What Avicenna does that is original is apply his own, new distinction between essence and existence to the old Aristotelian problem of determining the nature of the complementarity between final and efficient causes. But Avicenna was almost certainly led to use his essence/existence distinction in this way by the Neoplatonists' own attempts to solve the complementarity problem by applying Alexander's *to einai/to eu einai* and *ousia/teleiotês* distinctions to procession and reversion.

Let me explain. As I showed earlier, Avicenna held that the efficient cause is the *explanans* of an *explanandum* insofar as the *explanandum* is viewed in light of its existence in an absolute sense (*al-wujūd al-muṭlaq*) or in light of its affirmative existence (*al-wujūd al-ithbātī*). That is, the efficient cause is the primary *explanans* when the *explanandum* is viewed as an existent (*mawjūd*). The final cause, by contrast, is the *explanans* of the very same *explanandum* insofar as that *explanandum* is now viewed in light of its essence (*māhiyya*) or thingness (*shayʾiyya*); that is, the final cause is the primary *explanans* when that very same *explanandum* is now viewed as having one type of existence as opposed to another (*al-wujūd al-khāṣṣ*), as being one thing (*shayʾ*) in contrast to another thing.

When put in terms of procession and reversion, the efficient cause is now held by Avicenna to be prior with respect to the downward procession of pure existence from one thing to another below it. In other words, the efficient cause is better suited to explaining a higher thing's passing absolute, undifferentiated existence down to a lower thing. By contrast, the final cause is held to be prior with respect to a thing's upward reversion towards its own well-being or perfection. In other words, the final cause is better suited to explaining a thing's striving to attain its substantial form or nature, or, more broadly, its striving to attain the complete inherence of its essence (*māhiyya*) or "X-ness".

For example, the Active Intellect is related to me as an efficient cause is related to its effect: by bestowing my substantial form – my humanity – to me, the Active Intellect has given me existence in an absolute sense (or more precisely, existence in an absolute sense has proceeded or issued from the Active Intellect to me). In this respect the Active Intellect is the efficient cause of my existence.

In another sense, the Active Intellect is related to me as a final cause (*qua to hou*) is related to its effect: the perfect rationality that is possessed by the Active Intellect and that signifies its eternality provides me with a model to imitate, and thereby attain individual immortality, which is my ultimate goal. Again, Avicenna's idea seems to be that the Active Intellect *qua* final cause best

[1] Ibn Sīnā, *al-Mabdaʾ wa-l-maᶜād*, 78,14-15; *K. ash-shifāʾ/Manṭiq (5): al-Burhān* 4.5, 299,17-18; and *K. ash-shifāʾ/Ilāhiyyāt (2)* 9.7, 424,3.

explains my own reversionary struggle to perfect my humanity. That is, the Active Intellect *qua* final cause best explains my striving to exist, as fully and as well as I can, as a human: by being perfectly rational, by focusing entirely on my rationality, which is the specific difference or essential characteristic that sets my species apart from other species of animal such as "cat".

With this in mind, the Neoplatonists' move to distinguish between *to einai* and *to eu einai*, and Avicenna's move to distinguish *wujūd* and *mahiyya*, were similar in that both moves were driven partly by the desire to avoid a situation in which the efficient cause and the final cause competed over the same *explanandum* (or, more precisely, over the same aspect of a single *explanandum*). What I mean is that if the efficient cause and the final cause are simply different ways of explaining the same *explanandum* – the existence of effect X – the final cause will inevitably lose to the efficient cause. This is because the efficient cause enjoys a built-in advantage over the final cause: whereas the efficient cause exists concretely in the extramental world before or at the same time as its effect, the final cause comes into existence concretely in the extramental world at the same time as or after its effect. Sometimes, when an end is unfulfilled, the final cause never comes into existence concretely in the extramental world at all: my motion to the refrigerator exists regardless of whether or not I eventually fulfill the aim which first caused that motion to exist, namely, quenching my thirst by drinking the can of soda that may or may not be in the refrigerator. With the cards stacked in the efficient cause's favor, the final cause will appear superfluous, and this will in turn undermine Aristotle's and Proclus' many assertions about the supremacy of the final cause, a supremacy that is most starkly evident in the fact both Aristotle and Proclus held God, the ultimate cause, to be a final cause; in Aristotle's terms, the Unmoved Mover, and in Proclus' terms, the Good.

If, on the other hand, the efficient cause and the final cause were not seen to compete over the same *explanandum* – the existence of the effect – but were instead seen to cause different *explananda* – or more precisely, different aspects of the same *explanandum* – there would be complementarity rather than competition between them. I could hold that the efficient cause was the primary *explanans* of *explanandum* X insofar as *explanandum* X was viewed in light of the downward procession of existence; while at the same time holding that the final cause was the primary *explanans* of *explanandum* X insofar as *explanandum* X was viewed in light of the upward reversion towards its well-being, that is, towards *explanandum* X's perfection, towards perfect X-ness.

Holding that there is a complementarity between the way an efficient cause explains its *explanandum* and the way a final cause explains its *explanandum*, rather than holding that the efficient and final causes compete over the same *explanandum*; and arguing that this complementarity is meaningful rather than trivial because existence and essence are conceptually distinct; are, in my opinion, Avicenna's attempt to come to grips with one of the major problems facing late-antique and medieval philosophers who tried to defend the coherence of Aristotelian teleology.

This is important partly because the question of whether or not Aristotle really thought teleological explanation was essential to scientific explanation has been the subject of fierce debate in recent Aristotle scholarship.[2] Nowadays the charges that historians of ancient philosophy either level at Aristotelian teleology or defend it against tend to revolve around the question of how philosophically coherent Aristotle was in maintaining that the final cause is compatible either with the material cause (generally understood by them as the problem of compatibility between *hypothetical necessitation* and *absolute necessitation*) or with the efficient cause (generally understood by them as the problem of compatibility between *teleological explanation* and *mechanistic explanation*).[3]

To my mind these debates reflect post-scientific-revolution concerns that would have appeared inappropriate to most Aristotelian philosophers from before the scientific revolution. In other words, the modern assumption that Aristotelian teleology was accepted blindly by most premodern philosophers (until, that is, the scientific revolution taught us that it was more important to answer the question "How?" than the question "Why?") confuses two issues. Philosophers before the scientific revolution, though committed to teleology generally, *were* worried about Aristotle's final cause, and particularly about how it could be seen to be compatible with other forms of causation or explanation. But the compatibility or complementarity problem that preoccupied most late-antique and medieval philosophers was not one that was located in the first instance in the sublunary world of coming-to-be and passing-away, such as the problem of compatibility between hypothetical and material necessitation, or the problem of compatibility between teleological and mechanistic explanation. The compatibility problem that most worried Neoplatonizing Aristotelians such as Avicenna a thousand years ago was one born of the larger project to harmonize Plato's and Aristotle's cosmologies: the problem of compatibility between the

[2] Following the taxonomy proposed by Hankinson 1995, 130-132, opinions on this issue can be divided along the following lines, from weakest to strongest: (1) *metaphorical teleology*: those who understand Aristotle as holding that the final cause is a cause only metaphorically, that it is a useful heuristic device but one which does not reflect the way things are in reality, that natural things are structured in such a way that it only *appears* as if they are directed towards some purpose; (2) *epistemological teleology*: those who understand Aristotle as holding that the final cause is one part of a full *explanation* of a natural thing, and thus accommodates our intuitions about nature's being end-directed; but still, in reality, final causation will not resist being reduced to material causation; (3) *concrete teleology*: those who understand Aristotle as holding that final causes are *irreducible* potentialities for form, and that final causation is found to be operating in this way in the real world. Proponents of (1) include Wieland 1975, and Nussbaum 1978, 59-99; proponents of (2) include Sorabji 1980, 165-166; and proponents of (3) include Gotthelf 1976.

[3] For various persepctives on this issue see Charles 1981, Boylan 1981, Lennox 1982, Bradie and Miller 1984, Friedman 1986 and 1987, Cooper 1987, Balme 1987, Gotthelf 1989 and Sauvé Meyer 1992.

procession of being, in which the efficient cause plays the primary role, and the reversion towards well-being, perfection and essence, in which the final cause plays the primary role.

Given Avicenna's inheritance and adaptation of the idea of complementarity between efficient and final causes, it should come as little surprise that like his Ammonian predecessors, Avicenna thought that God was at one and the same time efficient cause, the origin of all existence, and final cause, the good or end of all essential perfection. Avicenna says as much in the *Ilāhiyyāt* of the *Shifāʾ*:

L51

Ibn Sīnā, *Kitāb ash-shifāʾ/Ilāhiyyāt (2)* 8.6, 355,6-356,5
Avicenna, *Liber de philosophia prima sive scientia divina V-X*, 412,55-413,78

The Necessary of Existence is perfect of existence [*tāmmu l-wujūdi* = *perfectum esse*], because He is not deficient in any part of His existence or in any of the perfections of His existence [*kamālāti wujūdihi* = *perfectionibus sui esse*]; nor does any part of the genus of His existence fall outside His existence or exist on account of something else, as is the case with other things such as "human" (who is deficient in many of the perfections of his existence, not to mention the fact that his humanity exists on account of something other than him). In fact the Necessary of Existence is above perfection [*fawqa t-tamāmi* = *plus quam perfectum*], because not only does He possess the existence which He alone possesses, but all [other] existence is an overflow that comes from His existence, and is on account of it, and emanates from it. The Necessary of Existence in itself is pure good, and good, on the whole, is what everything desires. Now what everything desires is existence, or rather, the perfection of existence of the type of existence [which the thing has] [*aw kamālu l-wujūdi min bābi l-wujūdi* = *et perfectio esse inquantum est esse*]; non-existence, on the other hand, is not desired in so far as it is non-existence, but rather in so far as existence or the perfection of existence follows after it. So what is really desired is existence, and existence is a pure good and a pure perfection [*khayrun maḥḍun wa-kamālun maḥḍun* = *bonitas pura et perfectio pura*]. On the whole, the good is that which each thing desires in respect of its definition and is that by which its existence is perfected; evil, on the other hand, has no essence [i.e., to be pointed to with a definition] but rather is either the non-existence of a substance or the non-existence of the substance's proper state. Existence is a [type of] goodness, and the perfection of existence is the goodness of existence. Existence which is accompanied by no non-existence (be it the non-existence of a substance, or the non-existence of something possessed by the substance) but which is instead perpetually in act, is a pure good. The possible of existence in itself is not a pure good, because in itself it does not necessarily entail its own existence, and in itself it allows for non-existence; and whatever

> allows for non-existence in any way will not be in every respect free from evil and deficiency. Therefore there is no pure good other than the Necessary of Existence in itself.

Unsurprisingly, Avicenna's works contain many assertions that the good is equivalent to perfection, that God is "perfect of existence" (*tāmm al-wujūd*), that He possesses perfection or "pure perfection" (*al-kamāl al-maḥḍ*), and that He is only for the sake of His own perfection (*li-ajli kamāli dhātihi*).[4] For my present purpose, what is interesting about those assertions is the inference that if the Necessary of Existence is to be the initial source of existence on the one hand, and the ultimate good and perfection on the other; if He is to be both the beginning of procession and the end of reversion; and if He is to have no end above and beyond Himself; then He will need to be a final cause as well as an efficient cause. In the *Taʿlīqāt* Avicenna is much more explicit:

L52

Ibn Sīnā, *at-Taʿlīqāt*

> 18,4: If the Necessary of Existence in himself is the agent, then he is also the end and objective.
> 51,28: [In the First] there is no difference between end and agent.
> 62,3-5: Every end is a good, and the Necessary of Existence – given that the end of whatever issues from Him is the absolutely perfect good – is [Himself] the end of creation, since everything terminates in Him, as He says [Qurʾān 53:42] ["Does the apostate not have Moses' and Abraham's knowledge] that the end point is at your Lord?".
> 62,12-13: If the First is an end in terms of perfection and there is no perfection above and beyond Him which may be related to Him, then no perfection above His perfection is imaginable.
> 80,25-26: [The Creator] is the first and the last because He is agent and end, His end being His self, and because [He] is the source of everything and that to which everything returns.
> 160,5-6: One must know that He is Necessary of Existence, that He is a principle, that He is a good, that he is an agent, that He is an end, and that he is power.
> 178,25-26: In addition [to the agent], the end is a cause which is distinct from the effect, although in the case of the Necessary of Existence the end and agent are identical, for He is agent and end.

Although Avicenna's position that God is both efficient and final cause seems like a natural consequence of his cosmology of procession and return, and is perfectly in line with the tradition of the Ammonian synthesis, as described in

[4] A thing's good (*nīkī*) is its perfection (*kamāl*): *Dānishnāma-yi ʿAlāʾī: Ilāhiyyāt*, 117,7-9. The Necessary of Existence is pure or absolute perfection: *K. al-hidāya*, 262,2-3; *ar-Risālat al-ʿarshiyya fī ḥaqāʾiq at-tawḥīd wa-ithbāt an-nubuwwa*, 21,2-4; and *Dānishnāma-yi ʿAlāʾī: Ilāhiyyāt*, 148,9-10. God has no perfection or final cause other than Himself: *ar-Risālat al-ʿarshiyya fī ḥaqāʾiq at-tawḥīd wa-ithbāt an-nubuwwa*, 22,18-20 and 29,3-4; *al-Mubāḥathāt*, 300,4-7 (= *Mubāḥatha* 6, #840).

Chapter 3, many interpreters have accepted without question the view of the Shiᶜite philosopher and theologian aṭ-Ṭūsī (d. 1274), in his commentary on a rather cryptic line in Avicenna's *Ishārāt*, that the Necessary of Existence is *only* an efficient cause.[5]

Partly as a result of aṭ-Ṭūsī's interpretation – or in my view, aṭ-Ṭūsī's misinterpretation – the little scholarly attention that has been paid to Avicenna's discussions of causality has focused on his theory of efficient causation, even despite Avicenna's bald assertion, mentioned above, about the primacy of final causality.[6] This focus is symptomatic of a broader tendency among historians of philosophy to reduce Neoplatonic cosmology to God's efficient causation of existence, in order to contrast it with an Aristotelian cosmology in which God's final causation of motion is paramount. As a result many historians of philosophy have ignored Neoplatonic teleologies such as Proclus' and Avicenna's, in which the final causation of existence – or rather, of "well-being" or "special existence" (*to eu einai = al-wujūd al-khāṣṣ*, i.e., *al-māhiyya*) – is meant to complement the efficient causation of existence (*to einai = al-wujūd*).[7]

[5] Naṣīr al-dīn aṭ-Ṭūsī (d. 1274), *Sharḥ al-Ishārāt*, 194,13-17 (inside box); in his own comments on this passage (194,23-33, outside box) Fakhr al-dīn ar-Rāzī (d. 1210) had refused to commit himself to naming one cause or the other. Avicenna's rather cryptic "Pointer" (*Ishāra*) is "If there is a First Cause, it will be a cause of every existence, and of the cause of the reality of every existence in existence (*in kānat ᶜillatun ūlā fa-hiya ᶜillatun li-kulli wujūdin wa-li-ᶜillati ḥaqīqati kulli wujūdin fī l-wujūdi*)" (*Ishārāt*, 140,10-11). Now in the three chapters immediately preceding this one Avicenna distinguishes between causes of existence (the efficient and final causes) and causes of essence (the formal and material causes), and also argues for the complementarity of efficient and final causes (the efficient is the cause, in terms of its *wujūd*, of the existence of the final, and the final is the cause, in terms of its *ḥaqīqa*, *māhiyya* and *maᶜna*, of the causality and efficiency of the efficient) (*Ishārāt*, 139,14-140,9). In this light the line should be understood as claiming that if there is a first cause, it will be a cause of existence (that is, it will be an efficient and final cause), and it will also be the cause of the cause of essence (that is, it will be the cause of the formal and material causes). The point is that given the proximity of these arguments to the line in question (not to mention the explicit statements in the *Taᶜlīqāt*; the clear implication of *K. ash-shifāʾ/Ilāhiyyāt* 8.6 that as the Good, God is the culmination of all the universe's perfections; and Avicenna's statement at the end of *K. ash-shifāʾ/Ilāhiyyāt* 6.5 that the final is the highest of the causes) I find it hard to understand how a close reader such as aṭ-Ṭūsī could argue so blithely that God could not be a final cause because of the fact that the other causes precede it in existence (reading *bi-l-wujūd* for the text's *bi-l-wujūb*); with eternal things such as God, after all, there is no temporal beforeness. The first half of Avicenna's apodosis must refer to God's being an efficient cause, and the second half must refer to God's being a final cause; otherwise, there would be a respect in which God's efficient causality was the effect of another cause, which is impossible. A later commentator on the *Ishārāt*, al-Āghā Ḥusayn al-Khʷānsārī (d. 1686), tries to correct what he regarded as his predecessors' error on this issue, claiming that Avicenna simply meant to deny that God was a *particular type* of final cause, since the other causes are prior to the final not in an absolute sense but only with respect to a certain category of final causes, namely, the non-essential final causes found in the world of coming-to-be and passing-away; the earlier commentators should be understood as denying merely that God was a final cause of that category, not as denying that God was a final cause in an absolute sense: *al-Ḥāshiya ᶜalā shurūḥ al-ishārāt (2)*, 39,3-5.

[6] See, for example, Gilson 1960 and 1962, and Marmura 1981 (esp. 65-72) and 1984b.

[7] See, for example, Sorabji 1990. Even authors who take into account Neoplatonic teleology tend either to ignore (e.g., Lovejoy 1936, 24-98) or to offer only cursory treatments of (e.g.,

Apart from the question of whether or not God is a final cause as well as an efficient cause, an important piece of evidence illustrating Avicenna's absorption of Neoplatonic cosmology can be gleaned from L51. Given the fact, discussed in Chapter 3, that in Neoplatonic cosmology the perfect corresponds to or to implies efficient causation, while perfection corresponds to or implies final causation, it should be no surprise that in L51, where Avicenna holds God to be both the source of existence and the ultimate goal of all perfection, the extent to which "perfect" and "perfection" may correctly be predicated of God is also discussed.

In L51 Avicenna starts by saying that God is perfect (*tāmm*), in the sense that He does not lack anything and is by implication causally self-sufficient. He then adds that God is in fact "above perfection" (*fawqa t-tamām*), by which Avicenna seems to mean that God is not simply full of existence and hence causally self-sufficient, but is also overflowing with existence, and hence a cause of others. The rest of this chapter is devoted to examining the tension in Avicenna's thought between these two conceptions of God, one as "perfect", complete in Himself, self-sufficient and unrelated to any effect, the other as "above perfection", overflowing with existence, and related to His effects; Avicenna's sources for the two ideas; and Avicenna's attempt to side-step the problems associated with them by using a new formula to describe God.

What precisely does Avicenna intend when he distinguishes between "perfect" and "above perfection" in L51?[8] Avicenna follows the *Metaphysics* translations of *teleion* as *tāmm* and of *telos* as *tamām* in his own discussion of the perfect, *Ilāhiyyāt* 4.3, and begins his treatment of *at-tāmm* in a way that is quite similar to Aristotle's treatment of *to teleion* in L4. However, Avicenna seems to follow Euclid – and Euclid's commentator, Nicomachus – in the sense that Avicenna thinks that numerical perfection (the quality by which a number is equal to the sum of its divisors, as 6 is equal to 1 + 2 + 3) is the most primitive sense of the term. This is in contrast to Aristotle, who introduces L4 with the idea of quantitative completeness (the quality by which a whole is in possession of all its parts).

Avicenna then proceeds, somewhat opaquely, to discuss the implications of viewing numerical perfection as being the most basic sense of perfection. Avicenna introduces the notion of *fawqa t-tamām* first in this numerical context, as equivalent to *zāʾid*, "superabundant" (that is, a number the sum of whose divisors is greater than itself), which suggests that he had Nicomachus' use of *hupertelês* in mind, even though Thābit b. Qurra, the translator of Nicomachus'

Blanchette 1992, 164 and 276-277) the contributions of late-antique philosophers such as Proclus and Ammonius, let alone the contributions of Arabic philosophers such as al-Fārābī and Avicenna.

[8] Avicenna also uses the phrase *tāmm bal fawqa t-tamām* at *at-Taʿlīqāt*, 16,26-27. At *Dānishnāma-yi ʿAlāʾī: Ilāhiyyāt*, 108,10-11, Avicenna says that the Necessary of Existence is "most perfect" (*tamāmtarīn*); at 116,9-117,5, Avicenna gives a synopsis of the distinction between deficient, sufficient, perfect and above perfection.

Introduction to Arithmetic, rendered *hupertelês* into Arabic as *zā'id ʿalā t-tamām* rather than *fawqa t-tamām.*[9] Avicenna then abruptly dismisses the numerical discussion he has just had as nothing but the silly notions of common people:

L53

Ibn Sīnā, *Kitāb ash-shifā'/Ilāhiyyāt (1)* 4.3, 188,3-189,11
Avicenna, *Liber de philosophia prima sive scientia divina I-IV*, 215,13-217,47

Having now brought [you] to this point, let us leave it behind, since we are not accustomed to talking about things such as this, which are based upon rhetorical conjectures and do not derive from the methods of scientific syllogisms. So we say instead: Philosophers have also extended "perfect" to cover the reality of existence [*ilā ḥaqīqati l-wujūdi* = *ad certitudinem essendi*]. In one sense, they say, the perfect is that whose characteristic is not to lack anything by which its existence is perfected [*inna t-tāmma huwa lladhī laysa shay'un min sha'nihi an yukmala bihi wujūduhu bi-mā laysa lahu* = (lacuna in Latin)]; on the contrary, everything such as this has come to be contained in it. In another sense they say that the perfect is that which has this characteristic but with the condition that its existence, in itself, is in the most perfect state it can possess [*ʿalā akmali mā yakūnu lahu* = *quantum perfectius esse potest*]; that it alone has it [this existence]; that there is no part of it which it does not have; that in the genus of existence nothing superior to it is related to it in any primary way; and that it is not on account of anything below it. "Above perfection" [*fawqa t-tamāmi* = *Plus quam perfectum*] is whatever has the existence which it needs to have, and from which there is existence left over for other things. It is as if it has the existence which it needs to have as well as some extra existence which it does not need and which is left over for [other] things, this being something that comes from itself.

They then posited that this rank – namely, being that which is above perfection [*fawqa t-tamāmi* = *ultra perfectionem*] – applies to the First Principle, given that in itself and not on account of anything else, a part of its existence is to emanate existence from its own existence to all things. They held that the rank of "perfect" belongs to a separate intellect [*li-ʿaqlin mina l-ʿuqūli l-mufāraqati* = *intelligentiae ei quae ex intelligentiis separatis*] which is untouched by anything potential at the origin of its existence in act, and which is not mindful of any other existence which exists as a result of it; for in fact everything other [than it] comes from the existence that issues from the First. They held that below the perfect were the sufficient and the deficient [*wa-jaʿalū dūna t-tamāmi shay'ayni l-muktafiya wa-n-nāqiṣa* = *sufficiens et insufficiens*]. The sufficient is what is given [the ability] to produce its own perfection. In a strict sense the deficient is what

[9] Nīqūmākhis al-Jārāsīnī, *K. al-madkhal ilā ʿilm al-ʿadad*, 36,11; 37,5.15; 40,14.

> needs something else to extend one perfection after another to it. An example of the sufficient is the rational soul which belongs to the universe, I mean the heavens. For in itself it [the rational soul] performs the activities which pertain to it and causes the existence of the perfections it needs to possess in a piecemeal fashion, without all of them being brought together at once, and without their remaining in perpetuity; otherwise those perfections which are in its substance and form, would not be distinct from what is potential, even though they contain within themselves a principle which makes them emerge from potency into act, as you will learn later on. As for the deficient, it is like the things which are in the world of coming-to-be and passing-away.

Avicenna's frustration at the beginning of the passage could be directed at the Neoplatonists' inconsistency over the question of what constituted a perfect number, which differed depending on the context in which perfect number was introduced.[10]

In any case, Avicenna claims that what is above perfection is whatever has all the existence it needs, and then some extra existence left over to spill onto things below it. This obviously refers to God. That which is perfect in existence is whatever does not exist on account of what is below it, and refers to the celestial intellects. What the sufficient refers to is slightly unclear: we are told that it refers to any of the celestial souls, since it has it in itself to attain its perfection – by causing its sphere's eternal circular motion, one assumes – without requiring the help of anything outside. In other words, the sufficient has a potentiality which it is able to exercise without relying on external things, whereas the perfect has no potentiality whatsoever. The deficient clearly refers to sublunary things, things like horses and trees which are subject to coming-to-be and passing-away.

I think that Avicenna's debt in this passage to the Neoplatonists is undeniable. Avicenna has applied Neoplatonic, and particularly Proclan, ideas – discussed in Chapter 3 – of *to autarkes* to the perfect, and of *to authupostaton* to the sufficient, in an effort to create a clearer distinction between the ways in which things are spoken of as being perfect. Just as Proclus had done, Avicenna applied the concepts of *to autarkes* and *to authupostaton* to the various inhabitants of

[10] As I mentioned at the end of Chapter 4, figuring out the perfect number of transmigrations of the soul, as well as the perfect number of revolutions of the universe, was a Neoplatonic preoccupation. The Neoplatonists seemed unable to decide on whether to understand perfect number in the Euclidean sense (that is, as the sum of its divisors, as 6 is the sum of 1, 2 and 3), or in a more mystical, Pythagorean sense (with the number 10 usually taken to possess true perfection). The Euclidean sense is in the foreground at Iamblichus, *Theol. Arithm.*, 42,19 and 17,13; and Proclus, *in Parm.*, 767,30-32; and *in Tim.*, Vol. 3, 168,17-20. The Pythagorean sense is in the foreground at Syrianus, *in Metaph.* 13.8 (*ad* 1084a29), 149,27; Proclus, *in Remp.*, Vol. 2, 81,9 and 121,4 (where Porphyry is said to have claimed that 12 represents perfection); *Theol. Plat.*, Vol. 4.29, 87,7-8 (citing *Resp.* VIII 546B3-4); *in Tim.*, Vol. 3, 94,32-95,6; and Asclepius, *in Metaph.* 1.5 (*ad* 985b23), 37,14-15 and 1.8 (*ad* 989b29), 65,18-19.

the superlunary realm partly in order to find some way round the problem of differentiating between things which are all eternal and actual and, in that sense, perfect.[11] Avicenna also seems to have followed Iamblichus' and Proclus' attempts to Pythagoreanize (by which I mean their attempts to assign ontological and cosmological value to categories of number) Euclid's and Nicomachus' distinction between superabundant, perfect, and deficient number.[12]

In short, Avicenna has used the concept of "that which is above perfection" in order to distinguish the causal self-sufficiency of the Intellects, which is not in itself productive of the existence of anything else, from the causal self-sufficiency of God, which is in itself productive of the existence of other things.[13] The idea that God is *above* perfection is not found in *Metaphysics* 12, where God and the celestial substances or movers (Aristotle never uses intellects in the plural in this context) are often described as being completely actual, but never as being *above* actuality.[14] Yet in the Arabic *Liber de causis*, a paraphrase of sections of Proclus' *Elements of Theology*, but attributed to Aristotle and called *Kitāb al-īḍāḥ fī l-khayr al-maḥḍ li-Arisṭūṭālīs* (*Aristotle's Book on The Exposition of the Pure Good*), God is described as being above perfection:

L54

(Ps.-)Arisṭūṭālīs, *Kitāb al-īḍāḥ fī l-khayr al-maḥḍ li-Arisṭūṭālīs* 21, 22,12-23,5[15]

corr. Proclus, *Inst. Theol.* 115, 100,28-102,12

The first cause is above every name predicated of it. This is in view of the fact that deficiency is not worthy of it, nor even perfection alone. [This is] because what is deficient is not perfect, and since it is deficient it is unable to carry out a perfect act; and what is perfect <in our opinion> – although it is self-sufficient [*wa-in kāna muktafiya bi-nafsihi*] – is unable to originate anything else, nor to emanate from itself anything whatsoever. If this is so, we shall return and say that the first cause is not deficient, nor perfect

[11] In addition to the Proclan ideas of *to autarkes* and *to authupostaton*, the idea of "the self-perfect" (*to autoteles*) – referring to something which has it in itself to come to perfection – also suggests itself as an antecedent to Avicenna's *muktafin* and *tāmm*; cf. Proclus, *Inst. Theol.*, Prop. 64, 60,25-31.

[12] See, for example, Iamblichus' distinction between *huperteles, teleion* and *ateles*, at *Theol. Arithm.* 18.17; and Proclus' distinction between "the full" (*to plêres*) and "that which is above fullness" (*to huperplêres*) at *Inst. Theol.*, Prop. 131, 116,15-27.

[13] Al-Fārābī uses *muktafin* at *K. as-siyāsat al-madaniyya*, 53,11-54,11, but differently from Avicenna: al-Fārābī's *muktafin* refers to the fact that celestial substances *in general* are sufficient to produce – i.e., capable of producing – other things; compare al-Fārābī, *R. fī al-ᶜaql*, 33,5-11, where he argues that the Active Intellect cannot be God because the Active Intellect does not possess the self-sufficiency (*kifāya*) to be its own cause, as a result of the unreliability of receptive sublunary matter and intellect always to receive its eternal emanation.

[14] Though Asclepius distinguishes between the celestial Intellect, which is completely actual and has no potentiality, and the First Cause, which is above actuality (*huper energeian*): *in Metaph.* 3.1 (*ad* 996a9), 148,30-34.

[15] *fawqa t-tamām* appears at 23,1; <ms b adds what is between brackets>.

> alone; rather, it is above perfection [*fawqa t-tamāmi*] <because it originates things and emanates goods to them in a perfect emanation> because it is an infinite and inexhaustible good.

Although the terms *huperousios* ("above being"), *huperzôos* ("above life"), *hupernous* ("above intellect") and *autotelês* ("self-perfecting"), all appear in the corresponding Greek chapter of Proclus' *Elements of Theology*, the term *huperteleion* does not; nor does it appear anywhere else in the *Elements*, as far as I can tell. The term *huperteleion* can be found, however, in Proclus' commentary on Plato's *Timaeus*, though applied in a different way.[16] I do not know whether the abridger of the *Liber de causis* applied the phrase *fawqa t-tamām* with Proclus' *in Timaeum* usage in mind, or whether he invented it in light of the other "hyper"-qualities described in the *Elements*. In any case the phrase also appears – far more often than in the *Liber de causis* – in *Mīmār* 10 of the *Uthūlūjiyā*, sometimes on its own as *fawqa t-tamām*, other times as a hendiadys with *kamāl*:

L55

(Ps.-)Arisṭūṭālīs, *Uthūlūjiyā 10*, 134,16-135,12[17]
corr. Plotinus, *Enneads* V.2.1,4-8

> I say too that the absolute One is above perfection [*fawqa t-tamāmi wa-l-kamāli*]. The sensible world is defective because it is originated from the perfect thing, which is mind; mind is perfect because it is originated from the true absolute One, which is above perfection. It is not possible that the thing which is above perfection should originate the defective thing directly, nor is it

[16] Proclus, *in Tim.*, Vol. 3, 10,22-11,4. The reason why Proclus uses *huperteleion* in this context is different from Avicenna's reason for using *fawqa t-tamām* in L53. In his *Timaeus* commentary, Proclus is discussing the nature of time, and is trying to distinguish Eternity (*ho aiôn*) from Living-in-Itself (*to autozôion*): Eternity is superior to Living-in-Itself, Proclus says, for various reasons; what then to do with *Tim.* 30D2, where Plato says that *to autozôion* is "the most beautiful of the objects of intellection and perfect in every respect (*kai kata panta teleion*)"? Well, Proclus argues, most beautiful does not mean best, and Eternity is best. As for the latter qualification, that which is "perfect in every respect" is not necessarily first and foremost (*prôtiston*); for "the perfect" possesses all things inasmuch as it possesses first, middle and final parts. Now, whatever is above this divisibility into beginning, middle and end, will therefore be "above perfection" (*epeita de ouk anangkê prôtiston einai to kata panta teleion; to men gar teleion panta ekhei, hôste kai prôta kai mesa kai teleutaia; ho de estin huper tautên tên tomên, huperteleion an eiê*). Proclus' argument here corresponds to his distinction between (1) the type of perfection that is prior to (meaning above) being divided into parts; (2) the type of perfection that wholes possess, that is, the perfection which is made up of parts; and (3) the type of perfection that each of the parts making up a whole possesses: Proclus, *Theol. Plat.* 4.25, 74,6-75,2 and 75,21-76,13. This distinction is articulated elsewhere as one between different types of "wholeness" (*holotês*): *Inst. Theol.*, Prop. 67, 64,1-14; and *Theol. Plat.* 3.25, 87,26-89,2. It would be tempting to postulate some kind of filiation between Proclus' tripartite distinction between types of perfection or wholeness, and Avicenna's tripartite distinction – in *Madkhal* 1.12, mentioned in Chapter 7 – between types of universal, but upon closer examination, the distinctions appear to have little in common apart from being tripartite.

[17] *fawqa t-tamām* appears at 134,16 and 135,2(*bis*).5.7.8.9.11. As with L7, the translation, with some variations, is that of Lewis 1959, 291-2.

> possible for the perfect thing to originate anything complete like itself, because origination is deficiency, by which I mean that the originated is not of the rank of the originator but is beneath it. The proof the *absolute One is perfect* and above perfection *is that it has no need of anything and does not seek to acquire anything, and because of* the intensity of *its perfection and superabundance another thing is produced from it.* For the thing which is above perfection cannot produce unless the thing be perfect: otherwise it is not above perfection. For if the perfect thing produces anything, then a fortiori the thing which is above perfection produces perfection, because it produces the perfect thing than which none of the things produced can be more powerful, more splendid or more sublime. For when the true One which is above perfection originates the perfect thing, *that perfect thing turns to its originator and casts its gaze on it and is filled* with light and splendor from it *and becomes mind.*

As was the case with L54, the Arabic phrase *fawqa t-tamām* in L55 does not correspond to an instance of *huperteleion* in Plotinus' Greek. But since by Plotinus' reckoning intellect is perfect, and because intellect looks *up* at what originates it, it would not have been too much of a stretch for the compiler of the *Uthūlūjiyā* to paraphrase him as holding that what originates mind must be *above* perfection.

It is hard to avoid the conclusion that all the conceptual fine-tuning undertaken by philosophers from Proclus to Avicenna in order to create a coherent scheme of differentiating between the various types of perfection and self-sufficiency enjoyed by superlunary beings, cried out for a clear, simple and watertight way to distinguish God from other perfect, self-sufficient and eternally actual things. The problem is that making such a clear, simple and watertight distinction forces a Neoplatonic philosopher to decide which is more basic: God's transcendence of the world or His involvement in the world. If I – as a Neoplatonist – were to opt for transcendence, I should naturally be drawn to emphasizing God's perfection: His self-sufficiency, His lack of nothing, and His not requiring any cause to sustain His existence. If, on the other hand, I were to opt for God's involvement, I should naturally be drawn to emphasizing God's being above perfection: His productivity, His being related to the world as its cause. Is there any way for me to strike a balance between God's transcendence and God's involvement and thereby avoid having to chuck out one in favor of the other; apart from making the fence-straddling assertion – as Avicenna did – that God is on the one hand perfect and on the other hand above perfection?

This dilemma came to a head because Avicenna, like other philosophers before him in the Ammonian synthesis, was committed to seeing God as both efficient and final cause. But since God's perfection, the ultimate goal of reversion, acted on its effect as a final cause acts on its effect, while God's being above perfection, the initial source of procession, acted on its effect as an efficient cause acts on its effect, Avicenna was forced to decide whether reversion culminates in the celestial Intellects or in God. On the one hand, the Intellects are perfect, Avicenna says, and hence possess perfection; therefore reversion should culminate in them, or in the highest of them. On the other hand, God is both perfect and hence possesses perfection, so reversion should culminate in Him; yet God is also above perfection, so reversion should not quite reach Him.

Avicenna's ambivalence about whether God as well as the Intellects, or the Intellects alone, should be regarded as being perfect and possessing perfection is a sign that like Proclus before him, he was torn between viewing perfection and the perfect as univocal terms or as equivocal terms. Avicenna seems to be struggling with this uncertainty when he says in the *Ta^c līqāt*:

L56

Ibn Sīnā, *at-Ta^c līqāt*, 62,11-24

> Imagining one perfection coming above another [*kamālun fawqa kamālin*] in those things that possess perfection, and the dissimilarity each has compared with others, is possible only in respect of the relation the perfections have to complete perfection [*ilā l-kamāli t-tāmmi*], since the dissimilarity is [only] with reference to that [complete perfection]. If the First is an end [or "limit"] in terms of perfection [*in kāna l-awwalu ghāyatan fī l-kamāli*] and there is no perfection above Him which may be related to Him, then no perfection above His perfection will be imaginable.

In other words, Avicenna, like Proclus, could not decide if a single basic meaning of "perfection" and "perfect" ought to be applied consistently to all subjects of which those terms are predicated – to sublunary souls and superlunary souls, to sublunary intellects and superlunary intellects, to sublunary bodies and superlunary spheres – or if, on the other hand, each subject of which "perfection" and "perfect" is predicated should be understood as being a perfection or as being perfect in different ways: as referring, for example, to activity or to actuality, to efficient causality or to final causality, to numerical wholeness or to self-sufficiency. Proclus and Avicenna devoted a great deal of effort to showing that all those apparently different meanings of perfection and the perfect in fact implied each other, or were reducible to one or the other of them. The effort to determine what Aristotle scholars would call a "focal meaning" for perfection and the perfect began, of course, with Alexander's comments on L4, as I showed in Chapter 2. Nevertheless, it is hard to avoid concluding that as a result of their very mutability – and hence their usefulness both with regard to the lesser *sumphônia* of reconciling Aristotle with himself and with regard to the greater *sumphônia* of reconciling Aristotle with Plato – the terms "perfection" and "perfect" came to be applied to so many different things in so many different ways that the terms were eventually rendered trivial.

I believe that it is partly as a result of Avicenna's frustration with the fact that perfection and the perfect had become such blunt philosophical tools, so incapable of chiseling the fine distinctions required to differentiate between various eternal things such as God and the Intellects, that Avicenna's new idea of *wājib al-wujūd bi-dhātihi*, "that which, in itself, necessarily exists", grew to enjoy such prominence in the middle and late parts of his career. Fleshing out the philosophical background to Avicenna's concept of necessary existence – actually a matrix of distinctions, between necessary existence and possible existence, between in itself and through another, between uncaused and caused, and between eternal and originated – and tracing its evolution in Avicenna's works is my task in the next four chapters.

11. Necessity and Possibility (A)
Materials from the Arabic Aristotle

In Chapters 7 to 10 I argued that while Avicenna's distinction between essence and existence appears to have originated in Māturīdite and Ashᶜarite *kalām*, the fact that he applied his distinction to the Aristotelian problem of the compatibility between efficient and final causes is best understood in light of intervening Neoplatonic attempts to construct a meaningful complementarity between the procession of existence from an efficient cause to its effect, and the reversion towards perfection of an effect to its final cause.

I also showed that several Neoplatonists, including Proclus, perhaps drawing from Aristotle's discussions of happiness in the *Nicomachean Ethics*, claimed that the idea of self-sufficiency – *autarkeia* in Greek, *istighnāʾ* in Arabic – was implied in the idea of perfection; and furthermore that self-sufficiency should be primarily construed to refer to uncausedness, and hence to a kind of existential necessity. I then showed that Avicenna was unhappy with the idea of God's possessing only perfection, because while that could explain His causal self-sufficiency (that is, His freedom from being caused to exist by other things) it could not explain his causal productivity (that is, His causing other things to exist). For this reason Avicenna borrows from the Arabic Neoplatonica and asserts that God is both perfect and above perfection (*fawqa t-tamām*).

Avicenna's discomfort with the dualism – conceptual, if not real – that results from holding that God is both final *and* efficient cause, and from holding that He can be seen as both possessing perfection *and* being above perfection, led him to search for an alternative to the old paradigm which had dominated metaphysical speculation throughout the period of the Ammonian synthesis. The question to be answered in the next four chapters is, how and why did Avicenna come up with his alternative paradigm? More specifically, I shall examine Avicenna's construction of a matrix of distinctions between "necessary of existence" (*wājib al-wujūd*) and "possible of existence" (*mumkin al-wujūd*), and between "in itself" (*bi-dhātihi*) and "through another" (*bi-ghayrihi*); his integration of older distinctions – between uncaused and caused, and between eternal and originated – into that new matrix of distinctions; and finally his use of that new matrix of distinctions to confront the old challenge of reconciling one's assertions about *what God is* with one's assertions about *how God causes the world*.

A number of scholars have treated this topic before, which is unsurprising given its centrality in Avicenna's thought and its influence on subsequent thinkers. Goichon views Avicenna's matrix of distinctions as basic, yet treats it almost as a corollary to Avicenna's distinction between essence and existence.[1]

[1] Goichon 1937, 156-180.

Davidson subjects it to a penetrating analysis, detecting two ways Avicenna's matrix of distinctions is put to use in proofs of God's existence, one articulated in the *Najāt* and the *Ishārāt*, the other in the *Shifāʾ* (explicitly) and the *Dānishnāma* (implicitly).[2] But because Davidson's main concern is determining how the question of the world's eternity played out in proofs of God's existence, he is able to group the Avicennian texts together in this way, and thereby does not address the question of whether there might be any evolution in Avicenna's thinking about this issue. Nor does Davidson examine Avicenna's treatments of the matrix of distinctions, and his application of it to the God-world relationship, in early works such as the *Ḥikma ᶜArūḍiyya* and the *Mabdaʾ wa-maᶜād*, both of which precede the *Shifāʾ*, *Najāt*, *Dānishnāma* and *Ishārāt*, and from both of which Avicenna copied whole passages to paste into the pages of his *Najāt*. In focusing exclusively on works from Avicenna's middle and late periods, Davidson follows Goichon, as well as other scholars who have weighed in on the topic.[3] As far as I know Gutas is the only scholar who has raised the issue of a possible evolution in Avicenna's thinking about necessary and possible existence, and called for further research on it.[4]

To a great extent the next four chapters revolve around that developmental question. I shall show that there is richer evidence of philosophical evolution from the works of Avicenna's early period (namely, the *Ḥikma ᶜArūḍiyya* and the *Mabdaʾ wa-maᶜād*) to the works of Avicenna's middle period, than there is of a philosophical development from the middle-period works to the late-period works. But the fact that the early-period works have been ignored (apart from Gutas' brief discussion) insofar as they bear on the issue of the development of Avicenna's matrix of distinctions and his application of that matrix to the God-world relationship, has prevented us not only from determining whether or not an evolution in Avicenna's thought on this topic can be detected. Our relative ignorance of the early-period works hinders us from determining precisely the sources Avicenna drew on when he first articulated the matrix of distinctions, and first applied that matrix to the God-world relationship. Davidson has made some useful suggestions as to possible sources for Avicenna's discussions. But without knowing how Avicenna *first* conceived of this issue, they remain tentative. Before showing how Avicenna's thought evolves from his early period to his middle and late periods, and showing how that evolution is linked to a contemporaneous progression in his thought about essence and existence, I shall present the *Ḥikma ᶜArūḍiyya* passage in which he first formulates his matrix of distinctions and applies them to the God-world relationship, and take stock of the sources that appear to have shaped that very early discussion.

[2] Davidson 1987, 281-310 and 350-361.

[3] Hourani 1972, 74-75, claims that no progression is detectable; see also Hyman 1987.

[4] Gutas 1988, 261-265.

In his autobiography Avicenna famously claimed that at the age of 18, following an 18-month period of intensive philosophical study:

L57

Ibn Sīnā, *Autobiography*

> 30,5-6: All that I knew at that time is just like what I now know: until today I have not become greater in respect of it [i.e., in knowledge] at all.
> 36,8-38,2: When I reached my eighteenth year I was done with all these sciences. And while at that time I had a better memory for [such] knowledge, I am more mature today; otherwise the knowledge [itself] is one and the same thing, nothing new having come to me afterwards [i.e., after the age of 18].

Avicenna's assertion is contradicted by the evidence of a progression in his thought from *shayʾiyya* to *māhiyya*, which I described in the previous chapter, as well as by recent research on other aspects of his philosophy which lend themselves to developmentalist interpretations.[5] So what could Avicenna have meant? Gutas has already attacked the tendency of earlier interpreters to ascribe Avicenna's assertion to an intellectual arrogance and immodesty supposedly common among "Orientals".[6] Gutas reasons that Avicenna must instead have been referring to his theory of intuition, which by Gutas' reckoning is the "core theory" of Avicenna's philosophical system.[7]

My guess, however, is that Avicenna was referring to a metaphysical rather than an epistemological insight: his distinction between necessary and possible existence, and specifically his equation of that which is necessary through another and that which is possible in itself. What I mean is that when, at around the age of 50 (the age he composed the *Autobiography*) Avicenna looked back at his philosophical career, and thinking of himself (to use Isaiah Berlin's distinction) as a hedgehog rather than a fox, he had to admit that his big idea – the idea which he knew was his most original and which he reckoned would be his most influential – came to him at the very young age of 18. That is not to say that this idea did not evolve in his subsequent thought; in fact I hope to show in the next four chapters that his distinction between necessary and possible existence did mature in subtle but important ways. Rather, what Avicenna meant is that after the age of 18 he had no other ideas which were both as big and as original as that one.

There is unequivocal evidence that Avicenna came to his distinction very early in his career. Immediately after the second assertion above in L57, Avicenna goes on to describe his first commissioned *summa*, *The Compilation* (*al-Majmūʿa*), which he composed for a neighbor of his in Bukhārā, Abū l-Ḥasan

[5] See, for example, Gutas 2001 and Hasse 2001.
[6] Gutas 1988, 159-160, esp. 159n.28.
[7] Gutas 1988, 160-176.

al-ᶜArūḍī, and which is known as *al-Ḥikmat al-ᶜArūḍiyya*, or *The ᶜArūḍian Philosophy*. Avicenna asserts that he was 21 when he finished it, that is, around the year 1001. In the section on metaphysics – which, as I noted in Chapter 6, is modeled after *Metaphysics* 5, Aristotle's philosophical lexicon – Avicenna devotes a paragraph to the necessary:

L58

Ibn Sīnā, *al-Ḥikmat al-ᶜArūḍiyya*, 3v16-4r12

"The Necessary" [*al-wājib*] is that which is necessary of existence in respect of the way it is [*aḍ-ḍarūriyyu l-wujūdi ᶜalā mā huwa ᶜalayhi*], this being either in itself [*bi-dhātihi*] (such as the principle of existents [*ka-mabdaʾi l-mawjūdāti*]) or through another (such as the fact that two and two are four). The necessary is either eternal (such as the principle of existents) or is at one time and not another [*fī ḥālin dūna ḥālin*] (such as the eclipse of the moon at that moment). All that is necessary of existence in itself has no cause. Whatever has a cause will be neither necessary of existence in itself nor impossible of existence in itself (for otherwise, it would never come to exist); with respect to itself [*fī ḥaythu dhātihi*], therefore, it [i.e., that which has a cause] will be possible of existence [*mumkinu l-wujūdi*], while [at the same time] being necessary of existence through its cause. Now the existence of whatever has no cause is not itself divisible into two states [*wa-mā lā ᶜillata lahu fa-inna wujūda dhātihi lā yanqasimu min ḥālatayni*], in virtue of which it [i.e., the existence of whatever has no cause] would come to be caused in both states; for there would be no way out of being caused, nor any escape from causedness. All that is subject to change is in these two states, neither one of which it possesses in itself; rather, it possesses both of them through a cause (there being no alternative to them [i.e., there being no alternative to being in the two states]). Thus all that is subject to change will itself be caused and possible, whereas all that is necessary of existence in itself will be necessary of existence in every respect, and no type of change whatsoever will be attributable to it. "The possible" is the existent which is not necessary [*laysa bi-ḍarūriyyin*]. "The possible" is said to be whatever is not impossible; and "the possible" is said to be whatever is not impossible and which exists and [then] is non-existent, and [in general] whatever does not exist at some time or other.

I shall defer until Chapter 14 explaining what Avicenna could have meant in this passage, and how the passage ought to be seen as a first, slightly incoherent attempt to formulate his new matrix of modal distinctions, one which he improved on in subsequent works such as the *Mabdaʾ wa-maᶜād*, the *Ilāhiyyāt* of the *Shifāʾ*, and the *Ishārāt wa-tanbīhāt*. My task now is to provide an inventory of the sources which Avicenna drew from to express the new ideas he articulates in the passage above. The sources include discussions of necessity and necessitation contained in the Arabic Aristotle, which I shall discuss in this chapter; the digested versions of those discussions contained in al-Fārābī's works, which I shall discuss in Chapter 12; and discussions of the eternality of God's attributes contained in tenth-century *kalām* works, which I shall discuss in Chapter 13.

Aristotle speaks at length about necessity in various contexts, but nowhere more canonically than in *Metaphysics* 5.5, the chapter of his philosophical lexicon on the necessary. Since the different ways Aristotle understands and applies the idea of necessity in other works can, with a little effort, be subsumed under the categories he sets out in *Metaphysics* 5.5, I shall begin my discussion with that chapter:

L59

Arisṭāṭālīs, *Mā ba^cda ṭ-ṭabī^ca II*, 515,7-517,7

Aristotle, *Metaph.* 5.5, 1015a20-b15

[**1**] The necessary is that without which a thing cannot exist, such as the cause [*al-muḍṭarru huwa lladhī laysa yumkinu an yakūna sh-shay'u illā bihi wa-huwa ka-l-^cillati = anankaion legetai hou aneu ouk endekhetai zên hôs sunaitiou*], just as breathing and nourishment are with respect to the animal: they are necessary since the animal cannot exist without them. [**2**] Next, the necessary is that without which a good, or the negation or non-existence of an evil, cannot exist or come to be; such as when it is said that ingesting a drug is necessary for an illness not to appear, or as embarking on a boat to Athens [*ilā Āthīniyā = eis Aiginan*] is necessary for someone to obtain some money which is owed to him. [**3**] Next, what is necessary for something is that which compels and compulsion [*al-qāhiru wa-l-qahru = to biaion kai hê bia*], this being what stands in the way of an act of will or impulse. For something which compels is said to be necessary, and for this reason it is also [said to be something] distressing [*muḥzinun = luperon*]; as Adonis [*Ādīnīs = Euênos*] says, "Everything which is necessary is painful and distressing". Compulsion is a kind of necessity; as Qurqalis [*Qurqālīs = Sophoklês*] also says, "Compulsion necessitated that I do this". Necessity is also thought to obtain when someone cannot be dissuaded from holding a firm belief in the correctness of his opinion, because it is the opposite of motion which comes about through an act of will of deliberation. [**4**] The necessary is also said of something which cannot exist in any other way [*ash-shay'u lladhī laysa yumkinu an yakūna bi-naw^cin ākhara = to mê endekhomenon allôs ekhein*]. It is by analogy to this "necessary" [*bi-mithli hādhā l-muḍṭarri = kata touto to anankaion*] that all other things which are necessary in some way [are held to be necessary]. For necessary action or passion is said to obtain when an impulse cannot be fulfilled because of something which compels it [not to be fulfilled], since necessity is that on account of which a thing cannot exist in any other way. And similarly with regard to the

> causes of life and the good, for when the good on the one hand, or life and coming to be on the other, cannot exist without certain things, those things are necessary, and the cause is a kind of necessity. [**5**] There is [also] the logical demonstration of necessary things [*fa-hādhā īḍāḥu l-muḍṭarrāti = eti hê apodeixis tôn anankaiôn*], in the sense that they cannot exist in any way other than what has been demonstrated in a simple [i.e., absolute] fashion, the cause [of this] being the first [premises], if the things which are combined [to form the syllogism, i.e., the major and minor premises] cannot exist in any other way. [**Corollary**] With some necessary things there is another cause [of their being necessary]; with others there is no [other cause], but instead it is on account of them that other things are of necessity. [**Summary**] It is clear, then, that what is necessary in a primary and real sense is the simple [*al-mabsūṭ = to haploun*]; for that [i.e., what is simple] cannot exist in many ways, nor even in one other way (for otherwise it will exist in many ways). So if there are certain things which are simple, eternal and not subject to change [*in kānat ashyāʾu mabsūṭatan wa-azaliyyatan wa-ghayra mutaḥarrikatin = ei ara estin atta aïdia kai akinêta*], none of them will be subject to compulsion nor [will they be] outside nature [*khārija ʿani ṭ-ṭibāʿi = para phusin*].

Let me sum up this complex passage. Aristotle distinguishes five senses in which something may be spoken of as being necessary.[8] The first two can be combined to form one category, which I shall call the indispensable. The example given in [1] is breathing and eating, which are indispensable if an animal is to exist, or, to be more precise, to continue to exist. The example given in [2] is ingesting a drug, which is indispensable if an ill person is to get better. Together [1] and [2] form a single category, which Aristotle refers to elsewhere – most prominently in *Physics* 2.9 and *Parts of Animals* 1.1 – as hypothetical or conditional necessity.

Hypothetical necessity in Aristotle is distinguished from absolute or material necessity. An explanation involving hypothetical necessity begins with the end-state – continued existence, in the case of [1], and health or well-being in the case of [2] – and then determines what causal conditions are required in order for that end-state to be realized. An explanation of this form will generally run along the following lines: "In order for X to exist, it is necessary that A, B and C exist". In other words A, B and C – be they materials, processes or events – are indispensable if X is to exist. In this light the main difference between [1] and [2] is that category [1] is the kind of hypothetical necessity that takes into account the end-directedness found in the organs and processes of a living thing, while [2] is the kind of hypothetical necessity that allows for the end-directedness found in the intentional actions of a human being. In another sense categories [1]

[8] Here I follow Alexander (*in Metaph.* 5.5 [*ad* 1015a20], 360,19) rather than Ross 1924, 299, who not only collapses [1] and [2] but also [4] and [5].

and [2] appear to prefigure Alexander's and the Neoplatonists' distinction between existence (*to einai*) and well-being (*to eu einai*): [1] is what is necessary for existence, and [2] is what is necessary for well-being.

Category [3] is the compulsory, and seems to need little explanation. I was inclined to watch television at home all day, but something compulsory (in this case, not losing my job) stood in the way of that impulse, and necessitated that I come to the classroom to teach my students. Like category [2], category [3] appears to be restricted to the intentional actions of human beings; but whereas category [2] refers to the necessity possessed by something which ensures that an end be realized, category [3] refers to the necessity possessed by something which frustrates an end from being realized. It is possible, however, to imagine cases where category [3] might apply to natural phenomena. A clump of lava spewed from a volcano into the air is compelled to move in the direction – up – which is contrary to the direction in which the lava's nature would naturally impel it. No intentionality obtains in this case, yet the conditions required to satisfy category [3] appear to be met.

Category [4] covers things which cannot be other than they are, which I shall call the invariable. Necessary things which fall into this category will be simple rather than complex; eternal rather than mortal; and immutable rather than changeable. Nor can a thing which is necessary according to category [4] be subject to the compulsion which is necessary according to category [3].

Category [5] is somewhat problematic. Attentive readers may have noticed that the extremely compressed Arabic of L59 slightly distorts the Greek of categories [3] and [4]. However, the only instance where the Arabic translator has made a decision which actually limits the philosophical options that had been open to a Greek reader of L59 occurs in category [5]. This is where the *tôn anankaiôn* in the first phrase (*eti hê apodeixis tôn anankaiôn*) can be understood as a partitive genitive, meaning "And demonstration is *among* the things which are necessary", a sense which the Arabic translator could have rendered only by a preposition such as *min* (e.g., *fa-hādhā l-īḍāḥu [huwa] mina l-muḍṭarrāti*). As the Arabic translation stands, however, the phrase *fa-hādhā īḍāḥu l-muḍṭarrāti* can only be construed with the genitive of belonging, to mean "There is [also] the logical demonstration *of* necessary things".

The upshot is that the Arabic of L59 may have led its Greekless readers to think that Aristotle meant for category [5] to refer to the necessity *that is possessed by* the conclusion of a valid syllogism (what the Latins would name *necessitas consequentis*), a necessity which follows from the necessity *that is possessed by* that valid syllogism's premises; rather than to the necessity *that obtains in the act of inferring* a conclusion from premises (what the Latins would name *necessitas consequentiae*). What I mean is that in the following valid syllogism:

"animal" holds of every "dog" [major premise]
"dog" holds of every "dachshund" [minor premise]

"animal" holds of every "dachshund" [conclusion]

the Arabic version of L59 probably pushed a close reader of the *Metaphysics* such as Avicenna in the direction of thinking that the "necessary things" (*al-muḍtarrāt*) of category [5] referred to a valid syllogism's conclusion and premises, all of which *possess* necessity, with the conclusion's necessity now seen as the *product* of the premises' necessity.

As I mentioned in the footnote, Ross collapses [4] and [5], while Alexander keeps them separate. I think Alexander is correct in distinguishing them because category [4] refers to what appear to be the essential characteristics of being necessary, namely simplicity, eternality and immutability. Category [5], by contrast, refers – at least in the Arabic version – to a derivative characteristic of being necessary, namely, being the necessary effect of a cause, with the conclusion's necessity now seen as the effect and the premises' necessity now seen as the cause. In other words, category [4] refers to being necessary, whereas category [5] refers to being necessitated, which I shall also refer to at times as the inevitable.

To sum up, then, Aristotle speaks of five types of necessary things, the first two of which may be reduced to the indispensable, the third of which is the compulsory, the fourth of which is the invariable, and the fifth of which is the inevitable. Aristotle then makes two very important general claims about the necessary. First, he asserts that category [4], the invariable, is the most basic type of necessary thing, that is, the category to which the other categories of the necessary ultimately refer. As I shall show, this prompted later commentators such as Alexander and Asclepius to make explicit Aristotle's implication that category [4] refers to the kind of necessity possessed by divine things. Aristotle's claim that category [4] is the necessary in a primary sense, and the commentators' interpretation of category [4] as referring to divine things, will play some role in helping shape Avicenna's claim that God is necessary of existence (*wājib al-wujūd*) in some primary or absolute way.

The second general claim Aristotle makes is that the necessary may refer either to something which is necessary because a cause other than itself has made it necessary, or to something which is itself necessary and which makes other things necessary. This claim, I believe, is one of the main sources of Avicenna's distinction between that which is necessary of existence in itself (*wājib al-wujūd bi-dhātihi*) and that which is necessary of existence through another (*wājib al-wujūd bi-ghayrihi*).[9]

But how exactly do we get from *Metaphysics* 5.5 to Avicenna's idea that God is the only being that is necessary of existence in itself (*wājib al-wujūd bi-*

[9] Davidson 1987, 291, mentions this in passing.

dhātihi)? Answering that question requires that I first turn to other passages in Aristotle where the types of necessity distinguished in *Metaphysics* 5.5 (apart from the compulsory, which is not relevant) are decompressed, as well as to some of the commentaries on those passages. I shall then need to review how the language of the Arabic translations of these other Aristotelian works is or is not reflected in Avicenna's discussions of necessity.

Physics 2.9 is where Aristotle discusses most explicitly his distinction between necessity in a hypothetical sense and necessity in an absolute sense. Here is the passage in question:

L60

Arisṭūṭālīs, *aṭ-Ṭabīʿa*, 158,4-160,7 and 163,9-164,7
Aristotle, *Phys.* 2.9, 199b33-15 and 200a31-b8

We must investigate whether necessity [*aḍ-ḍarūra* = *to d'ex anankês*] is hypothetical [*ʿan waḍʿin* = *ex hupotheseôs*] or absolute [*ʿalā l-iṭlāq* = *haplôs*]. For they [viz., natural philosophers such as Empedocles and Anaxagoras] believe that necessity is found in coming-to-be in such a way that one might think that a wall is a necessity because the heavy naturally descends downwards and the light naturally rises upwards; and for this reason the stones and foundation are at the bottom of it [i.e., the wall], while the mortar and cement are above [that] on account of their lightness, and the timber is at the top because it is lightest of all. Needless to say the wall will not exist without these [materials]; yet its existence is not on account of these [materials] (except of course in the sense that by "cause" you might be referring to the matter), but rather on account of, and for the sake of [*min ajli* = *heneka*], protection and safety. And it is in this manner that all other things which are for the sake of something proceed. It [the end] will not [come to] exist without things which have the necessary and required nature, although its [the end's] [coming into] existence is not for the sake of these [materials] (except by way of [their being] the matter), but [the coming-to-be] is for the sake of something else. An example of this [is the question] "Why does the saw come to have this characteristic?" So that it performs this [function], or for the sake of this [function]. To perform this [function, i.e., of cutting] – which is what it is for the sake of – it can be fashioned only out of iron. Therefore it will follow of necessity that it be made of iron [*fa-yajibu idhan ḍarūratan an yakūna min ḥadīdin* = *anankê ara sidêroun einai*] if it is saw and if it is to perform its function. Thus the necessity is hypothetical [i.e., it derives from having first postulated a condition], it [the necessity] not being like an intended end; this is because the necessity is found in the matter, while the that for the sake of which is found in the definition ....

It is clear, therefore, that the necessity found in natural things is what is so called in the sense of the matter and its motions. The natural philosopher must concern himself with both of these two

> causes [i.e., the matter and the end], although he must be more concerned with the cause that is "that for the sake of which", because this is the cause of the matter, while the matter is not the cause of the end, by which I mean the "that for the sake of which". [the Arabic omits 200a35] For example, because a house has such-and-such a characteristic, it is necessary that X and Y [first] come to be, or that X and Y [first] exist; because health is such-and-such [a thing], it is necessary that X and Y must [first] come to be, or that X and Y must [first] exist [*wa-li-anna ṣ-ṣiḥḥata kādhā, fa-wājibun ḍarūratan an yakūna kādhā wa-kādhā wa-an yūjada kādhā wa-kādhā = kai epei hê hugieia todi tade dei gignesthai ex anankês kai huparkhein*]. Similarly, if this is what "human" is, then it is necessary that X must [first come to be or exist], and [in general terms] if A is B, then it is necessary that X must [first come to be or exist]. It is likely, in fact, that the necessary enters into the definition as well. This is because if we define the activity of sawing as dividing in such-and-such a manner, this [activity] can come about only through the saw's having teeth with such-and-such a characteristic, and these [teeth] can only have such-and-such a characteristic by being made out of iron. For a definition also contains parts which are analogous to matter.[10]

Hypothetical and absolute necessity are distinguished along similar lines in *Parts of Animals* 1.1.[11] What is made more explicit in the *Parts of Animals* passages, however, is the linkage between absolute necessity and divine, eternal things. Hypothetical necessity, by contrast, applies to natural things down here in the world of generation and destruction. The distinction between absolute and hypothetical necessity is also alluded to in *Posterior Analytics* 2.11.[12]

In nature it is the postulating of an end which makes the materials necessary since it is possible (at least according to Aristotle's reasoning) to imagine a situation where all the materials that make up a human body are present – flesh, bone, nerves, blood, etc. – but for the end – the concrete existence of the form "human" – *not* to exist. This is because the materials must first be set in motion towards attaining that end; and given the fact that it is in view of the end that the materials have been made to come together in the first place, the end is what makes the materials (hypothetically) necessary.

That is Aristotle's theory, at least. The problem is that in almost all cases where Aristotle actually applies this theory to examples in the natural world, it is possible to appeal only to absolute, material necessitation, and dispense with the end. One well-known example is the shedding of deer antlers: Aristotle claims that the shedding takes place both because of absolute, material necessity

[10] cf. *Metaph.* 7.12, 1038a6-8, where he says that in a definition, the genus is analogous to the matter and the differentia is analogous to the form.

[11] *PA* 1.1, 639b21-640a9 (= *Fī aʿḍāʾ al-ḥayawān*, 6,24-7,16); cf. also *PA* 1.1, 642a2-13 (= *Fī aʿḍāʾ*, 12,8-19).

[12] *An. Post.* 2.11, 94b27-95a9 (= *Taḥlīlāt thāniyya*, 433,8-434,11).

(the earthy matter that constitutes the antlers having grown too heavy) and for an end (in order that the deer's head be lighter).[13] As I mentioned in Chapter 10, scholars of ancient philosophy nowadays disagree over whether or not – and if so, to what degree – the latter type of explanation (i.e., "In order that the deer's head be lighter") is an essential component of Aristotle's theory of how we know or understand something scientifically.

In any case, one final question arises from the Arabic of L60: should we view certain phrases in Isḥāq b. Ḥunayn's translation, such as *wājibun ḍarūratan an yakūna*, as somehow prefiguring Avicenna's formula of *wājib al-wujūd*? This might be tempting given the fact that the *Metaphysics* translation, in which *to anankaion* is rendered as *al-muḍtarr*, appears to be an unfruitful source, at least lexically speaking. But because Aristotle is speaking in *Physics* 2.9 of hypothetical and not absolute necessity, L60 will be valuable as a source only in the limited sense that Avicenna's concept of *wājib al-wujūd bi-ghayrihi*, the necessary of existence through another, could be conceived as being necessary in the way that organic matter in nature is necessary: as hypothetically necessary, that is. A natural thing in the world of coming-to-be and passing-away is *wājib al-wujūd bi-ghayrihi* because the materials that constitute it are caused to be necessary by the end they serve. As I shall show in Chapter 13, however, the main benefit Avicenna saw in *wājib al-wujūd bi-ghayrihi* was its use in solving a *kalām* problem: distinguishing between two or more eternal things.

I mentioned earlier in this chapter that Aristotle asserts in *Metaphysics* 5.5 that the necessity possessed by simple, eternal and immutable things is the most basic type of necessity, to which all other types may be referred. Aristotle's implication that this most basic type of necessity is one of the essential characteristics, if not *the* essential characteristic, of divine things, is made explicit by later commentators on *Metaphysics* 5.5, including Alexander and Asclepius. They were justified in making this connection because Aristotle himself alludes to the Unmoved Mover's necessity in *Metaphysics* 12.7. Much has been made of Aristotle's assertion at 1072b2 that God *ex anankês ara estin on*, particularly by those who see in it the most obvious antecedent of Avicenna's *wājib al-wujūd*.[14] But it seems unlikely to me that Aristotle's little assertion had anything more than a coincidental relation to Avicenna's formula.

The first reason why this is so is because what Aristotle means by divine necessity is so different from what Avicenna means by divine necessity. This will be brought out better by quoting the passage in full.

[13] *PA* 3.2, 663b10-14 (= *Fī aᶜḍāᵓ al-ḥayawān*, 64,15-18).
[14] Davidson 1987, 282, citing Ibn Sīnā, *Sharḥ ḥarf al-Lām*, 23,21-22.

L61

Arisṭāṭālīs, *Mā baʿda ṭ-ṭabīʿa III*, 1607,11-1608,5
Aristotle, *Metaph.* 12.7, 1072b4-11

> If something is moved it can be in various states. Therefore if locomotion is the primary activity by which it [i.e., heaven] is moved, it is possible that with respect to place [at least] it will be in various states, even if with respect to substance there is no variability. Because that which moves it is [itself] unmoved (since it exists actually), it cannot possibly be in any state other [than the one it is in]. The primary type of change is locomotion, and [more specifically] circular motion; and this [Unmoved Mover] is the mover of that [circular motion]. It is therefore of necessity that it [the Unmoved Mover] exist as a good, and in this way [i.e., as a good] it is of necessity that it be a principle [*fa-mina l-iḍṭirāri idhan yūjadu jayyidan* <replacing Bouyges' *mabdaʾan*> <*wa-*> *ayḍan huwa mina l-iḍṭirāri hakādhā mabdaʾan = ex anankês ara estin on kai hêi anankêi kalôs kai houtôs arkhê*].

Once again, the Arabic of the *Metaphysics* translation reflects an interpretation on the part of the translator, an interpretation that may not accurately express what Aristotle himself meant in this rather compressed passage. Attentive readers will have noted that in L61 I emended Bouyges' text to read *fa-mina l-iḍṭirāri idhan yūjadu JAYYIDAN* instead of Bouyges' *MABDAʾAN*. This is an emendation which the apparatus suggests could be justified on manuscript grounds; it is certainly justified on the basis of content, since the Greek *kalôs* must have been rendered by a term like *jayyidan*, the skeleton of which is almost identical to that of *mabdaʾan*. In any case what Aristotle probably meant by *ex anankês ara estin on kai hêi anankêi kalôs* is simply that the Unmoved Mover must be necessary in the sense of simple and invariable: necessary in the sense of L59's category [4], that is. Aristotle adds the epexegetical *kai hêi anankêi kalôs* to ensure that his reader understands that he means "necessary" here in the *nice* sense of category [4], and not in the *nasty* sense of category [3], which would entail that God be constrained or compelled in some way.

However, the Arabic of L61 – assuming that I am correct in emending *mabdaʾan* to read *jayyidan* – lends itself to a rather more specific interpretation of those crucial lines. According to this interpretation, Aristotle begins by describing the necessity of the Unmoved Mover in line with the conception of necessity articulated in L59 as category [4]. The Unmoved Mover is invariable, since it is only mover and not moved. Given that the Unmoved Mover is not subject to change of any sort – not even the highest form of change, circular motion – it is necessary in the sense that it is invariable.

Then Aristotle appeals to the conception of necessity articulated in L59 as category [5]. Given the fact that the Unmoved Mover is necessary in the sense that it is invariable, the Unmoved Mover will, by necessity, act as a principle – that is, it will cause its effects – *as a good.* In other words, it is only as a good, as an object of desire or thought, that a thing can move another without itself moving, and hence without being moved by another. According to this interpretation, the sense of necessity appealed to at the end of the passage falls under category [5] because it is a logically necessary consequence of the premises (1) the Unmoved Mover is invariable; (2) the Unmoved Mover is a cause; and (3) the only cause that can move things without itself moving is the final cause. Let me recapitulate: given that the Unmoved Mover is not subject to change, and given the fact that the Unmoved Mover causes motion, it follows of necessity that the Unmoved Mover causes motion as a final cause, since only final causes can move other things without themselves moving. To be more precise, it is only a final cause in the sense of *that in view of which* (i.e., *qua to hou*), and not in the sense of *that for the benefit of which* (i.e., *qua to hôi*), that can cause other things without itself being caused. Aristotle makes this explicit at 12.7, 1072b2-3 (= *Mā baᶜda ṭ-ṭabīᶜa III*, 1599,3).

In other words, the Arabic Aristotle's aim in this passage does not come across as a general one. It is not to introduce the notion that the Unmoved Mover is a necessary existent, that it *must be* in some bald sense. Rather, it is to draw, from what he has just discussed, the necessary conclusion that the Unmoved Mover *must be* a final cause *qua to hou.*[15]

How then to reconcile the Unmoved Mover's being a final cause, and its necessitation of other things? After all, there seems to be a contradiction. On the one hand, we are given a description in *Physics* 2.9 of how final causes necessitate their effects hypothetically, not absolutely. Hypothetical necessity is the kind in which materials are made necessary only by postulating an end towards which they are set in motion. In *Metaphysics* 5.5 hypothetical necessity is covered by categories [1] and [2]. Aristotle also makes clear in *Physics* 2.9 that hypothetical necessitation is the kind that is in operation among natural things like animals and plants, as well as among artifacts. By contrast, the way simple, eternal and immutable things necessitate their effects seems much more likely to be the kind of absolute necessitation covered by category [5] in *Metaphysics* 5.5. That is, simple, eternal and immutable things should necessitate their effects the way that premises necessitate their conclusions. The problem, then, is that if the Unmoved Mover is related to its effects as a final cause, and if final causes necessitate their effects hypothetically, the Unmoved Mover will necessitate its effects hypothetically and not absolutely; not, that is, in the way premises necessitate conclusions.

[15] The sense in which the necessity which Aristotle appeals to in the second part of the passage is that of category [5] – that of a logically necessary inference – is brought out in Thāmasṭiyūs, *Sharḥ ḥarf al-Lām min Kitāb Mā baᶜda ṭ-ṭabīᶜa li-Arisṭū*, 14,18-19. However Themistius understands Aristotle to be making the general claim that "it follows necessarily that there exists an unmoved mover" (*fa-in kāna yūjadu shayʾun yataḥarraku wa-yuḥarriku maᶜan wa-yūjadu shayʾun yataḥarraku faqaṭ min ghayri an yuḥarrika, fa-yajibu ḍarūratan an yūjada muḥarrikun ghayru mutaḥarrikin*), and not the specific claim that "it follows necessarily that the unmoved mover is a final cause *qua to hou*".

One could argue, of course, that unlike natural things subject to coming-to-be and passing-away, the Unmoved Mover is eternal. Because it already exists, its future coming-to-be need not be postulated for its effect to exist, and therefore its necessity is not hypothetical. But however convincing that might be, it is still difficult to conceive of how any final cause, even an eternal one such as the Unmoved Mover, could necessitate its effect in an absolute way.

It is in trying to cope with this problem that Alexander takes one step further than Aristotle when he links together the ideas of necessity and necessitation by arguing that the other categories of necessity derive their necessity from – that is, they are necessitated by – the necessity that category [4] possesses. In other words, the other categories of necessity are not only referable in a logical sense to category [4] – that is, not only is category [4] logically prior to the other categories of necessity – their necessity is *caused* by category [4]'s necessity. This is an important move. Alexander can now apply Aristotle's distinction between things whose necessity is the cause of other things' necessity and things whose necessity derives from something outside themselves, to the distinction between category [4] and the other categories. Aristotle – or at least the Arabic Aristotle, as I showed earlier – seems to have meant for the distinction between necessitating and necessitated to be applied respectively to premises, whose necessity is the cause of the conclusion's necessity; and to conclusions, whose necessity is derived from the premises' necessity. What I am getting at is that Alexander is the first to draw an explicit connection between divine necessity and divine necessitation. Because of their significance for Avicenna, Alexander's comments are worth quoting:

L62

Alexander, *in Metaph.* 5.5 (*ad* 1015b9-11), 361,24-36

> But eternal things are also necessary in this way [viz., in the way necessary premises are necessary], for they have no cause extrinsic to them and they are of necessity causes of being for other things too; for all things that are naturally constituted owe to the gods the fact that they are immediately necessary because they have a cause of their being that is eternal. Moreover, that which either cannot be or be in a good state without something else has from that other of necessity the cause both of its being and of its well-being [*ex anankês par' ekeinou tên aitian to men tou einai to de tou eu einai ekhei*] .... Only the eternal beings, those that are divine, do not have another thing as cause of their eternal being, and it is because of them that the things naturally constituted are and come to be of necessity.[16]

In other words, Alexander has appealed to his explicitly articulated distinction between being (*to einai*) and well-being (*to eu einai*) in order to incorporate the

[16] The translation is Dooley 1993, 32-33.

conception of necessity articulated in L59 as category [1] – the causation or necessitation of being (*to einai*) – and the conception of necessity articulated in L59 as category [2] – the causation or necessitation of well-being (*to eu einai*) – into an overarching scheme whereby the necessity of [1] and [2] is *caused* by the category-[4] necessity possessed by divine things. Alexander then adds to the mix the intrinsic necessity/extrinsic necessity distinction of the corollary that appears to modify category [5]: the necessity of the premises is intrinsic to them, while the necessity of the conclusion comes from outside, viz., from the premises' necessity.

Let me recapitulate Alexander's understanding of this passage. The divine things' necessity (i.e., category [4]) is the cause of all other things' necessity – both the necessity of things which are necessary for being (i.e., category [1]) as well as the necessity of things which are necessary for well-being (i.e., category [2]) – just as the necessity of premises is the cause of the necessity of the conclusions that follow from them (i.e., category [5]). Since the necessity that premises possess is intrinsic to them, while the necessity that conclusions possess comes from outside, the necessity possessed by divine things will be intrinsic to them, while the necessity possessed by all other necessary things will come from outside of them. Alexander's move to theologize category [4] gains momentum from Asclepius' comments on L59, where Asclepius explains that the necessity of simple things does not come from outside, but is in their very being; thus we say that God is good of necessity, since God's substance is goodness. [17] All of these interpretive trends seem to me to be reflected in the Arabic translations of L59 and L61.

When I labeled category [5] in Aristotle's list of the different ways we speak of a thing's being necessary as the "inevitable", I meant to distinguish between the absolute necessity possessed by something simple, eternal and immutable, and the necessity possessed by a conclusion which cannot help but follow from its premises. By applying the necessitating/necessitated distinction, we can infer that category [5] can apply to necessary things (such as premises) which necessitate as well as to necessary things (such as conclusions) which are necessitated. After all, the conclusion of a syllogism fulfills category [4]'s criteria of invariability just as much as its premises do. Therefore it would be correct to say that the necessity articulated in category [4] does not belong exclusively to causes. Taken in itself, category [4] refers only to simplicity, eternality and immutability. When those criteria are satisfied by a cause, it signifies that they will be productive of the same criteria in an effect; when those criteria are satisfied by an effect, it signifies that they will have been produced by a cause which also satisfies those criteria.

[17] Asclepius, *in Metaph.* 5.5 (*ad* 1015a33-34), 309,10-15 (*theôria*) and 313,2-3 (*lexis*).

In itself, therefore, category [4] seems closer to the idea of self-sufficiency, of immunity from causation, than it does to the idea of causal productivity, because neither being a cause nor being an effect appears to be essential to category [4]. We are still faced, then, with the same disjunction between self-sufficiency and productivity which forced Avicenna to appeal to the fence-straddling idea that somehow God both possesses perfection yet is also above perfection. Where else in Aristotle's writings could Avicenna find a way to fuse the notion of *necessitating* more tightly into the notion of *being necessary*?

In *Posterior Analytics* 1.30, Aristotle says:

L63

Arisṭūṭālīs, *Taḥlīlāt thāniyya*, 397,4-9
Aristotle, *An Post.* 1.30, 87b19-25

> There is no demonstrative knowledge of something which arises by chance, since something which is by chance is neither necessary or for the most part [*laysa huwa ḍarūriyyan wa-lā ᶜalā akthari l-amri = oute gar hôs anankaion outh' hôs epi to polu*], but is instead what falls outside of these two [categories]. Demonstration, however, applies to either of these two [categories], because every [demonstrative] syllogism has either necessary premises or premises which are for the most part. If the premises are necessary, the conclusion will be necessary as well [*fa-in kānati l-muqaddimātu ḍarūriyyatan fa-n-natījatu hiya ayḍan ḍarūriyyatun = kai ei men hai protaseis anankaiai, kai to sumperasma anankaion*]; and if they are for the most part, then the syllogism will be this way as well.

It seems true that the necessity which the premises possess can be reduced to Aristotle's category [4]. At the beginning of *An. Post.* 1.4, and again in 1.6, Aristotle argues that since demonstration treats only simple or absolute things, – things which cannot be otherwise, that is – what comes to be known through demonstration will be necessary knowledge. But what is being discussed in *An. Post.* 1.30 and in category [5] is necessitation, not necessity: a pair of necessary premises *necessitate* the conclusion that follows from them, that is to say, their necessity produces the necessity of the conclusion. Yet even though necessary premises satisfy the main criterion of category [4], in that they cannot be otherwise, what this means in a premise is different from the criteria of simplicity, eternality and immutability which Aristotle listed in *Metaphysics* 5.5. For a premise to be necessary its predicate must hold of its subject *necessarily*. To find out precisely what that means we must turn to *De Interpretatione* 12-13.

For readers unfamiliar with the treatise, the *De Interpretatione* is meant to determine what makes up a proposition. That is not an aim in itself, however: Aristotle is interested ultimately in determining what kind of propositions can serve as premises in a syllogism. A large part of the *De Interpretatione* is devoted to analyzing the elements of a proposition, such as verbs and nouns; to distinguishing between different types of propositions, such as those that exclaim ("Stop biting your fingernails!") and those that assert ("Biting one's fingernails is bad"); and to distinguishing between assertoric propositions that are affirmative ("Biting one's fingernails is bad") and those that are negative ("Biting one's fingernails is not good").

Finally, Aristotle hopes to distinguish between propositions which contradict each other and those which are contrary to each other. Contradictory propositions are so related that if one of the two is true the other will be false, and if one is false the other will be true, as for example the propositions "Rob is white" and "Rob is non-white". Contrary propositions, on the other hand, are so related that though both may be false they cannot both be true, as for example the propositions "Rob is white" and "Rob is black"; after all, Rob could be green, or slightly pink.

This is complicated stuff, and problems arise. First, Aristotle has to decide in fact whether the contradictory of "Rob is white" is "Rob is non-white" or "Rob is not white". Then Aristotle has to decide what happens if he tosses in adverbs or adjectives that in some way qualify the proposition, such as the temporal operators "always", "sometimes" or "never"; and their parallel modal operators "necessary", "possible", and "impossible". How do you go about making the contradictories of propositions that have these qualifiers in them?

The reason that the modal operators "necessary", "possible" and "impossible" are particularly important to Aristotle is that he wants to winnow down the vast number of propositions available to him to a smaller number which he can use as premises in demonstrative syllogisms, the only type of syllogism which he reckons is guaranteed to produce a scientific understanding of a thing. As I mentioned above in discussing *An. Post.* 1.6, Aristotle feels that the propositions that can be used as premises in a demonstrative syllogism will have to be necessary in the sense of being primary and true in some unshakeable way. After all, we learned already in *Metaphysics* 5.5 that it is only when the premises of a syllogism are necessary that the conclusion produced from them will be necessary. In *De Interpretatione* 12-13 Aristotle therefore needs to come to grips with what it means when we assert that X is P necessarily, that is, when we assert that the predicate "P" holds of the subject "X" in a necessary way. In short, Aristotle wants to determine as precisely as he can the properties of necessary propositions.

Part of his effort in this direction, as I said above, is focused on determining what the contrary and contradictory of "It is necessary that X is P" are. (I shall leave aside for a moment the question of whether the contradictory of "X is P" is "X is not P" or "X is non-P".) Two options immediately present themselves as possibly serving in the role of contrary and contradictory of "It is necessary that X is P": "It is not necessary that X is P", "It is necessary that X is not P". Aristotle eventually determines that the contrary of "It is necessary that X is P" is "It is necessary that X is not P"; and that the contradictory of "It is necessary that X is P" is "It is not necessary that X is P". This is because, as I mentioned above, a contrary pair of propositions is so related that though both may be false they cannot both be true; while a contradictory pair of propositions is so related that if either is true the other will be false.

In the case of the proposition "It is necessary that X is not P", the idea of impossibility is being expressed. In the case of the proposition "It is not necessary that X is P", however, the idea of possibility is being expressed. With that in mind, it is easier to see why the idea of possibility expressed in the proposition "It is not necessary that X is P" is the contradictory of the necessity expressed in the original proposition, "It is necessary that X is P". There is no middle ground between the two propositions – either something is necessary or it is possible – and therefore they are contradictories, since contradictory propositions are so related that if either is true the other will be false.

By contrast, there is a middle ground between the necessity expressed in the original proposition, "It is necessary that X is P", and the impossibility expressed in the proposition "It is necessary that X is not P". This is because it is possible to imagine X's being Q or R. Therefore, since it is possible to imagine a situation where the propositions "It is necessary that X is P" and "It is necessary that X is not P" are *both* false (even though they cannot both be true at the same time), the two propositions are contraries. This is because, once again, a pair of contrary propositions are so related that though both may be false they cannot both be true.

In short, the contradiction derives from a negation of the *mode*, whereas the contrariety derives from a negation of the *copula*. One crucial ambiguity arises, however. We have just decided that the possibility expressed in the proposition "It is not necessary that X is P" is the contradictory of the necessity expressed in the proposition "It is necessary that X is P". But the term Aristotle uses for impossible, *adunaton*, seems to be a straightforward negation of the term he uses for possible, *dunaton*. If a thing is either *dunaton* or *adunaton*, then the contradictory of the possibility expressed in the proposition "It is not necessary that X is P" will be the impossibility expressed in the proposition "It is necessary that X is not P", instead of the necessity expressed in the proposition "It is necessary that X is P". The upshot is that "the possible" (*to dunaton*) and "the impossible" (*to adunaton*) seem to be just as completely opposed to each other as "the possible" (*to dunaton*) and "the necessary" (*to anankaion*) are.

Deciding whether or not possibility is "one-sided" (that is, opposed only to impossibility) or two-sided (that is, opposed to both impossibility and necessity) is a problem that Aristotle takes a while to work out in *De Interpretatione* 12-

13.[18] As Ackrill points out, the first and third tables of propositions which Aristotle sets out in *Int.* 13, 22a24-31 will be truly compatible only if possibility is understood as being two-sided, while the second and fourth tables will be truly compatible only if possibility is understood as being one-sided. Eventually Aristotle reconfigures the tables so that they are truly compatible, but in so doing he is forced to chuck out two-sided possibility in favor of one-sided possibility.[19]

Now none of what Aristotle actually thought about these complex issues concerns me in and of itself. What I am interested in uncovering instead is how Aristotle's presentation of these issues, and his ambivalence over whether to think of possibility as one-sided or two-sided, may have influenced the way Isḥāq b. Ḥunayn, the Arabic translator of the *De Interpretatione*, chose to render the relevant terms. First of all, I maintain that Aristotle's ambivalence regarding whether or not to see possibility as one-sided or two-sided is reflected in a gradual evolution in the Arabic translations of *De Interpretatione* 12-13, from a rendering of *einai* as the more copulative (or at least amphibolous) *k-w-n*, to a rendering of *einai* as the more existential *w-j-d*. This is because, as I shall show, an existential rendering of *einai* makes it easier to see possibility as opposed to necessity, in that it flushes out the sense in which *dunaton* means "contingent" (and hence as being naturally opposed to "necessary") as well as "possible" (and hence as being naturally opposed to "impossible").

The other factor pushing Isḥāq b. Ḥunayn to use *w-j-d* instead of *k-w-n* is that in *De Interpretatione* 13 Aristotle begins to use a kind of shorthand, saying, for example, *anankaion einai* instead of the more explicitly copulative *ex anankês X esti Y*. This may have led Isḥāq to think it better to render the *einai* with the more existential *mawjūd* instead of the strictly copulative *huwa* or the amphibolous *yakūnu*. Let me show how the terms are transformed in Arabic.

In the first list of modal expressions we come across in *De Interpretatione* 12, the one at 21a36-8 (= *Fī l-ᶜibāra*, 86,4-6), *einai* is rendered by the copulative, or at least neutral, verb *k-w-n*. Thus:

to dunaton einai = *mā yumkinu an yakūna*
to mê dunaton = *mā lā yumkinu*
to endekhomenon = *mā yuḥtamalu an yakūna*
to mê endekhomenon = *mā lā yuḥtamalu*
to adunaton = *mā kāna fī l-mumtaniᶜ*
to anankaion = *mā kāna fī ḍ-ḍarūrī*

Only one line later, however, at 21a39 (= *Fī l-ᶜibāra*, 86,8), *einai* is rendered by the more existential verb *w-j-d*:

[18] The distinction between one-sided and two-sided possibility can be found at *An. Pr.* 1.3, 25a37-40 and 1.13, 32a18-21, though in both those passages Aristotle uses *to endekhomenon* instead of *to dunaton*.

[19] Ackrill 1963, 151-153.

to einai = mawjūd
to mê einai = lā mawjūd

At 21b23-27 (= *Fī l-ᶜibāra*, 87,15-18), Isḥāq begins to apply the new verb *w-j-d* to modal propositions (*yumkinu an yūjada* instead of *yumkinu an yakūna* and *yuḥtamalu an yūjada* instead of *yuḥtamalu an yakūna*); and at 21b27 (= *Fī l-ᶜibāra*, 87,18) Isḥāq also begins using the term *al-wājib* to render *anankaion* – instead of the previous *aḍ-ḍarūrī* – when drawing a contrast with *al-mumtaniᶜ* (*adunaton*). And even though at 22a4-7 (= *Fī l-ᶜibāra*, 88,14-17), in his discussion of the contradictories that arise from using the modal operator "necessary", Isḥāq uses both *w-j-b* and *ḍ-r-r* (*wājibun ḍarūratan an yūjada*), in the list of expressions at 22a12-13 (= *Fī l-ᶜibāra*, 89,7-11), we have the following:

dunaton/ou dunaton = mumkin/lā mumkin
endekhomenon/ouk endekhomenon = muḥtamal/lā muḥtamal
adunaton/ouk adunaton = mumtaniᶜ/lā mumtaniᶜ
anankaion/ouk anankaion = wājib/lā wājib
alêthes/ouk alêthes = ḥaqq/lā ḥaqq

with the result that at least in these new passages *wājib* has eclipsed *ḍarūrī*. More evidence of Isḥāq's move from *k-w-n* to *w-j-d* and from *ḍ-r-r* to *w-j-b* can be seen in the fourth table of compatible propositions in *De Interpretatione* 13, at 22a28-31 (= *Fī l-ᶜibāra*, 90,11-15):

(1) *ou dunaton mê einai = laysa mumkinan allā yūjada*
(2) *ouk endekhomenon mê einai = laysa muḥtamalan allā yūjada*
(3) *adunaton mê einai = mumtaniᶜun allā yūjada*
(4) *anankaion einai = wājibun an yūjada*

Why does using *w-j-d* to render *einai* allow Isḥāq to interpret Aristotle as advocating two-sided possibility in these passages more easily than using *k-w-n* would? My sense is that when *dunaton* (= *mumkin*) is used in opposition to *anankaion* (= *wājib*), what is being implied is contingency rather than possibility. That is to say, when *dunaton* (= *mumkin*) is used in opposition to *anankaion* (= *wājib*), the contrast which is implied is one between necessity in the sense of *uncausedness* and contingency in the sense of *causedness*. It is in this respect that *w-j-d* has an advantage over *k-w-n*, because *w-j-d* carries greater existential weight than *k-w-n* does. In order to accommodate the idea of contingency, *dunaton* (= *mumkin*) had to be understood with the more existential *w-j-d*, because with an existential verb the idea of causedness – that is, of being a thing whose existence is caused – is more justifiable than it would have been with the more copulative *k-w-n*.

What about *w-j-b*? What advantage did *wājib* have over *ḍarūrī* in rendering *anankaion*? I would guess that unlike *ḍarūrī* (or the Arabic *Metaphysics*' *muḍṭarr*), *wājib* accommodated a broad enough sense of logical necessity that it could include in its semantic range the necessity which obtained in propositions such as the ones being discussed in the *De Interpretatione*. This is because the standard way to render the idea of syllogistic *necessitation* was by the use of *w-j-b*. The idea that the conclusion follows necessarily from the premises was generally expressed by the phrase *yajibu* X *min* A *wa*-B, where X is the conclusion and A and B are the premises. Although the root *l-z-m* is sometimes used instead of *w-j-b* to express logical entailment, I am not aware of any instances where *ḍ-r-r* is used in this way.

Since what is being discussed in *De Interpretatione* 12-13 is the necessity that obtains when, in a proposition, a predicate holds necessarily of a subject; since Aristotle is interested in determining the nature of that necessity because he wants to employ necessary propositions as premises in syllogisms; and since Aristotle is interested in using necessary propositions as premises in syllogisms because they are the only ones, according to *An. Pr.* 1.6 and *Metaph.* 5.5 (remember category [5]), which produce conclusions which are necessary; Isḥāq turned to *w-j-b* rather than *ḍ-r-r*, because *w-j-b* was the standard verb used to render that very sense of syllogistic necessitation, that sense of the inferential necessity (*necessitas consequentiae*) by which necessary premises cause or produce the necessity possessed by the conclusion (*necessitas consequentis*).

What makes the *De Interpretatione* translator's use of the active participle *wājib* to render *anankaion* striking is that, as I shall show in Chapter 13, *wājib* had been used by *mutakallimūn* primarily to render the idea of moral obligation rather than logical necessity. It is true that knowledge (*ᶜilm*) was sometimes held by the *mutakallimūn* to be *wājib*, but this was generally construed to refer to the quasi-religious obligation not to be ignorant. Lexically speaking, the Arabic version of *De Interpretatione* 12-13 thus seems to have been the most significant Aristotelian source from which Avicenna drew in his attempt to construct a matrix of distinctions around the new concept of *wājib al-wujūd*. Conceptually speaking, however, *Metaphysics* 5.5 is at least as significant a source as the *De Interpretatione* passages. Chapters 12 and 13 will determine how two more immediate sources – al-Fārābī and the tenth-century Sunnī *mutakallimūn* – influenced the formation of Avicenna's new concept.

12. Necessity and Possibility (B)
Materials from al-Fārābī

I have just argued that one reason why Isḥāq b. Ḥunayn chose the Arabic root *w-j-d* to render *einai* in much of *De Interpretatione* 12-13 was because the existential momentum carried by *w-j-d* propelled an interpreter towards viewing possibility as two-sided. This is because *mumkin* will more plausibly contain the sense of contingency (that is, the sense of *being caused*) in its semantic range when it is used in conjunction with an existential "is" verb, than it would with a more purely copulative "is" verb. With *mumkin* understood as contingent, it becomes easier to view it as the contradictory of *wājib*, now understood as necessary (that is, as *being uncaused*). In other words, I will have an easier time of arguing that "necessary" and "possible" are contradictory terms if I can reduce their meanings, respectively, to "being uncaused" and "being caused". When placed in opposition with *mumtaniᶜ*, on the other hand, *mumkin* can retain what seems to have been its previously more basic meaning of "possible", and therefore serve plausibly as the contradictory of impossible.

In his *Commentary on the De Intepretatione*, al-Fārābī takes a couple of steps further in this direction than the Arabic translator of the *De Interpretatione* had. The first step which al-Fārābī takes – and Avicenna, as I shall show, follows him in this respect – is to make the opposition between the possible and the necessary the *basic* type of contradiction, with possible and impossible now relegated to second place. In fact, al-Fārābī refers to the possible and the necessary (*al-mumkin wa-ḍ-ḍarūrī*) as the primary or basic modes (*al-jihāt al-uwal*), the other modes being reducible to them.[1] Aristotle, by contrast, sees the possible first and foremost as the contradictory of the impossible in contexts where possibility is clearly taken to be one-sided. In other words, when the possible is viewed as one-sided rather than two-sided, Aristotle chooses the impossible, rather than the necessary, to be the more basic contradictory of the possible. It is only when Aristotle allows that possibility may be two-sided that its opposition with necessity is explicitly allowed for. One effect of al-Fārābī's having taken the step to view possibility and necessity as the more basic pair of contradictories, is that the idea of an opposition between necessary *existence* and possible *existence* becomes more expressly articulated than it had ever been before.

The second step which al-Fārābī takes in his *Commentary on the De Interpetatione*, in addition to the now more expressly articulated opposition between necessary existence and contingent existence, is to introduce another distinction which will play a major role in Avicenna's discussions. This time,

[1] al-Fārābī, *Sharḥ li-kitāb Arisṭūṭālīs fī l-ᶜibāra*, 163,16-19 (*ad* 21a34-37).

the distinction is between being necessary of existence in itself (*ḍarūrī al-wujūd fī nafsihi*) and being possible of existence in itself (*mumkin al-wujūd fī nafsihi*). To be sure, al-Fārābī does not articulate the linkage between being possible of existence in itself and being necessary of existence through another as expressly as Avicenna later will, but the linkage is implied in al-Fārābī's discussions. The following is an inventory of such passages.

In the first passage, al-Fārābī criticizes previous commentators for not distinguishing clearly enough the subject matter of metaphysics from logic:

L64

al-Fārābī, *Sharḥ Kitāb Arisṭūṭālīs fī l-ᶜibāra* (*ad* 18a33), 84,12-19

> Their approach, apart from the fault already mentioned, entails their making logic an investigation into the nature and mode of being of existing things. In this they go wrong. Their own principles would oblige them to reject this approach. For in the *Categories*, they refuse to give an account of entities in terms of their [modes of] existence. Their refusal to make any part of logic an investigation into the intrinsic nature of entities is more appropriate [than the approach adopted by them here]. To examine something as to whether its existence is a matter of intrinsic possibility or necessity [*fa-inna l-faḥṣa ᶜani sh-shayʾi hal huwa mumkinu l-wujūdi fī nafsihi aw ḍarūriyyu l-wujūdi fī nafsihi*] is to examine the mode of existence of the entity in question; which is outside the proper domain of logic. We must therefore ignore the commentators' line of interpreting this text and take the approach outlined above.[2]

In the second passage, al-Fārābī paraphrases Aristotle's claim at *De Interpretatione* 19a25-26/*Fī l-ᶜibāra* 74,16-75,1 that there is a difference between being necessary in an absolute sense (*to haplôs einai ex anankês* = *anna wujūdahu ḍarūratun ᶜalā l-iṭlāq*) and being necessary as long as it exists (*ḍarūratun idhā wujida*):

L65

al-Fārābī, *Sharḥ Kitāb Arisṭūṭālīs fī l-ᶜibāra* (*ad* 19a25-26), 95,18-19

> Aristotle divides necessary existence into two kinds, of which one is necessary as long as it lasts, the other necessary without qualification [*qad qassama l-wujūda aḍ-ḍarūriyya ilā ḍarbayni ḍarbun huwa ḍarūriyyun mā dāma mawjūdan wa-l-ākharu ḍarūriyyun ᶜalā l-iṭlāqi*].[3]

[2] The translation is Zimmermann 1981, 78. Zimmermann 1981, xxxviii-xli, contextualizes al-Fārābī's criticism of previous commentators.

[3] The translation is Zimmermann 1981, 90.

As I mentioned before, al-Fārābī only implies the idea of something which is necessary through another; and it is true that in this context, what is at issue is not so much the opposition between causedness and uncausedness but the relation between the temporal qualifiers "always" and "sometimes" on the one hand, and the modal qualifiers "necessary" and "possible" on the other.

In contrast to Avicenna, al-Fārābī seems mainly interested in articulating a distinction between necessity and possibility which will be consistent with the ideas of necessity and possibility that appear in the "tomorrow's sea-battle" discussion of future contingent events in *De Interpretatione* 9. What is at issue there is the precise manner in which the truth of my knowing or asserting yesterday that there will be a sea-battle tomorrow makes the fact of its occurring necessary. For if I do claim that the truth of my saying yesterday that there will be a sea battle tomorrow makes the fact of its occurring necessary, I shall be forced to deny that there is any contingency in the world; the basis on which I claim to act voluntarily will be pulled out from under me, and everything will be predetermined. As al-Fārābī says:

L66

al-Fārābī, *Sharḥ Kitāb Arisṭūṭālīs fī l-ʿibāra* (*ad* 19a32-b4), 98,12-15

Thus the existence of what exists in the future will be necessary [*ḍarūriyya l-wujūd*] if an anterior statement is true. Everything will be intrinsically necessary [*ḍarūriyyatan fī anfusihā*] again, being possible only in terms of our knowledge. Free will, deliberation and everything else that Aristotle has mentioned will again be eliminated.[4]

If, on the other hand, I claim that the truth of my saying yesterday that there will be a sea battle tomorrow does not make its occurring necessary, I shall be forced to maintain that there is no necessary relation between a statement's truth and the reality it truthfully describes; the basis on which I claim to understand a thing scientifically is pulled out from under me, and I will be left with mere opinion.

With the stakes so high it is not surprising that commentators energetically strove to create new distinctions that could resolve the dilemma, or at least blunt its horns. It is in this context that al-Fārābī introduces a more explicit distinction between being necessary in itself and being necessary through another:

[4] The translation is Zimmermann 1981, 93.

L67

al-Fārābī, *Sharḥ Kitāb Arisṭūṭālīs fī l-ʿibāra* (*ad* 19a32-b4), 99,1-8 and 99,18

No, the right answer lies in arguing that if something follows of necessity from something else, this does not mean that it is necessary in itself [*ḍarūriyyan fī nafsihi*]. For if it is true to affirm something, it follows of necessity that it is the case. Yet it does not follow that its being the case is intrinsically necessary [*wa-laysa yalzamu an yakūna l-amru ḍarūriyya l-wujūdi fī nafsihi*]. What follows is that its following from the truth of the affirmation is necessary. It is not the case that, if something follows from something else necessarily, the thing that follows is itself necessary. Take the case of intrinsically possible conclusions [*an-natāʾiju llatī hiya mumkinatun fī dhawātihā*]. They follow necessarily in the syllogisms that lead to them, yet a conclusion following of necessity is not intrinsically necessary. For its possibility is not eliminated by the necessity with which it follows from the premises ....

If something follows from something else of necessity, this does not mean that it is in itself a necessity [*fī dhātihi iḍṭirāriyyan*].[5]

Al-Fārābī's point is that the conclusion of a syllogism is not intrinsically necessary, but is *made* necessary by the necessity of the premises from which it follows necessarily. This obviously brings to mind *Metaphysics* 5.5, and particularly the concept of necessity articulated as category [5], that is, the necessity that obtains when a conclusion is necessitated by its premises, or, more strictly, when the necessity of a conclusion is the product of the necessity of its premises. In the present context, al-Fārābī is trying to find some way to resolve the sea-battle dilemma by maintaining that future contingent events have *both* possibility and necessity. The necessity of future contingent events derives from their being necessitated by – that is, their following necessarily from – the truth of our prior knowledge of and assertions about them. But that is not to claim that *in themselves* these future events are necessary, for they are made necessary by something else. The obvious next step for al-Fārābī would then be to claim that future events are *in themselves* possible. Once he had done that, he could – like Avicenna – judge that something whose existence is possible in itself will also be necessary of existence through another.

But al-Fārābī resists being forced to articulate a concept of the possible of existence in itself. One reason for this is that al-Fārābī is not in fact talking here about *necessitas consequentis*, the necessity possessed by the conclusion of a valid syllogism and which is the type of necessity suggested by the genitive of possessing in the Arabic translation of L59. Instead, al-Fārābī merely suggests that these future events can be said to be necessary only in the sense that *their*

[5] The translation is Zimmermann 1981, 94.

following from the truth of our prior knowledge of or assertions about them is necessary. In other words, al-Fārābī is speaking about *necessitas consequentiae*, the necessity that obtains in the act of inferring a conclusion from premises, and not *necessitas consequentis*, the necessity possessed by the conclusion itself. It is that latter type of necessity – *necessitas consequentis* – which Avicenna has in mind when he equates the possible of existence in itself with the necessary of existence through another.

Another reason why al-Fārābī resists taking the step that Avicenna would later take, is that al-Fārābī, like contemporary Muᶜtazilite thinkers of the early–tenth century, was torn between maintaining God's omnipotence and God's justice. If God is all-powerful, and therefore causes all our actions, including our evil actions, how then can God be just when He punishes us for those evil actions? One solution to this old dilemma would be to appeal to the distinction between God's foreknowledge of future events and His causal determination of future events. In the context of this discussion, it would seem perfectly natural to make the claim that God's foreknowledge of future events makes them necessary of existence, but not in themselves. Rather, they are necessary of existence in the sense that they follow necessarily from the truth of God's foreknowledge of their existence; in themselves, they are possible of existence. The question of God's causation of the events, as opposed to His foreknowledge of them, would be left open, in order that He not be directly implicated in our evil acts.

Again, al-Fārābī is reluctant to take that extra step. Partly this is because he seems to have thought that the concept of being possible of existence in itself somehow undermined the idea that future events are possible of *both* existence *and* non-existence.[6] Al-Fārābī says that possibility lies:

L68

al-Fārābī, *Sharḥ Kitāb Arisṭūṭālīs fī l-ᶜibāra* (*ad* 19a32-b4),
99,22-25 and 100,1-4

... not in the event itself, but in the fact that it follows from a true statement [about it]. If so, a state of affairs can become one of necessary existence [*fa-qad yakūnu sh-shayʾu ḍarūriyya l-wujūdi*], having had, up to the time of its existence, the possibility of not existing and not having existed. There is little objection to this if you bear in mind that the element of necessity which comes into it does not affect its possibility .... [7]

In this sense the prior knowledge of or assertion about a future event causes that event to be both necessary of existence and possible of existence, and therefore

[6] For a discussion of the history of how the problem of future contingents in *Int.* 9 was viewed in the context of discussions of God's foreknowledge of events, see Zimmermann 1981, lxvii-lxviii and lxxxvi, n.1; and cxvi-cxvii.

[7] The translation is Zimmermann 1981, 93-94.

the event will be both necessary of existence through another and possible of existence through another.

Why should al-Fārābī so resist the idea of a thing's being possible of existence in itself? I believe the reason for al-Fārābī's reluctance to use the terms "existence" and "in itself" together in a single phrase is that he thinks it might commit him to the idea that whatever had "existence in itself" – even things which are *possible* of existence in themselves – would be uncaused. In the *Kitāb al-ḥurūf*, he claims that one of the two basic senses of "that which exists in itself" (*al-mawjūd bi-dhātihi*) is that whose essence is independent (*mā māhiyyatuhu mustaghniyyatun*) of a relation to anything else, namely, to a cause. The opposite of "that which exists in itself" is "the existent which has some cause or other".[8] Given this assertion, al-Fārābī may have worried that calling anything a *mawjūd bi-dhātihi* or a *mawjūd bi-nafsihi* – regardless of whether it was *mumkin al-wujūd bi-dhātihi* or *ḍarūrī al-wujūd bi-dhātihi* – would force him to see the "possible of existence in itself" as causally independent. In other words, anything which can be spoken of as existing in itself will be causally independent. The implication is that only God fits al-Fārābī's description of *mawjūd bi-dhātihi*, strictly understood.

Al-Fārābī resists describing God as necessary of existence in itself because for him necessity and possibility still carry too many strictly logical connotations, despite the increasingly existential understanding of those modes that resulted from the infiltration of the root *w-j-d* into discussions. As discussed above, God comes into the Fārābian picture only in the sense that God's foreknowledge of future events could be described as consisting in truthful, and hence necessary, assertions, assertions which in a way cause the event to be necessary.

In his *Siyāsa madaniyya*, al-Fārābī does at one point (47,11-12) make the claim that the existence of the world follows necessarily (*lazima ḍarūratan*) from the existence of the First, and does use the terms *al-mawjūdāt al-mumkina* and *al-wujūd al-mumkin* in referring to material things and to various types of materiality (56,13 and 57,1-58,14). In the former case, however, this expression is an isolated occurrence, at least in comparison to his extensive discussion in the *Commentary on the De Interpretatione* of how the existence of future events follows necessarily from God's foreknowledge of them. And in the latter case, it seems clear that for al-Fārābī, necessary and possible are subordinate to the primary existential distinctions which he lists in his *Aghrāḍ*. There, as I mentioned in Chapter 5, actual and potential, perfect and deficient, and prior and posterior are presented as the modes of existence the study of which is the business of the metaphysician; necessary and contingent are not included.[9] Nor,

[8] al-Fārābī, *K. al-ḥurūf*, 124,8-11.

[9] *Maqāla ... fī aghrāḍ al-ḥakīm fī kulli maqālatin min al-kitāb al-mawsūm bi-l-ḥurūf*, 35,8-11. It is true that at *Int.* 13, 23a22-23 (= *Fī l-ᶜibāra*, 94,16-95,1), for example, Aristotle states that "It is clear from what has preceded that what exists of necessity, will be actual" *(phaneron dê ek tôn eirêmenôn hoti to ex anankês on kat' energeian estin = qad ẓahara mimmā qulnā anna mā*

as far as I know, does al-Fārābī ever describe God as the necessary of existence in itself, even though he does claim in the *Ārā'* (37,14-38,1) that God is perpetual of existence in His substance and self (*dā'imu l-wujūdi bi-jawharihi wa-dhātihi*).

The upshot is that for al-Fārābī, to be necessary in itself is still a modal category that applies primarily to propositions, and only secondarily to beings; and that the distinction between "necessary" and "possible", insofar as it can be applied to beings, is subordinate to more basic distinctions, be they Aristotelian, such as that between actual and potential, or Neoplatonic, such as that between perfect and deficient. Yet al-Fārābī's claim that God is the eternal of existence is an echo of what were, in al-Fārābī's time, intense discussions among the *mutakallimūn* about what it is for something to be eternal in itself. More specifically, al-Fārābī's use of the phrase "eternal of existence in itself" is a reflection of the tendency of *mutakallimūn* before, during and after his lifetime, to appeal to that idea in order to solve the problem of the relationship between God's self (*dhāt*) and God's attributes (*ṣifāt*). The history of that problem will be the subject of the next chapter.

wujūduhu wājibun ḍarūratan fa-huwa bi-l-fi'l). Although Ackrill 1963, 153, claims that this passage must be a later addition (he says the whole paragraph "reeks of notions central to the *Metaphysics*"), the commentators appear to have accepted it as a genuinely Aristotelian doctrine. See, for example, Ammonius *in Int.* 247,3-5. By contrast Philoponus (*in Phys.* 4.12 (*ad* 221b7-8), 755,26-29), as the *mutakallimūn* and Avicenna will, ties the necessary of existence to the eternal, rather than to the actual. In this respect Philoponus may have had in mind Aristotle's distinction, at *GC* 2.9, 335a33-35, between things which exist of necessity, such as eternal things (*ta men gar ex anankês estin hoion ta aïdia*), and things which do not exist of necessity, presumably refering to natural things in the sublunary world, that is, things which come-to-be and pass-away (cf. Philoponus, *in GC* 2.9 [*ad* 335a32], 284,14-21). The equation of what is "always" or "eternal" and what is "necessary" is asserted again at *GC* 2.11, 337b33-338a5.

13. Necessity and Possibility (C)
Materials from the Kalām

In Chapter 7 I argued that Avicenna's distinction between essence and existence owed as much to preceding *kalām* discussions about things and existents as it did to preceding Greek treatments of this issue. In some texts, in fact, Avicenna's position on how things and existents relate to each other is closer to that of tenth-century Ashᶜarite and Māturīdite *mutakallimūn* than it is to that of al-Fārābī, his fellow *faylasūf*. In much the same vein I shall now argue that Avicenna's matrix of distinctions – between necessary of existence (*wājib al-wujūd*) and possible of existence (*mumkin al-wujūd*), between in itself (*bi-dhātihi*) and through another (*bi-ghayrihi*), between uncaused and caused, and between eternal and originated – can be understood fully only when viewed in the context of the evolution of classical Sunnī theology.

In order to explain the nature of the eternality possessed by God and His attributes, Sunnī *mutakallimūn* moved away from earlier, pre-Avicennian attempts to argue that when we define an eternal thing as "that whose existence has no beginning in time" (*mā lā awwala li-wujūdihi*), what we really mean is that an eternal thing *is uncaused*; to later, post-Avicennian attempts to argue that when we define an eternal thing as "that which has never ceased to be nor will ever cease to be" (*mā lam yazal wa-lā yazālu*), what we really mean is that an eternal thing *cannot possibly not exist*, and that therefore an eternal thing *is necessary of existence*. Many of the different ways Avicenna constructed his matrix of distinctions should, it seems to me, be seen as responses to earlier *kalām* ideas and as influences on later *kalām* ideas. It is those earlier *kalām* ideas which I shall focus on here.

During the ninth and tenth centuries God's eternality (*qidam*) was held to be the most important of the divine attributes. This was because when a theologian said that God is eternal (*qadīm*) he used it for two distinct purposes. The Muᶜtazilite and then the Sunnī *mutakallimūn* based one of their proofs for the existence of God on the contradictory nature of the opposition between the eternal and the originated. Given the fact that nothing exists apart from what is eternal (*qadīm*) and what is originated (*muḥdath*); and given the fact that everything originated (*muḥdath*) requires an originator (*muḥdith*); then, in order to avoid an infinite regress, the chain of originated things and originators must terminate in an originator that is not originated. Since there is nothing – apart from the eternal – that is not originated, this ultimate originator must be eternal. This eternal, ultimate originator is God.

The Sunnī *mutakallimūn* also used God's eternality for another purpose: to stress their basic difference with the Muᶜtazilites concerning the issue of the reality of divine attributes such as God's knowledge (*ᶜilm*), power (*qudra*), life (*ḥayāt*) and so on. The Sunnīs, calling themselves "Upholders of the attributes" (*Aṣḥāb aṣ-ṣifāt*) and following the early anti-Muᶜtazilite *mutakallim* Ibn Kullāb (d. ca. 855), held that God's attributes (*ṣifāt*) were entities whose existence was real enough that they could not simply be identified with or subsumed under God's self (*dhāt*), as early Muᶜtazilites such as Abū l-Hudhayl (d. 841) and an-Naẓẓām (d. ca. 840) had maintained. The Sunnīs reasoned that since the attributes were both real and divine, they were eternal just as God Himself is eternal.

In short, God's eternality did double service to Sunnī theologians, helping them prove the world's need for an eternal Creator, and helping them argue for the eternal, and in some sense separate, reality of God's attributes. I shall now argue that a fundamental incompatibility existed between these two uses of eternality – the first directed against atheist Materialists (*dahriyya*), who believed in the eternity of the world, the second directed against the Muᶜtazilites, who denied the separate, eternal reality of the divine attributes – and that resolving, or at least skirting, this problem of incompatibility served as the main catalyst in spurring the Avicennian turn in Sunnī theology.[1]

One of the consequences of the use to which both Muᶜtazilite and Sunnī *mutakallimūn* put God's eternality in their proofs of His existence, was that the term *qidam* (eternality) underwent a semantic shift, from referring to *beforeness* to referring to *uncausedness*.[2] According to ᶜAbd al-Jabbār (d. 1025), the Muᶜtazilite al-Jubbāʾī (d. 915), who taught al-Ashᶜarī (d. 935) before al-Ashᶜarī's defection to Kullābism, defined *qadīm* as "that which comes before in existence" (*mutaqādim fī l-wujūd*).[3] In other books, according to ᶜAbd al-Jabbār, al-Jubbāʾī defined *qadīm* as "that whose existence has no beginning" (*mā lā awwala li-wujūdihi*).[4] Despite al-Ashᶜarī's defection from the Muᶜtazilites, both of al-Jubbāʾī's definitions turn up in the works of later Ashᶜarites. Ibn Fūrak (d. 1015), for example, uses the "existential beforeness" definition, implying that it is the one al-Ashᶜarī himself used.[5] Another Ashᶜarite, al-Ḥalīmī (d. 1012), applied the "beginningless" definition to *qadīm*; but al-Ḥalīmī uses the term *ibtidāʾ* ("origin") in place of *awwal* ("beginning"), reflecting, I believe, the beginnings of the semantic shift I mentioned.[6] This is because "origin" is ambiguous: like the Greek term *arkhê*, the Arabic *ibtidāʾ* can mean both a starting-point in time (*awwal*), as well as a principle (*mabdaʾ*).

[1] For Avicenna's influence on subsequent *kalām* discussions of God, eternality and the divine attributes, see Wisnovsky 2003b.
[2] On *qidam* in general see Gimaret 1988, 164-169.
[3] ᶜAbd al-Jabbār, *al-Mughnī V*, 233,17-18; 234,15 and 235,1; see also *at-taqaddum fī l-wujūd* at 234,6.11.
[4] ᶜAbd al-Jabbār, *al-Mughnī V*, 233,1-2 and 234,7-9.
[5] Ibn Fūrak, *Mujarrad maqālāt al-Ashᶜarī*, 26,19-20; 27,19-20; and 42,19-20.
[6] al-Ḥalīmī, *K. al-minhāj fī shuᶜab al-īmān* (*ap.* al-Bayhaqī, *K. al-asmāʾ wa-ṣ-ṣifāt*, 29,12-30,5).

The rationale for this shift from beginninglessness to uncausedness is quite plain. If, as a *mutakallim*, my main interest in the concept of eternality is using it in proofs of God's existence, I shall want the contradictory nature of the opposition between eternal (*qadīm*) and originated (*muḥdath*) to be basic to the meaning of the two terms. In other words, I shall have an easier time proving God's existence if I define *qadīm* in such a way that it means not only "beginningless" but also "uncaused". This is because "uncaused" will satisfy my intuitions about what an opposite of the passive participle *muḥdath* ("originated") should look like, far more completely than "beginningless" will.

According to ᶜAbd al-Jabbār, al-Jubbāʾī had treated *qadīm* (eternal) and *muḥdath* (originated) as contradictories: holding a single thing to be *qadīm* and *muḥdath* results in mutual contradiction (*yatanāqaḍu*).[7] And for a Muᶜtazilite, this seems obvious enough, given that God is the only thing which is eternal, everything other than God being originated. As with all contradictories, there is no middle ground between *qadīm* and *muḥdath*. As a Sunnī *mutakallim*, however, I shall have made another commitment concerning eternality which dulls this otherwise sharp opposition. For unlike my Muᶜtazilite counterpart, I believe that God Himself is not the only subject to which the attribute "eternal" (*qadīm*) may be predicated: God's attributes (*ṣifāt*), after all, are said to be eternal as well. I shall briefly review the history of the problem of the divine attributes' eternality, and then explain why this produced a dilemma for Sunnī theologians.

In order to buttress their strict understanding of God's unity, the Muᶜtazilites had divided God's attributes into "attributes of the self" (*ṣifāt adh-dhāt*) and "attributes of the act" (*ṣifāt al-fiᶜl*). Attributes of the self, such as God's "knowledge" (*ᶜilm*), could be predicated of God without referring to His creation. Attributes of the act, such as God's "providing" (*rizq*), could be predicated of God only with reference to His creation.

According to the Muᶜtazilites, the attributes of the self, including God's knowledge, power and life, were in no sense to be understood as separate entities. Instead, God is "a knower in Himself" (*ᶜālimun bi-nafsihi*).[8] Abū l-Hudhayl went so far as to claim that an attribute of the self was identical to God, asserting that God is "a knower through a knowledge which is identical to Him" (*ᶜālimun bi-ᶜilmin huwa huwa*).[9] An-Naẓẓām phrased it differently, saying that God "never stops being" His attributes of the self. For example, God "never stops being a knower in Himself" (*lam yazal ᶜāliman bi-nafsihi*).[10] Included in Abū l-Hudhayl's and an-Naẓẓām's lists of attributes of the self was God's being eternal (*qadīm*). According to Abū l-Hudhayl's formula, therefore, God is

[7] ᶜAbd al-Jabbār, *al-Mughnī V*, 233,5.
[8] al-Ashᶜarī, *Maqālāt al-islāmiyyīn*, 164,13-14. On Muᶜtazilite theories of attributes, see generally *Maqālāt al-islāmiyyīn*, 164,10-165,13 and 484,5-487,14.
[9] al-Ashᶜarī, *Maqālāt al-islāmiyyīn*, 165,5.
[10] al-Ashᶜarī, *Maqālāt al-islāmiyyīn*, 486,11-12.

"eternal through an eternality which is identical to Him" (*qadīmun bi-qidamin huwa huwa*); according to an-Naẓẓām's formula, God "never stops being eternal in Himself" (*lam yazal qadīman bi-nafsihi*).

At first glance Ibn Kullāb's view seems like a combination of Abū l-Hudhayl's and an-Naẓẓām's formulae. According to Ibn Kullāb, God "never stops being a knower through a knowledge" (*lam yazal ᶜāliman bi-ᶜilmin*). However, Ibn Kullāb resists Abū l-Hudhayl's identification of the attribute with God, saying instead that God is a knower through a knowledge which "He possesses (*lahu*)", and which "is subsistent in [or 'with'] Him (*qāʾim bihi*)". Ibn Kullāb's new formula applies in an identical way to 29 further attributes which he lists in addition to knowledge. In general, he claims, the attributes "belong to His self" (*li-dhātihi*) and are "neither identical to God nor other than He" (*lā hiya llāhu wa-lā hiya ghayruhu*).[11] What is striking about the description of Ibn Kullāb's doctrine is that "eternal" is not included in his list of 30 attributes. Instead, Ibn Kullāb appends a rather cryptic parenthesis to the end of his list, saying about God that "He is an eternal [thing] who never stops being [so] in [or 'with'] His names and attributes [*innahu qadīmun lam yazal bi-asmāʾihi wa-ṣifātihi*)".[12]

Why did Ibn Kullāb single out "eternal" for special treatment when Abū l-Hudhayl and an-Naẓẓām had seen the eternal as just another attribute of the self?[13] My guess is that Ibn Kullāb is hinting that *qadīm* is special because it is a meta-attribute rather than a regular attribute. The most important characteristic of meta-attributes such as *qadīm* is that they are attributable not only to God Himself but also to some or all of God's regular attributes. For example, once a Sunnī *mutakallim* had determined that God was a *mawjūd* (existent), and that God therefore possessed the attribute of *wujūd* (existence), he had to decide whether or not each of God's attributes likewise possessed the attribute of *wujūd*.

[11] al-Ashᶜarī, *Maqālāt al-islāmiyyīn*, 169,2-170,3.

[12] al-Ashᶜarī, *Maqālāt al-islāmiyyīn*, 169,9-10.

[13] I shall leave aside the problem of whether all or some of the attributes are eternal. As far as the classical Ashᶜarites were concerned, only the attributes of the self could be called eternal, the attributes of the act being originated. Their reasoning was that if an attribute of the act, such as "providing" (*rizq*), were eternal, then the object of that act – namely, the creatures for whom God provides – would also have to be eternal. According to the Māturīdites, attributes of the act as well as attributes of the self are eternal. The Māturīdites explained the eternality of the attributes of the act by appealing to a distinction which for all intents and purposes is the same as Aristotle's distinction between first *entelekheia* and second *entelekheia* as articulated in L1. According to the Māturīdites, the transition from possessing the capability to provide (first *entelekheia*) to exercising that capability (second *entelekheia*), like the transition from knowing how to write but not writing, to writing, does not involve a change from one thing to another (as would be the case with one of Aristotle's four types of change), but rather a transition from one thing to itself. On this issue see, for example, the Māturīdite scholar Abū l-Layth al-Samarqandī (d. 983): "So the correct doctrine is that God is characterized by all His attributes for eternity, be they of the self or of the act" (*thumma l-madhhabu ṣ-ṣaḥīḥu anna llāha taᶜālā mawṣūfun bi-jamīᶜi ṣifātihi fī l-azali dhātiyyatan kānat aw fiᶜliyyatan*): *Sharḥ al-fiqh al-absaṭ li-Abī Ḥanīfa*, lines 527-626 (= 138,4-160,3) at 568-569 (= 147,4-148,1).

The reason why *qadīm* came to be seen by Ibn Kullāb as a meta-attribute, when the Muᶜtazilites by contrast had seen it merely as one of several attributes of the self, is that Ibn Kullāb was so firmly committed to affirming the attributes' eternality. This was a stance he took in opposition to the ᶜAbbāsid Inquisition (*miḥna*) of 833-848, during which time jurists were forced to confess the Muᶜtazilite dictum that the Qurʾān was created.[14] By Ibn Kullāb's reckoning, the Qurʾān, conceived of as God's attribute of speech (*kalām*), was not only separate in some sense from Him, but also co-eternal with Him. For this reason, it seems, Ibn Kullāb wished to distinguish God's attribute of eternality from His other attributes.

But the special status which Ibn Kullāb assigned to *qadīm* confused his followers, who had to decide between two alternatives. The first alternative was to hold that Ibn Kullāb's general principle of attributes, that "God is X through an X-ness which he possesses", applied equally to "eternal"; in this case God will be eternal (*qadīm*) through an eternality (*bi-qidamin*) which He possesses. The second alternative was to hold that God's eternality (and by extension, His other meta-attributes, such as existence) was exempt from Ibn Kullāb's general principle of attributes; in this case God will be eternal in Himself (*bi-nafsihi*), and not through an eternality which He possesses.[15]

Neither alternative was free from difficulties. Although the first alternative enjoys the benefit of consistency, it forces its adherents into a sticky situation: let us allow, for the purpose of argument, that God is eternal through an eternality which He possesses. What about the other attributes, such as God's knowledge, power and speech – are they eternal or not? If they are not eternal, then God's attribute of speech will not be eternal either, and nor, therefore, will the Qurʾān be eternal. But this is precisely the Muᶜtazilite position a Kullābite is so keen to steer clear of.

If, on the other hand, the attributes are eternal; and if it is correct to infer that since God is eternal through an eternality which He possesses, each attribute will similarly be eternal through an eternality which it possesses; then all the attributes will possess their own individual meta-attributes of eternality. Now what about the meta-eternalities which each of the regular attributes possesses – will each of these meta-eternalities also be eternal through a further meta-meta-eternality which each meta-eternality possesses? It seems that if a Kullābite goes down this route a proliferation of eternalities will be hard to avoid.[16]

The upshot was that in order to steer clear of the Muᶜtazilite position that the Qurʾān is created, and in order to pre-empt the infinite-regress problem just

[14] On this see Madelung 1974a; van Ess 1965-66 and 1982; and Wolfson 1976, 235-303. On the attributes in general, see Wolfson 1959 and 1976, 112-234; and Allard 1965.

[15] al-Ashᶜarī, *Maqālāt al-islāmiyyīn*, 170,4-6; 171,16-172,3; 517,14-16.

[16] For evidence that an infinite regress of meta-eternalities was a real worry to Sunnī thinkers, see the Ashᶜarite *mutakallim* and mystic al-Qushayrī (d. 1072), *Sharḥ asmāʾ Allāh al-ḥusnā*, 55,8 and 392,5-7.

described, a follower of Ibn Kullāb will be forced to maintain that Ibn Kullāb's general principle of attributes, that "God is X through an X-ness which he possesses", does *not* apply to meta-attributes, and that God is eternal not through an eternality but in Himself. True, the formula that God is eternal in Himself smacks of Muᶜtazilism, since for all intents and purposes it is identical to an-Naẓẓām's formula mentioned above. Nevertheless, the specific concern with upholding the Qurʾān's uncreatedness at all costs and with avoiding a proliferation of eternalities trumped the worries about sounding too much like an-Naẓẓām.

Having decided in favor of God's being "eternal in Himself" (*qadīm bi-nafsihi*), a Kullābite is still left with the problem of how to describe the eternality which His attributes enjoy. Two options present themselves. On the one hand a Kullābite could claim that like God, each attribute (*ṣifa*) is eternal in itself (*qadīma bi-nafsihā*). This raises a serious problem, however. First of all, attributes are not, strictly speaking, selves (*anfus* or *dhawāt*), but only things which are predicated of selves. Second, the more explicitly a Kullābite affirms that God's attributes are eternal, the more causally independent the attributes might appear to be, given the trend, described earlier, towards seeing uncausedness and not simply beginninglessness as basic to the idea of eternality. In other words, if a Kullābite explicitly asserts that the attributes are all eternal in themselves, he will run the risk of painting a picture in which all God's attributes can be viewed as separate, uncaused divinities; and that in turn will expose him to accusations of *shirk*, or polytheism.[17]

On the other hand a Kullābite could stick like glue to Ibn Kullāb's rather ambiguous formula – that God "is an eternal [thing] who never stops being [so] in [or 'with'] His names and attributes (*innahu qadīmun lam yazal bi-asmāʾihi wa-ṣifātihi*)" – and thereby dodge any accusations of *shirk* which might arise as a result of explicitly affirming that each of God's attributes is eternal.[18] The only danger of adhering to Ibn Kullāb's formula – apart from its opaqueness – is that it might tempt anti-Kullābites to misrepresent the Kullābite position by claiming that Kullābites hold God to be *caused* to be eternal *by* His attributes. This is because one of the derived meanings of the preposition *bi-* (at least in theological and philosophical texts) is causal: "by", "through" or "by means of". In short, if a Kullābite holds that God is eternal *bi-ṣifātihi*, he runs a risk – admittedly slight – of being accused of implying that God is eternal *through* or *by* His attributes, when what he means is simply that God is eternal *in* or *with* His attributes.

When al-Ashᶜarī abandoned Muᶜtazilism in favor of Kullābism, these were the dilemmas he found himself facing. If al-Ashᶜarī held both that God was eternal

[17] This is precisely the trap which the Muᶜtazilite-influenced Shīᶜī *mutakallim* ash-Shaykh al-Mufīd (d. 1022) accuses al-Ashᶜarī of having fallen into: ash-Shaykh al-Mufīd, *Awāʾil al-maqālāt fī l-madhāhib wa-l-mukhtārāt*, 11,20-12,8.

[18] al-Ashᶜarī, *Maqālāt al-islāmiyyīn*, 172,1-3.

through an eternality (*qadīm bi-qidamin*) and that the divine attributes were eternal, he might be seen to be committing himself to the position that each of God's attributes was eternal through a further attribute of eternality (*qadīma bi-qidamin*); and an infinite regress of meta-eternalities would result. If, on the other hand, al-Ashᶜarī held that God was eternal in Himself and that the divine attributes were eternal, he might be seen to be committing himself to the position that each of God's attributes was eternal in itself (*qadīma bi-nafsihā*); and a pleroma of causally independent attribute-divinities would result. Al-Ashᶜarī could, of course, avoid this particular dilemma by denying that the attributes were eternal at all; but that was unacceptable because it would force him to admit that the Qur°ān, *qua* God's attribute of speech, was created. Alternatively, he could adhere to Ibn Kullāb's cryptic formula – that God "is an eternal [thing] who never stops being [so] in [or 'with'] His names and attributes (*innahu qadīmun lam yazal bi-asmā°ihi wa-ṣifātihi*)" – and leave it at that; but philosophically speaking that would represent a retreat into ambiguity rather than an advance towards greater precision, an ambiguity which opponents could exploit.

Al-Ashᶜarī clearly saw himself as a Kullābite as far as the eternality of the divine attributes was concerned, claiming at one point that the "evidence points to the eternity of the Creator *and* His knowledge".[19] But al-Ashᶜarī never decided whether God should be seen as "eternal through an eternality" or "eternal in Himself", probably because of the serious consequences that arose from choosing one option or the other. In fact the Ashᶜarite *mutakallim* Ibn Fūrak admitted that opponents were correct in criticizing al-Ashᶜarī for flip-flopping on this issue. According to Ibn Fūrak, al-Ashᶜarī adopts a strict-constructionist interpretation of Ibn Kullāb's view (that God is "eternal through an eternality" – *qadīm bi-qidamin*) in some texts, and a loose-constructionist interpretation (that God is "eternal in Himself" – *qadīm bi-nafsihi*) in other texts.[20] (In commenting on al-Ashᶜarī's ambivalence Ibn Fūrak confirms that the strict-constructionist interpretation is the one that reflects Ibn Kullāb's genuine opinion.) Ibn Fūrak's contemporary, al-Bāqillānī (d. 1013), however, follows the loose-constructionist line, holding that God is eternal in Himself (*idh li-nafsihi kāna qadīman*).[21]

A Sunnī *mutakallim* such as al-Bāqillānī could feel that, having departed from Ibn Kullāb's formula by maintaining that God is eternal in Himself and not through an eternality, he had at least skirted the old Kullābite dilemma, namely, affirming God's eternality without allowing an infinite proliferation of meta-

[19] al-Ashᶜarī, *K. al-lumaᶜ*, 12,21-13,2.

[20] Ibn Fūrak, *Mujarrad maqālāt al-Ashᶜarī*, 326,7-12; see also 28,12-17. The texts Ibn Fūrak refers to explicitly are *al-Īḍāḥ* (= *K. īḍāḥ al-burhān fī r-radd ᶜalā ahl az-zaygh wa-ṭ-ṭughyān*: Ibn ᶜAsākir, *Tabyīn kadhib al-muftarī fī-mā nusiba ilā l-Imām Abī l-Ḥasan al-Ashᶜarī*, 130,3-4), where al-Ashᶜarī adopts the *qadīm bi-qidamin* view; and *al-Mukhtazan* (Ibn ᶜAsākir, 133,2-5), where he follows the *qadīm bi-nafsihi* line.

[21] al-Bāqillānī, *K. at-tamhīd*, 29,18.

eternalities. This choice, however, forced Sunnī *mutakallimūn* not only to come to grips with the obvious question of whether or not God's attributes were similarly "eternal in themselves", but also to rethink their use of *qadīm* in proofs of God's existence.

As I mentioned earlier, the Muᶜtazilite al-Jubbāᵓī had treated *qadīm* (eternal) and *muḥdath* (originated) as contradictories: holding a single thing to be *qadīm* and *muḥdath* results in mutual contradiction (*yatanāqaḍu*). But a Sunnī *mutakallim*, having avoided the old Kullābite dilemma by holding that God is eternal in Himself (*qadīm bi-nafsihi*) rather than eternal through an eternality (*qadīm bi-qidam*), will now be inclined to articulate the two opposites as eternal in itself (*qadīm bi-nafsihi*) and originated in itself (*muḥdath bi-nafsihi*), and this is precisely what al-Bāqillānī does (though using the slightly less causative *li-nafsihi*).[22]

Strictly speaking, however, al-Bāqillānī's opposition between *qadīm li-nafsihi* and *muḥdath li-nafsihi* is one between contraries, not contradictories, because there is a middle position between them. For although it is impossible to be both *qadīm li-nafsihi* and *muḥdath li-nafsihi* at the same time, it is possible to be neither. One of God's attributes (*ṣifāt*), for example, is eternal (*qadīma*) – it most certainly is not originated (*muḥdatha*) – but it is difficult to see how an attribute can be eternal in itself (*qadīma li-nafsihā*). As I mentioned above, this is because attributes in general, and the divine attributes in particular, are not selves, but only things which are predicated of selves; and also because holding that an attribute is eternal in itself would assign it too much causal independence, given that uncausedness was so basic to the *kalām* conception of eternality.

This raised a problem precisely because, as mentioned above, it was the contradictory, not contrary, nature of the opposition between the terms *qadīm* and *muḥdath*, which served as the basis for the *mutakallimūn*'s proof of God's existence: given that everything which is *muḥdath* (originated) requires a *muḥdith* (originator), we must terminate eventually in something which is not *muḥdath* in order to avoid an infinite regress. And since the only thing which is not *muḥdath* is *qadīm*, the ultimate *muḥdith* will be *qadīm*. But this proof will not work if the terms in use are contraries rather than contradictories. If the terms are contraries, as *qadīm li-nafsihi* and *muḥdath li-nafsihi* appear to be, there will be things – the divine attributes, at least according to the Sunnīs – which are eternal but not eternal in themselves. Put another way, there will be things which are eternal, but not causally independent. The proof will only work if a new category is created – "eternal through another" (*qadīm li-ghayrihi*) – which could then somehow be identified with "originated in itself" (*muḥdath li-nafsihi*). Only then will *qadīm li-nafsihi* and *muḥdath li-nafsihi* cover all

[22] al-Bāqillānī, *K. at-tamhīd*, 29,17-30,2.

possible entities, such that the contradictory nature of their opposition be preserved.

The first of these two steps – creating a new category of "eternal through another" (*qadīm li-ghayrihi*) – was certainly acceptable to some Sunnī *mutakallimūn*. In his Qur'ān commentary, entitled *Interpretations of the Sunnīs*, al-Māturīdī (d. 944) claims that the verse "And therein [viz., in Heaven] shall they dwell forever" (*wa-hum fīhā khālidūna* = *Sūrat al-baqara* 25) can be understood as a refutation of the Jahmites who, in their zealousness to protect God's being the First, the Last, and the Eternal *a parte post* (*al-awwalu wa-l-ākhiru wa-l-bāqī*), felt constrained to maintain that Heaven would pass away. Otherwise, the Jahmites reasoned, both Heaven and God would be Eternal *a parte post*, and that would be a sin of *tashbīh*, or "likening" – likening anything created to God, that is.

Where the Jahmites got it wrong, al-Māturīdī reckons, is that they did not make the requisite distinction between *bi-dhātihi* ("in itself") and *bi-ghayrihi* ("through another"). If they had understood and applied this distinction they would have realized that God is eternal *a parte post* in Himself (*al-bāqī bi-dhātihi*), just as He is First in Himself (*al-awwalu bi-dhātihi*); whereas Heaven and all that it contains are eternal *a parte post* through something other than they (*bāqiyatun bi-ghayrihā*).[23]

It would be too bold to call the distinction which al-Māturīdī offers in this passage a full-fledged and coherent theory. First of all, as the later Ashᶜarite scholar al-Bayhaqī (d. 1066) would point out, God's attribute of *baqā'* can be seen to encompass His eternality *a parte ante* as well as His eternality *a parte post*; whereas the *baqā'* of heaven and hell, which are created things, can refer only to their eternality *a parte post*.[24] Nor is al-Māturīdī's *bi-nafsihi/bi-ghayrihi* distinction here meant to help explain how an eternal God and His eternal attributes are eternal in different ways, the former eternal in Himself, the latter eternal through another. Finally, even if we allow the creation of a new category of thing, "eternal through another", identifying that new category with "originated in itself" (*muḥdath li-nafsihi*) will still run counter to a *mutakallim*'s basic intuition that *qadīm* and *muḥdath* ought to be distinguished on temporal as well as causal grounds.

In the metaphysics section of his earliest philosophical *summa*, the *Ḥikma ᶜArūḍiyya*, composed in 1001 when he was 21, Avicenna, like al-Māturīdī before him, embraces the distinction between "eternal in itself" and "eternal through another" which is implicit in al-Bāqillānī's attachment of the rider *li-nafsihi* ("in itself") to *qadīm* ("eternal"). However, Avicenna resists applying the distinction between "in itself" and "through another" to *muḥdath* ("originated"),

[23] al-Māturīdī, *Ta'wīlāt ahl as-sunna*, vol. 1, 76,16-77,4. Al-Māturīdī also appeals to the *bi-dhātihi/bi-ghayrihi* distinction at *K. at-tawḥīd*, 43,8-9.

[24] al-Bayhaqī, *K. al-asmā' wa-ṣ-ṣifāt*, 33,6-12.

let alone equating *qadīm bi-ghayrihi* ("eternal through another") with *muḥdath bi-nafsihi* ("originated in itself"):

L69

Ibn Sīnā, *al-Ḥikmat al-ᶜArūḍiyya*, 4r14-17

> "Eternal" is said of all that has never been non-existent. Something may be eternal in itself [*qadīman bi-dhātihi*] and it may be eternal through another [*qadīman bi-ghayrihi*]. Now "originated" [*al-muḥdath*] and "brought-into-being" [*al-mutakawwin*] consist in that which did not exist at some time or other [*alladhī kāna laysa fī waqtin mā*], and which will not exist, except through another. It cannot escape coming from matter, because all that is brought into being has been preceded by the possibility of some existence [*fa-qad taqaddamahu imkānu wujūdin*]; otherwise it would not exist.

The problem remains, then, that even if by identifying "originated in itself" with "eternal through another", we were seen to be referring to an intelligible category of thing, an Ashᶜarite such as al-Bāqillānī will resist describing the attributes as either *muḥdatha li-nafsihā* ("originated in themselves") or *qadīma li-ghayrihā* ("eternal through another"), because doing so raises further *kalām*-specific problems, some familiar, others new. On the one hand, if an attribute is said to be *muḥdatha li-nafsihā* or *li-dhātihā*, its possessing a *nafs* or *dhāt* ("self") will assign it too much ontological independence, when – as mentioned above – an attribute is not, strictly speaking, a self but only something predicated of a self. What is more, given that *muḥdath* must mean originated *in time* if it is to be useful in proofs of God's existence which rely on an equation of prior non-existence and causedness, the attributes, if described as *muḥdatha*, will be seen to be temporally bounded rather than eternal, and the Qurᵓān, understood as God's attribute of speech, will be seen to be created instead of uncreated.

On the other hand, if the attributes are *qadīma li-ghayrihā*, an alarming degree of otherness (*ghayriyya*) will infect the relationship between God's attributes and God's self, with the result that the attributes will fail to satisfy Ibn Kullāb's criterion of being neither identical to nor other than God. What is worse, positing a significant degree of otherness between God and His attributes will run the risk of allowing a host of eternal divinities to proliferate – entities which are caused by something other than they, it is true, but which are still eternal and separate. In sum, the ambiguous status of the attributes – eternal, yet not causally independent – flushes out the problems latent in the pre-Avicennian Sunnī trend towards seeing uncausedness as basic to eternality.

In attempting to grapple with this problem the Ashᶜarites al-Bāqillānī and al-Ḥalīmī offer another meaning for *qadīm*, one that should be familiar from my discussion in Chapter 11 of modality and *De Interpretatione* 12-13: "that whose non-existence is impossible".[25] They could even cite the founder of their school for support of their new definition:

L70

al-Ashᶜarī, *Kitāb al-lumaᶜ*, 11,14-15

If the opposite of knowledge were eternal [*qadīm*], it would be impossible for it not to exist [*la-staḥāla an yabṭula*].

At first glance, it is hard to see how this new definition does al-Bāqillānī and al-Ḥalīmī much good. For even if they apply the new understanding of the eternal as that whose non-existence is impossible, to their argument for God's existence, they will still run aground on the rocky shores of the divine attributes. This is because their proof remains reducible to an appeal to the impossibility of an infinite regress of causes and effects, so whichever phrase is chosen to describe the eternal, the term's basic meaning must remain "uncaused" if it is to be opposed to *muḥdath* and thereby useful in their proof of God's existence. As before, the problem arises when that newly chosen phrase – "impossible not to exist" – is similarly applied to the attributes.

Nevertheless, there is a sense in which, if another little step is taken, and being "necessary of existence" (*wājib al-wujūd*) – not just being "impossible of non-existence" (*mustaḥīl al-ᶜadam*) – is held to be the basic criterion of eternality, the horns of the old Kullābite dilemma will at least be blunted. Eternality, let us recall, was held to be predicable both of God's self and of His attributes, though perhaps in different ways. Necessity, by contrast, is not merely a meta-attribute but also a mode of predication, since necessity can be seen to govern the very act of predicating attributes of a subject.

What I mean is that in propositions such as "God is an existent", "God is a knower" and "God is a provider", the modal qualifier "necessary that" (or "necessarily") could be added to describe *how* each of the predicates or attributes holds of its subject: for example, it is necessary that God be (or "exist as") a knower (*wājibun an yakūna* [or *yūjada*] *llāhu ᶜāliman*). The result is that "necessity of existence" can be seen to obtain in the copula which binds the predicates (i.e., God's attributes) to the subject (i.e., God's self), and not simply to be predicable of the subject and of each of the attributes in turn, as was the case with meta-attributes. In short, necessity of existence blunts the horns of the old Kullābite dilemma better than eternality does, because unlike eternality, necessity of existence can be held to describe the divine attributes *only* insofar as they are predicated of God's self.

[25] al-Bāqillānī, *K. at-tamhīd*, 29,5: "because the non-existence of the eternal is not possible (*li-anna l-qadīma lā yajūzu ᶜadamuhu*)"; al-Ḥalīmī, *K. al-minhāj fī shuᶜab al-īmān* (*ap.* al-Bayhaqī, *K. al-asmāʾ wa-ṣ-ṣifāt*, 33,1-5): "If He is existent neither from a beginning nor through a cause, then neither extinction nor non-existence will be possible for Him (*li-annahu idhā kāna mawjūdan lā ᶜan awwala wa-lā bi-sababin lam yajuz ᶜalayhi l-inqiḍāʾu wa-l-ᶜadamu*)".

Given the clear advantages of necessity over eternality, why were pre-Avicennian Sunnī *mutakallimūn* so reluctant to take that little step and assert openly that since eternality is now to be defined as impossibility of non-existence, and since impossibility of non-existence is identical to necessity of existence, God's eternality will refer at the most basic level to His necessity of existence? The short answer is that they were uncomfortable using the term *wājib* in this way. When the early *mutakallimūn* wished to refer to a proposition's being axiomatic or intuitively necessary, in the sense that a necessary proposition expresses an *a priori* truth, they turned to the term *ḍarūrī*. For example, the proposition "the whole is greater than any of its parts" is *ḍarūrī*.[26] (The precise date when *ḍarūra* first came to be used this way is a matter of mild debate among historians of early *kalām*.[27])

By contrast, early *mutakallimūn* had understood the active participle *wājib* as connoting religious or moral obligation (*farḍ*), and used *wājib* with the preposition *ᶜalā* to mean "morally incumbent upon".[28] It is true that many of those same *mutakallimūn* turned to the root *w-j-b* – most commonly in the form of *yajibu* X *min* A *wa*-B ("[Conclusion] X follows necessarily from [premises] A and B") – to render the idea of syllogistic necessitation. For example, in his *Vindication of the Science of Kalām*, al-Ashᶜarī uses *wajaba* in this way:

L71

al-Ashᶜarī, *Risālat istiḥsān al-khawḍ fī ᶜilm al-kalām*, 92,12-16

> We say: If God were to resemble something, He would resemble it either in every respect or in one respect. If He resembled it in every respect, it would follow necessarily [*wajaba*] that He be originated in every respect. And if He resembled it in one respect, it would follow necessarily [*wajaba*] that like it He be originated to the extent that He resembled it, given that each of two similar things will be judged to be similar in the respect in which it

[26] Examples of *bi-ḍ-ḍarūra*, *ḍarūratan*, *ḍarūrat al-ᶜaql*, *ḍarūrī* (and, less often, *bi-l-iḍṭirār*, etc., which is usually paired with *bi-ṭ-ṭabᶜ*, etc., "by nature", and contrasted with *bi-l-ikhtiyār*, etc., "by choice") in an epistemological context in pre-Avicennian *kalām* include al-Ashᶜarī, *Maqālāt al-islāmiyyīn*, 136,10-15; 393,5-14; 480,6-10; an-Nāshiʾ al-Akbar (d. 906), *al-Kitāb al-awsaṭ fī l-maqālāt*, 109,13-110,11 (= #148); Saᶜdiyā al-Fayyūmī (i.e., Saadia Gaon), *Kitāb al-amānāt wa l-iᶜtiqādāt*, 12,17-13,10; 16,19-20,18; and al-Māturīdī, *K. at-tawḥīd*, 5,13; 7,11; 8,14.17; 42,20; al-Ashᶜarī, *K. al-lumaᶜ*, 41,10-42,15; Bāqillānī, *K. at-tamhīd*, 7,4-10; 8,6-13; 9,2-15; 52,4-7; Ibn Fūrak, *Mujarrad maqālāt al-Ashᶜarī*, 12,1-20; 13,25-14,20; 18,21-19,6; 20,9-21,13; 222,16-19; 247,17-249,22; 284,15-18; 324,4; 328,14-19.

[27] Rudolph 1992, 83n.37, and 1996, 252, argues that the distinction between *ḍarūrī* (necessary) and *muktasab* (acquired) knowledge is a product of late-ninth/early-tenth-century Muᶜtazilite epistemology; see also Frank 1974, 142n.26. However, according to Tritton 1940, 253, the late-Umayyad *mutakallim* Jaᶜd b. Dirham (d. 743) advocated a version of *ᶜilm ḍarūrī*; and van Ess 1966, 114-118, argues that the *ḍarūrī/muktasab* distinction had been in circulation since the very beginnings of *kalām*. On this issue see also Abrahamov 1993.

[28] On the distinction between *wājib* and *ḍarūrī*, see van Ess 1966, 118-119. Instances where *wājib* and *farḍ* appear to be interchangeable include Ibn Fūrak, *Mujarrad maqālāt al-Ashᶜarī*, 16,3-6; 32,7-17; 180,17; and 199,8-9; and al-Bāqillānī, *K. at-Tamhīd*, 187,1.

resembles the other. Yet it is impossible for what is originated to be eternal, and for what is eternal to be originated.

The later *mutakallimūn* could, of course, justify adding syllogistic necessity to *wājib*'s semantic field by stressing the rather Muᶜtazilite idea that knowledge of the concepts of right and wrong was both morally incumbent and intellectually necessary, since a human endowed with responsibility for his actions (a *mukallaf*, that is) both possessed an intuitive knowledge of right and wrong, and was under a moral obligation to act according to that intuitive knowledge.[29] Still, using the active participle *wājib* – as opposed to the verb *wajaba/yajibu* – to denote syllogistic necessity remained rare in pre-Avicennian Sunnī *kalām*.

Unlike most *mutakallimūn*, a number of polymaths and litterateurs of the late-tenth and early-eleventh centuries had no qualms about asserting that since God is impossible of non-existence, He is necessary of existence. For example, the Ikhwān aṣ-Ṣafā᾽ (fl. ca. 985?) at one point refer to God as *al-wājib al-wujūd* in their *Rasā᾽il.*[30] Ibn Miskawayh (d. 1030), who despite his death date was a generation or two older than Avicenna, also argues that "If, as we asserted, the existence in Him is essential, He could not possibly be imagined to be non-existent; thus He is necessary of existence, and whatever is necessary of existence will be perpetual of existence, and whatever is perpetual of existence will be eternal (*wa-idhā kāna l-wujūdu fīhi ka-mā qulnā dhātiyyan fa-laysa yajūzu an yutawahhama maᶜdūman fa-huwa wājibu l-wujūdi wa-mā kāna wājiba l-wujūdi fa-huwa dā᾽imu l-wujūdi wa-mā kāna dā᾽ima l-wujūdi fa-huwa azaliyyun*)".[31] And the phrase *wājib al-wujūd* appears with the rider *bi-dhātihi*, again in reference to God, in the *K. al-amad ᶜalā l-abad* of al-ᶜĀmirī.[32]

Al-ᶜĀmirī in fact appears to be the most likely direct source of Avicenna's distinction, for a number of reasons. First of all, al-ᶜĀmirī was the first to predicate the entire expression *wājib al-wujūd bi-dhātihi* ("necessary of existence in itself") of God. Second, though trained in Baghdad, al-ᶜĀmirī moved to Bukhārā, and was active in the same Sāmānid court, and studied in the same Sāmānid library where, only a decade or so later, the 21-year-old Avicenna would write his first philosophical *summa*, the *Ḥikma ᶜArūḍiyya*, which is also the first Avicennian text in which *wājib al-wujūd bi-dhātihi* appears. Finally, in his *Kitāb at-taqrīr li-awjuhi t-taqdīr*, al-ᶜĀmirī again makes the distinction between necessary, possible and impossible of existence, and illustrates what he

[29] Ibn Fūrak, *Mujarrad maqālāt al-Ashᶜarī*, 285,7-20; al-Bāqillānī, *K. at-Tamhīd*, 8,4-5; 379,11-380,15.

[30] Ikhwān aṣ-Ṣafā᾽, *Rasā᾽il II*, 471,1.

[31] Rowson (*al-Amad*, 233) refers to the Cairo, 1907, edition of Ibn Miskawayh's *K. al-fawz al-asghar*: 15f.; in the edition I have access to (*K. al-fawz al-asghar*, Beirut, 1901), this sentence appears on 20,10-12.

[32] al-ᶜĀmirī, *K. al-amad ᶜalā l-abad*, 78,12; *wājib al-wujūd* appears without the rider *bi-dhātihi* at 170,12.

means by necessary of existence with the example "2+2=4", the same example which, as will be shown in the next chapter, Avicenna later used in both his *Ḥikma ᶜArūḍiyya* and in his *Mabdaʾ wa-maᶜād*.[33] (I admit that "2+2=4" is such a prosaic example that its use in two or more texts does not constitute definitive proof of some kind of filiation between them.)

Al-ᶜĀmirī also makes the distinction in the *Kitāb at-taqrīr li-awjuhi t-taqdīr* between that which is necessary of existence in itself (*bi-dh-dhāt*) and that whose existence is necessary as a consequence of a relation (*bi-l-iḍāfa*), the same distinction which Avicenna was to make in his *Mabdaʾ wa-maᶜād*.[34] (I shall discuss the *Mabdaʾ wa-maᶜād*, and this passage in particular – L75 – in Chapter 14.) Of course it is not certain whether Avicenna derived his matrix of distinctions directly from the courtesy copy of *al-Amad* which al-ᶜĀmirī doubtless left in the Sāmānid library, or whether Avicenna and al-ᶜĀmirī read the same texts there and were independently influenced by them.

In fairness to the *mutakallimūn* I should mention that the appearance of "necessary of existence" (*wājib al-wujūd*) – sometimes with the rider "in itself" (*bi-dhātihi*), other times without – in descriptions of God, is also a characteristic of a small number of theological texts produced during the thirty years between 985 and 1015, including those by the Muᶜtazilite ᶜAbd al-Jabbār and the Ashᶜarite belletrist ar-Rāghib al-Iṣfahānī.[35] In fact, some scholars have wondered whether there might be a causal link between, on the one hand, ᶜAbd al-Jabbār's presence in Rayy between 1013 and 1015 and the presence of terms such as *wujūb al-wujūd* in ᶜAbd al-Jabbār's works, and, on the other hand, Avicenna's presence in Rayy around 1014-1015 and Avicenna's own evolving ideas about necessary and possible existence. The assumption has been that if there were any influence, it must have come from the older ᶜAbd al-Jabbār and towards the younger Avicenna. This perception is reinforced by Averroes' famous comment in the *Tahāfut at-tahāfut* that Avicenna pinched the idea of distinguishing necessary and possible existence from the Muᶜtazilites (*wa-huwa ṭarīqun akhadhahu bnu Sīnā mina l-mutakallimīna ... hādhā huwa ᶜtiqādu l-Muᶜtazilati qabla l-Ashᶜariyyati*).[36]

What truth might there be to Averroes' claim? In the *Kitāb al-majmūᶜ fī l-muḥīṭ bi-t-taklīf* ᶜAbd al-Jabbār does seem to toy with the idea that God's eternality (*qidam*) can somehow be explained by referring to the necessity of His existence (*wujūb al-wujūd*).[37] ᶜAbd al-Jabbār also comes close to making a distinction in that work between intrinsic and derivative necessity (*al-wujūbu li-*

[33] al-ᶜĀmirī, *Kitāb at-taqrīr li-awjuh at-taqdīr*, 28-30 [MS Princeton 2163 (393B), 26-76]; here I am following the synopsis by Rowson in his commentary on the *Amad*, 232-233.

[34] Ibn Sīnā, *al-Mabdaʾ wa-l-maᶜād*, 3,2-15.

[35] I have been told that the phrase *wājib al-wujūd* also appears in the Longer Version of the *Uthūlujiyā*, but I have not been able to check the manuscript.

[36] Ibn Rushd, *Tahāfut at-tahāfut*, 276,4-9.

[37] *ap.* Ibn Mattawayh, *K. al-majmūᶜ fī l-muḥīṭ bi-t-taklīf I*, 50,24; 99,21-22; 141,10-12; and 142,1.

dhātihi lā li-shay'in siwāhu).[38] In his *Mughnī* the two trends are joined together a little more closely.[39] But as far as I can tell, in neither work does ᶜAbd al-Jabbār articulate a matrix of distinctions (necessary of existence vs. possible of existence, in itself vs. through another, uncaused vs. caused), nor apply that matrix to the problem of God's relationship to the world, in a way that even approached the clarity and completeness found in Avicenna's discussions. It is difficult to be definitive about this question because we do not possess the first three volumes of the *Mughnī*, the volumes which cover the topic of *tawḥīd* (divine oneness) and hence those which would be the obvious context for ᶜAbd al-Jabbār to expound most fully on the issue of *wājib al-wujūd*.

Of course, if we accept (as I think we should) that the Uppsala *Ḥikma ᶜArūḍiyya* manuscript we now have access to is really a copy of the very text which Avicenna composed when he was 21, in the year 1001, then the matrix of distinctions appears in Avicenna's work – in L58, that is – a dozen years before Avicenna ever could have laid eyes on ᶜAbd al-Jabbār in Rayy, and we can dismiss any claim of ᶜAbd al-Jabbār's personal influence on purely historical grounds. This is not to say, of course, that ᶜAbd al-Jabbār's works, or other Muᶜtazilite works which are now lost, may have been contained in the Sāmānid library and read by Avicenna before he composed the *Ḥikma ᶜArūḍiyya*. But given the lack of textual evidence that other Muᶜtazilites thought of this matrix of distinctions first; and given the hints at that matrix of distinctions by al-ᶜĀmirī, who worked in the Sāmānid library only a dozen years before Avicenna; my tentative conclusion has to be either that Ibn Sīnā's work influenced ᶜAbd al-Jabbār's, or, as seems more likely, that Ibn Sīnā and ᶜAbd al-Jabbār came up with the idea independently, the former in a sustained and precise way and building on earlier work by al-ᶜĀmirī, and the latter almost in passing. My guess is that Averroes' comment might well be an expression of his discomfort at the astonishingly rapid and widespread incorporation of Avicenna's matrix of distinctions into Sunnī-*kalām* proofs of God's existence and into their discussions of epistemology and God's attributes, in the century or so following Avicenna's death.[40]

The one Ashᶜarite contemporary of Avicenna who uses the phrase *wājib al-wujūd* to describe God is ar-Rāghib al-Iṣfahānī. I shall not go into too much detail concerning the uncertainty over Rāghib's death date. Rowson, in the most recent synopsis of this question, reckons that he flourished around 1010, and I am convinced by his arguments, which build upon earlier work by Madelung.[41] In his *Iᶜtiqādāt*, Rāghib argues that existents and originated things cannot help but terminate eventually in an existentiator and originator (*ilā mūjidin wa-*

[38] *ap.* Ibn Mattawayh, *K. al-majmūᶜ fī l-muḥīṭ bi-t-taklīf I*, 51,20-21.
[39] ᶜAbd al-Jabbār, *al-Mughnī IV*, 250,4-15; and *XI*, 432,11-15.
[40] See Wisnovsky 2003b.
[41] Rowson 1995 and Madelung 1974b.

muḥdithin), and that this existentiator and originator must be One, Eternal, and Necessary of Existence in Himself (*wa-anna dhālika l-mūjida wa-l-muḥditha yajibu an yakūna wāḥidan azaliyyan wājiba l-wujūdi li-dhātihi*).[42] Later on, Rāghib explains what he means when he says that God is necessary of existence:

L72

ar-Rāghib al-Iṣfahānī, *al-Iᶜtiqādāt*, 56,9-57,11

Proof that He, may He be exalted, is an existent which is necessary of existence [*mawjūdun wājibu l-wujūdi*] consists in the fact that whenever we assume or imagine Him to be an existent, it must be in one of three ways: necessary of existence, impossible of existence, or possible of existence [*immā wājibu l-wujūdi aw mumtaniᶜu l-wujūdi aw mumkinu l-wujūdi*]. The necessary of existence is that which, when postulated as non-existent, an absurdity is logically entailed, e.g., [when] the occurrence of four from the existence of two and two [is postulated as non-existent] [*fa-l-wājibu l-wujūdi huwa lladhī idhā furiḍa ghayra mawjūdin lazima minhu muḥālun ka-ḥuṣūli arbaᶜatin min wujūdi ithnayni wa-ithnayni*]. The impossible of existence is that which, when postulated as existent, an absurdity is logically entailed, e.g., [when] the occurrence of four from the existence of two and three [is postulated as existent]. The possible of existence is that which, when postulated as existent or non-existent, no absurdity is logically entailed, e.g., [when] the coming of rain in the winter [is postulated as existent or non-existent].

The necessary of existence is of two types: the necessary of existence not in itself but through something else [*wājibu l-wujūdi lā li-dhātihi bal li-amrin ākhara*], such as the existence of four which follows necessarily from the occurrence of two and two; and the necessary of existence in itself, not through anything else, namely the Creator, may He be exalted [*wa-wājibu l-wujūdi li-dhātihi lā li-shayʾin ākhara wa-huwa l-bārī taᶜālā*]. The necessary of existence is that which, when postulated as non-existent, an absurdity occurs [*idhā furiḍa ghayra mawjūdin ḥaṣala minhu muḥālun*]; nor does it need, in its existence, anything to make it exist; and it is eternal, this being God, may He be exalted [*wa-lā muḥtājun fī wujūdihi ilā shayʾin yūjiduhu wa-yakūnu azaliyyan wa-dhālika huwa llāhu taᶜālā*] .... The necessary of existence is that which has no need, in terms of its existence, for anything other than itself [*wa-l-wājibu l-wujūdi huwa lladhī lā yaftaqiru fī wujūdihi ilā shayʾin ghayri dhātihi*]. It is established therefore that it is correct to say that there is only one necessary of existence in itself, this being God, may He be exalted.

The wording of Rāghib's explanation – which we can date, following Rowson's conjecture, to around 1010 – is strikingly similar to that found in yet another passage from Avicenna's *al-Mabdaʾ wa-l-maᶜād* (L74), composed around 1013

[42] ar-Rāghib al-Isfahānī, *al-Iᶜtiqādāt*, 48,15-20.

(that is, twelve years after his first stab at the idea of necessary existence in the *Ḥikma ᶜArūḍiyya*), and which I shall discuss in the next chapter.

As with ᶜAbd al-Jabbār, because of the absence of whose *Mughnī I-III* we cannot definitively solve the problem of who influenced whom, so the uncertainty over Rāghib's dates forces us to be agnostic about who came up with the new formulation first, Avicenna or Rāghib. Nevertheless, I believe the burden of proof lies with those who deny that al-ᶜĀmirī is the most likely direct source of Avicenna's matrix of distinctions, since he is the one author whose works were almost certainly in the right place (Bukhārā) at the right time (ca. 1000) to spark the young Avicenna's metaphysical imagination. My task in Chapter 14, then, is to survey Avicenna's major discussions of necessary and possible existence, mindful of the strong possibility that his views on this topic may have evolved over his lifetime.

14. Necessity and Possibility (D)
The Question of Evolution

As a way of starting this final chapter, I shall dissect the main reason which prompted Avicenna – and al-ᶜĀmirī before him – to seize upon *wājib* with such enthusiasm. In my opinion *wājib* came to enjoy prominence as a technical term at the end of the tenth and beginning of the eleventh century, because it is more syntactically amphibolous than its main rival, *ḍarūrī*, and therefore could be used to signify a wider range of referents. What I mean is that unlike *ḍarūrī*, *wājib* could be construed not only intransitively but transitively as well; and that in its transitive sense *wājib* could be construed in the active voice as well as in the passive voice.

Let me list the different types of necessity (*wujūb*) which *wājib* could plausibly refer to:

1. Intransitive

(i) The modal *wujūb* of a proposition taken in itself: *WĀJIBUN an yūjada S P* ("it is NECESSARY that S is [or 'exists as'] P"), or *fa-yūjadu S P WĀJIBAN* ("S is [or 'exists as'] P NECESSARILY"), where S is a subject and P a predicate.

(ii) The absolute *wujūb* of simple, eternal and immutable things: *X huwa WĀJIBU l-wujūd* ("X is NECESSARY of existence"), where X is a simple, eternal and immutable thing.

(iii) The perfect *wujūb* of a causally self-sufficient thing: *X huwa WĀJIBU l-wujūd* ("X is NECESSARY of existence"), where X possesses perfection understood as uncausedness.

2a. Transitive (active)

(i) The inferential *wujūb* of a valid syllogism: *YAJIBU C min A wa-B* ("C FOLLOWS NECESSARILY from A and B"), where C is a conclusion and A and B are premises (i.e., *necessitas consequentiae*).

(ii) The productive *wujūb* of a proposition taken as a premise: *yajibu wujūbu C min WUJŪBI A wa-min WUJŪBI B* ("C's necessity follows from A's NECESSITY and B's NECESSITY"), where C is a conclusion and A and B are premises.

2b. Transitive (passive)

(i) The derived *wujūb* of a proposition taken as a conclusion (e.g., *yajibu WUJŪBU C min wujūbi A wa-min wujūbi B* ("C's NECESSITY follows from A's necessity and B's necessity"), where C is a conclusion and A and B are premises (i.e., *necessitas consequentis*).

(ii) The hypothetical *wujūb* of generable and perishable things (e.g., *li-an yūjada E WĀJIBUN an yūjada M^1 wa-M^2 wa-M^3* ("In order that E exist, it is NECESSARY that M^1 and M^2 and M^3 exist"), where E is an intended end, and M^1 and M^2 and M^3 are the materials necessary for that end to exist, or to exist well.

In other words, *wājib* could serve in almost all the major roles a *faylasūf* or *mutakallim* might require of it. Understood intransitively, *wājib* could be construed as referring to the necessary *qua* modal qualifier "necessary that" or "necessarily" (i.e., *qua wājibun* or *wājiban* = *Int.* 12-13); the necessary *qua* "invariable" (i.e., *qua wājib al-wujūd* = *Metaph.* 5.5 category [4]); and the necessary *qua* "causally self-sufficient" (i.e., *qua wājib al-wujūd* = Neoplatonic perfection). Understood transitively, *wājib* could be construed as referring to the necessary *qua* "necessary inference" (i.e., *qua ījāb* = *Metaph.* 5.5 category [5]); the necessary *qua* "necessitating cause" (i.e., *qua mūjib* = *Metaph.* 5.5 category [5]); the necessary *qua* "necessitated effect" (i.e., *qua mūjab* = *Metaph.* 5.5 category [5]); and the necessary *qua* "indispensable" (i.e., *qua mūjab* = *Metaph.* 5.5 categories [1] and [2] and *Phys.* 2.9).

The only sense of the necessary which the older term *ḍarūrī* seemed to express better than *wājib* did was the compulsory (= *Metaph.* 5.5 category [3]). And in fact Avicenna regularly refers to accidental material factors which prevent a cause from producing its effect as *ḍarūriyyāt*. But that was a relatively small price to pay for all the benefits he accrued by using *wājib*. Most important of these is that *wājib* was amphibolous enough to be used in a context where causal relationships are not at issue as well as in a context where causal relationships are at issue. The chasm between the self-sufficiency of that which possesses perfection and the productivity of that which is above perfection could be bridged by employing *wājib* to describe both types of necessity. This allowed Avicenna to use *wājib* in the phrase *wājib al-wujūd bi-dhātihi* to refer to God's intrinsic self-sufficiency at the same time as he used it to refer to God's causal productivity.

What is more, *wājib* could express the derived necessity of an effect as well as the productive necessity of a cause. This allowed Avicenna to use *wājib* in the phrase *wājib al-wujūd bi-ghayrihi* ("necessary of existence through another") to refer to the necessity an effect derives from its cause. Avicenna thereby gained a decisive advantage over the *mutakallimūn*, because while Avicenna could make a case for identifying *wājib al-wujūd bi-ghayrihi* ("necessary of existence through another") and *mumkin al-wujūd bi-dhātihi* ("possible of existence in itself"), given that the latter referred to the effect's intrinsic contingency, there was little chance – as I showed in the previous chapter – that a *mutakallim* could plausibly identify *qadīm bi-ghayrihi* ("eternal through another") and *muḥdath bi-dhātihi* ("originated in itself").

Having taken stock of the numerous advantages which impelled Avicenna to construct his matrix of distinctions around the term *wājib*, I shall now turn to the question of whether or not – and if so, how – Avicenna's uses of that matrix of distinctions in different works might represent an evolution in his views. For the sake of convenience I shall repeat what Avicenna says in the *Ḥikma ᶜArūḍiyya*:

L73 (= L58)

Ibn Sīnā, *al-Ḥikmat al-ᶜArūḍiyya*, 3v16-4r12

"The Necessary" [*al-wājib*] is that which is necessary of existence in respect of the way it is [*aḍ-ḍarūriyyu l-wujūdi ᶜalā mā huwa ᶜalayhi*], this being either in itself [*bi-dhātihi*] (such as the principle of existents [*ka-mabdaʾi l-mawjūdāti*]) or through another (such as the fact that two and two are four). The necessary is either eternal (such as the principle of existents) or is at one time and not another [*fī ḥālin dūna ḥālin*] (such as the eclipse of the moon at that moment). All that is necessary of existence in itself has no cause. Whatever has a cause will be neither necessary of existence in itself nor impossible of existence in itself (for otherwise, it would never come to exist); with respect to itself [*fī ḥaythu dhātihi*], therefore, it [i.e., that which has a cause] will be possible of existence [*mumkinu l-wujūdi*], while [at the same time] being necessary of existence through its cause. Now the existence of whatever has no cause is not itself divisible into two states [*wa-mā lā ᶜillata lahu fa-inna wujūda dhātihi lā yanqasimu min ḥālatayni*], in virtue of which it [i.e., the existence of whatever has no cause] would come to be caused in both states; for there would be no way out of being caused, nor any escape from causedness. All that is subject to change is in these two states, neither one of which it possesses in itself; rather, it possesses both of them through a cause (there being no alternative to them [i.e., there being no alternative to being in the two states]). Thus all that is subject to change will itself be caused and possible, whereas all that is necessary of existence in itself will be necessary of existence in every respect, and no type of change whatsoever will be attributable to it. "The possible" is the existent which is not necessary [*laysa bi-ḍarūriyyin*]. "The possible" is said to be whatever is not impossible; and "the possible" is said to be whatever is not impossible and which

> exists and [then] is non-existent, and [in general] whatever does not exist at some time or other.

In this passage Avicenna presents both in itself/through another and always/sometimes as alternative ways of distinguishing between types of necessary existence. He opts for the in itself/through another distinction, and holds it to be equivalent to uncaused/caused. This appears to be because of his reluctance to advocate a bald parallelism between the modal operators "necessary", "possible" and "impossible" and the temporal operators "always", "sometimes" and "never". As Bäck has shown, in later works such as the *Shifāʾ* Avicenna will distinguish between six ways necessity operates in predications when it is tied to varying time periods.[1] Even at this early stage Avicenna seems aware that if linking the modal operators to the temporal operators produces so many alternative types of necessity, the in itself/through another distinction will be easier to mesh with the desired uncaused/caused distinction than the always/sometimes distinction will.

What I mean is that "necessary eternally" and "necessary sometimes" will entail uncausedness and causedness, respectively, far less strictly than "necessary in itself" and "necessary through another" will. As we saw with the *mutakallimūn*'s struggle to determine the precise nature of the divine attributes' eternality, there are things which are eternal but which are *not* uncaused. For Avicenna, of course, it is the heavens rather than the divine attributes which fit this category. But the fundamental challenge remains the same for the *mutakallimūn* and for Avicenna: to find a coherent way to distinguish between eternal things which *are* uncaused and eternal things which are *not* uncaused.

So how exactly does one go about establishing a strict equivalence between "being necessary of existence in itself" and "being uncaused", and between "being necessary of existence through another" and "being caused"? It is in response to this question that Avicenna begins to articulate – in the *Ḥikma ʿArūḍiyya* and the *Mabdaʾ wa-maʿād* – the two approaches which Davidson would differentiate in Avicenna's later works.

Avicenna claims in the *Ḥikma ʿArūḍiyya* passage above (i.e., L58/L73) that "the existence of whatever has no cause is not itself divisible into two states [or 'modes'] (*wa-mā lā ʿillata lahu fa-inna wujūda dhātihi lā yanqasimu min ḥālatayni*), in virtue of which [two states] it [the existence of whatever has no cause] would come to be caused in both states; for there would be no way out of being caused, nor any escape from causedness". The question arises, how ought we to interpret Avicenna's phrase "divisible into two states [or 'modes']" (*yanqasimu min ḥālatayni*)? Two alternatives present themselves. The first alternative (1) takes the "two states" to refer to (i) the state of non-existence which precedes X's coming-to-be or which follows X's passing away, and (ii)

[1] Bäck 1992.

the state of existence currently possessed by X. The advantage of this interpretation is that it coheres with the final assertion of L58/L73, that the "possible" refers to that which "exists and [then] is non-existent (*yūjadu wa-yaᶜdamu*), and [in general to] whatever does not exist at some time or other".

Nevertheless, alternative (1) suffers from some grave flaws. First, Avicenna does not claim that *X* is divisible into two states, but that the *existence* of X is divisible into two states. It is difficult to imagine Avicenna's making the assertion that the existence of something is divisible into non-existence and existence. An advocate of interpretation (1) might argue that within X itself existence is mixed with non-existence, since X is infected with some degree of non-existence by virtue of the fact that at one point in the past X was non-existent and at some point in the future X will once again be non-existent. But even if we were to concede this point, it is X, and not X's existence, which would be divisible into non-existence and existence.

The second flaw is that interpretation (1) fails *prima facie* to solve one of the main philosophical challenges facing the Sunnī *mutakallimūn* and Avicenna, namely, figuring out a way to distinguish eternal things which *are* uncaused (God's self; God) from eternal things which are *not* uncaused (God's attributes; the heavens). Because interpretation (1) takes the two states to refer to the non-existence and existence possessed by things that come-to-be and pass-away at different points in time, the divisibility cannot apply to eternal things which never come to be or pass away. The upshot is that if (1) is the correct interpretation of what Avicenna meant when he said "divisible into two states [or 'modes']", being necessary of existence in itself will entail uncausedness no more strictly than being eternal will. This is because eternal things which are not uncaused – God's attributes, or the heavens – will not be accounted for in Avicenna's scheme, since they cannot be described as being divisible into the two states of non-existence and existence.

Let us turn then to the second alternative, interpretation (2). Interpretation (2) takes Avicenna's assertion that "the existence of whatever has no cause is not itself divisible into two states [or 'modes'], in virtue of which [two states] it [the existence of whatever has no cause] would come to be caused in both states; for there would be no way out of being caused, nor any escape from causedness", to be a somewhat tentative attempt to appeal to the old "every composite requires a composer" axiom, common to both Neoplatonists and *mutakallimūn*, the gist of which is that everything simple is uncaused, while everything composite or complex is caused.[2] Two further lines of interpretation – (2a) and (2b) – can be distinguished.

The first line of interpretation – (2a) – holds that Avicenna is referring to the fact that the existence of all beings in the world other than God is conceptually divisible into the two modes (i) "necessary through another" (*wājib al-wujūd bi-*

[2] On the history of this argument, see Davidson 1987, 146-153.

ghayrihi) and (ii) "possible in itself" (*mumkin al-wujūd bi-dhātihi*). God's existence, by contrast, is *not* conceptually divisible into two modes, since God's existence is only ever "necessary in itself" (*wājib al-wujūd bi-dhātihi*). The conceptual divisibility of the existence possessed by all beings other than God into the two modes "necessary of existence through another" and "possible of existence in itself", entails that their existence be thought of as a composite of those two modes, just as the conceptual divisibility of each sublunary substance into form and matter entails that it be thought of as a composite of matter and form.

According to interpretation (2a), Avicenna's train of thought is that since being a composite entails being caused; and since everything composite requires a composer (the same Arabic term – *murakkab* – means both "composite" and "composed"); all existence which is conceptually divisible into, and thus a composite of, the two modes "necessary through another" and "possible in itself" will therefore be caused. By contrast, all existence which is *not* conceptually divisible into and thus *not* a composite of the two modes, will be uncaused. The only being whose existence fits that latter category is God.

As attractive as (2a) might be, it, like interpretation (1), suffers from a serious difficulty. In the very next line after Avicenna states that the existence of whatever is divisible into two states or modes will be caused, he asserts that "All that is subject to change (*kullu mutaghayyarin*) is in these two states, neither one of which it possesses in itself" (*laysa wa-lā wāḥidata minhumā lahu bi-dhātihi*). An opponent of (2a) could argue, then, that if the two states or modes into which the existence of all beings other than God is divisible, were meant to refer to "necessary through another" and "possible in itself", Avicenna would not have claimed so baldly that such a thing possessed *neither* state in itself. The reason, of course, is that a being whose existence is both "necessary through another" and "possible in itself", *does* possess one of the two states in itself: namely, being possible.

If the "two states" should not be taken to refer to the two modes "necessary of existence through another" and "possible of existence in itself", I am left with interpretation (2b). This alternative holds that the "two states" refer to (i) the state of potentiality or imperfection that characterizes the existence of a changeable thing – X – when X is understood as a potential or imperfect Y; and (ii) the state of actuality or perfection that characterizes the existence of a changeable thing – X – when X is understood as an actual or perfect X.

What makes interpretation (2b) plausible is that it coheres with Avicenna's immediately preceding assertion that everything which is *changeable* (*kullu mutaghayyarin*) is in these two states. As with interpretation (2a), interpretation (2b) takes the two states – potentiality/actuality or imperfection/perfection – which characterize the existence of a changeable thing at a given time, to entail compositeness, and thus causedness.

Nevertheless, like interpretation (1), interpretation (2b) fails *prima facie* to address one of the main challenges facing Avicenna and the *mutakallimūn*, which is, once again, figuring out a way to distinguish eternal things which *are* uncaused (God's self; God) from eternal things which are *not* uncaused (God's attributes; the heavens). This is because Avicenna's assertion that everything which is changeable falls into these two states could be taken to restrict "divisibility into two states" to sublunary things which come to be and pass away. A defender of (2b) could argue, I suppose, that the existence of some eternal things – celestial spheres and celestial souls – can still be characterized by potentiality and imperfection, and that therefore their existence can be taken to be divisible into, and hence a composite of, actuality and potentiality, or perfection and imperfection.

But the defender of interpretation (2b) will still be unable to account for the celestial intellects, which Avicenna clearly takes to be entirely actual and perfect, at least according to L53. That is why, after all, he felt the need to appeal to the idea of God's being not only perfect but also *above* perfection. If the existence of the celestial intellects is not, therefore, a mixture of actuality and potentiality, or a mixture of perfection and imperfection, they will not be divisible into, and hence composites of, those states. And if their existence is not composed of those states, it will be uncaused just as God's existence is uncaused. So while interpretation (2b), with a little tweaking, is better than interpretation (1) at accommodating at least *some* eternal things (i.e., the celestial spheres and the celestial souls), interpretation (2b) still fails to entail a distinction between caused and uncaused among eternal things which are all fully actual and perfect; between the celestial intellects and God, that is.

The upshot is that none of these interpretations – (1), (2a) or (2b) – is entirely satisfactory. Let us assume that this ambiguity, or perhaps confusion, is real, and not the result of a scribal error which has corrupted the *Ḥikma ᶜArūḍiyya* manuscript we have and left it without some key phrases or sentences. We then seem to have little choice but to view L58/L73 as nothing more than the young Avicenna's first stab at his new matrix of distinctions. L58/L73 should be taken as evidence, in other words, that at this very early stage of his career Avicenna still inhabited the thought-world of tenth-century *kalām*, a world in which the notions of eternality and uncausedness were bound so closely together that they were held to be mutually implicative; yet at the same time he struggled to flesh out and usefully apply al-ᶜĀmirī's new and exciting suggestion that God is necessary of existence in Himself.[3]

[3] In fact Avicenna's assertion (*Ḥikma ᶜArūḍiyya* 82r5-6) that "*It has already been said* that the First is necessary of existence in itself (*wa-qad qīla inna l-awwala wājibu al-wujūdi bi-dh-dhāti*)", could be taken to refer to al-ᶜĀmirī's earlier use of that phrase to describe God. Alternatively the *qad qīla* may refer merely to Avicenna's own identification of the First with the necessary of existence in itself in L58/73. If that were the case, however, I would have expected to see the first-person *qad qulnā* ("we have already said") rather than the impersonal *qad qīla*.

The rest of this chapter focuses on Avicenna's attempts to sort out this confusion by applying his matrix of distinctions in a more coherent way. In the *Mabdaʾ wa-maʿād*, Avicenna will use a more purely ontological method of constructing the matrix of distinctions; and then, in the *Ilāhiyyāt* of his *Shifāʾ*, he will view his newly sharpened distinction between essence and existence as a new and better way to provide the conceptual divisibility, compositeness and causedness that he appealed to in the *Ḥikma ʿArūḍiyya*. Finally, in the *Ishārāt wa-tanbīhāt*, Avicenna will allude, in a very compressed manner, to many of the different approaches he articulated in preceding works.

Although from later descriptions of the work Avicenna almost certainly discussed metaphysical issues in *The Available and the Valid* (*al-Ḥāṣil wa-l-maḥṣūl*), a book he composed immediately following the *Ḥikma ʿArūḍiyya*, it is sadly lost, and we must jump ahead 12 years, to 1013, when Avicenna composed his next *summa*, *The Origin and the Destination* (*al-Mabdaʾ wa-l-maʿād*). Given the fact that the *Ḥāṣil wa-maḥṣūl* is not extant, and given the fact that Avicenna's correspondence with al-Bīrūnī (which was also composed soon after the *Ḥikma ʿArūḍiyya*) contains no information directly relevant to the distinctions between necessary existence and possible existence and between being in itself and being through another, it is difficult to say whether or not there were any intermediate steps which Avicenna took between his discussion in the *Ḥikma ʿArūḍiyya* and his discussion in the *Mabdaʾ wa-maʿād*.

In any case, Avicenna takes a very different approach in the *Mabdaʾ wa-maʿād* to describing and applying his matrix of distinctions. To be precise, he employs some terminology (e.g., *matā/idhā furiḍa ghayra mawjūdin*) which is identical to that employed by ar-Rāghib al-Iṣfahānī in L72; refers to a concept (viz., the inconceivability of the necessary's non-existence) which is identical to that proposed by Ibn Miskawayh; and appeals to an example (viz., 2+2=4) which is identical to that offered by al-ʿĀmirī:

L74

Ibn Sīnā, *al-Mabdaʾ wa-l-maʿād*, 2,4-17

> *1. On defining the necessary of existence and the possible of existence*
>
> The Necessary of existence is the existent which, when postulated as non-existent [*matā furiḍa ghayra mawjūdin*], an absurdity occurs. The possible of existence is that which, when postulated as either non-existent or existent, no absurdity occurs. The necessary of existence is the necessary [*aḍ-ḍarūrī*], while the possible of existence is that in which there is no necessity at all [*alladhī lā ḍarūrata fīhi*], i.e., neither in its existence or in its non-existence. This is what we mean by "possible of existence" in this context. If what is in potentiality were what is meant by "possible of existence", "possible" would be said of all that could correctly

[be said] to exist [*ʿalā kulli ṣaḥīḥi l-wujūdi*], this having been explained in detail in the *Logic*.[4]

Next, the necessary of existence may be in itself [*bi-dhātihi*] and it may be *not* in itself [*lā bi-dhātihi*]. That which is necessary of existence in itself [*wājibu l-wujūdi bi-dhātihi*] is that on whose account [*li-dhātihi*] (and not on account of anything else, whichever thing that might be) postulating its non-existence becomes absurd. The necessary of existence *not* in itself is that which becomes necessary of existence on account of postulating [the existence of] something which is not [identical to] it, such as the fact that four is necessary of existence not in itself, but [only] when two and two are postulated; and the fact that being burned and burning [i.e., burning something else] are necessary of existence not in themselves, but [only] when contact between the natural active potentiality and the natural passive potentiality (I mean [the potentiality] to burn and be burned) is postulated.

In L74 the matrix of distinctions articulated so tentatively in L58/L73 is restructured. The most striking difference between Avicenna's first discussion of necessary and possible existence in the *Ḥikma ʿArūḍiyya* (i.e., L58/L73), composed around 1001, and his discussion here in the *Mabdaʾ wa-maʿād* (i.e., L74), composed around 1013, lies in the fact that in the *Ḥikma ʿArūḍiyya* Avicenna begins by distinguishing between the necessary of existence in itself and the necessary of existence through another, whereas in the *Mabdaʾ wa-maʿād* Avicenna begins with a distinction between the necessary of existence and the possible of existence.

What is the significance of this change? My sense is that in the *Mabdaʾ wa-maʿād* Avicenna is formulating an alternative approach to the idea of the necessary of existence in itself, an approach which he would modify and partially abandon in the *Ilāhiyyāt* of the *Shifāʾ*, and then return to in the *Najāt*, into which work this and the following *Mabdaʾ wa-maʿād* passage were copied and pasted. Let me explain. As I discussed above, Avicenna began in the *Ḥikma ʿArūḍiyya* with a distinction between the necessary of existence in itself, and the necessary of existence through another. He then went on immediately to imply that the former is uncaused and the latter is caused because the former is simple and the latter composite; composed, that is, of two modes of existence, necessary of existence through another and possible of existence in itself, if interpretation

[4] This may refer to the *Shorter Summary of Logic* (*al-Mukhtaṣar al-asghar fī l-manṭiq*), composed at roughly the same time as the same time as the *Mabdaʾ wa-maʿād*; see Gutas 1988, 112. Given the fact that Avicenna copied the *Shorter Summary* and pasted it into the first section of the *Najāt*, which is devoted to logic; given the fact that this passage (i.e., L74) is itself copied and pasted into the *Najāt* (*K. an-Najāt*, 366,3-367,1); and given the fact that Avicenna did not excise the internal reference in the copied-and-pasted version in the *Najāt*; the *Shorter Summary* passage to which Avicenna seems to refer in L74 above is almost certainly that reproduced in *K. an-Najāt*, 38,7-39,9.

(2a) is correct; or composed of the states of potentiality and actuality, or of perfection and imperfection, if interpretation (2b) is correct.

In the *Mabdaʾ wa-maʿād* (2,5-11), on the other hand, Avicenna begins with the claim that the basic distinction is between the necessary of existence, which *by definition* is that whose non-existence is inconceivable; and the possible of existence, which *by definition* is that whose non-existence and whose existence are conceivable. In other words, Avicenna appeals to what he seems to think is an *a priori* difference between necessary and possible existence. It is only in the second half of the chapter (2,12-17) that we encounter the distinction between the necessary of existence in itself and the necessary of existence through another, the distinction which fronted the discussion in the *Ḥikma ʿArūḍiyya*. In other words, Avicenna now seems to feel that the ontological distinction between necessary of existence and possible of existence is sufficiently intuitive that he need not appeal to the latter's compositeness to explain its causedness, a move which would have pushed the in itself/through another distinction to the fore, as was the case with L58/L73, assuming interpretation (2a) or (2b) is correct.

One effect of this new move is that Avicenna can identify the necessary of existence through another and the possible of existence in itself more strictly in the *Mabdaʾ wa-maʿād* than he had been able to in the *Ḥikma ʿArūḍiyya*. In the *Mabdaʾ wa-maʿād* Avicenna not only claims that the two modes "necessary of existence through another" and "possible of existence in itself" appear to be extensionally identical (that is, any being of which one mode is predicated will also be subject to predication by the other mode), he hints that the two modes are intensionally identical as well (that is, being necessary of existence through another has the same meaning as being possible of existence in itself). Remember that in the *Ḥikma ʿArūḍiyya* Avicenna highlighted the intensional difference between being necessary of existence through another and being possible of existence in itself, in order to flush out the compositeness, and hence causedness, of any being of which both modes are predicated (assuming, that is, that interpretation [2a] is correct). In the *Mabdaʾ wa-maʿād*, by contrast, compositeness is no longer needed to explain the causedness of all beings other than God, so the two modes can now be identified intensionally.

In the *Mabdaʾ wa-maʿād* a new argument is introduced to identify the necessary of existence through another with the possible of existence in itself:

L75

Ibn Sīnā, *al-Mabdaʾ wa-l-maʿād* 1, 3,2-15

3. On the fact that the necessary of existence through another is possible of existence in itself

All that is necessary of existence through another is possible of existence in itself, because the necessity of the existence of whatever is necessary of existence through another, is a consequence of some relation and some connection [*tābiʿun li-nisbatin mā wa-iḍāfatin*]. Taking into consideration relation and

> connection is something other than taking into consideration the very thing itself which possesses a relation and a connection. So necessity of existence is established [in this case] only by considering this relation. Taking into consideration the self alone will logically entail either necessity of existence, possibility of existence or impossibility of existence [*fa-ᶜtibāru dh-dhāti waḥdahā lā yakhlū immā an yakūna muqtaḍiyan li-wujūbi l-wujūdi aw muqtaḍiyan li-imkāni l-wujūdi aw muqtaḍiyan li-mtināᶜi l-wujūdi*]. Now it cannot logically entail the impossibility of existence, because everything whose existence is impossible either in itself or through another will not exist; nor can it entail necessary existence, since we have already asserted that [with regard to] that whose existence is necessary in itself, the necessity of its existing through another is impossible. It remains therefore that taking into consideration itself [alone], it will be possible of existence; taking into consideration the appearance of the relation to that other, it will be necessary of existence, and taking into consideration the disappearance of the relation which is to that other, it will be impossible of existence; [all this] given that its self, in itself, with no conditions [attached], is possible of existence. It is now clear that all that is necessary of existence through another is possible of existence in itself.[5]

Following upon the *a priori* distinction between being necessary of existence and being possible of existence articulated the first *Mabdaʾ wa-maᶜād* passage (i.e., L74), Avicenna argues in the second *Mabdaʾ wa-maᶜād* passage (i.e., L75) that we can conceive of the existence of something which is possible of existence only in the context of a causal relation, a causal relation which *makes* the possible of existence in itself necessary of existence through another. The necessary of existence, by contrast, can be imagined to exist entirely on its own, without any causal relation having been supposed.

The causedness of that which is necessary of existence through another and possible of existence in itself therefore derives from the fact that its necessary existence is only ever a consequence of a relation, and not from the fact that possessing two mutually implicative modes (being necessary of existence through another and being possible of existence in itself, according to interpretation [2a]) or states (being potential and being actual, or being perfect and being imperfect, according to interpretation [2b]) entails a compositeness which requires a composer, and hence a cause.

The difference between the *Ḥikma ᶜArūḍiyya*'s appeal to compositeness to explain the causedness of the necessary of existence through another and the possible of existence in itself, and the *Mabdaʾ wa-maᶜād*'s appeal to our intuition that whatever is necessary of existence through another will by definition be contingent upon that relation with the other and hence caused, is one that will play out in the middle part of Avicenna's career. As I mentioned

[5] This passage is reproduced in *K. an-najāt*, 367,7-368,9.

above, this is mainly because the *Mabda*ʾ *wa-ma*ʿ*ād*'s treatment of this issue was lifted and plopped into the *Najāt*.

How does Avicenna's construction of the matrix of distinctions change from the *Ḥikma* ʿ*Arūḍiyya* and the *Mabda*ʾ *wa-ma*ʿ*ād* to the *Ilāhiyyāt* of the *Shifā*ʾ? In *Ilāhiyyāt* 1.6, Avicenna begins as he did in the *Mabda*ʾ *wa-ma*ʿ*ād*, by making an ontological distinction; but he phrases it slightly differently:

L76

Ibn Sīnā, *Kitāb ash-shifā*ʾ*/Ilāhiyyāt (1)* 1.6, 37,7-11
Avicenna, *Liber de philosophia prima sive scientia divina I-IV*, 43,8-15

Things which fall into [the category of] existence bear dividing in the mind into two subdivisions [*inna l-umūra llatī tadkhulu fī l-wujūdi taḥtamilu fī l-*ʿ*aqli l-inqisāma ilā qismayni = Dicemus igitur quod ea quae cadunt sub esse possunt in intellectu dividi in duo*]. One is that which, when considered in itself, its existence does not follow necessarily [*mā idhā* ʿ*tubira bi-dhātihi lam yajib wujūduhu = quod, cum consideratum fuerit per se, eius esse erit necesse*] (and obviously its existence is not impossible either, for otherwise it would not fall into [the category of] existence), and this thing is found to be in the domain of possibility [*fī ḥayyizi l-imkāni = in termino possibilitas*]. The other is that which, when considered in itself, its existence follows necessarily. We say that the necessary of existence in itself has no cause, and that the possible of existence in itself has a cause.

After listing the various implications of the fact that the necessary of existence in itself is uncaused – such as being necessary of existence in all respects, and not being equivalent to anything else, or composed of several other things, or essentially similar to anything else – Avicenna then goes on to explain why the necessary of existence in itself is uncaused:

L77

Ibn Sīnā, *Kitāb ash-shifā*ʾ*/Ilāhiyyāt (1)* 1.6, 38,1-5
Avicenna, *Liber de philosophia prima sive scientia divina I-IV*, 44,24-31

Now the fact that the necessary of existence in itself has no cause is obvious, because if the necessary of existence had a cause for its existence, its existence would be through it [i.e., through that cause]; and everything whose existence is through something, when it is considered in itself apart from anything else, existence will not follow necessarily for it. Everything which, when considered in itself apart from anything else, and for which existence does not follow necessarily, will not be necessary of existence in itself. Thus it is clear that the necessary of existence has no cause.

Even though Avicenna's structuring of his matrix of distinctions in the *Ilāhiyyāt* is very close to that found in the *Mabdaʾ wa-maᶜād*, there seems even so to be a subtle development. Avicenna does not appeal in the *Ilāhiyyāt* to the idea that a logical absurdity will occur when the necessary of existence is held to be non-existent, an appeal which is prominent in the first *Mabdaʾ wa-maᶜād* passage (i.e., L74). Here in the *Ilāhiyyāt*, in fact, Avicenna seems to be combining elements from the two *Mabdaʾ wa-maᶜād* passages discussed above. From the first *Mabdaʾ wa-maᶜād* passage (i.e., L74) Avicenna draws the ontological basis for the distinction; it appears in the *Ilāhiyyāt* passage as an appeal to the permissibility in the mind (*taḥtamilu fī l-ᶜaql*) of making the distinction. From the second *Mabdaʾ wa-maᶜād* passage (i.e., L75) Avicenna draws the considered in itself/considered in relation distinction.

Later on in the chapter, however, Avicenna makes an important move: he introduces the term *māhiyya* (essence) into the discussion. Avicenna makes a distinction between a *māhiyya* which is sufficient for a thing to exist and a *māhiyya* which is not sufficient for it to exist (38,17-18). The existence of that which has a *māhiyya* sufficient for it to exist will be uncaused (38,18-39,1); whereas the existence of a thing which has a *māhiyya* insufficient for it to exist will be caused (39,2-4).

Avicenna's distinction is less important for what it actually expresses than what it may have brought to his mind. What I mean is that Avicenna tosses the term *māhiyya* into this discussion almost as an afterthought. Nevertheless, his appeal to *māhiyya*, however incidental it may be to his present argument, is highly significant, because it is at this point, I believe, that it occurs to him that he can appeal to the distinction between essence and existence – so clearly held in the previous chapter (*Ilāhiyyāt* 1.5) to be intensionally distinct yet extensionally identical – in much the same way that he appealed to the notion of divisibility into two modes or states in the *Ḥikma ᶜArūḍiyya*: to explain causedness through compositeness.

It is true that in *Ilāhiyyāt* 1.6 Avicenna's equation of being necessary of existence in itself and being uncaused rested on much the same basis as it had in the *Mabdaʾ wa-maᶜād*. But in *Ilāhiyyāt* 8.4 Avicenna will make the claim, when discussing why the First is necessary of existence in itself, and why the First is the only thing in the universe which is necessary of existence in itself, that the First is not distinguishable into *māhiyya* (essence) and *wujūd* (existence) (343,10-15); that the necessary of existence cannot be a composite (345,6-346,8); that therefore *māhiyya* and *wujūd* are identical in the necessary of existence in itself (346,8-12); and that everything else is caused, because in them *māhiyya* must be combined with *wujūd* in order to exist (346,13-347,16).

What Avicenna has done in the *Ilāhiyyāt* is to add the essence/existence distinction to the matrix of distinctions he structured in the *Mabdaʾ wa-maᶜād*. As I just mentioned, the essence/existence distinction is not crucial to *Ilāhiyyāt* 1.6's articulation of the matrix of distinctions, since Avicenna could have left it out of that passage without creating any fatal weaknesses in his arguments. So why should it appear in the first place? To my mind Avicenna brought up the essence/existence distinction in order to side-step the objections of critics who could have argued either that the link between being possible of existence and being caused was not as intuitive as Avicenna seemed to be taking for granted; or that the link between being necessary of existence through another and being caused was so intuitive as to smack of circularity. Were he ever to be attacked in this way, Avicenna could now appeal to the causedness of everything composed of essence and existence. And with space not an issue in the *Shifāʾ*, Avicenna had the luxury of including arguments which he may have felt compelled to excise in the more compressed *Mabdaʾ wa-maʿād* and *Najāt*.

Most compressed of all was Avicenna's late work, the *Ishārāt wa-tanbīhāt*. Here is what he says there about being necessary of existence:

L78

Ibn Sīnā, *Kitāb al-ishārāt wa-t-tanbīhāt*, 140,12-151,2

> Warning: When you examine every existent in and of itself and apart from any other, it is such that the existence it possesses follows necessarily, or does not [follow necessarily]. If it [i.e., the existence it possesses] does follow necessarily, then it [the existent] is what is real in itself [*al-ḥaqqu bi-dhātihi*] and that whose existence is necessary in itself, namely, the Self-subsisting [*al-qayyūm*]. If it [existence] does not follow necessarily, it cannot be said to be impossible in itself after having been assumed to be an existent. On the contrary, if a condition is added [*in qurina ... sharṭun*] to taking it in itself, such as the condition that its cause be non-existent, then it would become impossible; or [if] the condition that its cause exist [is added], then it would become necessary. Now if no condition is attached – neither the existence or non-existence of its cause – it will, in itself, be left with the third alternative, namely, possibility, because taken in and of itself, it will be the thing which is neither necessary nor impossible. Every existent is thus either necessary of existence in itself, or possible of existence in itself.

In the *Ishārāt* Avicenna's approach has changed. He introduces the distinction between necessary and possible existence following discussions of two other distinctions. The first distinction he discusses is that between essence and existence (138,2-139,13). In this sense the *Ishārāt* follows the pattern of the *Shifāʾ*, in which the discussion of necessary and possible existence (*Ilāhiyyāt* 1.6) follows immediately upon a discussion of essence and existence (*Ilāhiyyāt* 1.5).

The *Ishārāt* departs from the pattern of the *Ilāhiyyāt*, however, in that a discussion of the different types of causes (139,14-140,9) is interposed between the *Ishārāt*'s discussion of essence and existence and its discussion of necessary and possible existence. In that discussion of causation Avicenna distinguishes between causes of essence (the formal and material) and causes of existence (the efficient and final). Avicenna also makes the claim, examined in Chapters 8, 9 and 10, that the two causes of existence are complementary, in the sense that the final is prior in terms of its essence and the efficient is prior in terms of its existence. In other words Avicenna inserts, in summary fashion, the results of his discussion of the four causes in *Ilāhiyyāt* 6.1 and 6.5. The only difference is that in *Ilāhiyyāt* 6.1, Avicenna had distinguished between causes that are *intrinsic to* the effect (formal and material) and causes that are *extrinsic to* the effect (efficient and final), whereas in the *Ishārāt* Avicenna distinguishes between causes *of essence* (formal and material) and causes *of existence* (efficient and final).[6]

The reason why Avicenna structures his discussions in the *Ishārāt* this way is that he wishes to press his distinction between necessary and possible existence into the immediate service of proving God's existence, a task he was willing to separate into two different chapters – 1.6 and 8.4 – in the *Ilāhiyyāt*. To do this he must introduce the distinction between essence and existence in the context of causation. The underlying message of the *Ishārāt* passage is that the distinction between essence and existence is crucial to his argument for the existence of God, since everything other than God requires something to combine its essence with its existence.

The argument in *Ilāhiyyāt* 8.4 for the uncausedness of the necessary of existence in itself, which rests on the fact that the necessary of existence in itself is not a composite of essence and existence and thus requires no composer, is merely an adjunct to the ontological argument for the uncausedness of the necessary of existence in itself which appears in *Ilāhiyyāt* 1.6 and which derives from the *Mabdaʾ wa-maʿād*. In the *Ishārāt*, by contrast, the distinction between essence and existence and the discussion of the necessary of existence in itself are joined together by a discussion of causation.

The essence/existence distinction thus appears to be more integral to the *Ishārāt*'s discussion of the necessary of existence in itself than it had been to the parallel discussion of the necessary of existence in itself in *Ilāhiyyāt* 1.6. Whether or not this is because Avicenna felt that pressing the essence/existence distinction into service in this way really made his discussion of the necessary of existence in itself more coherent, is very difficult to say, because the *Ishārāt* does not contain philosophical arguments *per se* but rather reminders – almost mnemonic devices, like bulleted lecture notes – of those arguments.

The most that can be said about this series of discussions in the *Ishārāt*, perhaps, is that we find there, in extremely condensed form, threads from all the strands of thought expressed in previous works: the *Ḥikma ʿArūḍiyya*'s linking of causedness to being composed of two modes or states of existence; the

[6] On this development see again Wisnovsky 2003a.

Mabdaʾ wa-maᶜād's appeal to our *a priori* intuitions about the causedness of the possible of existence; *Ilāhiyyāt* 1.5's claims that essence and existence are intensionally distinct but extensionally identical; and *Ilāhiyyāt* 6.5's and the *Najāt*'s distinction between the complementary ways final and efficient causes cause their effects, the former in terms of essence, the latter in terms of existence.

I mentioned at the beginning of Chapter 11 that Davidson detected two ways Avicenna's matrix of distinctions is put to use in proofs of God's existence, one articulated in the *Najāt* and the *Ishārāt*, the other in the *Shifāʾ* (explicitly) and the *Dānishnāma* (implicitly).[7] In the *Shifāʾ* and *Dānishnāma*, Davidson claims, we find the distinction between necessary and possible existence juxtaposed with Avicenna's argument for God's existence from the impossibility of an infinite regress of efficient causes. In the *Najāt* and the *Ishārāt*, by contrast, the distinction between necessary and possible existence is juxtaposed with Avicenna's argument for God's existence from the impossibility of a self-sufficient totality of possible things. In the *Shifāʾ* and *Dānishnāma*, the distinction between necessary and possible existence is a rather redundant supplement to what is a more purely cosmological argument for God's existence. In the *Najāt* and *Ishārāt*, however, the distinction between necessary and possible existence is crucial to what amounts to a combined ontological-cosmological argument for God's existence.

I also pointed out at the beginning of Chapter 11 that Davidson's analysis, though philosophically acute, was based only on works from Avicenna's middle and late periods. My claim was that ignoring the works from the early period, such as the *Ḥikma ᶜArūḍiyya* and the *Mabdaʾ wa-maᶜād*, weakened Davidson's analysis in two ways. The first is that it is in Avicenna's earliest works that we can expect to find the rawest evidence of the sources of his thinking on this complex of problems. Any conclusions about sources and influences drawn only from Avicenna's middle and late works, will therefore end up being tentative. The second weakness is that the earliest works are the only evidence we have of Avicenna's starting-point, that is, the origin from which his theories evolved.

What do these early works tell us about the sources of Avicenna's matrix of distinctions and of the different ways he applied that matrix in his works? And how might that information allow us to revise Davidson's hypothesis? In Chapters 12-14 it has emerged that the background to Avicenna's matrix of distinctions was very complex. The Arabic version of *De Interpretatione* 12-13, mediated through al-Fārābī's commentary, allowed Avicenna to think that the primary modal opposition was between the contradictory terms *mumkin* (possible) and *wājib* (necessary), rather than between *mumkin* (possible) and *mumtaniᶜ* (impossible). This move, combined with Isḥāq b. Ḥunayn's and al-

[7] Davidson 1987, 281-310 and 350-361.

Fārābī's use of the existential root *w-j-d* in contexts where Greek authors had understood *einai* only in its copulative sense, encouraged Avicenna to hold that not only "possible" but "contingent" was included in *mumkin*'s semantic field; and thus to think that "caused" might be an intuitively apprehended characteristic of something which is *mumkin al-wujūd.*

In his *Commentary on the De Interpretatione* al-Fārābī also came up with a distinction between *mumkin al-wujūd bi-nafsihi* and *wājib al-wujūd bi-nafsihi.* But al-Fārābī introduced his distinction in the context of the problem of future contingents, and of the effect that God's foreknowledge of those future events might have on the question of determinism. This is *not* the context in which Avicenna devises and employs his matrix of distinctions. Although al-Fārābī and the Arabic *De Interpretatione* may have supplied the terminology, the context was supplied by *Metaphysics* 5.5 and by the *mutakallimūn.*

The Arabic version of *Metaphysics* 5.5, mediated by Alexander and Ammonius, provided Avicenna with the idea that the necessity which God possesses consists in invariability: to be more specific, the qualities of simplicity, eternality and immutability. From the Neoplatonists Avicenna inherited a tradition which elevated simplicity above the other characteristics of the divine. In Neoplatonic terms God's simplicity was often expressed as His perfection, now understood as referring to His being whole and non-composite, and hence causally self-sufficient.

Divine simplicity was not only a tenet of Neoplatonists. The *mutakallimūn* had vigorous debates about the extent to which divine simplicity was infringed upon by holding that God's attributes of knowledge and power, for example, enjoyed some kind of separate reality instead of being distinguishable from the divine self only conceptually. From the Ashᶜarites and Māturīdites Avicenna inherited a tradition of discussions about how to distinguish between two or more eternal things. God, they claimed, was eternal in Himself (*qadīm bi-nafsihi*). And though they could not quite bring themselves to say that the attributes were eternal through another (*qadīma bi-ghayrihā*), al-Māturīdī did hold that Heaven was eternal *a parte post* through another (*bāqiya bi-ghayrihā*).

I believe that what this background tells us is that the distinction which Avicenna was searching for above all others was one which could differentiate between an eternal thing which is causally self-sufficient and an eternal thing which is not causally self-sufficient. This is precisely the distinction which the Neoplatonists and the *mutakallimūn* were searching for. The only difference in their searches was that Avicenna had in mind the heavens when he thought of things which were eternal but not causally self-sufficient; the Neoplatonists had in mind the full complement of gods, minds, souls and demiurges; and the *mutakallimūn* had in mind the divine attributes. The Neoplatonists, committed as they were to integrating Plato's and Aristotle's cosmologies, were ultimately incapable of overcoming the duality that resulted from seeing God as both final and efficient cause, as causally self-sufficient but also causally productive. The

Sunnī *mutakallimūn* held back from making a clean jump to holding that the attributes were eternal through another (*qadīma bi-ghayrihā*) because they worried that it would imply too much otherness in the relationship between God's self and His attributes. It would also complicate their attempts to use *qadīm* in the sense of uncaused in their proofs of God's existence.

The conclusion we can draw from Avicenna's early works about the sources of his matrix of distinctions is that the Neoplatonists and the *mutakallimūn* defined the problem for Avicenna, while the Arabic Aristotle, mediated through al-Fārābī, provided the terminology and some of the conceptual tools he used to solve it. Finally, by applying the phrase "necessary of existence in itself" to God, al-ᶜĀmirī provided the young Avicenna with a crucial element of his matrix. This conclusion about sources does not, in itself, invalidate Davidson's hypothesis of a two-track approach in Avicenna's middle and late works towards the use of the necessary of existence/possible of existence distinction in proofs of God's existence.

What it does show is that the problem of the eternity of the *world* is less overarching than Davidson makes it out to be, and consequently that the opposing positions of the *mutakallimūn* and the philosophers on this particular issue should not be seen as signifying some basic or "natural" opposition in their philosophies. Avicenna's position on the distinction between essence and existence was shown in Chapter 7 to be closer in important ways to that of the Ashᶜarites and Māturīdites than it was to al-Fārābī's position, which in turn was closer in important ways to that of the Muᶜtazilites than it was to Avicenna's. In the same vein I have shown that while Avicenna employs the terminology and a number of important conceptual tools from the Arabic Aristotle, al-Fārābī and the Neoplatonists to construct his matrix of distinctions, the question he originally wanted to use that matrix to answer was posed to him by the *mutakallimūn*. The enthusiasm with which post-classical Sunnī *mutakallimūn* and Shiᶜite *falāsifa* – not to mention medieval Latin theologians and philosophers – later employed Avicenna's matrix of distinctions in their proofs of God's existence and in their discussions of epistemology and the divine attributes, is a clear sign that Avicenna's matrix transcended the particular debate over the createdness or eternality of the world.

Now to the question of development. Can the series of different ways Avicenna articulates and employs his matrix of distinctions be described as an evolution in his views? And how might our conclusions about that allow us to revise Davidson's hypothesis? I believe that the different ways Avicenna structured his matrix of distinctions do constitute evidence of evolution. But I must say precisely what I mean by "evolution". I use the term carefully, to refer to the fact that the different ways Avicenna structured his matrix of distinctions were both responses to environmental stimuli and the results of a self-propelled algorithm.

External factors which helped to shape the ways Avicenna structured his matrix of distinctions and employed it in different texts include, for example, the length of the text and the intellectual level of the intended audience. In a relatively brief compendium, such as the *Mabdaʾ wa-maʿād* or the *Najāt*, Avicenna allowed himself less space to explore interesting implications of his arguments than he did in the much lengthier *Shifāʾ*. In the *Ishārāt*, a text intended for very advanced students of philosophy, Avicenna's argumentation is so compressed that it can be interpreted in very different ways; this is much less the case in the *Mabdaʾ wa-maʿād*, written for a civilian patron.

By "self-propelled algorithm" I simply refer to an internal continuum in all Avicenna's texts: the degree of philosophical coherence Avicenna expected of himself. Even this continuum changed in subtle ways. For example, in some texts, such as the *Mabdaʾ wa-maʿād*, Avicenna felt that the link between being possible of existence and being caused was so intuitive that he did not need to appeal to an argument for compositeness to forge that link. In other texts, such as the *Ḥikma ʿArūḍiyya* and the *Ilāhiyyāt* of the *Shifāʾ*, he felt the need to buttress that intuition with an argument for compositeness. In the *Ḥikma ʿArūḍiyya*, that argument for compositeness was based on the premise that what is necessary of existence through another and possible of existence in itself is a composite of those two existential modes, or of the states actuality/potentiality or perfection/imperfection. In the *Ilāhiyyāt* of the *Shifāʾ*, the argument for compositeness was based on the premise that what is necessary of existence through another and possible of existence in itself is a composite of essence and existence.

In short, as long as we resist thinking about Avicenna's intellectual development in teleological terms, as long as we are clear that evolution does not necessarily mean resolution, I think it can safely be said that the way Avicenna structured his matrix of distinctions and employed it in different texts evolved over his lifetime. Once again, this conclusion about evolution does not, in itself, invalidate Davidson's hypothesis of a two-track approach in Avicenna's middle and late works towards the use of the necessary of existence/possible of existence distinction in proofs of God's existence.

What it does show is that the seeds of what Davidson sees as a two-track approach can be found in two of Avicenna's earliest works, the *Ḥikma ʿArūḍiyya* and the *Mabdaʾ wa-maʿād*. In addition, taking these two works into account, and showing how Avicenna's thinking on this issue evolves over his lifetime, weakens Davidson's hypothesis in the sense that the external and internal factors which combined to produce a certain structure of the matrix of distinctions in a particular text at a particular time now appear to be very complex. Given this complexity, the discussions in which Avicenna's matrix of distinctions appears will resist being divided according to a single, all-governing criterion: usefulness or superfluousness in proofs of God's existence.

Conclusion

What have I accomplished in this book? In an effort to analyze the sources and evolution of Avicenna's metaphysics, I focused on the answers Avicenna and his predecessors gave to two fundamental pairs of questions: what is the soul and how does it cause the body; and what is God and how does He cause the world? To respond to these challenges Avicenna invented new concepts and distinctions and reinterpreted old ones.

In Part I I traced the complicated history of one such concept, "perfection", and of the distinctions associated with perfection. I began by discussing how Aristotle's varied uses of the Greek term *entelekheia* ("actuality") and of a cluster of other terms related to *entelekheia* – such as *energeia* ("activity"), *to teleion* ("the complete"), *teleiôsis* ("completion") and *teleiotês* ("completeness") – were interpreted by late-antique commentators, both Peripatetic and Neoplatonist. I showed that the commentators juggled all these terms around in an effort to reconcile what appeared on the surface to be incompatible views. Peripatetic commentators focused their attention on reconciling Aristotle's seemingly inconsistent uses of *entelekheia* to define the soul and to define change. Neoplatonic commentators focused their attention on reconciling two larger inconsistencies, which appeared to divide Plato (at least as understood by Neoplatonists such as Plotinus) and Aristotle (at least as understood by Peripatetics such as Alexander). The first was the inconsistency between the Aristotelian doctrine that God operated as a final cause, and the Platonic doctrine that God operated as an efficient cause. The second was the inconsistency between the Aristotelian doctrine that the soul is inseparable from the body, and the Platonic doctrine that the soul is separable from the body. Finally I described how the commentators' reconciliation work shaped the way these terms were translated into Arabic in the ninth and tenth centuries, and I explained the ways in which Avicenna, in his own discussions of the soul, appropriated the conceptual and terminological legacy he inherited from earlier thinkers and translators.

In Part II I argued that Avicenna's famous distinction between essence (*māhiyya*) and existence (*wujūd*) owes a great deal to earlier debates within Islamic doctrinal theology, or *kalām*, concerning the relationship between "thing" (*shayʾ*) and "existent" (*mawjūd*). I also described how Avicenna integrated his distinction between essence and existence into the cosmology of procession and reversion bequeathed to him by the Neoplatonic commentators; and how this integration led to an unacceptable dualism in God, now seen to be a composite of efficient and final causality, of involvement with and transcendence of the world. Finally, I analyzed the background to and development of the matrix of distinctions Avicenna devised to skirt this dualism, a matrix constructed around the idea that God is the only being which, by virtue of itself, exists necessarily (*wājib al-wujūd bi-dhātihi*). Once again, Avicenna is shown to have drawn much inspiration from preceding *kalām* debates, this time about how divine attributes (*ṣifāt*) such as knowledge (*ᶜilm*) and power (*qudra*) relate to the divine Self (*dhāt*), and about the status of what I have called "meta-attributes" such as eternality (*qidam*), which are attributable not only to the divine Self but to the divine attributes as well.

My general conclusion is that Avicenna's innovations are a turning point in the history of metaphysics. Avicenna is the culmination of one period of synthesis – I refer to it as the "Ammonian" synthesis, after the Neoplatonic commentator Ammonius (d. ca. 521 AD), son of Hermeias – during which philosophers succeeded in incorporating the larger, Neoplatonic project of harmonizing Plato with Aristotle, into the smaller, Peripatetic project of harmonizing Aristotle with himself. Yet Avicenna also stands at the beginning of another period of synthesis, during which philosophers sought to fuse together the Arabic version of the Ammonian synthesis with the ontology and theology of the Muslim *mutakallimūn*. Avicenna's metaphysical theories, translated into Latin, greatly influenced European scholastic thought, but they had an even more profound impact on Islamic intellectual history: the philosophical problems and opportunities engendered by the Avicennian synthesis continued to be debated in the Islamic world up to the end of the nineteenth century.

It is up to the reader to judge whether I have proven or merely suggested the particular hypotheses set out in the Introduction and argued for in the different chapters, as well as the general hypothesis that Avicenna serves as the culmination of the Ammonian synthesis and as the initiator of the Avicennian synthesis. Assuming that I *have* proven them, what are the lessons that different readers can take from my book?

Those scholars of late antiquity and of medieval Europe who ponder about when the late-antique era ended and the medieval began, can infer from my book that at least as far as the history of metaphysics is concerned, the decisive moment occurred around 1001, in the Sāmānid library in the city of Bukhārā in the Central Asian province of Transoxania, far outside their traditional area of focus. For historians of philosophy, the lesson is that Avicenna's thought cannot be properly understood when it is ripped out of the context in which it emerged, and thrust, lifeless, into comparison with earlier thinkers such as Aristotle and later thinkers such as Aquinas. Avicenna read Aristotle very carefully, to be sure; but he read an Arabic version of Aristotle, and viewed Aristotle through the prism of the late-antique commentators. What is more, some of Avicenna's most important ideas were inspired by preceding *kalām* debates. Similarly, Aquinas read Avicenna very carefully; but he read a Latinized version of Avicenna, and viewed Avicenna through the prism of Averroes, among others. And again, some of Aquinas' most important ideas were inspired by preceding debates in Christian theology. My point is that comparative work which decontextualizes the philosophers under examination runs the risk of comparing what in the end are mere metonyms for a cluster of philosophical concepts or arguments selected precisely for their usefulness in serving the comparativist's aim. Such metonymy rarely evokes the rhetoric, complexity, evolution and ultimately underdetermined nature of the philosophy of thinkers as creative and prolific as Aristotle, Avicenna and Aquinas.

Some Arabists may feel that the paucity of reliably edited texts of Arabic philosophy and theology makes a project such as mine so tentative and premature that we should postpone our analyses until some future date when all the relevant works have been subject to critical edition. I can only say in response that I suffer from no delusion about the definitiveness of my treatment of Avicenna's metaphysics; far from it. What I do hope is that readers will find my discussion and analysis thought-provoking, and mostly convincing, and that proving my hypotheses wrong will itself spur the creation of newer and better theories. As Sabra says, regarding the study of Arabic science:

> As for the argument that "we do not yet know enough to ask the big questions", my answer is this: it is only by attempting to formulate appropriate questions that can be fruitfully examined in light of what we now know that we make it possible for others to come up with deeper and more probing questions in the future. We do not know much (that is for certain), but the day when we know "enough" will never come. On the other hand, by altogether abandoning all programs of full-fledged historical research, we only tempt others to fill the vacuum with easy and useless essentialist generalizations.[1]

Ultimately, I shall judge my book a success if readers come away from it with the sense of a moment in the thought-world of a philosopher from a thousand years ago, a moment when the tools which had been crafted to solve old metaphysical problems and to reconcile old metaphysical inconsistencies, themselves became so interesting and powerful that problems and inconsistencies associated with those tools now became the stuff of a new metaphysics: the metaphysics of Latin scholasticism in Europe, and the metaphysics of post-classical *kalām* in the Islamic world.

[1] Sabra 1996, 664.

Appendix I
Tables of Greco-Arabic Translation

T1 *telos* in the Arabic *Metaphysics*

Metaph. = Aristāṭālīs {*ap.* Averroem}, *{Tafsīr} Mā baᶜda ṭ-ṭabīᶜa I-III* [*MBṬ I-III*]

Metaph. 2.1, 993b21 *ghāya*: *MBṬ I* 11,3(*bis*)
Metaph. 2.2, 994b5 *nihāya*: *MBṬ I* 24,8
Metaph. 2.2, 994b9 *eti de to hou heneka telos* = *fa-inna sh-shayʾa lladhī bi-sababihi takūnu l-ashyāʾu huwa ghāyatun*: *MBṬ I* 30,10
Metaph. 2.2, 994b16 *to gar telos peras estin* = *wa-dhālika anna n-nihāyata hiya l-ghāyatu l-maqṣūdatu ilayhā*: *MBṬ I* 33,12-13
Metaph. 3.1, 995b1 *ghāya*: *MBṬ I* 166,7
Metaph. 3.2, 996a24 *ghāya wa-tamām*: *MBṬ I* 183,14
Metaph. 3.2, 996a26 *al-ghāya*: *MBṬ I* 183,15
Metaph. 3.2, 996a26 *tamām*: *MBṬ I* 183,15
Metaph. 3.2, 996b12 *at-tamām*: *MBṬ I* 185,4
Metaph. 3.4, 999b10 *ghāya wa-tamām*: *MBṬ I* 236,4
Metaph. 5.2, 1013a33 *hôs to telos* = *ka-t-tamāmi*: *MBṬ II* 482,3
Metaph. 5.2, 1013a36 *at-tamām*: *MBṬ II* 482,6
Metaph. 5.2, 1013b2 *at-tamām*: *MBṬ II* 482,8
Metaph. 5.2, 1013b11 *at-tamām*: *MBṬ II* 483,1
Metaph. 5.2, 1013b25 *hôs to telos* = *ka-t-tamāmi*: *MBṬ II* 488,1
Metaph. 5.2, 1013b26 *tamāman*: *MBṬ II* 488,3
Metaph. 5.4, 1015a11 *to telos tês genêseôs* = *nihāyatu t-takawwuni*: *MBṬ II* 507,9
Metaph. 5.6, 1016a20 *at-tamām*: *MBṬ II* 532,6
Metaph. 5.16, 1021b23 *at-tamām*: *MBṬ II* 622,3
Metaph. 5.16, 1021b25 *bi-tamāmihā*: *MBṬ II* 622,3
Metaph. 5.16, 1021b25 *at-tamām*: *MBṬ II* 622,3
Metaph. 5.16, 1021b29 *at-tamām*: *MBṬ II* 622,7
Metaph. 5.16, 1021b29 *tamām*: *MBṬ II* 622,6
Metaph. 5.17, 1022a6 *tamām*: *MBṬ II* 628,5
Metaph. 5.24, 1023a34(*bis*) *telos men gar estin hê morphê, teleion de to ekhon telos* = *fa-inna ṣ-ṣūrata tamāmun wa-t-tāmmu huwa lladhī lahu tamāmun*: *MBṬ II* 655,9-10
Metaph. 8.1, 1042a4 *bi-t-tamāmi*: *MBṬ II* 1023,3
Metaph. 8.4, 1044b1 *at-tamām*: *MBṬ II* 1074,2
Metaph. 9.8, 1050a8 *tamām*: *MBṬ II* 1186,6
Metaph. 9.8, 1050a8 *at-tamām*: *MBṬ II* 1186,7
Metaph. 9.8, 1050a17 *tamāmuhā*: *MBṬ II* 1190,9
Metaph. 9.8, 1050a18 *bi-t-tamāmi*: *MBṬ II* 1190,10
Metaph. 9.8, 1050a21 *tamām*: *MBṬ II* 1191,1
Metaph. 9.8, 1050a27 *tamām*: *MBṬ II* 1191,6
Metaph. 9.8, 1050a28 *bi-tamām*: *MBṬ II* 1191,6
Metaph. 9.8, 1051a16 *at-tamām*: *MBṬ II* 1210,10
Metaph. 10.4, 1055a12 *at-tamām*: *MBṬ III* 1301,5
Metaph. 10.4, 1055a13 *at-tamām*: *MBṬ III* 1301,6
Metaph. 10.4, 1055a14 *tamāman*: *MBṬ III* 1301,6

Metaph. 10.4, 1055a15 *at-tamām*: *MBṬ III* 1301,7
Metaph. 12.8, 1074a23 *tamām*: *MBṬ III* 1678,4
Metaph. 12.8, 1074a30 *tamām*: *MBṬ III* 1678,10
Metaph. 12.10, 1075b1 *hôs telos* = *ka-t-tamāmi*: *MBṬ III* 1720, 6

T2 *entelekheia* in the Arabic *Metaphysics*

Metaph. = Arisṭāṭālīs {*ap.* Averroem}, *{Tafsīr} Mā baᶜda ṭ-ṭabīᶜa I-III* [*MBṬ I-III*][1]

Metaph. 4.4, 1007b28 *entelekheiâi* = *bi-l-fiᶜli*: *MBṬ I* 381,12
Metaph. 4.5, 1009a36 *entelekheiâi* = *bi-l-fiᶜli*: *MBṬ I* 409,17
Metaph. 5.4, 1015a19 *entelekheiâi* = *bi-l-fiᶜli*: *MBṬ II* 507,15
Metaph. 5.7, 1017b1 *entelekheiâi* = *bi-l-fiᶜli*: *MBṬ II* 555,18
Metaph. 5.11, 1019a7 *kat' entelekheian* = *bi-l-fiᶜli*: *MBṬ II* 570,1
Metaph. 5.11, 1019a8 *kata entelekheian* = *bi-l-fiᶜli*: *MBṬ II* 570,3
Metaph. 5.11, 1019a10(*bis*) *kat' entelekheian* = *bi-l-fiᶜli*: *MBṬ II* 570,3 and 4
Metaph. 7.9, 1034b17 *entelekheiâi* = *bi-l-fiᶜli*: *MBṬ II* 887,7
Metaph. 7.13, 1039a4 *entelekheiâi* = *bi-l-fiᶜli*: *MBṬ II* 970,8
Metaph. 7.13, 1039a5(*bis*) *entelekheiâi* = *bi-l-fiᶜli*: *MBṬ II* 970,8 and 9
Metaph. 7.13, 1039a7 *entelekheia* = *al-fiᶜl*: *MBṬ II* 970,11
Metaph. 7.13, 1039a14 *entelekheiâi* = *bi-l-fiᶜli*: *MBṬ II* 970,12
Metaph. 7.13, 1039a17 *entelekheiâi* = *bi-l-fiᶜli*: *MBṬ II* 971,2
Metaph. 7.16, 1040b12 *entelekheiâi* = *bi-l-fiᶜli*: *MBṬ II* 997,1
Metaph. 8.3, 1044a9 *entelekheia* = *fiᶜl*: *MBṬ II* 1064,10
Metaph. 9.1, 1045b34 *kata ... entelekheian* = *bi-t-tamāmi wa-l-fiᶜli*: *MBṬ II* 1103,10
Metaph. 9.1, 1045b35 *peri ... entelekheias* = *fī t-tamāmi*: *MBṬ II* 1103,10
Metaph. 9.3, 1047a30 *hê pros tên entelekheian suntithemenê* = *alladhī tarakkaba maᶜa t-tamāmi*: *MBṬ II* 1133,6
Metaph. 9.3, 1047b2 *entelekheiâi* = *bi-t-tamāmi*: *MBṬ II* 1133,11
Metaph. 9.7, 1049a5 *entelekheiâi* = *bi-t-tamāmi*: *MBṬ II* 1165,8
Metaph. 9.8, 1050a21-23 *to gar ergon telos, hê de energeia to ergon, dio kai tounuma energeia legetai kata to ergon kai sunteinei pros tên entelekheian* = *fa-inna l-ᶜamala tamāmun wa-l-fiᶜla l-ᶜamalu wa-li-dhālika ismu l-fiᶜli ayḍan yuqālu ᶜalā l-ᶜamali bi-l-yūnāniyyati wa-yasluku maslaka t-tamāmi*: *MBṬ II* 1191,1-2
Metaph. 12.5, 1071a36 *eti to prôton entelekheiâi* = *wa-ayḍan awwalu fī l-kamāli*: *MBṬ III* 1549,7
Metaph. 12.8, 1074a35-36 *to de ti ên einai ouk ekhei hulên to prôton; gar entelekheia* = *wa-amma mā huwa bi-l-anniyyati l-ūlā fa-laysa lahu ᶜunṣurun li-annahu tamāmun*: *MBṬ III* 1683,8-9

[1] *Metaph.* 11 (*K*), which recapitulates much of Book 9, does not appear to have been translated into Arabic, so the renderings of *entelekheia* at 1065b15.21.22.25.27.33.35, 1066a27.29, and 1066b18 cannot be checked.

T3 *entelekheia, teleiotês and teleiôsis* in the Arabic *De Anima*

DA = Arisṭūṭālīs, *Fī n-nafs* [*FN*]
+ Themistius, *in De Anima* [*TG*] = Thāmasṭiyūs, *Sharḥ Kitāb an-nafs li-Arisṭūṭālīs* [*TA*]
+ Ibn Sīnā, *at-Taᶜlīqāt ᶜalā ḥawāshī Kitāb an-nafs li-Arisṭū* [*MN*]

DA 1.1, 402a26 *entelekheia* = *bi-l-fiᶜli*: *FN* 4,10
+ *MN*: *bi-l-istikmāli* at 75,22 and *bi-l-fiᶜli* at 76,2

DA 2.1, 412a10 *entelekheia* = *anṭalākhiyā yaᶜnī at-tamām*: *FN* 29,11-12
+ *TG* (*ad* 412a6-10), 39,9-10: *to de eidos hê teleiotês kai hôsper anaplêrôsis tês euphuias kai tou dunamei pros to telos proagôgê* = *wa-amma ṣ-ṣūrata fa-hiya l-kamālu wa-ka-annahā tatimmatu t-tahayyuʾi wa-[nqiyādu] ma bi-l-quwwati ilā ghāyatihi*: *TA* 43,5-6
+ *TG* (*ad* 412a10-11), 39,17: *tautên oun tên morphên kai to eidos ei tis entelekheian onomazoi* = *wa-hādhihi l-khilqatu <wa-> ṣ-ṣūratu in sammāhā musamm<ā> anṭalākhiyā ay istikmālan*: *TA* 43,12-13
+ *TG* (*ad* 412a10-11), 39,18: *teleiôsis* = *kamāl*: *TA* 43,15
+ *TG* (*ad* 412a10-11), 39,19-20: *sêmainoi an ouden allo hê entelekheia ê tên hexin tês teleiotêtos* = *fa-laysa yadullu qawluhu anṭalākhiyā fī lisāni l-yūnāniyyīn ᶜalā shayʾin ghayri malakati l-kamāli mina l-khilqati*: *TA* 43,15-44,1
+ *TG* 39,20 (*ad* 412a10-11): *teleiotês* = *kamāl*: *TG* 44,1
+ *TG* (*ad* 412a10-11), 39,21: *entelekheia* = *istikmāl*: *TA* 44,1
+ *TG* (*ad* 412a13-16), 40,3: *anankaion ara tên psukhên eidos einai kai entelekheian kai houtôs ousian hôs eidos* = *fa-qad yajibu ḍarūratan an takūna n-nafsu ṣūratan wa-stikmālan wa-takūna jawharan ᶜalā ṭarīqi ṣ-ṣūrati*: *TA* 45,7-8
+ *TG* (*ad* 412a16-20), 40,12-13: *anankê pasa <to> eidos einai tên psukhên kai entelekheian* = *fa-qad yajibu ḍarūratan min kulli wajhin an takūna n-nafsu hiya ṣ-ṣūratu wa-l-istikmālu*: *TA* 45,18-46,1
+ *MN* : *bi-l-istikmāli* at 91,3.8

DA 2.1, 412a21 *entelekheia* = *anṭalāshiyā*: *FN* 29,19

DA 2.1, 412a22 *entelekheia* = *al-anṭalāshiyā*: *FN* 29,19

DA 2.1, 412a27 *entelekheia* = *anṭalāshiyā wa-huwa awwalu tamāmin*: *FN* 30,3
+ *TG* (*ad* 412a22-28), 41,8: *entelekheia* = *istikmāl*: *TA* 47,16
+ *TG* (*ad* 412a22-28), 41,12: *entelekheia* = *istikmālan*: *TA* 48,1
+ *TG* (*ad* 412a22-28), 41,15: *têi entelekheiâi* = *istikmāl*: *TA* 48,4
+ *TG* (*ad* 412a22-28), 41,20: *entelekheian* = *istikmāl*: *TA* 48,10
+ *TG* (*ad* 412a22-28), 41,24: *entelekheia hê prôtê* = *al-istikmāl al-awwal*: *TA* 48,14
+ *TG* (*ad* 412a22-28), 42,1: *entelekheia* = *istikmāl*: *TA* 49,16
+ *MN al-istikmāl* at 91,3.10.12(*tris*)

DA 2.1, 412b5 *entelekheia* = *anṭalāshiyā*: *FN* 30,8
+ *TG* (*ad* 412b4-9), 42,18-19: *all' homôs eph' hapantôn to eidos amphoin aition kai hên legomen entelekheian* = *lakinnahu wa-in kāna ka-dhālika fa-fī jamīᶜihā ṣ-ṣūratu wa-sh-shayʾu lladhī nusammīhi stikmālan huwa sababuhumā* *TA* 51,1-2

DA 2.1, 412b9 *entelekheia* = *al-anṭalāshiyā*: *FN* 30,12

DA 2.1, 412b28 *entelekheia* = *anṭalāshiyā*: *FN* 31,10
+ *TG* (*ad* 412b11-17), 42,33: *entelekheia prôtê* = *istikmāluhu l-awwalu*: *TA* 51,17
+ *TG* (*ad* 412b25-27), 43,6: *tou sômatos nekrou entelekheia* = *istikmālu l-jismi l-mayyiti*: *TA* 52,12
+ *TG* (*ad* 412b27-413a3), 43,15: *entelekheia* = *istikmāl*: *TA* 53,4:
+ *TG* (*ad* 412b27-413a3), 43,17: *entelekheia* = *al-istikmāl*: *TA* 53,5
+ *TG* (*ad* 412b27-413a3), 43,17-18: *psukhê men oun amphô hai entelekheiai kai mallon hê prôtê* = *fa-n-nafsu hiya l-istikmālāni jamīᶜan wa-ka-annahā l-awwalu wa-th-thānī* [sic]: *TA* 53,5-6
DA 2.1, 413a7 *entelekheias* = *anṭalāshiyā*: *FN* 31,14
DA 2.1, 413a8 *entelekheia* = *anṭalāshiyā*: *FN* 31,15
+ *TG* (*ad* 413a3-8), 43,24: *entelekheia kai teleiotês* = *istikmālan wa-kamālan*: 53,11-12
+ *TG* (*ad* 413a8-9), 43,27: *entelekheia* = *istikmālan*: *TA* 53,14
+ *TG* (*ad* 413a8-9), 43,27-30: *houtô de kai ho nous ekhein dokei. oupô gar dêlon, ei kai houtos sômatos tinos entelekheia ara toiautê hôste akhôristos einai, ê hôste khôrizesthai, hôsper ho kubernêtês tou ploiou. houtos gar entelekheia men, alla khôristê* = *fa-inna l-ᶜaqla qad yuẓannu annahu laysa yajrī majrā sh-shakli wa-l-mithāli li-annahu lam yubayyin baᶜdu annahu istikmālun li-jismin mā fa-in kāna istikmālan yajrī majrā mā yufāraqu bi-manzilati r-rubbāni ᶜinda s-safīnati fa-inna hādhā huwa stikmālun illā annahu mufāraqun*: *TA* 53,15-54,2
+ *MN kamāl bi-l-fiᶜli* at 93,12 and *al-kamālāt* at 93,17
DA 2.2, 413b18 *entelekheiâi* = *al-anṭalāshiyā llatī hiya tamāmun*: *FN* 33,5
+ *TG* (*ad* 413b11-27), 45,20: *entelekheias* = *istikmālayni*: *TA* 58,10
+ *TG* (*ad* 413b11-27), 45,24: *entelekheias* = *istikmālāt*: *TA* 58,13
+ *TG* (*ad* 413b11-27), 45,33: *entelekheiâi* = *bi-l-istikmāli*: *TA* 59,4
DA 2.2, 414a17 *to de eidos entelekheia* = *wa-anna ṣ-ṣūrata anṭalāshiyā*: *FN* 34,10
DA 2.2, 414a18 *ou to sôma estin entelekheia psukhês, all' hautê sômatos tinos* = *wa-anna l-jirma laysa tamāma n-nafsi wa-li-dhālika lan yaqaᶜa ᶜalayhi maᶜnā l-anṭalāshiyā bali n-nafsu anṭalāshiyā jirmin bi-ṣifati kadhā wa-kadhā*: *FN* 34,11-12
+ *TG* (*ad* 414a14-19), 46,29: *to de eidos entelekheia* = *wa-ṣ-ṣūratu stikmālun*: *TA* 61,3
DA 2.2, 414a26 *entelekheia* = *anṭalāshiyā*: *FN* 34,18
DA 2.2, 414a27 *entelekheia* = *al-anṭalāshiyā*: *FN* 34,19
+ *TG* (*ad* 414a27-28), 47,5: *entelekheia* = *istikmāl*: *TA* 61,16
DA 2.4, 415b15 *entelekheia* = *anṭalāshiyā*: *FN* 38,9
+ *MN kamāl* at 95,1
DA 2.5, 417a9 *entelekheiâi* = *bi-l-fiᶜli*: 42,2
DA 2.5, 417a21 *peri dunameôs kai entelekheias* = *al-quwwa wa-l-fiᶜl*: *FN* 42,11
+ *TG* (*ad* 417a21-b2), 55,17: *entelekheias* = *al-istikmāl*: *TA* 80,6
+ *TG* (*ad* 417a21-b2), 55,23: *entelekheiâi* = *bi-l-istikmāli*: *TA* 80,18
DA 2.5, 417b4 *hupo tou entelekheiâi ontos* = *min dhī l-fiᶜli*: *FN* 43,2
DA 2.5, 417b7 *eis entelekheian* = *al-anṭalāshiyā wa-huwa l-fiᶜlu t-tāmmu*: *FN* 43,4
DA 2.5, 417b10 *eis entelekheian* = *ilā l-anṭalāshiyā*: *FN* 43,7
DA 2.5, 417b13 *hupo tou entelekheiâi ontos* = *min ... dhī l-anṭalāshiyā*: *FN* 43,9
+ *TG* (*ad* 417b8-16), 56,12: *teleiotês* = *kamāl*: *TA* 82,6
DA 2.5, 418a4 *entelekheiâi* = *bi-l-fiᶜli*: *FN* 44,4
+ *TG* (*ad* 418a31-b4), 59,9: *energeia tis kai teleiotês* = *fiᶜlun wa-kamālun*: *TA* 89,14

DA 2.7, 418b12 *entelekheiâi* = *bi-l-fiᶜli*: *FN* 45,19
+ *TG* 59,33 (*ad* 418b9-12): *entelekheia tis kai teleiotês* = *istikmālun mā wa-kamālun*: *TA* 91,2
+ *TG* 59,34 (*ad* 418b9-12): *teleiotês* = *kamāl*: *TA* 91,4-5
+ *TG* 59,35 (*ad* 418b9-12): *teleiotês* = *kamāl*: *TA* 91,6
DA 2.7, 418b30 *entelekheiâi* = *bi-l-fiᶜli*: *FN* 46,11
+ *TG* (*ad* 418b12-13), 60,2: *entelekheiâi* = *bi-l-istikmāli*: *TA* 91,9
DA 2.7, 419a11 *entelekheia* = *fiᶜl*: *FN* 46,20
DA 2.10, 422b1 *entelekheiâi* = *bi-l-fiᶜli*: *FN* 55,18
DA 2.10, 422b16 *entelekheiâi* = *ilā l-fiᶜli*: *FN* 56,9
+ *TG* (*ad* 422a34-b10), 71,33: *entelekheiâi* = *bi-l-istikmāli*: *TA* 118,2
DA 3.4, 429a28 *entelekheiâi* = *bi-l-fiᶜli*: *FN* 73,2
+ *MN bi-l-fiᶜli*: 100,23
DA 3.4, 429b31 *entelekheiâi* = *bi-l-fiᶜli*: *FN* 74,11
+ *TG* (*ad* 429b31-430a2), 97,22: *entelekheiâi* = ? [The Arabic text diverges from the Greek of Themistius from *TG* 91,7-97,27]
DA 3.4, 430a1 *entelekheiâi* = *bi-l-fiᶜli*: *FN* 74,13
+ *TG* (*ad* 430a10-14), 98,13: *teleiotês* = *at-tamām*: *TA* 169,5
+ *TG* (*ad* 430a14-19), 106,10: *teleiotês* = *kamāl*: *TA* 193,1
DA 3.7, 431a3 *entelekheiâi* = *bi-l-anṭalāshiyā*: *FN* 76,20
+ *MN bi-l-fiᶜli*: 105,22-23
DA 3.8, 431b25-26 *hê d'entelekheiâi eis ta entelekheiâi* = *wa-mā kāna fī ḥaddi l-fiᶜli kānat qismatuhu li-dhawī l-afᶜāli*: *FN* 78,21-79,1

T4 *entelekheia* in the Arabic *Physics*

Phys. = Arisṭūṭālīs, *aṭ-Ṭabīᶜa* [*Ṭ*]

Phys. 1.2, 186a3 *entelekheiâi* = *bi-l-istikmāli*: *Ṭ* 16,13
Phys. 2.1, 193b7 *entelekheiâi* = *bi-stikmālihi*: *Ṭ* 86,11
Phys. 3.1, 200b26 *entelekheiâi* = *ᶜalā l-kamāli*: *Ṭ* 168,2
Phys. 3.1, 200b27 *entelekheiâi* = *bi-l-kamāli*: *Ṭ* 168,3
Phys. 3.1, 201a10 *entelekheiâi* = *bi-l-kamāli*: *Ṭ* 171,1
Phys. 3.1, 201a11 *entelekheia* = *kamāl*: *Ṭ* 171,2
Phys. 3.1, 201a17 *entelekheiâi* = *bi-l-fiᶜli*: *Ṭ* 172,14
Phys. 3.1, 201a20 *entelekheiâi* = *bi-l-kamāli*: *Ṭ* 177,3
Phys. 3.1, 201a21 *entelekheiâi* = *bi-l-kamāli*: *Ṭ* 177,5
Phys. 3.1, 201a28 *entelekheiâi* = *bi-l-kamāli*: *Ṭ* 178,1
Phys. 3.1, 201a30 *entelekheia* = *kamāl*: *Ṭ* 178,4
Phys. 3.1, 201a34 *entelekheia* = *kamālahu*: *Ṭ* 178,8
Phys. 3.1, 201b5 *entelekheia* = *kamāl*: *Ṭ* 178,15
Phys. 3.1, 201b6 *entelekheia* = *fī l-kamāli*: *Ṭ* 179,2
Phys. 3.2, 202a7 *entelekheia* = *kamāl*: *Ṭ* 184,7
Phys. 3.2, 202a11 *entelekheiâi* = *bi-l-kamāli*: *Ṭ* 184,12
Phys. 3.3, 202a14 *entelekheia* = *kamāl*: *Ṭ* 191,5
Phys. 3.3, 202a16 *entelekheian* = *kamālan*, 191,7
Phys. 3.3, 202b26 *entelekheia* = *kamāl*: *Ṭ* 195,4
Phys. 3.5, 204a28 *entelekheiâi* = *bi-l-kamāli*: *Ṭ* 224,1
Phys. 3.6, 206a15 *entelekheiâi* = *bi-l-kamāli*: *Ṭ* 250,12

Phys. 3.6, 206b13 *entelekheiâi* = *fī l-kamāli*: *Ṭ* 253,4-5
Phys. 3.6, 206b22 *entelekheiâi* = *bi-l-kamāli*: *Ṭ* 254,1
Phys. 3.6, 206b25 *entelekheiâi* = *bi-l-kamāli*: *Ṭ* 254,4
Phys. 3.6, 207a22 *entelekheiâi* = *bi-l-kamāli*: *Ṭ* 260,5
Phys. 4.5, 213a7 *entelekheia* = *kamāl*: *Ṭ* 333,4
Phys. 4.5, 213a8 *entelekheiâi* = *bi-l-kamāli*: *Ṭ* 333,5
Phys. 8.5, 257b7 *entelekheiâi* = *bi-l-istikmāli*: *Ṭ* 856,4
Phys. 8.5, 257b8 *eis entelekheian* = *ilā l-istikmāli*: *Ṭ* 856,5
Phys. 8.5, 257b8 *entelekheia* = *istikmāl*: *Ṭ* 856,6
Phys. 8.5, 258b2 *entelekheiâi* = *bi-l-istikmāli*: *Ṭ* 862,1
Phys. 8.8, 263a29(*bis*) *entelekheiâi* = *bi-l-istikmāli*: *Ṭ* 901,5.6
Phys. 8.8, 263b5 *entelekheiâi* = *bi-l-istikmāli*: *Ṭ* 901,15

T5 *telos* in the Arabic *Physics*

Phys. = Arisṭūṭālīs, *aṭ-Ṭabīʿa* [*Ṭ*]

Phys. 2.2, 194a27 *al-ghāya*: *Ṭ* 95,12
Phys. 2.2, 194a28 *ghāya*: *Ṭ* 95,13
Phys. 2.2, 194a29 *ghāya*: *Ṭ* 95,14
Phys. 2.2, 194a32 *ghāya*: *Ṭ* 96,3
Phys. 2.2, 194a35 *ghāya*: *Ṭ* 96,7
Phys. 2.3, 194b32 *al-ghāyat al-maqṣūda*: *Ṭ* 102,2
Phys. 2.3, 194b36 *al-ghāyat al-maqṣūda*: *Ṭ* 102,6-7
Phys. 2.3, 195a2 *al-ghāya*: *Ṭ* 102,9
Phys. 2.3, 195a10 *ghāya maqṣūda*: *Ṭ* 103,12
Phys. 2.3, 195a24 *al-ghāyat al-maqṣūda*: *Ṭ* 104,12
Phys. 2.3, 195a25 *ghāya*: *Ṭ* 104,13
Phys. 2.5, 197a1 *al-ghāya*: *Ṭ* 121,8
Phys. 2.7, 198b3 *ghāya*: *Ṭ* 140,13
Phys. 2.8, 199a8 *ghāya*: *Ṭ* 147,5
Phys. 2.8, 199a25 *al-ghāyat al-maqṣūda*: *Ṭ* 150,12
Phys. 2.8, 199a31 *al-ghāya*: *Ṭ* 151,20
Phys. 2.8, 199a32 *al-ghāya*: *Ṭ* 151,21
Phys. 2.8, 199b6 *al-ghāyat al-maqṣūda*: *Ṭ* 152,11
Phys. 2.8, 199b17 *ghāya*: *Ṭ* 155,2
Phys. 2.9, 200a14 *al-ghāyat al-maqṣūda*: *Ṭ* 160,6
Phys. 2.9, 200a20 *al-ghāyat al-maqṣūda*: *Ṭ* 161,3
Phys. 2.9, 200a22 *al-ghāya*: *Ṭ* 161,6
Phys. 2.9, 200a27 *al-ghāyat al-maqṣūda*: *Ṭ* 162,12
Phys. 2.9, 200a34 *al-ghāya*: *Ṭ* 163,14
Phys. 3.3, 202a24 *ergon de kai telos* = *wa-yakūnu l-ʿamalu nafsuhu wa-t-tamāmu*: *Ṭ* 192,2
Phys. 3.4, 203b9 *ākhir*: *Ṭ* 212,9
Phys. 3.6, 207a14 *teleion d'ouden mê ekhon telos; to de telos peras* = *wa-t-tāmmu lā yakūnu illā mā lahu tamāmun wa-t-tamāmu nihāyatun*: *Ṭ* 259,10-11
Phys. 4.1, 209a22 *tamām*: *Ṭ* 279,15
Phys. 6.5, 236a10 *kata to telos tês metabolês* = *min qibali ntihāʾi t-taghayyuri*: *Ṭ* 674,7

Phys. 6.5, 236a12 *metabolês telos* = *ākhir at-taghayyur*: *Ṭ* 674,8
Phys. 6.9, 239b13 *ākhir*: *Ṭ* 713,10
Phys. 6.9, 239b34 *apo telous tou stadiou* = *min ākhiri l-mīdāni*: *Ṭ* 715,3
Phys. 8.8, 262b31 *anankê gar epi telos elthein* = *fa-wājibun ḍarūratan an yantahiya ilā ghāyatihi* [reading *ilā ghāyatihi* instead of Badawī's *ilā ghayri ʿillatihi*, because of the Greek]: *Ṭ* 899,4
Phys. 8.9, 265a30 *al-inqiḍāʾ*: *Ṭ* 917,11
Phys. 8.9, 265a34 *ākhir*: *Ṭ* 918,3
Phys. 8.9, 265b4 *ākhir*: *Ṭ* 918,8
Phys. 8.9, 265b13 *inqiḍāʾ*: *Ṭ* 919,7
Phys. 8.9, 265b15 *inqiḍāʾ*: *Ṭ* 919,9
Phys. 8.10, 267a9 *telos de pauetai* = *wa-yakuffu bi-akharatin*: *Ṭ* 930,1

Appendix II

Transcriptions of Lemmata from MS Uppsala Or. 364

4v16-5r5 (L31)

المبدأ هو ما يتعلق | وجود الشيء به وهو اما مادّته ان كان مادّياً واما صورته ان كان مركّباً || من مادّة وصورة واما غايته ان كان لغاية ما وجد والمُيَسِّر والمُعين | والالة تلتحق بالفاعل والمثال لنقصان ذات الفاعل عن ان يصدر عنه | ‹وَ›يوجد منه ما ‹هو› الفعل ‹وَ› الجوهر المركّب له سببان مقارنان مادّته وصورته | وسببان مفارقان فاعله وغايته والعرض له ثلثة اسباب ليس | فيها الصورة والصورة والمفارقات لها سببان الفاعل والغاية

3v16-4r12 (L58/L70)

الواجب هو الضروريّ الوجود على ما هو عليه وذلك امّا بذاته كمبدأ | الموجودات وامّا بغيره ككون اثنين واثنين اربعة والواجب امّا دايما || كمبدأ الموجودات وامّا في حال دون حال ككسوف القمر في وقته | وكلّ ما هو واجب الوجود بذاته فلا علّة له فما له علّة فليس بواجب الوجود | بذاته ولا ممتنع الوجود بذاته والا لما كان يوجد فهو اذاً في حيث ذاته | ممكن الوجود وهو واجب الوجود بعلّته وما لا | علة له فان وجود ذاته لا ينقسم من حالتين يصير بهما معلولا في كلتا | الحالتين فيكون لا بدّ له من ان يكون معلولا ولا يخلو عن المعلوليّة وكلّ | متغيّر فانه يكون على حالتين ليس ولا واحدة منهما له بذاته فكلّ | واحدة منهما بعلة ولا يخلو عنهما فكلّ متغيّر معلول الذات وممكنها | وكلّ ما هو واجب الوجود بذاته فهو واجب الوجود من جميع | جهاته فليس يوصف البتة بنحو من انحاء التغيّر والممكن هو | الموجود الذي ليس بضروريّ ويقال ممكن لما ليس بممتنع ويقال ممكن | لما كان غير ممتنع يوجد ويعدم وليس موجودا في الحال .

4r14-17 (L69)

يقال قديم لكلّ ما لم يكن قط ليساً وقد يكون الشي قديماً بذاته وقد يكون قديماً | بغيره كما يتبيّن واما المحدث والمتكوّن فهو الذي كان ليس في وقت ما | ولن يكون الا بغيره ولا بدّ له من مادة لان كلّ متكوّن فقد تقدّمَه | امكان وجودٍ والا لم يكن وذاك الامكان يكون عرضاً فيكون في موضوع || لانه لا واحدَ من الجواهر يكون قوامه بالاضافة الى غيره ما هو جوهر | والامكان امكان بالقياس الى الممكن ولا يتوهم له البتة وجود مفرد غير منقاس | فليس البتة جوهراً فهو على كلّ حالٍ عرض او شيء في المادّة فعلى كل حالٍ كل متكون | فله مادّة وهذا مبدأ للطبيعيّات

Bibliography

PRIMARY SOURCES CITED IN THE NOTES

ʿAbd al-Jabbār, *al-Mughnī fī abwāb at-tawḥīd wa-l-ʿadl* ed. M.M. Ḥilmī et al., Cairo, 1958f.

(Ps.-)Abū Ḥanīfa, *al-Fiqh al-akbar* ed. M.M. ash-Shaʿʿār (= Mullā ʿAlī b. Sulṭān Muḥammad al-Qārī, *Sharḥ al-fiqh al-akbar*), Beirut, 1997

Albert of Saxony, *Expositio et quaestiones in Aristotelis Physicam ad Albertum de Saxonia attributae I*, ed. B. Patar, Louvain, 1999

Alexander, *DA* (*CAG* Suppl. I.1), ed. I. Bruns, Berlin, 1887

Alexander, *in Metaph.* (*CAG* I), ed. M. Hayduck, Berlin, 1891

Alexander, *in Meteor.* (*CAG* III.1), ed. M. Hayduck, Berlin, 1899

Alexander, *in Sens.* (*CAG* III.1), ed. P. Wendland, Berlin, 1901

Alexander, *in Top.* (*CAG* II.2), ed. M. Wallies, Berlin, 1891

Alexander, *Quaest.* (*CAG* Suppl. I.2), ed. I. Bruns, Berlin, 1892

Alexander, *Maqālat Aliskandar fī anna l-fiʿl aʿammu mina l-ḥaraka ʿalā raʾy Arisṭū*, ed. ʿA. Badawī (*Arisṭū ʿinda l-ʿArab*), Cairo, 1947

Alexander, *Maqālat Aliskandar fī l-ḥiss*, ed. H.-J. Ruland (*Die arabische Übersetzung der Schrift des Alexander von Aphrodisias über die Sinneswahrnehmung*), Gottingen, 1978

Alexander, *Risāla fī l-ʿaql ʿalā raʾy Arisṭūṭālīs*, ed. ʿA. Badawī (*Commentaires sur Aristote perdus en grec et autres épîtres*), Beirut, 1971

Alexander of Hales, *In XII Aristotelis Metaphysicae libros*, Venice, 1572

Algazel, *Intentiones philosophorum*, ed. J. Muckle (*Algazel's Metaphysics*), Toronto, 1933

al-ʿĀmirī, *Kitāb al-amad ʿalā l-abad*, ed. E. Rowson, New Haven, Conn., 1988

Ammonius, *in Isag.* (*CAG* IV.3), ed. A. Busse, Berlin, 1895

Ammonius, *in Int.* (*CAG* IV.5), ed. A. Busse, Berlin, 1897

Anonymous, *Late-Antique Paraphrase of and Commentary on the De Anima*, ed. R. Arnzen (*Aristoteles De anima: eine verlorene spätantike Paraphrase in arabischer und persischer Überlieferung: arabischer Text nebst Kommentar, quellengeschichtlichen Studien und Glossaren*), Leiden, 1998

Arisṭāṭālīs {*ap.* Ibn Rushd}, *{Tafsīr} Mā baʿda ṭ-ṭabīʿa I-III*, ed. M. Bouyges, Beirut, 1938-48

Arisṭūṭālīs, *Fī aʿḍāʾ al-ḥayawān*, ed. R. Kruk (*Aristoteles Semitico-Latinus: The Arabic Version of Aristotle's Parts of Animals*), Amsterdam, 1979

Arisṭūṭālīs, *Fī kawn al-ḥayawān*, ed. J. Brugmann and H. Drossaart Lulofs, Leiden, 1971

Arisṭūṭālīs, *Fī l-ʿibāra*, ed. ʿA. Badawī (*Manṭiq Arisṭū I*), Cairo, 1948-1952

Arisṭūṭālīs, *Fī n-nafs*, ed. ʿA. Badawī, Cairo, 1954

Arisṭūṭālīs, *aṭ-Ṭabīʿa*, ed. ʿA. Badawī, Cairo, 1964

Arisṭūṭālīs, *Taḥlīlāt thāniyya*, ed. ʿA. Badawī (*Manṭiq Arisṭū II*), Cairo, 1948-1952

Arisṭūṭālīs, *Ṭibāʿ al-ḥayawān*, ed. ʿA. Badawī, Kuwait, 1977

Arisṭūṭālīs, *Ṭūbīka*, ed. ʿA. Badawī (*Manṭiq Arisṭū II*), Cairo, 1948-1952

(Ps.-)Arisṭūṭālīs, *Uthūlūjiyā*, ed. ʿA. Badawī (*Plotinus apud Arabes*), Cairo, 1955

(Ps.-)Arisṭūṭālīs, *Kitāb al-īḍāḥ fī l-khayr al-maḥḍ li-Arisṭūṭālīs*, ed. A. Badawī (*Neoplatonici apud Arabes*), Cairo, 1955

Asclepius, *in Metaph.* (*CAG* VI.2), ed. M. Hayduck, Berlin, 1888

al-Ashʿarī, *Maqālāt al-islāmiyyīn I-II*, ed. H. Ritter, Istanbul, 1929-30

al-Ash^c^arī, *Kitāb al-luma^c^* and *Risālat istiḥsān al-khawḍ fī ^c^ilm al-kalām*, ed. R.J. McCarthy (in his *The Theology of al-Ash^c^arī*), Beirut, 1953
Averroes, *Aristotelis opera cum Averois commentariis*, Venice, 1562-1574
Avicenna, *Liber de anima seu sextus de naturalibus I-III*, ed. S. van Riet, Leiden, 1972
Avicenna, *Liber de philosophia prima sive scientia divina I-IV*, ed. S. van Riet, Leiden, 1977
Avicenna, *Liber de philosophia prima sive scientia divina V-X*, ed. S. van Riet, Leiden, 1980
Avicenna, *Liber primus naturalium: Tractatus primus de causis et principiis naturalium*, ed. S. van Riet, Leiden, 1992
Avicenna, *Liber quartus naturalium de actionibus et passionibus qualitatum primarum*, ed. S. van Riet, Leiden, 1989
al-Baghdādī, Awḥad az-zamān Abū l-Barakāt *Kitāb al-mu^c^tabar fī l-ḥikma III*, no ed., Hyderabad, 1938-39
al-Baghdādī, al-Khaṭīb *Tārīkh Baghdād 6*, no ed., Beirut, 1968
Bahmanyār ibn al-Marzubān, *at-Taḥṣīl*, ed. M. Muṭahharī, Tehran, 1997
al-Bāqillānī, *Kitāb at-tamhīd*, ed. R.J. McCarthy, Beirut, 1957
al-Bayhaqī, *Kitāb al-asmā^ɔ^ wa-ṣ-ṣifāt*, ed. M.Z. al-Kawtharī, Beirut, 1970
Buridan, John, *in Metaphysicen Aristotelis questiones*, Paris 1588 (i.e., 1518), repr. Frankfurt a.M., 1964
Damascius, *Treatise on First Principles*, ed. L. Westerink, Paris, 1986-1991
Duns Scotus, *Quaestiones super libros Metaphysicorum Aristotelis I-IX*, New York, 1997-1998
al-Fārābī, *Epitome of Aristotle's* Physics, ed. A. Birkenmajer, "Eine wiedergefundene Übersetzung Gerhards von Cremona", *Beiträge zur Geschichte der Philosophie und Theologie des Mittelalters* (*Suppl.* 3.1), 1935, 472-481
al-Fārābī, *Kitāb al-ḥurūf*, ed. M. Mahdī, Beirut, 1969
al-Fārābī, *Kitāb al-jam^c^ bayna ra^ɔ^yay al-ḥakīmayni Aflāṭūn al-ilāhī wa-Arisṭūṭālīs*, ed. F. Dieterici (*Alfārābī's philosophische Abhandlungen*), Leiden, 1890
al-Fārābī, *Kitāb ārā^ɔ^ ahl al-madīnat al-fāḍila*, ed. A. Nādir, Beirut, 1968
al-Fārābī, *Kitāb īsāghūjī ay al-madkhal*, ed. and trans. D. Dunlop, "Al-Fārābī's *Eisagoge*", *Islamic Quarterly* 3 (1956), 117-138.
al-Fārābī, *Kitāb as-siyāsat al-madaniyyat al-mulaqqab bi-Mabādi^ɔ^ al-mawjūdāt*, ed. F. Najjār, Beirut, 1964
al-Fārābī, *Maqāla ... fī aghrāḍ al-ḥakīm fī kulli maqālatin mina l-kitāb al-mawsūm bi-l-ḥurūf*, ed. F. Dieterici (*Alfārābī's philosophische Abhandlungen*), Leiden, 1890
al-Fārābī, *Risāla fī l-^c^aql*, ed. M. Bouyges, Beirut, 1938
al-Fārābī, *Risāla fī jawāb masā^ɔ^il su^ɔ^ila ^c^anhā*, ed. F. Dieterici (*Alfārābī's philosophische Abhandlungen*), Leiden, 1890
al-Fārābī, *Sharḥ li-kitāb Arisṭūṭālīs fī l-^c^ibāra*, ed. W. Kutsch and S. Marrow, Beirut, 1971
(Ps.-)al-Fārābī, *Risāla fī l-^c^ilm al-ilāhī*, ed. ^c^A. Badawī, *Neoplatonici apud arabes*, Cairo, 1955
Giles of Rome, *Errores Philosophorum*, ed. J. Koch, Milwaukee, 1944
al-Ghazālī, *Tahāfut al-falāsifa*, ed. M. Bouyges, Beirut, 1927, 358,8-11
al-Ghazālī, *Maqāṣid al-falāsifa*, ed. S. Dunyā, Cairo, 1961
Henry of Ghent, *Quodlibet XIII*, ed. J. Decorte, Leuven, 1985
Ḥunayn ibn Isḥāq, *al-Masā^ɔ^il fī ṭ-ṭibb li-l-muta^c^allimīn*, ed. M. Abū Rayyān et al., Cairo, 1978
Iamblichus, *Theologumena Arithmeticae*, ed. F. Ast, Leipzig, 1817

Ibn ᶜAsākir, *Tabyīn kadhib al-muftarī fī-mā nusiba ilā l-Imām Abī l-Ḥasan al-Ashᶜarī*, no ed., Damascus, 1928
Ibn Bābawayh aṣ-Ṣadūq, Abū Jaᶜfar Muḥammad *Kitāb at-tawḥīd*, Bombay (?), 1903
Ibn Fūrak, *Mujarrad maqālāt al-Ashᶜarī*, ed. D. Gimaret, Beirut, 1987
Ibn Khallikān, *Wafayāt al-aᶜyān wa-anbāʾ abnāʾ az-zamān*, 6 vols, ed. M. ᶜAbd al-Ḥamīd, Cairo, 1949
Ibn Mattawayh, *Kitāb al-majmūᶜ fī l-muḥīṭ bi-t-taklīf* 1, ed. J. Houben, Beirut, 1965
Ibn Miskawayh, *K. al-fawz al-asghar*, no ed., Beirut, 1901
Ibn an-Nadīm, *Kitāb al-fihrist*, ed. G. Flügel, Leipzig, 1871
Ibn Rushd, *Tafsīr Mā baᶜda ṭ-ṭabīᶜa I-III*, ed. M. Bouyges, Beirut, 1938-48
Ibn Rushd, *Tahāfut at-tahāfut*, ed. M. Bouyges, Beirut, 1930
Ibn Sīnā, *Autobiography*, ed. and trans. W. Gohlman (*The Life of Ibn Sina*), Albany, N.Y., 1974
Ibn Sīnā, *Dānishnāma-yi ᶜAlāʾī: Ilāhiyyāt*, ed. M. Muᶜīn, Teheran, 1331 (Shams)
Ibn Sīnā, *al-Ḥikmat al-ᶜArūḍiyya*, MS Uppsala Or. 364
Ibn Sīnā, *Ilāhiyyāt-i Dānishnāma-yi ᶜAlāʾī*, ed. M. Muᶜīn, Tehran, 1952
Ibn Sīnā, *Kitāb al-ḥudūd*, ed. A.-M. Goichon, Cairo, 1963
Ibn Sīnā, *Kitāb al-hidāya*, ed. M. ᶜAbduh, Cairo, 1974
Ibn Sīnā, *Kitāb al-ishārāt wa-t-tanbīhāt*, ed. J. Forget (*Ibn Sīnā: Le Livre des théorèmes et des avertissements*), Leiden, 1892
Ibn Sīnā, *Kitāb an-najāt mukhtaṣar ash-shifāʾ li-bn Sīnā*, Rome, 1593
Ibn Sīnā, *Kitāb an-najāt*, Cairo, 1913
Ibn Sīnā, *Kitāb ash-shifāʾ/Ilāhiyyāt (1)*, edd. G. Qanawātī and S. Zāyid, Cairo, 1960.
Ibn Sīnā, *Kitāb ash-shifāʾ/Ilāhiyyāt (2)*, edd. M.Y. Mūsā, S. Dunyā and S. Zāʾid, Cairo, 1960
Ibn Sīnā, *Kitāb ash-shifāʾ/Manṭiq (1): al-Madkhal*, edd. G. Qanawātī, M. al-Khuḍayrī and F. al-Ahwānī, Cairo, 1952
Ibn Sīnā, *Kitāb ash-shifāʾ/Manṭiq (5): al-Burhān*, ed. A. ᶜAfīfī, Cairo, 1956
Ibn Sīnā, *Kitāb ash-shifāʾ/Riyāḍiyyāt (2): al-Ḥisāb*, ed. A. Maẓhar, Cairo, 1985
Ibn Sīnā, *Kitāb ash-shifāʾ/Ṭabīᶜiyyāt (1): as-Samāᶜ aṭ-ṭabīᶜī*, ed. S. Zāyid, Cairo, 1983
Ibn Sīnā, *Kitāb ash-shifāʾ/Ṭabīᶜiyyāt (4): al-Afᶜāl wa-l-infiᶜālāt*, ed. M. Qāsim, Cairo, 1965
Ibn Sīnā, *Kitāb ash-shifāʾ/Ṭabīᶜiyyāt (6): an-Nafs*, ed. F. Rahman (*Avicenna's De Anima – Arabic Text*), Oxford, 1959
Ibn Sīnā, *Kitāb ash-shifāʾ/Ṭabīᶜiyyāt (8): al-Ḥayawān*, ed. ᶜA. Mustanṣir, S. Zāʾid and ᶜA Ismāᶜīl, Cairo, 1970
Ibn Sīnā, *al-Mabdaʾ wa-l-maᶜād*, ed. ᶜA Nūrānī, Tehran, 1984
Ibn Sīnā, *Mabḥath ᶜani l-quwā n-nafsāniyya*, ed. A. al-Ahwānī (*Aḥwāl an-nafs*), Cairo, 1952
Ibn Sīnā, *al-Mubāḥathāt*, ed. M. Bīdārfar, Qom, 1992
Ibn Sīnā, *al-Qānūn fī ṭ-ṭibb* (1), ed. I. al-Qashsh, Beirut, 1987
Ibn Sīnā, *ar-Risālat al-ᶜarshiyya fī ḥaqāʾiq at-tawḥīd wa-ithbāt an-nubuwwa*, ed. I Hilāl, Cairo, no date
Ibn Sīnā, *Risāla fī n-nafs wa-baqāʾihā wa-maᶜādihā*, ed. A. al-Ahwānī (*Aḥwāl an-nafs*), Cairo, 1952
Ibn Sīnā, *Risāla fī l-kalām ᶜalā n-nafs an-nāṭiqa*, ed. A. al-Ahwānī (*Aḥwāl an-nafs*), Cairo, 1952
Ibn Sīnā, *Risāla ilā Kiyā*, ed. ᶜA. Badawī (*Arisṭū ᶜinda l-ᶜArab*), Cairo, 1947
Ibn Sīnā, *Sharḥ ḥarf al-Lām*, ed. ᶜA. Badawī (*Arisṭū ᶜinda l-ᶜArab*), Cairo, 1947
Ibn Sīnā, *Risāla fī l-lugha*, ed. I. Yārshāṭir (*Panj Rasāʾil*), Tehran, 1332 (Shams)

Ibn Sīnā, *at-Ta^clīqāt*, ed. ᶜA. Badawī, Cairo, 1973
Ibn Sīnā, *at-Taᶜlīqāt ᶜalā ḥawāshī Kitāb an-nafs li-Arisṭū*, ed. ᶜA. Badawī, (*Arisṭū ᶜinda l-ᶜArab*), Cairo, 1947
Ibn Sīnā, *ᶜUyūn al-ḥikma*, ed. ᶜA. Badawī (*Avicennae Fontes sapientiae*), Cairo, 1954
Ikhwān aṣ-Ṣafāʾ, *Rasāʾil*, no ed., Beirut, 1957
(Ps.-)Isḥāq b. Ḥunayn, *Kitāb an-nafs*, ed. A. al-Ahwānī (*Talkhīṣ Kitāb an-nafs li-Abī l-Walīd ibn Rushd wa-arbaᶜ rasāʾil*), Cairo, 1950
Jābir b. Ḥayyān, *Kitāb al-ḥudūd, Kitāb al-baḥth, Kitāb ikhrāj mā fī l-quwwa ilā l-fiᶜl, Kitāb al-khawāṣṣ al-kabīr* and *Kitāb al-mīzān aṣ-ṣaghīr*, ed. P. Kraus (*Jābir ibn Ḥayyān: Essai sur l'histoire des idées scientifique dans l'islam. Vol. 1: Textes choisis*), Paris, 1935
al-Juwaynī, *ash-Shāmil fī uṣūl ad-dīn*, ed. ᶜA.M. ᶜUmar, Beirut, 1999
al-Khayyāṭ, *Kitāb al-instiṣār*, ed. H.S. Nyberg, Cairo, 1925
al-Khʷānsārī, al-Āghā Ḥusayn *al-Ḥāshiya ᶜalā shurūḥ al-ishārāt (2)*, ed. A. al-ᶜĀbidī, Qum, 1999
al-Khʷārazmī, *Mafātiḥ al-ᶜulūm*, ed. G. van Vloten, Leiden, 1895
al-Kindī, *Kitāb fī l-falsafat al-ūlā*, edd. R. Rashed and J. Jolivet (*Oeuvres philosophiques et scientifiques d'al-Kindī II: Métaphysique et cosmologie*), Leiden, 1998
al-Kindī, *Risāla fī l-fāᶜil al-ḥaqq al-awwal at-tāmm wa-l-fāᶜil an-nāqiṣ alladhī huwa bi-l-majāz*, edd. R. Rashed and J. Jolivet (*Oeuvres philosophiques et scientifiques d'al-Kindī II: Métaphysique et cosmologie*), Leiden, 1998
al-Kindī, *Risāla ilā Aḥmad b. al-Muᶜtaṣim fī l-ibāna ᶜan sujūd al-jirm al-aqṣā wa-ṭāᶜatihi li-llāh ᶜazza wa-jalla*, edd. R. Rashed and J. Jolivet (*Oeuvres philosophiques et scientifiques d'al-Kindī II: Métaphysique et cosmologie*), Leiden, 1998
(Ps.-?)al-Kindī, *Risāla fī ḥudūd al-ashyāʾ wa-rusūmihā*, ed. M. Abū ar-Rīda (*Rasāʾil al-Kindī al-falsafiyya* [2nd ed.]), Cairo, 1978
al-Kulaynī, Abū Jaᶜfar Muḥammad b. Yaᶜqūb *al-Uṣūl min al-kāfī*, ed. ᶜAlī Akbar al-Ghaffārī, Tehran, 1961
al-Masᶜūdī, *Murūj adh-dhahab wa-maᶜādin al-jawhar*, ed. C. Barbier de Meynard et A. Pavet de Courteille, Paris, 1864
al-Māturīdī, *Kitāb at-tawḥīd*, ed. F. Kholeif, Beirut, 1970
al-Māturīdī, *Taʾwīlāt ahl as-sunna* (= *Tafsīr al-Māturīdī al-musammā Taʾwīlāt ahl as-sunna*), Cairo, 1971
Mullā Mahdī Narāqī, *Sharḥ al-ilāhiyyāt min kitāb ash-shifāʾ*, ed. M. Muḥaqqiq, Tehran, 1986
Mullā Ṣadrā, *al-Asfār al-arbaᶜa II*, ed. H.H. al-Āmulī, Tehran, 1995
Mullā Ṣadrā, *Kitāb al-mashāᶜir*, ed. H. Corbin (*Le Livre des Pénétrations métaphysiques*), Paris/Tehran, 1964
Mullā Ṣadrā, *at-Taᶜlīqāt ᶜalā ilāhiyyāt ash-shifāʾ*, in Ibn Sīnā, *ash-Shifāʾ II*, Tehran, 1886
an-Nāshiʾ al-Akbar, *al-Kitāb al-awsaṭ fī l-maqālāt*, ed. J. van Ess, Beirut, 1971
Nīqūmākhis al-Jārāsīnī, *Kitāb al-madkhal ilā ᶜilm al-ᶜadad*, ed. W. Kutsch (*Thābit b. Qurra's arabische übersetzung der Arithmêtikê Eisagôgê des Nikomachos von Gerasa*), Beirut, 1959
Olympiodorus, *in Alc. I*, ed. L. Westerink, Amsterdam, 1956
Olympiodorus, *in Meteor.* (*CAG* XII.2), ed. W. Stuve, Berlin, 1900
Olympiodorus, *in Phaedonem*, ed. W. Norvin, Leipzig, 1913
Philoponus, *in DA* (*CAG* XV), ed. M. Hayduck, Berlin, 1897
Philoponus, *in GC* (*CAG* XIV.2), ed. H. Vitelli, Berlin, 1897

Philoponus, *in Phys.* (*CAG* XVI-XVII), ed. H. Vitelli, Berlin, 1887-1888
(Ps.-)Plutarch, *Fī l-ārā' aṭ-ṭabīʿiyya allatī tarḍā bihā l-falāsifa*, ed. ʿA Badawī (*Arisṭūṭālīs Fī n-nafs*), Cairo, 1954
Proclus, *in Alc. I*, ed. L. Westerink, Amsterdam, 1954
Proclus, *in Parm.*, ed. V. Cousin, Paris, 1864
Proclus, *in Remp.*, ed. W. Kroll, Leipzig, 1899-1901
Proclus, *Inst. Theol.*, (2nd) ed. E. Dodds, Oxford, 1963
Proclus, *in Tim.*, ed. E. Diehl, Leipzig, 1903-1906
Proclus, *Theol. Plat.*, edd. H. Saffrey and L. Westerink, Paris, 1968-1997
al-Qāsim ibn Ibrāhīm, *Kitāb ad-dalīl al-kabīr*, ed. B. Abrahamov, Leiden, 1990
al-Qushayrī, *Sharḥ asmā' Allāh al-ḥusnā*, ed. Ṭ.ʿA. Saʿd and S.Ḥ.M. ʿAlī, Cairo, 2001,
ar-Rāghib al-Iṣfahānī, *al-Iʿtiqādāt*, ed. Sh. al-ʿAjalī, Beirut, 1988
ar-Rāzī, Fakhr ad-dīn *Sharḥ al-ishārāt*, no ed. (*Sharḥay al-ishārāt li-l-Khʷāja Naṣīr ad-dīn aṭ-Ṭūsī wa-li-l-ʿImām Fakhr ad-dīn ar-Rāzī*), Qum, 1983 or 1984
ar-Rāzī, Fakhr ad-dīn *Kitāb lubāb al-ishārāt*, ed. ʿA.S. ʿAṭiyah, Cairo, 1936
ar-Rāzī, Fakhr ad-dīn, *al-Mabāḥith al-mashriqiyya I*, ed. M. al-Baghdādī, Beirut, 1990
ar-Rāzī, Muḥammad ibn Zakariyā' *Maqāla fī-mā baʿda ṭ-ṭabīʿa*, ed. P. Kraus (*Rasā'il falsafiyya li-Abī Bakr Muḥammad ibn Zakariyā' ar-Rāzī*, Part 1), Cairo, 1939
Sabzawārī, *Sharḥ ghurar al-farā'id*, ed. M. Muḥaqqiq and T. Izutsu (*Sharḥ-i manẓūmah)*, Tehran, 1969
Saʿdiyā al-Fayyūmī (i.e., Saadia Gaon), *Kitāb al-amānāt wa l-iʿtiqādāt*, ed. S. Landauer, Leiden, 1880
as-Samarqandī, Abū l-Layth *Sharḥ al-fiqh al-absaṭ li-Abī Ḥanīfa*, ed. H. Daiber (as *The Islamic Concept of Belief in the 4th/10th Century*), Tokyo, 1995
ash-Shahrastānī, *Kitāb al-milal wa-n-niḥal*, ed. M. Badrān, Cairo, no date
ash-Shahrastānī, *Kitāb nihāyat al-iqdām fī ʿilm al-kalām*, ed. A. Guillaume, no date
ash-Shaykh al-Mufīd, *Awā'il al-maqālāt fī l-madhāhib wa-l-mukhtārāt*, ed. M. Muḥaqqiq, Tehran, 1993
Sībawayhi, *al-Kitāb I*, ed. I.B. Yaʿqūb, Beirut, 1999
Siger of Brabant, *Quaestiones in metaphysicam* (Cambridge MS), ed. A. Maurer, Louvain, 1983
Simplicius, *in Cael.* (*CAG* VII.1), ed. J.L. Heiberg, Berlin, 1894
Simplicius, *in Cat.* (*CAG* VIII), ed. C. Kalbfleisch, Berlin, 1907
Simplicius, *in Phys.* (*CAG* IX-X), ed. H. Diels, Berlin, 1882-1895
(Ps.-?)Simplicius, *in DA* (*CAG* XI), ed. M. Hayduck, Berlin, 1882
Suarez, Francisco, *Disputationes metaphysicae,* edd. and trans, S. Rabade Romeo, S. Caballero Sanchez and A. Puigcerver Zanon (*Disputaciones metafisicas IV*), Madrid, 1962
Syrianus, *in Metaph.* (*CAG* VI.1), ed. W. Kroll, Berlin, 1902
aṭ-Ṭabarī, *Tafsīr aṭ-Ṭabarī*, ed. M.M. Shākir, Cairo, 1954
at-Tawḥīdī, *al-Ḥawāmil wa-sh-shawāmil*, no ed., Cairo, 1951
Thāmasṭiyūs, *Sharḥ ḥarf al-Lām min Kitāb Mā baʿda aṭ-Ṭabīʿa li-Arisṭū*, ed. ʿA. Badawī (*Arisṭū ʿinda l-ʿArab*), Cairo, 1947
Thāmasṭiyūs, *Sharḥ Kitāb an-nafs li-Arisṭūṭālīs*, ed. M. Lyons (*An Arabic Translation of Themistius' Commentary on Aristoteles De Anima*), Norfolk, 1973
Themistius, *in DA* (*CAG* V.3), ed. R. Heinze, Berlin, 1899
Themistius, *in Phys.* (*CAG* V.2), ed. H. Schenkl, Berlin, 1900
Thomas Aquinas, *in XII Libros Metaphysicorum Aristotelis Expositio*, Turin, 1950
Thomas Aquinas, *in VIII Libros Physicorum Aristotelis*, Turin, 1954

Thomas Aquinas, *Scriptum super libros Sententiarum*, ed. and trans. E.M. Macierowski (*Thomas Aquinas's Earliest Treatment of the Divine Essence*), Binghamton, NY, 1998

Thomas Aquinas, *Summa contra gentiles*, Rome, 1934

aṭ-Ṭūsī, Naṣīr ad-dīn, *Sharḥ al-ishārāt*, no ed. (*Sharḥay al-ishārāt li-l-Khʷāja Naṣīr ad-dīn aṭ-Ṭūsī wa-li-l-ᶜImām Fakhr ad-dīn ar-Rāzī*), Qum, 1983 or 1984

az-Zabīdī, *Tāj al-ᶜarūs min jawāhir al-qāmūs I*, ed. ᶜA. Shīrī, Beirut, 1994

SECONDARY SOURCES CITED IN THE NOTES

Abed, S. 1991. *Aristotelian Logic and the Arabic Language in Alfārābī*, Albany, N.Y.

Abrahamov, B. 1993. "Necessary knowledge in Islamic theology", *BJMES* 20, 20-32

Ackrill, J. 1963. (trans. and comm.) *Aristotle's Categories and De Interpretatione*, Oxford

Ackrill, J. 1972-73. "Aristotle's definitions of *psukhê*", *Proceedings of the Aristotelian Society (New series)* 73, 119-133

Adamson, P. 2000. "Two early Arabic doxographies on the soul: al-Kindī and the 'Theology of Aristotle'", *The Modern Schoolman* 77, 105-125

Allard, M. 1965. *Le problème des attributs divins dans la doctrine d'al-Ashᶜarī et de ses premiers grands disciples*, Beirut

d'Alverny, M.T. 1951. "L'introduction d'Avicenne en Occident", *Revue du Caire* 14/141, 130-139

d'Alverny, M.T. 1952. "Les traductions latines d'Ibn Sina et leur diffusion au Moyen Age", *Millénaire d'Avicenne*, Cairo, 59-69

Anawati, G. 1978. (trans. and comm.) *La Métaphysique du Shifāᵓ*, Paris

Bäck, A. 1992. "Avicenna's conception of the modalities", *Vivarium* 30/2, 217-255

Balme, D. 1987. "Teleology and necessity" in A. Gotthelf and J. Lennox, eds., *Philosophical Issues in Aristotle's Biology*, Cambridge, 275-285

Barnes, J. 1995. (ed.) *The Cambridge Companion to Aristotle*, Cambridge

Biard, J. 1997. "Le système des causes dans la philosophie naturelle de Jean Buridan", in A. Hasnawi et al., eds, *Perspectives arabes et médiévales sur la tradition scientifique et philosophique grecque*, Paris, 491-504

Black, D. 1997. "Avicenna on the ontological and epistemic status of fictional beings", *Documenti e studi sulla tradizione filosofica medievale*, 8, 425-453

Blair, G. 1967. "The meaning of 'energeia' and 'entelecheia' in Aristotle", *International Philosophical Quarterly* 7/1, 101-117

Blanchette, O. 1992. *The Perfection of the Universe according to Aquinas: A Teleological Cosmology*, University Park, PA

Blumenthal, H. 1990. "Neoplatonic elements in the *de Anima* commentaries", in Sorabji, ed., *Aristotle Transformed*, 305-324

Bolton, R. 1978. "Aristotle's definitions of the soul: *De Anima* II,1-3", *Phronesis* 23/3, 258-278

Boylan, M. 1981. "Mechanism and teleology in Aristotle's biology", *Apeiron* 15/2, 96-102

Bradie, M. and F. Miller, Jr. 1984. "Teleology and natural necessity in Aristotle", *History of Philosophy Quarterly* 1/2, 133-146

Bruni, G. 1960. "Note di polemica neoplatonica contro l'uso e il significato del termine *entelekheia*", *Giornale critico della filosofia italiana* 39, 205-236

Brunschwig, J. 1988 "La théorie stoïcienne du genre suprême et l'ontologie platonicienne", in J. Barnes and M. Mignucci, eds., *Matter and Metaphysics: Fourth Symposium Hellenisticum*, Naples, 19-127 (= J. Lloyd [trans.], "The Stoic theory of the supreme genus and Platonic ontology", in Brunschwig 1994, 92-157)

Brunschwig, J. 1990. "Sur une façon stoïcienne de ne pas être", *Revue de théologie et de philosophie* 122, 389-403 (= J. Lloyd [trans.], "On a Stoic way of not being", in Brunschwig 1994, 158-169)

Brunschwig, J. 1994. *Papers in Hellenistic Philosophy*, Cambridge

Burnett, C. 1997. *The Coherence of the Arabic-Latin Translation Programme in Toledo in the Twelfth Century*, Berlin

Burrell, D. 1986. "Essence and existence: Avicenna and Greek philosophy", *MIDEO* 17, 53-66

Carame, N. 1926. (trans.) *Avicennae metaphysices compendium*, Rome

Caston, V. 1999. "Something and nothing: The Stoics on concepts and universals", *Oxford Studies in Ancient Philosophy* 17, 145-213

Charles, D. 1981. "Teleological causation in the *Physics*", in L. Judson, ed. *Aristotle's Physics: A Collection of Essays*, Oxford, 101-128

Charlton, W. 1980. "Aristotle's definition of soul", *Phronesis* 25/2, 170-186

Chen, C. 1958. "The relation between the terms *energeia* and *entelecheia* in the philosophy of Aristotle", *Classical Quarterly* (New Series) 7/1, 12-17

Cooper, J. 1987. "Hypothetical necessity and natural teleology", in A. Gotthelf and J. Lennox, eds., *Philosophical Issues in Aristotle's Biology*, Cambridge, 243-274

Craemer-Ruegenberg, I. 1991. "'Ens est quod primum cadit in intellectu' – Avicenna und Thomas von Aquin", in U. Tworuschka, ed., *Gottes ist der Orient – Gottes ist der Okzident*, Köln, 133-142

Daiber, H. 1980. *Aetius Arabus: die Vorsokratiker in arabischer Überlieferung*, Wiesbaden

Davidson, H. 1987, *Proofs for Eternity, Creation and the Existence of God in Medieval Islamic and Jewish Philosophy*, Oxford

Des Chene, D. 1996. *Physiologia: Natural Philosophy in Late Aristotelian and Cartesian Thought*, Ithaca, NY

De Young, G.R. 1981. (ed., trans. and comm.) *The Arithmetic Book of Euclid's Elements in the Arabic Tradition*, Harvard University Ph.D. dissertation.

Dhanani, A. 1994. *The Physical Theory of Kalām*, Leiden

Dooley, W. 1989. (trans.) *Alexander of Aphrodisias: On Aristotle Metaphysics 1*, London

Dooley, W. 1993. (trans.) *Alexander of Aphrodisias: On Aristotle Metaphysics 5*, London

Druart, T.-A. 2000. "The human soul's individuation and its survival after the body's death: Avicenna on the causal relation between body and soul", *Arabic Sciences and Philosophy*, 10/2, 259-273

Emilsson, E. 1991. "Plotinus and soul-body dualism", in S. Everson, ed., *Psychology (Companions to Ancient Thought, Vol. 2)*, Cambridge, 148-165

Endress, G. 1966. "Die arabischen Übersetzungen von Aristoteles' Schrift *De Caelo*" (Dr.Phil. Diss.) Frankfurt am Main

Endress, G. 1973. *Proclus Arabus: Zwanzig Abschnitte aus der Institutio Theologica in arabischer Übersetzung*, Beirut

Endress, G. and Gutas, D. (eds) 1992-. *A Greek-Arabic Lexicon*, Leiden

Frank, R. 1958-59. "Some fragments of Isḥāq's translation of the *De Anima*", *Cahiers de Byrsa* 8, 231-251

Frank, R. 1974. "Notes and remarks on the *ṭabāʾiʿ* in the teaching of al-Māturīdī", in P. Salmon, ed., *Mélanges d'islamologie (Armand Abel Festschrift)*, Leiden, 137-149

Frank, R. 1980. "Al-maʿdūm wal-mawjūd", *MIDEO* 14 (1980), 185-210

Frank, R. 1999. "The Ashʿarite ontology: I. Primary entities", *Arabic Sciences and Philosophy* 9/2, 163-231

Franzen, W. and Georgulis, K. 1972. "Entelechie", in J. Ritter, ed., *Historisches Wörterbuch der Philosophie (Bd. 2)*, Basel, 506-507

Frede, M. 1980. "The original notion of cause", in M. Schofield et al., eds, *Doubt and Dogmatism*, Oxford, 217-249

Freeland, C. 1992. "Accidental causes and real explanations", in L. Judson, ed., *Aristotle's Physics*, Oxford, 49-72

Friedman, R. 1986. "Necessitarianism and teleology in Aristotle's biology", *Biology and Philosophy* 1/3, 355-365

Friedman, R. 1987. "Simple necessity in Aristotle's biology", in *International Studies in Philosophy* 19/1, 1-9

Gaiser, K. 1969. "Das zweifache Telos bei Aristotles" in I. Düring, ed., *Naturphilosophie bei Aristoteles und Theophrast*, Heidelberg, 97-113

Gätje, H. 1971. "Die vorhandenen Übersetzungen der Schrift über die Seele, Avicennas *Kitāb al-inṣāf* und die Autoren der Übersetzungen", in his *Studien zur Überlieferung der aristotelische Psychologie im Islam*, Heidelberg, 28-44

Gill, M.L. 1980. "Aristotle's theory of causal action in *Phys.* III.3", *Phronesis* 25, 129-147

Gilson, É. 1948. *L'Être et l'essence*, Paris

Gilson, É. 1960. "Avicenne et la notion de cause efficiente," *Atti del XII Congresso Internazionale di Filosofia*, Florence, 121-130

Gilson, É. 1962. "Notes pour l'histoire de la cause efficiente," *AHDLMA* 29, 7-31

Gimaret, D. 1980. *Théories de l'acte humain en théologie musulmane*, Paris

Gimaret, D. 1988. *Les noms divins en Islam*, Paris

Goichon, A.-M. 1937. *La distinction de l'essence et de l'existence d'après Ibn Sīnā (Avicenne)*, Paris

Goldschmidt, V. 1972. "*Huparkhein* et *huphistanai* dans la philosophie stoïcienne", *Revue des Études Grecques* 85, 331-344

Gotthelf, A. 1976. "Aristotle's conception of final causality", *Review of Metaphysics* 30, 226-254

Gotthelf, A. 1989. "Teleology and spontaneous generation in Aristotle: a discussion", in *Apeiron* 22/4, 181-193

Graeser, A. 1971. "À propos *huparkhein* bei den Stoikern", *Archiv für Begriffsgeschichte* 15, 299-305

Graham, D. 1988. "Aristotle's definition of motion", *Ancient Philosophy* 8/2, 209-215

Graham, D. 1989. "The etymology of Entelecheia", *American Journal of Philology* 110, 73-80

Gutas, D. 1987-1988. "Avicenna's *madhhab* with an appendix on the question of the date of his birth", *Quaderni di studi arabi* 5-6, 323-336

Gutas, D. 1988. *Avicenna and the Aristotelian Tradition*, Leiden

Gutas, D. 1994. "Pre-Plotinian philosophy in Arabic (other than Platonism and Aristotelianism): a review of the sources", *Aufstieg und Niedergang der römischen Welt* II.36.7, Berlin, 4939-4973

Gutas, D. 1998. "Tardjama", *Encyclopaedia of Islam (New Edition)*, Vol. 10, 225-231

Gutas, D. 2001. "Intuition and thinking: The evolving structure of Avicenna's epistemology", in R. Wisnovsky, ed., *Aspects of Avicenna*, Princeton, NJ

Hadot, P. 1969. "Zur Vorgeschichte des begriffes Existenz: *huparkhein* bei den Stoikern", *Archiv für Begriffsgeschichte* 13, 115-127

Hadot, P. 1980., "Sur divers sens du mot *pragma* dans la tradition philosophique grecque", in P. Aubenque, ed., *Concepts et catégories dans la pensée antique*, Paris, 309-319

Hager, F. 1964. "Die Aristotelesinterpretation des Alexander von Aphrodisias und die Aristoteleleskritik Plotins bezüglich der Lehre von Geist", *Archiv für Geschichte der Philosophie* 46, 174-187

Hamlyn, D. 1968. (trans. and comm.) *Aristotle's De Anima: Books II,III*, Oxford

Hankinson, R.J. 1995. "Philosophy of Science", in J. Barnes, ed., *The Cambridge Companion to Aristotle*, Cambridge, 109-139

Hankinson, R.J. 1998. *Cause and Explanation in Ancient Greek Thought*, Oxford

Haschmi, M.Y. 1956. "Die Bewegungstheorie Avicennas", *Sudhoffs Archiv für Geschichte der Medizin* 40, 115-118

Hasnawi, A. 1994. "Alexandre d'Aphrodise vs Jean Philopon: notes sur quelques traités d'Alexandre 'perdus' en grec, conservés en arabe", *Arabic Sciences and Philosophy* 4, 53-109

Hasnawi, A. 1998. "Le mouvement et les catégories selon Avicenne et Averroès", in *Oriens-Occidens: Sciences, Mathématiques et Philosophie d'Antiquité à l'Âge classique*, Paris, 2, 119-224

Hasnawi, A. 2001. "La définition du mouvement dans la *Physique* du *Shifāʾ* d'Avicenne", *Arabic Sciences and Philosophy* 11/2, 219-255

Hasse, D. 2000. *Avicenna's De anima in the Latin West*, London

Hasse, D. 2001. "Avicenna on abstraction", in R. Wisnovsky, ed., *Aspects of Avicenna*, Princeton, NJ

Heinaman, R. 1988. "*Eudaimonia* and self-sufficiency in the *Nicomachean Ethics*", *Phronesis* 33, 31-53

Hocutt, M. 1974. "Aristotle's four becauses", *Philosophy* 49, 385-399

Horten, M. 1907. (trans.) *Die Metaphysik Avicennas*, Halle

Hourani, G. 1972. "Ibn Sīnā on necessary and possible existence", *Philosophical Forum* 4/1, 74-86

Hussey, E. 1983. (trans. and comm.) *Aristotle's Physics: Books III and IV*, Oxford

Hyman, A. 1987. "Aristotle, Algazali and Avicenna on necessity, potentiality and possibility", in K.-L. Selig and R. Somerville, eds, *Florilegium Columbianum: Essays in Honor of Paul Oskar Kristeller*, New York, 73-88

Jadaane, F. 1968. *L'influence du stoïcisme sur la pensée musulmane*, Beirut

Jalbert, G. 1960. "Le nécessaire et le possible dans la philosophie d'Avicenne", *Revue de l'Université d'Ottawa* 30, 89-101

Janssens, J. 1986. "Le *Dānesh-nāmeh* d'Ibn Sīnā: Un texte à revoir?", *Bulletin de philosophie médiévale* 28, 163-177

Janssens, J. 1997. "Les *Taʿlīqāt* d'Ibn Sīnā: Essai de structuration et de datation", in A. de Libera et al., eds, *Langages et philosophies: Hommage à Jean Jolivet*, Paris, 109-122

Jolivet, J. 1984. "Aux origines de l'ontologie d'Ibn Sīnā", in. J. Jolivet and R. Rashed, eds, *Études sur Avicenne*, Paris, 19-28

Jolivet, J. 1991. "La répartition des causes chez Aristote et Avicenne: le sens d'un déplacement", in J. Jolivet, Z. Kaluza, and A. de Libera, eds, *Lectionum varietates: Homage à Paul Vignaux (1904-1987)*, Paris, 49-65

Keyt, D. 1978. "Intellectualism in Aristotle", *Paideia* 7, 138-157

Khodeiri, M. 1959-61. "Lexique arabo-latin de la Metaphysique du Shifā'", *MIDEO* 6, 309-324
Klein-Franke, F. 1994. "The non-existent is a thing", *Le Muséon* 104, 375-390
Kosman, L.A. 1969. "Aristotle's definition of motion", *Phronesis* 14, 40-62
Kostman, J. 1987. "Aristotle's definition of change", *History of Philosophy Quarterly* 4/1, 3-16
Kraus, P. 1942. "Plotin chez les Arabes", *Bulletin de l'Institut d'Égypte* 23, 263-295
Kutsch, W. 1954. "Ein arabisches Bruchstück aus Porphyrios (?) PERI PSUKHES und die Frage des Verfassers der 'Theologie des Aristoteles'", *Mélanges de l'Université Saint Joseph* 31/4, 265-286
Lennox, J. 1982. "Teleology, chance, and Aristotle's theory of spontaneous generation", *Journal of the History of Philosophy* 20/3, 219-238
Lettinck, P. 1994. *Aristotle's Physics and its Reception in the Arabic World*, Leiden
Lovejoy, A. 1936. *The Great Chain of Being*, Cambridge, Mass.
Lewis, G. 1959. (Trans.) (Ps.-)Arisṭūṭālīs, *Uthūlūjiyā*, in *Plotini Opera, Tomus II: Enneades IV-V*, edd. P. Henry and H.-R. Schwyzer, Paris, 1959
Madelung, W. 1971. "The spread of Māturīdism and the Turks", *Actas do IV Congresso de Estudos Árabes e Islâmicos Coimbra-Lisboa 1968*, Leiden, 109-168
Madelung, W. 1974a. "The origins of the controversy concerning the creation of the Koran," in J. Barral, ed., *Orientalia Hispanica: sive studia F.M. Pareja octogenario dicata*, Leiden, 504-525
Madelung, W. 1974b, "Ar-Rāghib al-Iṣfahānī und die Ethik al-Ghazālīs", in R. Gramlich, ed., *Islamwissenschaftliche Abhandlungen Fritz Meier zum 60sten Geburtstag*, Wiesbaden, 152-163
Madelung, W. 1991. "Māturīdiyya", *Encyclopaedia of Islam (New Edition)*, Vol. 6, 847-848
Mahdi, M. 1990. "Al-Fārābī's imperfect state," *JAOS* 110/4, 691-726
Maier, A. 1955. "Finalkausalität und Naturgesetz", in her *Metaphysische Hintergründe der spätscholastischen Naturphilosophie* (*Studien zur Naturphilosophie der Spätscholastik, Bd. 4*), Rome, 273-335
Maier, A. 1958a, "*Motus est actus entis in potentia* ....", in her *Zwischen Philosophie und Mechanik* (*Studien zur Naturphilosophie der Spätscholastik, Bd. 5*), 3-57
Maier, A. 1958b. "*Forma fluens* oder *fluxus formae*?", in her *Zwischen Philosophie und Mechanik* (*Studien zur Naturphilosophie der Spätscholastik, Bd. 5*), 61-143
Marmura, M. 1979. "Avicenna's chapter on universals in the *Isagoge* of his *Shifā'*", in A. Welch and P. Cachia, eds, *Islam: Past Influence and Present Challenge*, Edinburgh, 34-56
Marmura, M. 1981. "Avicenna on causal priority", in P. Morewedge, ed., *Islamic Philosophy and Mysticism*, Delmar, N.Y., 65-83
Marmura, M. 1984a. "Avicenna on primary concepts in the *Metaphysics* of his *al-Shifā'*", in R. Savory and D. Agius, eds, *Logos Islamikos: Studia islamica in honorem Georgii Michaelis Wickens*, Toronto, 219-239
Marmura, M. 1984b. "The metaphysics of efficient causality in Avicenna", in M. Marmura, ed., *Islamic Theology and Philosophy*, Albany, 172-187
Marmura, M. 1991-92. "Avicenna and the Kalām", *ZGAIW* 7, 172-206
Marmura, M. 1992. "Quiddity and universality in Avicenna", in P. Morewedge, ed., *Neoplatonism and Islamic Thought*, Albany, NY, 77-87
McCullough, E.J. 1980. "St Albert on motion as *Forma fluens* and *Fluxus formae*", in J. Weisheipl, ed., *Albertus Magnus and the Sciences*, Toronto, 129-153
McDermott, M.J. 1978. *The Theology of al-Shaykh al-Mufīd*, Beirut

Menn, S. 1994. "The origins of Aristotle's concept of *energeia*: *energeia* and *dunamis*", *Ancient Philosophy* 14, 73-114

Michot, J. 1997a. "Avicenne, *La définition de l'âme*, section I de l'*Épître des états de l'âme*: Traduction critique et lexique", in A. de Libera et al., eds, *Langages et philosophie: hommage à Jean Jolivet*, Paris, 239-256

Michot, J. 1997b. "La réponse d'Avicenne à Bahmanyār et al-Kirmānī", *Le Muséon* 110/1-2, 143-221

al-Miṣbāḥī, M. 1980-81. "*Dawr mafhūm al-kamāl fī ta^crīf an-nafs bayna Arisṭū wa-bn Sīnā*" ("The role of the concept of perfection in defining the soul: Aristotle and Avicenna"), *Majallat Kulliyyat al-ādāb wa-l-^culūm al-insāniyya bi-Fās* 4-5, 121-147. (The article also appears, with minor variations, in *A^cmāl nadwat al-fikr al-^carabī wa-th-thaqāfat al-yūnāniyya bi-munāsabat murūr alf sana ^calā mīlād Ibn Sīnā wa-thalātha wa-^cishrūn qarnan ^calā wafāt Arisṭū* [= *Actes du colloque pensée arabe et culture grecque organisé pour célébrer le millénaire de la naissance d'Ibn Sīnā et le 23ème siècle après la mort d'Aristote: Les 7-10 Mai 1980*], Casablanca, 1985, 427-450, and in the author's *Dalālāt wa-ishkālāt: Dirāsāt fī l-falsafat al-^carabiyyat al-islāmiyya*, Casablanca, 1988, 113-136.)

Moravcsik, J. 1975. "*Aitia* as generative factor in Aristotle's philosophy", *Dialogue* 14, 622-638

Moravcsik, J. 1992. "What makes reality intelligible? Reflections on Aristotle's theory of *aitia*", in L. Judson, ed., *Aristotle's Physics*, Oxford, 31-47

Morewedge, P. 1972. "Philosophical analysis of Ibn Sīnā's essence-existence distinction", *JAOS* 92/3, 425-35

Mure, G. 1975. "Cause and because in Aristotle", *Philosophy* 50, 356-357

Nasr, S.H. 1989. "Existence (*wujūd*) and quiddity (*māhiyyah*) in Islamic philosophy", *International Philosophical Quarterly*, 29/4, 409-428

Nussbaum, M. (trans. and comm.) 1978. *Aristotle's de Motu Animalium*, Princeton

Owens, J. 1978 "Aristotle – motion as actuality of the imperfect", *Paideia: Special Aristotle Issue*, 120-132

Pasquino, P. 1978. "Le statut ontologique des incorporels", in J. Brunschwig, ed., *Les Stoïciens et leur logique*, Paris, 375-386

Peck, A. 1972. "Aristotle on kinêsis", in J. Anton and G. Kustas, eds, *Essays in Ancient Greek Philosophy*, Albany, NY, 478-490

Pines, S. 1936. *Beiträge zur islamischen Atomenlehre*, Berlin

Rahman, F. 1952. (trans. and comm.) *Avicenna's Psychology*, Oxford

Rahman, F. 1958. "Essence and existence in Avicenna", *Mediaeval and Renaissance Studies* 4, 1-16

Rahman, F. 1981. "Essence and existence in Ibn Sīnā: the myth and the reality", *Hamdard Islamicus* 4, 3-14

Ross, D. 1924. (ed. and comm.) *Aristotle: Metaphysics I-II*, Oxford

Ross, D. 1936. (ed. and comm.) *Aristotle's Physics*, Oxford

Ross, D. 1961. (ed. and comm.) *Aristotle: De Anima*, Oxford

Rowson, E. 1988. (ed., trans. and comm.) *A Muslim Philosopher on the Soul and its Fate: Al-^cĀmirī's Kitāb al-Amad ^calā l-abad*, New Haven

Rowson, E. 1992. "The Theology of Aristotle and some other pseudo-Aristotelian texts reconsidered", *JAOS* 112/3, 478-484

Rowson, E. 1995. "al-Rāghib al-Iṣfahānī", *Encyclopaedia of Islam (New Edition) VIII*, 389-390

Rudolph, U. 1992. "Ratio und Überlieferung in der Erkenntnislehre al-Ash^carīs und al-Māturīdīs", *ZDMG* 142, 72-79

Rudolph, U. 1996. *Al-Māturīdī und die sunnitische Theologie in Samarkand*, Leiden

Sabra, A.I. 1987. "The appropriation and subsequent naturalization of Greek science in medieval Islam: A preliminary statement", *History of Science* 25, 223-243
Sabra, A.I. 1996. "Situating Arabic science: Locality versus essence", *Isis* 87, 654-670
Santas, G. 1989. "Desire and perfection in Aristotle's theory of the good", *Apeiron* 22, 75-99
Sauvé Meyer, S. 1992. "Aristotle, teleology and reduction", *Philosophical Review* 101, 791-825
Schofield, M. 1991. "Explanatory projects in *Physics* 2.3 and 7", *Oxford Studies in Ancient Philosophy (Supplement)*, 29-40
Sebti, M. 1999. "La signification de la définition avicenniene de l'âme comme 'perfection première d'un corps natural organique' dans le Livre I du *Traité de l'âme* du *Shifā*ʾ", *Bulletin d'Études Orientales* 51, 299-312
Shehadi, F. 1982. *Metaphysics in Islamic Philosophy*, Delmar, NY
Sorabji, R. 1980. *Necessity, Cause and Blame: Perspectives on Aristotle's Theory*, London
Sorabji, R. 1990. "Infinite power impressed: the transformation of Aristotle's physics and theology", in his *Aristotle Transformed: The Ancient Commentators and their Influence*, London, 181-198
Steigerwald, D. 1997. *La pensée philosophique et théologique de Shahrastānī*, Québec
Stern, S. 1962. "'The first in thought is the last in action': The history of a saying attributed to Aristotle", *Journal of Semitic Studies* 7/2, 234-252
Todd, R. 1974. "Lexicographical notes on Alexander of Aphrodisias' philosophical terminology", *Glotta* 52, 207-215
Tritton, A.S. 1940. "Theory of knowledge in early Muslim theology", in M. Shafi, ed., *Woolner Commemoration Volume*, Lahore
van Ess, J. 1965-66. "Ibn Kullāb und die Miḥna", *Oriens* 1965-66
van Ess, J. 1966. *Die Erkenntnislehre des ʿAḍudaddīn al-Īcī*, Wiesbaden
van Ess, J. 1982. "Ibn Kullāb", *Encyclopaedia of Islam (New Edition)*, Suppl., 391-392
van Ess, J. 1991-1997. *Theologie und Gesellschaft im 2. und 3. Jahrhundert Hidschra*, Berlin
Verbeke, G. 1971. "Les critiques de Plotin contre l'entéléchisme d'Aristote", in *Philomathes: Studies and Essays in the Humanities in Memory of Philip Merlan*, The Hague, 194-222
Verrycken, K. 1990. "The metaphysics of Ammonius son of Hermeias", in R. Sorabji, ed., *Aristotle Transformed: The Ancient Commentators and their Influence*, London, 199-231
Walzer, R. 1953. "New light on the Arabic translations of Aristotle", *Oriens* 6, 91-113
Waterlow, S. 1982. *Nature, Change and Agency*, Oxford, 1982
Weisheipl, J. 1981. "The specter of *Motor coniunctus* in medieval physics", in *Studi sul XIV secolo in memoria di Anneliese Maier*, Rome, 81-104
Whittaker, J. 1975. "The historical background of Proclus' doctrine of *Authupostata*", in B. Dalsgaard Larsen et al., eds, *De Jamblique à Proclus*, Geneva, 193-237
Wieland, W. 1975. "The problem of teleology", in J. Barnes et al., eds, *Articles on Aristotle I: Science*, London
Wisnovsky, R. 2000. "Notes on Avicenna's concept of thingness (*shay*ʾ*iyya*)", *Arabic Sciences and Philosophy*, 10/2, 181-221

Wisnovsky, R. 2001 (ed.) *Aspects of Avicenna* (*Princeton Papers: Interdisciplinary Journal of Middle Eastern Studies*, 9), Princeton, NJ

Wisnovsky, R. 2003a. "Towards a history of Avicenna's distinction between immanent and transcendent causes", in D. Reisman and A.H. al-Rahim, eds, *Before and After Avicenna*, Leiden

Wisnovsky, R. 2003b. "One aspect of the Avicennian turn in Sunnī *kalām*", *Arabic Sciences and Philosophy* 13/2

Wolfson, H. 1938. "The amphibolous terms in Aristotle, Arabic philosophy and Maimonides", *Harvard Theological Review* 31, 151-173

Wolfson, H. 1946. "The Kalam problem of nonexistence and Saadia's second theory of creation", *Jewish Quarterly Review* 36, 371-391

Wolfson, H. 1959. "Philosophical implications of the problem of the divine attributes in the Kalam", *Journal of the American Oriental Society* 79, 73-80

Wolfson, H. 1976. *The Philosophy of the Kalam*, Cambridge, Mass.

Zimmermann, F. 1981. (trans. and comm.) *Al-Fārābī's Commentary and Short Treatise on Aristotle's De Interpretatione*

Zimmermann, F.W. 1986. "The origins of the so-called *Theology of Aristotle*", in J. Kraye et al., eds, *Pseudo-Aristotle in the Middle Ages*, London, 110-240

Zimmermann, F. 1994. "Proclus Arabus rides again", *Arabic Sciences and Philosophy* 4, 9-47

Index of Lemmata

General Index